And these signs shall follow them that believe; In my name shall they cast out devils; they shall speak with new tongues; They shall take up serpents; and if they drink any deadly thing, it shall not hurt them; they shall lay hands on the sick, and they shall recover.
Mark 16: 17-18

Other Titles by Troy Taylor

* **The Devil and All His Works**
A History of Satan, Sin, Murder, Mayhem & Magic

* **Sex and the Supernatural**
The Haunted and Horrific History of Sex and the Occult

* **A Song of Dance and Death**
Magic, Murder, Mayhem and the Diabolical Notes of the Devil's Music

TAKING UP SERPENTS

American Cults, Messiahs and Madmen

An American Hauntings Ink Book

© Copyright 2020 by Troy Taylor
and American Hauntings Ink
All Rights Reserved, including the right to copy or reproduce this book, or portions thereof, in any form, without express permission from the author and publisher.

Original Cover Artwork Designed by
© Copyright 2020 by April Slaughter & Troy Taylor

This Book is Published By:
American Hauntings Ink
Jacksonville, Illinois | 217.791.7859
Visit us on the Internet at
http://www.americanhauntingsink.com

First Edition – April 2020
ISBN: 978-1-7324079-8-5

Printed in the United States of America

Table of Contents

Introduction – 7

Part One: The Great Awakening – 13
American Witch Trials – 13
A Growing Excitement – 24
The Burned-Over District – 28
The Wilderness Prophet – 31
The Publick Universal Friend – 33
The Utopians – 36
Worshippers of the Apocalypse – 39
The Millerite's Great Disappointment – 40
Doomsday and Corn Flakes – 47
The "Pocasset Horror" – 48
Knocking on Doors with the Jo-Ho's – 52
The Mark of the Beast – 55
The Prophet and the Antichrist – 61
Blinded by (Christian) Science – 73
The Amish: A Life Meant to be Simple – 78
Signs and Wonders: Pentecostals in America – 89
Speaking in Tongues – 96
Taking up Serpents with the Snake Handlers – 98
Faith Healers: Con Artists for the Lord – 104
God's Messenger – Father Divine – 110
Sister Aimee's Cult of Personality – 126
Man with the Golden Plates: Mormons in America – 153
America's Only "King" – 183

The Kirtland Cult – 187
Polygamy, "The Principle" and Child Brides – 196
The Church of the Lamb of God – 201
Warren Jeffs: Prophet of Evil – 209

Part Two: From the Fringes of Religious Belief – 219
Cyrus Teed and the Hollow Earth – 222
The Blackburn Cult of the Great Eleven – 242
The Madness of Jim Jones – 282
The "Orange People" of the Rajneesh – 300
The Ant Hill Kids – 311
David Berg and the Children of God – 320
David Koresh and the Inferno in Waco – 340
UFO Cults: Salvation from the Stars – 350
Mankind United – 351
Raëlism – 354
Heaven's Gate – 357
Xenu, Thetans, and Clams: Scientology, the Most Dangerous Cult in America - 363

Introduction

I thought I'd already seen everything. I hadn't.

About six months before this realization I'd made some new friends at work who invited me to go with them to their church. I'd already had more than my share of church as a kid – every Wednesday, twice on Sunday, and "youth meetings" in between, which all combined helped me kill it on all the Bible questions on *Jeopardy* – but I agreed to go with them anyway because these friends were, well, "different" might be the best way to put it.

The ladies that I worked with always wore dresses. They never cut their hair. They didn't wear jewelry. I'd met some of the guys from their church, too. They always wore long pants, never shorts, and were always clean-shaven with short hair. Modesty was a big thing with them. They assured me they weren't Amish or anything, they belonged to a Pentecostal church. Technically it was an Apostolic church, I would later find out, which is another branch of Pentecostals who have a lot of rules.

Whatever they were, it was a new one on me. This was in the late 1980s. I'd never heard of this kind of thing before. My parents had been dragging me to a standard Protestant church for years, so I figured that most people – except for the Catholic side of the family – all did things pretty much the same way.

Boy, I was about to find out how wrong I was about that.

The first visit to their church was an eye-opening experience. There was a lot of music. Almost every church has music, but not like this. The songs – which everyone seemed to already know the words to – were accompanied by a piano, guitar, bass, and drums. And those drums – they turned out to be very important. After the minister was finished things really got going. The tempo of the music picked up, and people started yelling and waving their arms. Everyone was clapping and standing up so they could bounce and sway in their pews. I was hesitant to stand but trust me when I tell you it's easier to go along with it and just stand up and clap, too. If you don't you feel like an uncomfortable diner in a Mexican restaurant as you awkwardly try and eat while being serenaded by a mariachi band.

The more people stomped their feet and waved their arms, the more excited they got. And the music picked up the pace. Soon they were jumping up and down and crying, flapping their hands, falling on the floor, and running up and down the aisles of the church building. People were yelling "Hallelujah!" and "Jesus!" and whooping and hollering like an audience at a rock concert. Or maybe a square dance in this case.

I wish that I could remember exactly what I was thinking and feeling at the time, but I can assure you that I was stunned, scared, and more than a little intrigued. I couldn't imagine what was next. It turned out the floor show was just getting started.

The minister had put out a call asking anyone who wanted to pray to come down to the front of the church. I saw a guy who was half-dragged out of his pew by a couple of other men and led down to the front. He dropped to his knees and started praying – or at least I think that's what he was doing. It was hard to tell since his eyes were closed, his hands were up in the air, and he looked like he was in a lot of pain. Tears were streaming down his face. He either needed Jesus or an ambulance.

This went on for a few minutes and soon the pastor came down from the stage and grabbed hold of one of the guy's arms. Two other men had a hold of him, too. Several of the women in the church, their long hair threatening to fall out of the huge buns at the back of their heads, were gathered around. Everyone was praying, waving their arms, and yelling for Jesus.

And then it got weird. Okay, weirder.

One of the women in front – I later found out this was the pastor's wife – started yelling out some sort of gibberish. It had a sort of speech pattern to it, but it was no language that I'd ever heard before. And then another woman started doing the same thing. One of the men started hollering in the same "language," mixed in with repeated calls for Jesus.

I had no idea what was going on, but this was terrifying.

I stood there, clapping my hands in stunned silence, and watched this as it went on for about 10 minutes or so. The guy who was kneeling on the floor looked ready to fall over. He'd been praying and weeping this whole time, but unlike everyone crowded around him seemingly urging him on, he'd never let out any of the nonsense words that the others had. To me he seemed like the only person in the front of the church who hadn't suffered a stroke.

When it was all over my friends shared with me that this guy had been attending their church for the last six months but had never been "filled with the Holy Spirit." They were starting to doubt his commitment to the faith. I'd later find out that "being filled with the Holy Spirit" was like an initiation into the club, so to speak. It didn't matter how often you came to church, that you followed all the Apostolic rules, or how nice of a person you were, if you didn't start "speaking in tongues" – the outward sign of the Holy Spirit's presence – you were always seen as somehow suspect.

My alarm bells should have been going off, but they weren't – at least not yet.

My head was spinning when I left the church that night, but I knew right then I'd be back. I was put off by all the rules the group had to follow – more of which I'd learn about later – but couldn't help but wonder if everything I'd seen was real. I had known a lot of religious people in my life – good, kind, sincere people – but had never really felt like getting involved. My interests were far too varied already about all kinds of things, so religion didn't interest me much. But what if these people were onto something? Were they really being "possessed," so to speak, so that they ended up speaking in foreign languages?

So, I went back and continued to do so for the next several months. I began absorbing all their philosophies and reasons behind everything from not cutting their hair to wearing skirts and speaking in tongues. But I had a tough time with the rules. As a man, of course I had a lot fewer rules than the women did. It's a very misogynistic faith – as most faiths seem to be – but even so I didn't like to be told what I had to wear, where I could go, how I shouldn't watch movies or television, or listen to the "wrong" kind of music, or read the "wrong" kind of books. At one point, I was literally told, "You think about things too much."

So, you can probably imagine that since I couldn't get behind the little things the big things really weren't going to work for me either. Before you ask, yes, I'd been taken down to the front of the church several times, but I never felt the urge to babble in "tongues." After a few tries I think the group considered me as suspicious as they did that poor guy I'd seen being worked over on my first visit. By the way, he never did manage to "be filled," and he eventually drifted away from the church.

Finally, after a few months, I stopped showing up. There were some calls of concern for a bit, and then that came to an end. Weirdly, I got fired from my job. One of the members of the church was my manager and she made some false accusations against me and I was out. I couldn't help but think it was all related somehow. It didn't matter. I quickly found another job with a rival company and a few years later I was self-employed anyway. Being sabotaged that way stuck with me, though. Before that, I'd been naïve enough to believe that religious equaled good. That was another part of my involvement with this church that opened my eyes.

But let's get back to my revelation of realizing that I'd hadn't seen everything.

The following summer – after I'd been away from the church for a few months – I got a call from one of my friends who I'd loosely stayed in touch with. The word was out about me in the church, though. Most of my old friends had parents in the church and they'd warned them about associating with me. But this call was different – they thought they might be able to lure me back. That summer there was a giant statewide camp meeting that was taking place in the area and that meant Apostolics from all over Illinois would be there. Would I like to come to one of the evening services?

Sure, I said, I'll come. I did consider some of the people that I'd met good friends and wanted to see them again. I made arrangements to meet them at the camp one evening that week.

When I arrived at the camp that night, I was amazed by the number of people who were there. The church that I had attended was fairly small, but I knew there were others in Illinois. I just didn't know how many at the time. The parking area around the camp buildings – and the gigantic open-air pavilion where the services were held – was packed with cars and RVs. Some people stayed in the nearby cabins for the week, others camped in tents and trailers, and others drove in just for the services. There were possibly hundreds – more likely thousands – of people in attendance. During the day there was a lot of long hair, denim skirts, and tennis shoes but at night everyone was in their best dresses and suits, waiting for the service to start.

And what a service it was. Music, shouting, more music, a preacher, praying, music, and then a lot more music. The end of the service was "praise" time, just like it had been in that little church with 50 or so people in attendance. At this place, though, there were hundreds, packed into folding chairs in row after row, all the way up to a "Pentecostal mosh pit" in front. That's the best way that I can describe what was happening. This was the first church service I attended, multiplied by 1,000.

Men, women, teenagers, and children were screaming, hollering, shaking, running around and around the auditorium, dancing, and falling on the floor. In addition to the music (full band this time) and the beating drums, the air was filled with the sounds of all the people crying, weeping, and shouting "Jesus!" and

"Hallelujah!" Hands and arms were waving wildly, and the crowd was singing. I have no idea what song was being played. There was too much noise to tell you.

Once again, I was pretty terrified. Sorry – but this did not seem normal to me. Years later, I would have the chance to attend a Voodoo ceremony and that was pretty close to what I saw that night at the camp meeting. I think that the Apostolics would shudder at the comparison, but really, it was pretty much the same thing.

And then I saw what I'd never seen before.

I'd heard all the stories about what people did when they were "overcome with the Spirit," and I'd seen it plenty of times. As I've mentioned, people ran around, danced, got slammed into walls, fell on the floor in a trance, spoke in tongues, and generally acted like lunatics. And all of this was going on, don't get me wrong.

But from where I was sitting, about half-way back in the auditorium, I had a pretty good view of the front of the pavilion. There were plenty of shenanigans going on all around me, but the "mosh pit" was insane. It really did look like a punk concert. People were twirling around, dancing, bumping into each other – nuts.

And then I saw the first one. A second one followed, then a third. There were only three of them, but that was enough. Three young men, dressed in white shirts, with their ties loosened and their sleeves rolled up – jumped into the air. And I'm not talking about mere "jumping." A lot of people were doing that. These were standing-in-one-spot, jumping-higher-than-an-NBA-player, at-least-12-feet-in-the-air kind of jumps that could never have been normally achieved by these guys, who looked like farmers in their J.C. Penney Sunday-go-to-meeting outfits.

This is not an exaggeration, by the way.

These were literally superhuman jumps. I saw them, with my own eyes, fly into the air, at least eight feet above the crowd, fall back down, and do it again. Call it flying, levitating, something – whatever it was, they were doing it.

That was it. I'd seen enough. I left the pavilion, walked to my car, got in, drove away, and never looked back. I've only told that story a couple of times before in my life, but it happened, and I've never forgotten it.

That was the moment that I decided that religion was not for me.

I've never regretted that decision, and yet I remain fascinated with American religion. Cults, would-be messiahs, manias like I witnessed that night – I found it all fascinating. I have always been a person who has considered blind faith in anything – religion, government, other people, etc. – to be terrifying. And yet, like so many things that terrify me, I can't help but be fascinated with it.

America has always been a nation of extremes, whether it deals with popular fads or religion – or both. We have created an array of religious faiths in this country that deal with everything from one God to multiple ones, ghosts, UFOs and aliens, snake handling, speaking in tongues, polygamy, and faith healing. And while not every faith that we have in this country originated here – some came with the arrivals in the New World – we have managed to twist and contort them to become uniquely American.

This is a country that promises to allow us to worship in whatever way we choose. America has long been a nation that offers a sanctuary for those who are persecuted elsewhere for their beliefs. As the immigrants streamed into the United States, we saw

Jews from across Europe who found refuge from hatred and the Holocaust. Centuries earlier the Puritans settled in America to escape persecution in England, only, ironically, to persecute others after they arrived.

At the base of the Statue of Liberty is a plaque inscribed with the words from Emma Lazarus's poem, "The New Colossus." Its final lines read, "Give me your tired, your poor, your huddled masses yearning to breathe free. The wretched refuse of your teeming shore. Send these, the homeless, tempest-tost to me. I lift my lamp beside the golden door!" In this welcoming spirit, the United States has cultivated an environment of religious tolerance – it's even in the First Amendment of the Constitution.

Many Americans – I probably wouldn't say "most" these days – defend the right to religious freedom, regardless of whether they agree with those beliefs or not. Part of being an American is saying that it's okay for you to do whatever you want to do with your religious faith, as long as it doesn't hurt other people, whether I believe in it or not.

And there's where we get into trouble.

This is not an argument about the fact that a very large number of fundamentalist Christians in this country have forgotten that we have religious freedom here. Let's leave that alone in this book. This isn't about intolerance for Muslims, Satanists, and anyone who doesn't believe in a strict, often wildly-skewed Protestant faith. This is about the other part of that earlier statement – unfortunately, some of America's religious practices have – and do – hurt other people.

Some of these religious groups, i.e. cults, are closed societies, allowing corruption and depravity to flourish. Our "freedom of religion" sometimes becomes an excuse to commit crimes under the guise of "worship." This freedom has become oppression for some people and many religious beliefs have endangered the lives, health, and sanity of their followers.

For many people religious beliefs – and by extension, religious practices – are seen as untouchable and sacred. It has become taboo to question someone's religious beliefs. Religion is too often indulged with unquestioning respect. When abuses occur within these communities, people, including the authorities, often look the other way and decide there is nothing that can be done.

Others argue – and have for decades – what's the harm? Today, I think we can look at the thousands of instances of abuse within the Catholic Church and quickly see "the harm." But it hasn't always been that way. Besides, since this book is about the fringes of American religious belief, we'll be taking a look at considerable harm that has been done in the name of religion, including underage marriage, rape, incest, risky rituals, animal sacrifice, financial scams, questionable faith healing., suicide, and even murder – all in the name of a god of some sort.

Despite the light approach that I try and take to some of the strangeness that is detailed in this book, I'm not attempting to make fun of anyone's beliefs. I have tried to present a factual look back at the history – and sometimes current activity – of various religious groups, cults, and faiths in America. Some of the stories are weird, others unbelievable, and others – well, simply terrifying. And yes, "terrifying" is a word that I use a lot when it comes to some of these faiths and their often wilder off-shoots. I think that you'll also find that this is an apt description of many of them.

Just remember as you delve into the chapters ahead — these stories are true. These people, and their beliefs, were genuine. Did some of them make up stories to deceive their followers or to bilk them out of their money? Of course. But, in far too many of these faiths, those who created them believed in their truth. Their belief system was real. Church was not just for Sundays; it was a way of life. Religion was heavily intertwined in their very existence, and their faith dictated everything they did — how they dressed, what they ate, who they married, and where they lived.

It was a belief system that often led to their destruction.

But not in every case, though. I wanted to present the reader with not only a historical look at what we often consider America's fringe religions — past and present — but a look at some of the non-traditional faiths that are still around today. The beginnings of some of them will shock you, and yes, it will terrify you, as well.

But nothing will shock you like the final section of the book will.

I have a feeling that the details of some of those faiths will give the reader your "terrifying moment" — like the one I had at the camp meeting that summer night. So, prepare yourself before you turn those pages.

People will often give you some pretty solid advice: Never talk about politics or religion. Usually I follow that advice, but this time I can't, not about religion anyway.

Hopefully, you'll still be speaking to me when this book is over.

Troy Taylor
Winter-Spring 2020

Part 1.
A Great Awakening

Historians are often fond of remarking that America, throughout its relatively short history, has been a nation of extremes. It should be no surprise that our homegrown religious faiths can also be described in the same way --- extreme.

Our first real taste of American religious mania came from a faith that had been imported to this country and yet made an impact on it that is still being felt today. The Puritans arrived in America in 1620, having fled England because of persecution. They wanted a place where they could worship as they saw fit, out from under the thumb of the Church of England. They'd grown disgusted with what they saw as the church's corruption and straying from the purity that they demanded from their faith.

The Puritans who settled in New England had no intention of letting go of their unyielding Bible-based convictions. Democracy, as we know it, was never considered. There was no separation between church and state. Their religious beliefs influenced all community and political decisions. As God-fearing Christians, the Puritans saw the Devil as their enemy whom they needed to be always vigilant against, for Satan always lurked nearby, ready to claim the souls of anyone at any time. For the Puritans fear and superstition were simply a part of their faith.

The village of Salem was settled in 1626. Four years later, the Puritans had dominated every aspect of its existence. Life there was not easy. Hard work and prayer consumed most of a person's time. There was a genuine fear of insufficient crops and food supplies. There were illnesses and epidemics, Indian attacks, and squabbles and disputes between neighbors. For the religious, they believed the wrath of God was responsible for nearly anything that went wrong, from inclement weather to disease. If the Puritans wanted to improve their fortunes, they believed, they should spend more time being prayerful in the worship of God.

Underlying many of the Puritan's problems was a feeling of helplessness and terror of the unknown. The uneasiness and anxiety of the village created the perfect climate for seeking scapegoats – any affliction could be attributed to the eccentric, the difficult, the elderly, or those not pious enough. It was convenient to accuse them of being witches or sorcerers, in league with the Devil and his demons, no matter how irrational it seems to us today.

While the adults in Salem faced both genuine and imagined stresses, children were permitted few, if any, of the joys or freedoms associated with childhood. They were to be seen and not heard, to be "obedient, industrious, and prayerful." Boys were taught skills they would need as adults – farming, building, and hunting. They learned to read and write so they could comprehend the Bible. Girls didn't need to be literate. They needed to learn cooking, sewing, and household skills. There was little else to break the grim monotony of their days and nights.

Not surprisingly, the tedious lives of Puritan children created boredom, especially during the long and dreary winter months. In turn, boredom led to mischief and created the witchcraft hysteria of 1692 – America's first religious mania that led to horror and death. It was started by several young girls in Salem whose innocent curiosity in something outside their religious faith spun wildly out of control.

The belief in witches – who carried out the Devil's evil deeds – was as real to the Puritans as the constant threat of the Devil himself. Witchcraft was against the law in most New England colonies and was punishable by death. And for good reason, it seems. The Puritans believed that witches could put spells on livestock that made animals become ill or die. Witches even had the power to deform or kill newborn babies. It was the Devil, they believed, not the high infant mortality rates of the era. An inappropriate look, a pointed finger, or harsh word might be construed as an evil curse.

There were other outbreaks of witchcraft in New England in the years before the Devil came to call in Salem Village, but none as famous. Salem was unique in some ways, not having the cosmopolitan or well-educated citizens of Boston, just 30 miles away. Salem Village was, as one historian put it, a "backwater." It was a small, rural village, with an adult population at the time of only 215 and was plagued by friction and quarrels between various factions, creating enough jealousy, hostility, and religious fervor to make it the perfect place for a witchcraft outbreak.

The events began, ironically, at the home of Reverend Samuel Parris, a relatively inexperienced but pious and strict Puritan minister. In the Parris household lived the reverend, his wife, his nine-year-old daughter, Elizabeth or "Betty," who was a quiet and nervous child, and his 11-year-old niece, Abigail Williams, a bold little girl who dominated her younger cousin. Elizabeth and Abigail were fully committed to the Puritan faith, with its fear of the Devil, demons, and witches. Of the reverend's wife we know little, except that she was a devout woman who spent most of her time doing charitable work in the village. Parris had lived for a time in Barbados and had brought two black slaves to Salem with him – John Indian, who did outside work, and his wife Tituba, who cooked and cleaned. The children were mostly cared for by Tituba, and with idle time on their hands they were always eager to be entertained with her stories about her island home, culture, and magic. She told fortunes and read palms and showed the girls how to cast harmless spells.

The girls were very proud of this secret knowledge, and they boasted about it to some of their older friends - Mary Walcott, Elizabeth Booth, and Susanna Sheldon – and later, to several others, including Ann Putnam, the malicious daughter of a neurotic, gossipy mother who was largely responsible for the ignorant rumors that later began to spread. Initially though, the girls all quietly joined Elizabeth and Abigail for stories and demonstrations of fortune-telling. The secret gatherings generated a lot of excitement but also feelings of fear, guilt, and sinfulness in children who had now gone beyond the boundaries of accepted Puritan faith.

The first sign of a serious problem occurred when Elizabeth and Abigail began displaying "peculiar" behavior. They gazed emptily at the ceiling above and seemed to be experiencing strange muscular contractions, twitches, and fits. Reverend Parris and his wife quickly summoned the village doctor for his advice but, not surprisingly since nothing like what we'd consider medicine was being practiced in those days, he had no idea what was wrong with them. His conclusion? "An evil hand is on them," he announced.

To everyone in the village it was clear – the children were victims of witchcraft.

No one knew what to do for the girls except to pray for them. Reverend Parris summoned several other ministers, and they offered sincere and fervent entreaties to God on behalf of the afflicted girls. But Elizabeth and Abigail seemed to worsen. Their bodies became oddly contorted, then stiffened. Their breathing was labored, and they cried loudly, complaining of horrible pains. They suffered fits of dizziness and spells during which they crawled about on all fours and made horrible animal noises. Prayer proved to be of no avail. Accounts stated that the girls screamed as though touched with burning coals whenever sacred words were said over their bodies.

It was clear that they were being bedeviled by witchcraft, but who was working with Satan in Salem Village? Who had bewitched the two girls? Whoever it was, that person had to be found and stopped.

The girls were asked who their tormentors were, but no one could not get a straight answer from either of them. Mary Walcott's aunt, Mary Sibley – described in one account as a "true Puritan busybody" – suspected Tituba and persuaded the slave to make a "witch cake" from an old country recipe, consisting of rye meal and the urine of the afflicted children. The idea was that if the family dog ate the cake made with the urine of the "possessed" girls, the dog would begin to act as if it were bewitched if the girls were truly under the influence of witchcraft. When Parris learned of this and accused his daughter of being involved with the making of the cake, she went into such terrible hysterics that he feared she would die.

The girls became increasingly frightened and agitated. They knew they were now in a position where they had to identify someone as a witch. They had no choice – their elders, who could be both intimidating and punishing, insisted on it. So, they accused not one, but three local women as those responsible for their suffering. They named Tituba, Sarah Good, and Sarah Osborne.

Why those three? Anyone who lived in Salem at the time could understand. Tituba was easy to explain. Her stories of the occult and magic had started it all. She was also a woman of color, which made her suspicious in the white Puritan, backwoods New England community. Sarah Good was a poor, disheveled, homeless woman who roamed the streets begging for shelter for herself and her children. Sarah Osborne's reputation was in question simply because she had stopped attending church.

Warrants were issued for the arrest of the three unfortunate women, and they were ordered to present themselves before two magistrates, John Hathorne and Jonathan Corwin. Allegations were being made by Elizabeth and Abigail, as well as eight other girls who were now "afflicted" by witchcraft. They included the girls who had come to the secret meetings at the Parris home, as well as Ann Putnam, 12, from a well-to-do Salem family; Mercy Lewis, a 17-year-old high-strung Putnam servant;

Mary Warren, 20, a servant for the John Proctor family; Elizabeth Booth, 18; Sarah Churchill, a 20-year-old servant for the George Jacobs family; Elizabeth Hubbard, 17, the niece of the doctor's wife; Susannah Shelton, 18; and 17-year-old Mary Walcott, whose father was the parish deacon.

The prisoners were allowed no defense counsel. It was enough for a witness to declare that he had seen the "shape" of the accused riding through the air on a broomstick for his or her word to be believed. It didn't matter how much the poor soul on trial protested the testimony.

During the questioning of the "afflicted," they suddenly fell into convulsions and screamed that they were in pain. They confirmed the accusations that had been made against the accused – their fits and convulsions confirmed it.

When Tituba was questioned, she maintained her innocence at first, then changed her testimony and admitted that she'd had contact with the Devil. Some believe that she was beaten into a confession by Reverend Parris but it's more likely that she was just telling the Puritan judges what they wanted to hear. She confessed to anything she could think of and once stayed was nearly impossible to stop. She claimed that a "tall man" had come to her and she signed the "Devil's Book." Among the other names listed there were those of Sarah Good and Sarah Osbourne. She had flown to Sabbaths with the Devil, accompanied by a hog, two red cats, and the winged head of a cat that belonged to Sarah Osbourne. Sarah Osborne also had a familiar that was a "yellow dog" and "a thing with a head like a woman, with two legs and wings." Sarah Good had a "yellow bird" that served her as her familiar. There was yet another demonic entity that walked erect, was covered in hair, and was perhaps two or three feet high. There were also "shapes" of red and black that beckoned to her, "Serve me." She claimed that these two shapes had tried to get her to bring them Elizabeth and Abigail, but she had resisted.

The court readily accepted her testimony. It was evident to them that the uneducated slave had been deceived by the Devil and was an innocent victim of the witches. Evidence of this was given as Tituba also became "possessed," rolling her eyes, frothing at the mouth, and screaming that she was being attacked by a demon for having spoken out against the forces of darkness. Her husband also got involved in the ruse and he roared, blasphemed, and threw himself onto the floor of the courtroom, also apparently in agony. The court believed that he, too, was also another victim of the horror that had come to Salem.

Hysteria soon gripped the village. The magistrates had noted that Tituba said nine marks had been made in the Devil's Book. That meant there were still six other witches in the village – who were they?

A dozen people came forward, including some who may have honestly believed what they were saying, claiming that they had seen the "shapes" of others sticking pins into dolls and taking a diabolical sacrament of red-colored bread and wine mixed with blood. Rebecca Nurse, a formerly respected old woman, was dragged from her sickbed to be charged as a witch. A farmer named John Proctor dared to declare that the girls were liars and that their "possession" was self-induced to draw attention to themselves. The result was that he was arrested as a witch and his property was confiscated before he had even been tried.

There were many illustrations created that depicted the witch trials in Salem. All of them were dramatic... and all inaccurate.

When Martha Corey was accused villagers were shocked. Unlike the dubious reputations of Sarah Good, Sarah Osborne, and Tituba, Mrs. Corey was an upstanding member of the community and church. But Mrs. Corey had made a serious error in judgment when witch hysteria gripped Salem – skeptical of the claims she neither attended the court appearances of the accused nor did she want her husband, Giles, to attend them. Rumors claimed that she was inclined not to believe in the accusations, and they spread through the village. This started further rumors that perhaps Martha Corey was a witch but for most this seemed too hard to believe. Before church leaders considered such an allegation, they thought it best to speak with her privately.

The visit went badly. Martha remained skeptical about the goings-on in town and overlooked the fact that those who believed in witchcraft could easily rationalize the idea that even a woman who appeared to be pious could still do the work of the Devil. Martha Corey was arrested on Monday. The previous day she had been in church, disregarding the rumors about her because she was certain of her innocence.

When taken before the magistrates she denied that she had tormented the girls with witchcraft. If she was not responsible, she was asked, who was? She replied, "I do not know. How should I know? I am a gospel woman."

The afflicted girls who were present immediately screamed, "Gospel witch! Gospel witch!" Ann Putnam added that she saw Martha Corey's specter and another woman invoked the Devil.

Martha was quick to reply, "We must not believe these distracted children!" But the girls showed no signs of calming down. They continued to scream and cry and were sufficiently convincing enough that Martha Corey joined the other accused in jail.

The hysteria gained strength in the village. Fire and brimstone sermons, the fear of lurking demons, and wild rumors created a troubled atmosphere in the village. This saw even more people accused of frolicking with the Devil.

Perhaps the most bizarre – and certainly most unjust – arrest for practicing witchcraft was that of Dorcas Good, the five-year-old daughter of Sarah Good. In my opinion, this marks the peak of the collective insanity in Salem. At trial little Dorcas "confessed" that she, like her mother, was a witch. She told the court that her familiar was a snake that sucked out her blood. As "proof" she showed the magistrates a small blister on her hand. That was enough to send her to jail.

Meanwhile, John Proctor's wife, Elizabeth, had also been accused and had joined her husband in jail. Rebecca Nurse's sister, Sarah Cloyse, was understandably distressed by the accusations made against her sister, knowing they were outrageous and untrue. During a church service she heard Reverend Parris make a biblical reference that was clearly an implication about Rebecca being in league with the Devil. In a fit of anger, she left the meetinghouse, banging the door when she exited so that everyone present heard the noise.

Any guesses as to the next person accused of witchcraft?

The afflicted girls soon claimed to have witnessed Sarah's specter, and Tituba's husband, John Indian, alleged that she used sorcery to harm him.

In court though Sarah stood her ground. "When did I hurt thee?" she demanded.

"A great many times," he replied.

"Oh, you are a grievous liar," Sarah snapped.

Asked by the judges the afflicted girls predictably answered that they had witnessed ceremonies in which the Devil gave communion to several witches, including Rebecca and Sarah.

Hearing the accusations Sarah collapsed. The afflicted girls reacted by mocking her. The meetinghouse burst into a commotion while the girls convulsed into fits and spasms.

The reaction of the girls was not an isolated incident. Their behavior did everything possible to unsettle the accused. If the prisoner lifted her eyes, the girls all lifted theirs; if she rubbed her face, the girls did the same; if she coughed, the girls all coughed, and so on. If the prisoner denied the charges brought against her, the girls went into a frenzy, howling and throwing themselves on the floor. Still worse, they became the jury and executioner of the accused. One by one the girls were carried to the prisoner and she was forced to take each of their hands. If an afflicted girl continued to rave and thrash about the accused was innocent, but if she became quiet it was assumed that the accused had removed the demon that had been sent to torture her and so was obviously guilty.

The girls had a terrifying effect on not only the trials but on the people of the village as well. They were constantly seeing "shapes" all over the place, and so unshakable had the belief in them become that at the girl's direction the villagers stabbed with swords and pitchforks at the empty air where the "shapes" were supposed to be.

People in Salem who feared being accused or "cried out," as it was called, began to leave the village. Among them was John Willard, the deputy constable, who had arrested several of the accused witches. In a sudden fit of disgust, he turned on the afflicted girls, accused them of being frauds, and said that they should be hanged for what they had done. The girls retaliated against him by claiming that they had seen his "shape" strangling his nephew, a young man who had recently died. Willard tried to flee but was captured and chained up in prison, accused of having witched to death several other people.

Around this time the afflicted girls decided to announce the identity of another prominent witch – The Reverend George Burroughs, who had been a minister in Salem several years before. Even though they were shocked at the idea that a minister would be involved, the magistrates quickly dispatched officers to the parish where Burroughs now lived. They stormed into his home in the middle of a meal and dragged him back to Salem. To Burroughs' amazement he was accused of murdering several soldiers who had been killed near his parish while fighting Indians – not physically, of course, but as a sinister "shape," just like the other alleged witches. Interestingly Burroughs' time in Salem had been unpleasant. He'd had a history of disagreements with many people, but especially with the Putnam family. There was quite a bit of animosity between the reverend and Ann's parents, which undoubtedly played a large part in the accusations against him.

More arrests were made on charges of witchcraft – Bridget Bishop, Abigail Hobbs, Martha Corey's 80-year-old husband Giles, and John Proctor's servant Mary Warren, herself one of the afflicted girls. There were questions about Mary's arrest – she had been an accuser, why was she now being charged? Likely she was badly shaken by the arrest of the Proctors for whom she'd worked. Her behavior became erratic and she was now confused about her time as a victim. When the other tormented girls got wind of Mary's doubts, they quickly tried to quiet her loose talk by claiming that she had bewitched them and has signed the Devil's Book.

When she was brought into court it only took a glance from her to cause the other girls to fall into another round of fits and screams. Mary became emotionally overwhelmed – and it wasn't an act. She was genuinely terrified and became so hysterical that she was removed from court and taken to jail. Several weeks later she admitted to being a witch but blamed John and Elizabeth Proctor – along with others – for her misfortunes. By confessing Mary probably saved her own life. She was freed and again considered one of the afflicted. Typically, those who confessed to being witches were spared the gallows. Those who maintained their innocence were invariably convicted and condemned to hang.

When Bridget Bishop, Abigail Hobbs, and Giles Corey were questioned, both Bishop and Corey insisted that they were not guilty of witchcraft. But their pleas were in vain – as soon as the afflicted girls looked at them the girls fell into outbursts of fits and contortions.

Abigail Hobbs, however, confessed to everything, telling the magistrates that she had "sold herself body and soul to the old boy." She said that's he practiced witchcraft, attending meetings of sorcerers, and drank "red wine with red bread." She was jailed along with the others, but during her confession she implicated nine more people. Arrest warrants were issued for Abigail's parents – William and Deliverance Hobbs – Susanna Martin, and Mary Esty, the sister of Rebecca Nurse and Sarah Cloyse.

Shaken by her arrest and the questioning that followed, Deliverance Hobbs began to question her own sanity – could she be a witch and not know it? Rattled and overwhelmed, she confessed to practicing witchcraft and offered the names of other witches in the village. Her husband William, outraged by the spectacle, insisted that he was innocent of all charges, which, of course, landed him in jail.

Mary Esty, when questioned, kept control of her emotions but was also jailed. Susanna Martin, on the other hand, didn't take the courtroom proceedings seriously at all and even laughed at one point. She doubted the afflicted girls and called them liars. As she was being taken away to jail, she remarked, "A false tongue will never make a guilty person."

When a short time later Mary Esty was released from the jail, her manner so impressed officials that they began to believe she was not guilty. But her freedom didn't last long. Whether genuinely fearful or just malicious, the afflicted girls grew hysterical, especially Mercy Lewis, whose fits frightened everyone who witnessed them. When she cried out Mary's name, the poor woman was placed back behind bars.

Meanwhile, a new governor had arrived from England, Sir William Phips, and he came to the village with Increase Mather, the father of Cotton Mather, and later president of Harvard University. Mather had been prominent in earlier witch trials in Boston, but Phips was only interested in getting together a military expedition against the French in Canada. He wanted nothing to do with what was going on in Salem Village.

After decreeing that all of those who had been accused of witchcraft be left chained in their cells, he left the business of trying them to the courts. A special court was formed with Deputy Governor William Stoughton as president and six other judges. Whether intentional or not, the fact that judges from a higher court came to Salem elevated the controversy to a new level. This was no longer a matter of village business – the mania became news that gripped the entire Massachusetts colony.

The accused were no longer being questioned – they were now going on trial.

Bridget Bishop was the first to be brought before the judges. Her position in the community had contributed to her dilemma. She was twice widowed and was the successful proprietor of a local inn. She also stood out in the community for her wearing of "brightly colored" clothes, which was abhorred by the Puritans who traditionally wore dark, modest clothing. She didn't help her case by appearing in court wearing a "lace-trimmed scarlet bodice." When women assigned by the court examined Bridget's body, they found an "excrescence of flesh," believed to be a teat or a nipple used by the witch's familiar to feed from her breast. She also didn't help herself by stating that she was innocent.

Bridget was pronounced guilty and hanged on Gallows Hill on June 10.

During the Salem trials religious hysteria peaked when the judges began allowing "spectral evidence" to be admitted in court. This evidence claimed that specters or apparitions of witches tormented and inflicted pain on the innocent. But the specters could only be seen by those who were bewitched. These claims – along with unsupported claims and hearsay – were allowed by the Salem judges. This seems mind-boggling to us today, but in the religious climate of New England in the seventeenth century it seemed perfectly reasonable.

In late June the fates of Sarah Good, Elizabeth Howe, Susanna Martin, Sarah Wilds, and Rebecca Nurse were also sealed. Four of them were found guilty and sentenced to hang. Only Rebecca Nurse had been found not guilty. Her good reputation served her well – at first. Her numerous friends and family were brave enough to testify on her behalf and she was found to be not guilty of the crimes for which she was accused. Instantly the courtroom was plunged into chaos. The girls howled, pulled their hair, and rolled around on the floor screaming that the woman was guilty. Unbelievably she was brought back into court and the jury was ordered to think things over again. This time they reversed their verdict and she was found guilty. On Tuesday, July 19, she and the other four women hanged as witches in Salem.

Sarah Good's last words proclaimed her innocence, and as the noose was placed around her neck, she rebuked the Reverend Nicholas Noyes, who stood nearby and had accused her of being a witch. "You are a liar," she shouted. "I am no more a witch than you are a wizard, and if you take away my life, God will give you blood to drink."

Eerily Sarah's prediction came true. Years later Noyes choked to death on his own blood following a throat hemorrhage.

The terror continued to spread. Scores of people were "cried out," and the court continued its travesty of justice. Prisoners who confessed could hope for clemency, but those who denied their guilt were condemned.

In July John Proctor, still in the dismal confines of the jail, wrote to Boston ministers to plead that the witch trials be held in Boston with new judges on the bench. He was certain that the "witch hunts" were based largely on lies and intimidation. But his letters had little effect. In early August, he and his wife, Elizabeth, stood trial, as did Reverend George Burroughs, and three others. More than 30 people from Ipswich, Massachusetts, where John Proctor once lived, appealed to the judges on his behalf, hoping to save his life. Nearly two dozen neighbors from Salem also offered support. But their efforts were in vain – John and Elizabeth were declared guilty, along with the others. Only Elizabeth was spared from being hanged. She was pregnant at the time and under Puritan law the killing of her innocent, unborn child was forbidden.

George Jacobs was convicted on the word of his granddaughter, Margaret. When she had been arrested on witchcraft charges, she had offered his name because she feared being tortured and hanged. Although she later stated in court that her confession had been coerced and that her testimony had been "false and untrue," it had no effect on the fate of her grandfather, who was condemned to die on the gallows.

The trials and executions continued. In September, 15 more people were sentenced to death. On just one day, September 22, eight were hanged including Martha Corey. Several of the convicted pleaded to the governor, judges, and clergy for clemency, but their appeals fell on deaf ears.

Giles Corey, Martha's husband, had also been accused of practicing witchcraft. Although the old man knew he was not guilty, he also understood that if he claimed to be innocent, he'd be convicted anyway. A proud man, he refused to falsely plead guilty just to save his life and satisfy his accusers. So, Corey refused to enter a plea at all. In fact, he did not utter a single word in court. Therefore, under Puritan law, he could not be brought to trial.

But he paid the price for his bold silence.

He was brutally punished, and the court made no allowance for Giles's advanced age. He was laid on the ground while heavy stones were placed on him until he was crushed to death under their weight. He lasted for two days of suffering before he finally died. His courage deeply affected the people of the village, as did his composure and refusal to lie.

The seeds of doubt had finally been sown in Salem Village.

Following the death sentences of September, the court recessed with plans to reconvene later in the fall – it never happened. There was a marked shift in the attitude of the villagers about the trials. People were beginning to speak out. Cotton Mather issued a warning about depending on "spectral evidence." An influential Boston merchant named Thomas Brattle wrote a letter in which he objected to the way that the Salem trials had been conducted. A magistrate from Salisbury, Robert Pike, wrote that he was skeptical of both what the afflicted girls claimed and the types of highly questionable evidence were permitted to convict someone of witchcraft. He did not doubt the reality of witches, he stated, but suggested the Devil was doing his nefarious work through the afflicted, not the witches. Because of this innocent people were being accused in some instances because the Devil was commanding the afflicted to falsely blame the righteous.

But it was Governor Phips who finally put the whole thing to an end. He returned from the Canadian border and was shocked to find that more than 150 people were still chained up in jail, waiting to be put on trial for witchcraft. He was dismayed that his special court had not found a solution to the problem. It seemed to have made things worse. In October he ordered that no one else would be jailed, except in extreme cases. He also decreed that, in the future, "spectral evidence" would be inadmissible in his courts. This made trying the other defendants nearly impossible, but laws had to be followed. Those that remained in jail finally had their day in court in January 1693. There were 52 people brought to trial, and three were convicted who confessed to witchcraft. All but those three were set free – the confessors were sentenced to hang.

But the royal attorney general ruled the evidence against those to be hanged was insufficient and Governor Phips commuted their sentences.

The Salem witch hysteria came to an end.

By the spring of 1693 the witch hunts were over, but the acrimony that they created between villagers would linger for years. The accusations, harsh words, and bitter memories created permanent rifts between former friends and neighbors. Many of those who fled Salem during the hysteria chose to never return.

Once public sentiment shifted away from the "afflicted girls," they withdrew from sight. Only Ann Putnam publicly admitted the wrong that she'd taken part in. In 1706, she requested to be allowed back as a member of the church in Salem Village, and Reverend Green read her apology from the pulpit. In the spirit of healing she was forgiven and allowed to return to the church.

But not all were forgiven. Many were angered at Reverend Parris for his rush in demanding that the children accuse others of supposedly bewitching them. The most furious were, of course, the relatives of those jailed, tortured, and executed. Parris was forced to leave Salem in 1697 and he never returned.

Eventually, most people came to realize that the Salem insanity was a deception instigated by fear and religious extremism. Throughout the Massachusetts colony the date January 4, 1797 was set aside as a day of fasting and prayer to ask "God's forgiveness" for the tragedy of the witch trials. One of the judges, Samuel Sewall, wrote a letter that his minister read to the congregation. Sewall acknowledged his terrible mistake when he condemned innocent people to death. All he could do now, he wrote, was plead for absolution from God and his fellow men and women. Also, on that same day, former trial jurors admitted their mistakes, especially in believing that "spectral evidence" was sufficient to send someone to the gallows. They begged for forgiveness and deeply apologized, saying they'd fall under the power of a strong "delusion."

But no number of apologies could erase the damage that had been done.

In all 20 people went to their deaths – 19 of them hanged and one crushed. Dozens and dozens had been jailed. Of those accused 50 confessed to being witches, likely under the threat of torture. Several died in jail, undoubtedly from the deplorable conditions. And then there was little Dorcas Good, the five-year-old sent to jail as a witch. She nearly went insane from her experiences and the subsequent trauma. She remained mentally ill for the rest of her life.

Sorry about that – an inadequate gesture considering the horror that occurred.

What happened in that small New England village? Experts have blamed fraud, class conflict, village factions fighting one another, sexual repression, accidental poisoning, hysteria, actual witchcraft, and, of course, religious extremism. Likely no one explanation will suffice. It was probably a combination of several things, but there is no doubt that the extreme faith of the Puritans was a strong factor. If not for their willingness to blame the Devil for every illness, crop failure, and storm that occurred in and around the village, the witch hunts would never have occurred at all.

The region teetered on the edge of madness and changed the way that Americans thought about religion for years to come. The reaction that so many people had to the rigid dogma of the Puritans, combined with a coming era of "enlightened" thinking, left little room for religious mania in the eighteenth century. America's Puritan heritage cast a shadow over the history of the country, and it influenced many opinions and fears about religion for more than a century.

A Growing Excitement

Witch hunt mania in America was not confined to Salem or even just the Massachusetts colony. The fervor for hanging witches swept the colonies in the latter years of the seventeenth century leading to tragedies and death. The madness that arose from this period drained America of its lust for religious mania for many years to come. There was a sobering that followed, guiding people into the sober church denominations that refused to make waves, question authority, or introduce anything too daring into the daily lives of those who worked hard to survive in the conditions of the era.

As time marched into the years of the eighteenth century, Americans were preoccupied with a war for independence from England, followed by the building of a new nation, and another war with Britain in 1812. This time of hardship, brutality, and war ushered in a new era of enlightenment for the country. In the 1820s and 1830s religious excitement began to sweep the country, and soon new groups, sects, and cults began to emerge.

Many factors led to this sudden "new age" that came to America, not the least of which was the public's fascination with "mesmerism." It was named for the man who developed it, Franz Anton Mesmer, who was born in Germany in 1734 and later earned a medical degree from the University of Vienna. He theorized that a magnetic fluid surrounds, or links, all things and beings on earth and in the heavens and that the "universal fluid" in the human body could be influenced to treat illnesses. Mesmer called his new method "animal magnetism," and he began to attract a huge following in Paris. In 1773 he produced his first cure when he applied "magnetic plates to a patient's limbs," but in 1778 he purportedly cured a blind girl, which won him even greater fame.

After an investigation Mesmer was branded a fraud – by none other than Benjamin Franklin himself – but in 1823 a French doctor, Alexander Bertrand, became curious about Mesmer's work and a renewed interest in "animal magnetism" emerged in Europe. During the experiments that followed subjects were placed in hypnotic trances and many of them demonstrated psychic abilities that they did not ordinarily have, such as telepathy, seeing objects when their eyes were closed, clairvoyant abilities, speaking in voices not their own, and even precognition of future events.

Mesmerism arrived in America at a perfect time. During the first half of the nineteenth century Americans were seeking and exploring new religious and spiritual ideas. Demonstrations of mesmerism became popular with the public in the 1830s and 1840s. There were as many as 30 different mesmerists on the lecture circuit in New England at one time, and in Boston alone at least 200 men who were practicing the trade.

No one could explain how mesmerism worked, which is why it not only provoked curiosity from audiences but frightened them, too. Some believed that the trances subjects entered could provide communication with God or, as the Spiritualists who came along a few years later believed, the spirit world. Not surprisingly others believed it the work of the Devil.

Regardless of what mesmerism was, it would be a great influence on those who became leaders and followers in the religious sects and groups that followed. Americans were seeking new spiritual ideas and while mesmerism was certainly strange and eye-opening, why not take things one step further?

Many would soon have that chance as they began to embrace what was known in the 1830s as "Mother Ann's Work."

The story of Ann Lee began in England in the eighteenth century. Ann lived in the industrial town of Manchester and spoke of magical visions and prophecies. She belonged to a radical religious sect that would come to be known as the Shakers and for her beliefs she was laughed at, beaten, and jailed on charges of sorcery and public disruption. Local authorities had no idea what to make of the otherworldly possession that seemed to grip her and the other Shakers when they quivered and shook in their spirit trances. Ann was determined not to become another victim of persecution and she fled from England.

Mother Ann Lee

In 1774 the woman now known as Mother Ann landed in New York with eight followers. They included her unfaithful husband with whom she had suffered through the births and deaths of four children, but he would not be around for long. According to legend their ship almost capsized in a storm but Ann, in a state of eerie calm, told the captain that no harm would come to them. She later claimed to see "two bright angels of God" on the mast. The ship made it safely to New York.

The group, which grew to include 12 people – minus Ann's husband, toiled at menial labor until 1776 when they managed to save enough money to form a small colony in the marshy fields of Niskayuna, near Albany, in New York's Hudson Valley. They anointed the place "Wisdom's Valley." It was a brutal 200 acres of swamp land that was punished by cold winds in the winter and transformed into a muddy, mosquito-infested field in the summer. The neighbors were no friendlier than the landscape. Rumors claimed that Mother Ann's flocks – all sworn pacifists – were British sympathizers or spies. Ann was briefly jailed in Albany on charges of sedition. She was released but treated horribly. During a missionary trip to Massachusetts a band of 30 men seized Ann and stripped her naked, claiming that they were checking to see if she was a British spy in women's clothing. She was accused of both witchcraft and heresy, and yet the odd little sect – celibate and steeped in a life of poverty and hard labor – began to grow.

Soon after a brutal upstate New York winter in 1780, two men from across the Hudson River in the farm community of New Lebanon took advantage of the spring thaw to visit the Shaker colony. The men were disappointed followers of one of the many Baptist revivals that had been sweeping the region, and they wanted to meet the woman whom followers called "Christ returned in female form." When they found Mother Ann and her colony in the wilderness, they could scarcely believe they had survived the winter. They were granted an audience with Ann and asked about her mystical teachings and the rumors of the sect's practices, in which they spoke of prophecies, saw visions of the dead, and danced, jumped, and shouted while possessed by the Holy Spirit. "We are the people who turn the world upside down," she told them.

The men returned to New Lebanon to tell of the people in the woods and soon more curiosity-seekers began arriving at "Wisdom's Valley." Strange natural events brought even more newcomers to Mother Ann's doorstep. On May 19, 1780, many parts of New England experienced what was called "The Dark Day" – a period when the daytime skies were mysteriously blackened. The cause may have been a rash of local fires to clear fields, but the effect was panic. Scores of people were convinced that it signaled the end of days. Mother Ann saw many new converts flock to her community. She had predicted it all and, to the Shakers, the dark days were expected. Soon New Lebanon itself grew into a much bigger colony and was eventually known for its immaculate whitewashed buildings, tidy yards, and brick meetinghouses. Each was filled with the simple, clean lines of furniture for which the Shakers became famous. It was as if the purity to which they aspired to was given life in the objects they created with their hands.

Mother Ann died in 1784, but her influence extended further after her death than it ever did in life. The late 1830s saw the dawn of an inspired and influential period of Shaker activity that became known as "Mother Ann's Work."

Shakers believed that their departed leader appeared as an otherworldly spirit guide, directing a wide range of supernatural activities and teachings. Shaker villages – which had now spread as far away as the wilds of Kentucky – recorded visits from the ghosts of historical figures and the spirits of vanquished Indian tribes. Mother Ann's followers claimed to receive ghostly visions and songs, which they turned into beautiful paintings and haunting songs that still survive today. They spoke in mysterious tongues, thrashing and rolling about on the floors during meetings that lasted all night. They were, it was believed, possessed by the spirits of those who passed away long before.

In an America that had not yet experienced the heyday of Spiritualism which would offer séances, table tilting, and conversing with the dead, the Shakers foretold that beings from the other side would soon "visit every city and hamlet, every palace and cottage in the land."

And Spiritualism made this prediction come true. The Spiritualist movement is a bit of an anomaly within the context of this book. Its beginnings occurred in the same part of the country where so many other sects, cults, and movements were born, and the movement began in 1848, a time when so many Americans were searching for answers when it came to religion and spirituality.

But Spiritualism was never meant to be a religious movement. It began in Hydesville, New York when two young girls began communicating with an unseen presence in their home. News of the communications spread and the movement that emerged went on to galvanize American society for nearly a century, fascinating people from every walk of life. It was founded on the belief that life existed after death and that the spirit could continue to exist outside of the body. Most importantly, Spiritualists maintained that these spirits could – and did – communicate with the living.

The spirits communicated through "mediums" – sensitive men and women who slipped into trances and passed along messages from the other side. Sometimes during séances (or "sittings") the dead produced physical phenomena like mysterious lights, unearthly music, levitating objects, disembodied voices, or actual apparitions.

Spiritualism took root in the American consciousness during a time of religious fervor in the country. The promises of life after death that the movement offered was its initial draw, but it saw an incredible resurgence after both the Civil War and World War I. Those two wars saw the wholesale slaughter of young men in America and Europe like nothing the world had witnessed before. But thanks to Spiritualism, lost loved ones were no longer lost at all. They could speak and be spoken to as if they were still alive. Spiritualism filled the huge void that death had made in the lives of the everyday person. They now had something to cling to and a belief that their family members and friends had gone on to a better place.

The movement swept across the country. People became obsessed with the idea that the living could communicate with the dead – and receive a reply.

However, it did not spread without opposition. Most of the attacks against Spiritualism in the early days came from the fundamentalist Christians. Conservative religious groups held the opinion that communion with the spirits was possible, but it was evil and dangerous to the welfare of one's soul. Many church leaders saw Spiritualism as a grievous threat to organized religion, but interestingly Spiritualism was never meant to turn into a faith or a religious movement.

In fact, it was quite the opposite of religion. Spiritualism never assumed the rigid structure of ordinary church denominations. It was accessible to everyone and while that openness appealed to many, ironically, the lack of organization may have been the movement's greatest weakness. It would not be able to withstand the changes that were coming in America in the decades that followed its birth. The country was experiencing unprecedented growth and mobility, and Spiritualism initially seemed to reflect the changes that America was going through. It was an age of religious and social agitation and excitement, coupled with new marvels in science and technology.

In 1859, barely a decade after Spiritualism began, Charles Darwin published his controversial book *Origin of Species*. The impact of his theory of evolution was stunning. Some said that by accepting Darwin's theory it meant that you were replacing a God in whose image man was created with the anatomical results of natural selection and an ape for an ancestor. In this heady mixture Spiritualism threatened to redefine man's very nature, abilities, and purpose. For if people did possess "other abilities" then the current concept of mankind, religion, and perhaps even God, would have to be changed or at least re-examined. Spiritualism became a starting point for a great many people in search of answers to some of the great mysteries of life and death.

Spiritualism replaced religion in other ways, too. For the bereaved it offered something no church could. The early and middle nineteenth century was a time of short life expectancy and high child mortality rates. Two out of every ten babies did not live to see their first birthday. It was not unusual for mothers to die during childbirth. Simply living to adulthood was a great achievement, and even then, a great many people did not live beyond their forties. Medical treatment was limited, painful, and often deadly. There were no therapists to help the grieving deal with death. Whether they knew it or not mediums were suddenly placed in the role of grief counselors. Spirit contact meant comfort, no matter what the church, the press, and the scientists said about it. Attending séances became more than mere entertainment. For many it became a necessity of life.

So, even though Spiritualism came to life out of the turmoil of religious excitement that was taking place at the time – and the methods that some followers used to try and turn it into a religious faith – it was never a religious movement. Opponents were correct in fearing that it might replace organized religion if it continued unchecked, but they need not have worried. Eventually Spiritualism as a national movement wore itself out and faded into history.

The Burned-Over District

Many wide-ranging social changes came to America in the first half of the nineteenth century. Long-established Christian denominations now faced the threat of new and emerging religious sects and utopian social movements as Americans looked for alternative ways to express their spirituality.

There was also a steady stream of immigrants arriving on American shores. The land, with its wide-open spaces, offered unprecedented freedom, opportunity, and expansion. These immigrants brought with them their own religious and cultural beliefs. Also, many people were finally starting to move westward from the cities and towns that crowded America's Atlantic coastline. They began seeking land and wilderness, like the frontiers of western New York, Ohio, and beyond. By 1800 the nation's population had increased to five million people – one million more than in 1790. In 1803 the Louisiana Purchase added more than 830,000 square miles to the country.

The mesmerists were also out and about with their lectures in the 1830s and 1840s and were immensely popular with the public, if less so with the scientists. They were the period's version of a "self-help" movement, which in those days meant creating a completely fresh and new perspective on life. The mesmerists claimed that they could restore a deeper sense of one's balance and an understanding between people and the unseen spirit world. Mesmerism, in its efforts to restore "health and virtue," was not unlike the religious revival sweeping America at the same time.

Christianity had long taught that the way to betterment was through God. America's religious teachings had always raised mistrust about the extent to which people could make personal improvements unless they did so through the intervention of the Holy Spirit. The revivalists offered the opportunity to be "born again" through fundamentalist Christianity, maintaining that people could "take responsibility" for seeking their own deliverance from sin and damnation. This is a common religious teaching today, but at the time, it was groundbreaking. It differed completely from the Puritan and Calvinist beliefs of an earlier era, but its focus was narrow, and anything that strayed from the fundamentalist belief system was considered the work of the Devil.

In 1825 the Erie Canal opened in Western New York and provided a direct east-west water route across the state from Albany to Buffalo. This new method of transportation meant improved services, more commerce, and growing cities and towns. One of the thriving communities was Rochester, New York which would become known, thanks to its mills, as the "Flour City." It would also be the center of a region that birthed great social movements, including abolitionism, women's suffrage, scores of religious sects, and Spiritualism.

As the people moved west to build the new towns, the religious men and women followed, arriving in the same place where the Shakers had already laid down their roots. This area would prove to be pivotal in America's culture, its influence vastly surpassing its size. No account of American religion is possible without taking stock of how important it was.

Traveling preachers found fertile territory in Western New York. They actively sought to convert as many people as possible to evangelical Christianity in the newly-settled communities. Some ministers preached fire and brimstone, hell and damnation, and the end of days. Traveling circuit riders crisscrossed the hills and valleys with news of the Holy Spirit. The itinerant ministers crossed and re-crossed the region, traveling along hills and valleys and spreading the word of God and the Holy Spirit. The preachers and their tent revival meetings ignited a fervent passion among the simple farmers and tradesmen. For days after they departed, without the prompting of the revivalists, men and women would speak in tongues or fall to the ground in religious ecstasy. Many reported visitations from angels and spirits.

Camp meetings could be wild and complicated affairs. They usually took place in a large open area, perhaps in a forest glade or clearing. They tended to last for about a week and were always held in late summer when farmers were able to take some time away from their fields. During the meetings the grounds were transformed into a kind of tent city – which is why they were often known as tent meetings – with large tents serving as makeshift hostels, taverns, and hospitals. Open-air kitchens were everywhere. Around the central meeting grounds was a circle of smaller tents where families slept and where peddlers put their wares on display. People who couldn't get a place among the tents – it was always overcrowded – usually just slept in the forest, which was not a hardship during the summer months. The meetings could be remarkably large with hundreds – occasionally, thousands – of worshippers in attendance.

A typical meeting always started in a low-key way. A preacher would offer a sermon of welcome and lead a prayer for peace and community. This was followed by the singing of hymns. Then there were more sermons. As the hours went by the atmosphere gradually began to change. The preachers became livelier and the audience got more excited. The most sensational preacher was always saved for last. He would clap his hands, yell, froth at the mouth, and encourage his audience to do the same. The sermons went on past sunset, and when they ended everyone broke off with the sense of a day well spent in the worship of God.

As more days passed the sermons grew increasingly sensational and impassioned. The excited response of the crowd was louder and went on longer with each passing day. By the third day, people were crying out during the sermons, shouting prayers, grabbing their neighbors, and desperately pleading with them to repent, sobbing uncontrollably, and running through the crowd, shoving everyone out of their path.

Eventually the crowds got so big and noisy that the preacher couldn't be heard across the whole field, so multiple preachers began sermonizing at the same time at different points on the meeting ground. As the preachers ranted without letting up the crowd was driven into a kind of collective ecstasy. People behaved as though possessed by something unknown and unfathomable. As they grew more frenzied, they had the irresistible urge to fall to the ground.

This was what was called the "falling exercise." It was a kind of violent fainting spell that came over people at the height of religious mania. It often started with a scream, after which they collapsed to the ground. They might remain that way for minutes or even hours. At some meetings men were in charge of dragging the fallers out of the way so that they would not be stepped on by the crowd.

Those that didn't fall might experience the "jerks." This was a convulsive movement that began in the arms, shoulders or legs, and then spread throughout the entire body. It was said that when the head alone was affected it would be jerked backward and forward, or from side to side, so quickly that the features of the face could not be distinguished. When people recovered from the jerks, they could not account for what had happened to them.

Somewhat like the jerks was the "rolling exercise." People would start by twisting their heads from side to side and rapidly nodding and snapping their heads back. They would throw themselves onto the ground and begin rolling over and over again. Sometimes they writhed and howled like they were being stabbed with something sharp or would bounce up and down and shake convulsively as if their limbs had come loose.

Others performed the "dancing exercise," a somber sequence of forward and backward steps. While smiles of radiant bliss were plastered on their face, the dancers might keep up this movement for hours until they dropped from exhaustion.

There was also the "laughing exercise," which is self-explanatory, and times when rapturous attendees would bark and howl like dogs. Others would begin to run wildly, shoving people aside, trampling on the fallers, and sprinting in circles until they dropped from exhaustion. Others gave in to the general mood of riot and began fighting and beating each other up over nothing.

But what made the camp meetings truly infamous were the orgies.

The meetings were always intensely erotic experiences. In the pervasive atmosphere of excitement, some simply didn't make a distinction between religious ecstasy and sexual need. The campgrounds were notoriously good places for prostitutes to do business. At the height of religious transport many camp attendees would simply go off into the woods together, day or night, in complicated and unthinking combinations. According to one scandalized report from a vigilance committee, a woman at a camp meeting invited six men to meet her in the woods at the same time. It became a standard joke that the local population always spiked nine months after any meeting. These children became known as "camp meeting babies."

The rumors of what went on at the meetings were what eventually led to a taming of the camp meeting traditions a few years later. Vigilance committees began to police the local meetings, and gradually they became calmer and more tedious. Preachers were still expected to be wildly dramatic – it was said that a preacher who didn't end a sermon by falling to the ground and rolling around was just lazy – but many of the more sordid traditions of the past began to disappear.

It was an unusual period in American history, which became known as the country's "Second Great Religious Awakening." Eventually so many fiery preachers flocked to Western New York that it seemed there was no one left to convert – some nicknamed it the "Burned-Over District."

But those camp meetings and the fires they awakened in people would open the door to practices that were far stranger and more disconcerting than the itinerant preachers could have ever dreamed of.

The Wilderness Prophet

From out of this era of religious mania came many so-called prophets and messiahs, but one of the most bizarre was likely Isaac Bullard. He appeared on the scene in the wake of the War of 1812, when traveling preachers were starting to make their way into the wilder reaches of the country, spreading the word of the Lord and the fiery brimstone that awaited those who failed to surrender to God's will.

Isaac Bullard was born in Canada, and his first appearance in New England was marked by a series of strange chants that were heard emanating from the woods outside of a small town. Bullard, a self-proclaimed prophet, had arrived. Once a mild-mannered farmer, he was now on a mission after receiving a direct command from God. He was convinced that the advancements of modern society were sure to lead to mankind's damnation.

Bullard claimed that he had been called by God while he was seriously ill – although he refused to elaborate what his illness may have been. To cure himself he shunned all man-made items and after a 40-day fast he had a vision. He began to preach that God had commanded him to interpret the Bible in a new way and had sent him out to build a model community in the wilderness. He cast off all traditional clothing, dressed in bearskins, and gave away all his possessions. He also stopped cutting his hair and shaving, which led to him growing a huge, bushy, flaming-red beard that complemented his piercing eyes and booming voice.

For the most part, Bullard scared people instead of enlisting them as his followers. Still, a few locals in almost every town he visited joined his sect. He began to be called the "new Prophet Elijah," and eventually his followers numbered more than 200. He promised to lead his disciples to a Promised Land and set up a commune. Because of their righteous living, they would be spared when Judgement Day came around.

Bullard was certain that his ideas would start a national sensation and be imitated by all, but Bullard's path was rigid and he demanded that his followers follow a life of rigid self-denial. They had to wear coarse, skin-irritating bearskins, as well as endure long fasts broken only by simple meals of gruel. He even thought his people might be corrupted by eating this plain fare with utensils, so he forbade the use of forks, spoons, and knives. They had to suck up the mush through a straw while standing. While Bullard's interpretation of the Bible didn't allow shaving or hair cutting, he also decided that bathing was wrong too. He encouraged his followers to roll in the dirt and mud as an act of repentance. The sight of wild-haired, mud-covered men, women, and children dressed in bearskins walking into any town never failed to draw a crowd.

The press was fascinated with Bullard and his sect. A reporter from the *Pittsburgh Gazette* wrote in 1817, "So incessant were their professed addresses to and communications with invisible beings, with whom they pretended at times to hold converse, their fame went abroad."

Even more attention was gained by Bullard and the group's strange chanting. Bullard would sometimes spontaneously stop and face his traveling congregation and ask his favorite rhetorical question: "My God, what wouldst thou have me do?" Each time the group would begin to sway and scream at the top of their lungs:

"Mummyjum, Mummyjum, Mummyjum!"

They would continue to scream this phrase over and over until they were stricken with exhaustion and fell to the ground. No one had any idea what the phrase meant, and when asked about it, Bullard would spread his arms around his followers and say that their lifestyle and beliefs were the answer. In other words, "Mummyjum."

Bullard led his followers from New England to the faraway Arkansas Territory outfitted with nothing other than their bearskin clothes, a few oxen, and the mystic power of "Mummyjum." They never asked for handouts, though they were routinely beaten, horsewhipped, and run out of most towns into which they ventured. They continued to soldier on, though, believing that someday their faith would spread across the country.

Little is known of what became of the "Wilderness Prophet" and his followers. Bullard and the others were last seen around 1824. Legend has it that Bullard walked across the Mississippi River and ascended to heaven. Others believe they were wiped out by Native Americans, which is probably more accurate.

In 1824 a traveler came across the last of the surviving cult members who were desperate and seemingly deranged, living in mud huts along the banks of the Mississippi. Reportedly, "Mummyjum" was the only word they uttered, no matter what they were asked.

Isaac Bullard left no writings behind to explain his visions or beliefs. We only have the stories reported in the newspapers of the day to chronicle his faith – oh, and his incantation of "Mummyjum," which has never been deciphered but remains mysteriously tantalizing all the same.

The Publick Universal Friend

One of the common threads among the dreamers and cultists who flourished in the early nineteenth century was the desire to split apart the already existing orthodoxies of standard religion and remake Christianity into a new source of magic and mystery. One woman in particular – who is largely forgotten today – created a new idea in the minds of her followers about what a divine messenger could be. She became the first American woman to found a new spiritual order. Unlike Mother Ann, who had proclaimed herself the female return of Christ, this woman claimed to be a channel who was possessed by the Divine Spirit. Her name was Jemima Wilkinson.

Born in 1752 to a moderately prosperous family in Rhode Island, Jemima lost her mother at 12 and was raised by her older sisters, riding horses, gardening, and learning the tenets of Quaker theology, to which her family subscribed.

The formal name of the Quakers was the Religious Society of Friends, and the movement was founded in England by John Fox in the seventeenth century. He and his early followers were persecuted for their beliefs, which included the idea that the presence of God exists in every person. "Quaker" began as a derisive nickname because of the belief in a biblical passage that said people should "tremble at the Word of the Lord." The group eventually embraced the term.

Quakers first arrived in America in the middle 1650s. Many of their beliefs were considered radical at the time, such as the idea that women and men were spiritual equals, and that women could speak out during worship. Quakers didn't have official ministers or religious rituals. Based on their interpretation of the Bible Quakers were pacifists and refused to take legal oaths.

As the Quakers moved throughout the colonies, they faced persecution in America, too. Particularly in Puritan-dominated Massachusetts, where many Quakers were executed.

In 1681 King Charles II gave William Penn – a wealthy English Quaker and the face on the box that leads most modern readers to connect Quakers to oatmeal – a large section of land in America to pay off a debt owed to his family. Penn, who had been jailed many times for his Quaker beliefs, founded Pennsylvania as a sanctuary for religious freedom and tolerance. Quakers were involved in Pennsylvania's new government and held positions of power there throughout the first half of the eighteenth century. In time, though, they decided that their political participation was forcing them to compromise some of their beliefs including pacifism. This did not stop them from becoming deeply involved in the fight to abolish slavery. Also, many of the leaders in the women's suffrage movement were Quakers.

Today there are believed to be more than 300,000 Quakers in the world. Most refer to their congregations as "meetings" and practice silent worship, where only those who are inspired to do so will speak.

Jemima Wilkinson's family were practicing Quakers, so she was raised in a different sort of household than most Colonial women. She learned to read and write and had hundreds of books at her disposal. She grew into a young woman of "personal beauty" who "took pleasure in adding to her good appearance the graceful drapery of

The genderless Publick Universal Friend, once known as Jemima Wilkinson

elegant apparel." Later in her life admirers commented on her fresh complexion and gently tanned skin, her chestnut-brown hair, and flashing black eyes. The attractive woman was a striking contrast to Mother Ann Lee, who was later described as a dark, straight-haired woman with an unusually large forehead, dull eyes, and thick, masculine lips. The description accurately captures the world-weariness of Ann's life, far different than that of Jemima Wilkinson, who was raised amidst the comforts of a successful New England farm.

By age 16 Jemima was well-educated, but after becoming immersed in the religious revival of the era her life took a dramatic turn. Jemima fell in with a group of revivalist Baptists and she began to comb through the Bible with a strange intensity. She often locked herself in her room, meditating for hours. Within a few years of her religious rebirth she became entangled in something else that was sweeping through the region – typhus fever.

On October 4, 1776, Jemima stumbled to her bed with a high temperature. Her skin clammy, wet, and burning from within she slipped in and out of delirium, returning to consciousness to describe dreams of being in heaven and speaking with the dead. Her health worsened, and she slipped into a coma. Her breathing grew faint and her pulse slowed. The end seemed near. But after 36 hours near death, she suddenly got out of bed with renewed energy. Jemima had "passed to the angel world," she told her family. She was now "reanimated with the spirit" and destined to "deliver the oracles of God." She was a new entity, she told her family and friends, and was no longer Jemima Wilkinson.

She would now only respond to the name "Publick Universal Friend."

On the Sunday after her seemingly miraculous recovery, still frail and washed-out from her illness, the Publick Universal Friend went to the local church that had become the center of the area's Baptist revival. The congregation was shocked by the reappearance of the young woman that nearly all assumed had died. After the service their shock was even greater as she walked out to a shady tree in the churchyard and began preaching. It was probably the first time that any of them had seen a woman deliver a sermon in public. Her message – repentance from sin, humility, and the Golden Rule – was little more than warmed-over Quakerism, but it electrified the crowd. They marveled at the confidence and eloquence of the girl returned from the dead, who now claimed to be the voice of God.

The Friend soon began traveling all over New England and down to Philadelphia, not exactly seeking converts to a religion but seeking followers of a direct line from God. While in Philadelphia she came under the influence of at least one admirer with ties to a mystic commune at Ephrata in Lancaster County. The commune had been founded in 1732 by Johann Conrad Beissel who had links to divine mystics from

Germany. Following the lead of the commune members, the Friend began to reject the formality of church services, liturgy, confessions of faith, and vows. She also changed the day of the Sabbath to Saturday. Also, like the German mystics, she encouraged – but stopped short of demanding – celibacy among her followers. If anything, the Friend's appeal was that she never required any kind of strict doctrine. She relied instead on the teachings of the scriptures and a simple do-unto-others ethic. Her teachings – in contrast to her extraordinary claims about herself – seemed downright ordinary, relying heavily on punctuality and being a good neighbor.

Unlike the intense devotees that had flocked around Mother Ann, the Friend attracted a circle made up of landowners and merchants. The Shakers, who had frequently run afoul of the authorities, were largely made up of kitchen maids, hired hands and hard-luck farmers, and had seen the inside of a jail on several occasions. Thanks to the status of her followers the Universal Friend moved freely about the region, even during the Revolutionary War, preaching to both American and British troops.

Even when the Friend did end up in court after the war, the results were laughable. In a dispute with an angry former follower the Friend was forced before the Central New York circuit court on charges of blasphemy, only to hear the presiding judge state that blasphemy was not an indictable offense in the new nation. Unbelievably, Judge Morgan Lewis, who later served as governor of the state, even invited the Friend to preach before the court and applauded her for her "good counsel." It was certainly not the kind of reception that Mother Ann could have expected under those circumstances.

Times were already beginning to change.

Influenced by the success of the Germans at Ephrata, the Friend's followers began to discuss creating a community of their own. By late 1788 a cluster of devotees journeyed to Central New York to break ground for a settlement where the Universal Friend could reside. They became some of the earliest white settlers in the area. Their community, called Jerusalem, eventually grew near Crooked Lake – now called Keuka Lake – and continues to exist today. Many of the descendants of the Friend's followers still live in the town.

As time passed, many Central New Yorkers began to have conflicting opinions about their spirit-possessed pioneer, who was a theatrical presence in her trademark cape and a wide-brimmed hat. Most of the ill feelings came from rumors that depicted the Friend as, at best a shrewd operator, and at the worst a con artist of massive proportions. A popular story was told about the Friend leading her followers to the lakeshore one day where she preached to them about the powers of faith. After the story, she proclaimed that she was going to walk on water. She asked her followers if they had faith that she could do it and they replied that they did. "Then, if you have faith," the Universal Friend replied, "there is no need for any vulgar spectacle." With that she climbed into her carriage and drove away.

There was also the shady business of her death, or so the stories went. Her critics claimed the Friend said she was immortal, so when she died in 1819 her minions snuck her body out of her basement in the night and buried her in a secret, unmarked grave. This wasn't true, though. Her followers never tried to hide her death. Jemima

Wilkinson's body was interred with several others in a traditional burial vault on her property. Several years later her remains were moved, in Quaker fashion, to an unmarked plot.

Legal battles over the township land began even before the Friend's death, but for the most part her followers and their families were able to keep a steady balance between their fantastical beliefs and their successful public lives. Following their teacher's death, the merchants and tradesmen that had believed in her remained to join many of the region's liberal and experimental religious communities. The Friend's ministry, which was both supernatural and down-to-earth, left a lasting impression on the Burned-Over District and on the utopian societies that sprang up in the years that followed.

The Utopians

Many of the faithful of the early nineteenth century believed in the power of ideas – whether political or spiritual – as the catalyst for the redemption of the soul. Rare was the person who was part of one of the region's mystical sects that did not also have a part in a social sect. For many the two worlds naturally blended.

One of the first utopian communities in America was founded by a German baker named Conrad Beissel, who migrated from Germany to Pennsylvania in 1720.

Although he favored seclusion as the path to spirituality, he initially joined a religious sect that was flourishing at the time called the "Dunkards." This Protestant offshoot had been established in 1708 by a German miller named Alexander Mack. Originally called the Church of the Brethren, the movement earned the nickname of "Dunkards" from their practice of dipping a convert underwater three times as a form of baptism. Adherents believed exclusively in the Bible's New Testament and were encouraged to avoid carnivals, swearing, filing lawsuits, or attending secular schools. Baptism was reserved until an age when prospects could choose for themselves whether to adhere to church doctrines.

This method of baptism may sound familiar to some readers because, while the sect didn't last, their methods were adopted by many other denominations who continue this ritual today.

No one knows what caused Beissel to become dissatisfied with this sect and others that he tried, but by 1732 he'd decided to start his own religious movement. He established a spiritual commune that he called the Ephrata Cloisters near Lancaster, Pennsylvania. He attracted followers by claiming revelations that he had personally received from God to start a new society.

Beissel was a striking man. When he delivered insights in his curt German-English accent he seemed believable. None doubted his sincerity or piousness. His reputation and character were widely admired, and he was uninterested in any sort of courtship or marriage. One of the stern requirements of membership in the commune was absolute celibacy. Beissel believed that to receive God's message a person must be free of all lustful distractions. Subsequently, living quarters within the commune were separated for men and women.

He also stated that vegetarianism was the best diet to cleanse the mind and body and make one better suited to hear God's instructions. His utopia became the first completely vegetarian commune in America – mostly. Every Easter, Beissel and his group ate lamb.

Beissel loved music, wrote hymns, and supported the commune through a printing company. The commune grew its own food and sold off the excess to nearby communities. Beissel insisted on complete silence inside of the commune, aside from the sound of his organ, which he played whenever he was inspired.

The cloistered and austere lifestyle at Ephrata continued after Beissel died in 1768. He had set up his finances so well that the group could continue without him. It went on to inspire other communes and societies, like the Publick Universal Friend, for a few decades. However, there were no spiritual leaders involved that were of Beissel's caliber, so they failed to attract new recruits. The utopian experiment limped along until the buildings deteriorated.

Without a new generation to carry on – there was no sex allowed, even to produce children – the order disbanded entirely by 1814. All is not lost, though. The grounds of the community are now owned by the Commonwealth of Pennsylvania and are administered by the Pennsylvania Historical and Museum Commission. The original buildings have been renovated, and a glimpse into the life at the Cloisters can still be experienced today.

Another utopian society created years later in the Burned-Out District has become known as America's longest-running and most economically successful commune – but it has its dark side.

The commune was founded at Oneida, New York. The Oneidans thrived from the manufacturing of animal traps, cutlery, and other high-quality goods, while experimenting with biblical communism, attempts at human perfectionism, and sexual liberation. It was at the Oneida commune where the term "free love" was coined.

From about 1848 to 1880 the commune was under the leadership John Humphrey Noyes, who had been expelled from the Yale School of Divinity after he claimed that all religions were flawed. He believed that if God did indeed give mankind free will, then everything that a person chose to do, in his reasoning, was divine. Noyes's path to God was achieved by striving toward "perfectionism" in both body and mind. He wanted to emulate the example of the first-century Christians, who, in the face of persecution, often survived in self-sustaining, tight-knit communities where everything was shared. Inspired, Noyes decided to form a similar utopian society. Noyes's troubles really began because of his broad definition of Christian love, which to him naturally included sex – and a lot of it. After his arrest for adultery in 1847, he and his followers fled Vermont and started a commune for like-minded "perfectionists" at Oneida.

The experimental community was a profitable one. Members worked diligently at farming or in manufacturing, and all worked without a salary. Noyes built a giant dormitory called "Mansion House" where more than 50 followers lived in "complex marriage" arrangements. Noyes considered sex with varying partners an antidote to selfishness. Sharing your husband or wife was one of the noblest demonstrations of

Christian love. Accordingly, he encouraged his followers to engage in sex as often as possible. Not surprisingly, branches of his commune quickly began establishing from Brooklyn to Ontario.

There was only one rule to sex at Oneida – have as much of it as you wanted, but a man always had to pull out before climax. This withdrawal method of birth control was part of Noyes's bigger plan, which was an attempt to engineer the perfect human being. He only selected those considered the most flawless and attractive to produce children. Noyes subsequently fathered nine of his own.

In 1879 a warrant was issued for Noyes's arrest for statutory rape. He fled Oneida for Canada and never returned. He soon sent instructions to the various communes to abandon "complex marriage" and accept traditional nuptial arrangements. He eventually gave ownership of the wide array of businesses to all the commune members in the form of stocks. In the early 1900s

Utopian, Free love advocate, and statutory rapist John Humphrey Noyes

one of his sons turned the original communal enterprise into Oneida Unlimited, which remains today one of the largest manufacturers of quality forks, knives, and spoons in the world. Interestingly, their "official" company history marks their founding date as 1880 – when John Noyes fled New York.

The Oneida commune may have been one of the only sects to survive into the twentieth century, but it was not alone in the Burned-Over District. By the middle nineteenth century there were at least 20 villages or active societies that were operating as utopian communities. Most were short-lived.

The Burned-Over District continued to attract the unusual and the bizarre. A wide range of reformist, civic, and spiritual movements shared members and blended together in the region. Suffragists, abolitionists, and temperance marchers each had deep footholds in the area. As people and ideas crossed the land on their way to the west, they left behind new ideas where strict beliefs in God were replaced by Transcendentalism, Unitarianism and Universalism, and other liberal ways of seeking spirituality. Freemasons and anti-Masonic activists clashed and eventually the Burned-Over District gave birth to one of the strangest and most influential of America's movements: Spiritualism.

Spiritualism shared a common trait with the utopian movements that dotted the region. Spiritualists had the familiar Yankee attitude that religion rested not just on faith, but on proof. Like many of the other religious sects that thrived in that time and place, Spiritualists found tantalizing "facts" to back up their belief in the reality of the afterlife: spirit raps, tilting tables, and messages through mediums.

The utopians maintained that they, too, were simply following a process of logic – in their case, the cause-and-effect of better styles of living creating better men and women. In the Burned-Over District, mystics and radicals had a shared stake in the prophecy of progress. They believed that spiritual and social forces, if they were properly used, could remake a person, inside and out.

It was a way of thinking that would certainly outlast the sects, cults, and movements that created it.

Worshippers of the Apocalypse

The idea of an imminent apocalypse has been rooted in American religious beliefs for centuries, and, of course, it's still there. Predictions of the end of the world, or at least the end of the world as we know it, date back thousands of years. Those who counted down the days to the predicted apocalypse on December 21, 2012 were following one of hundreds – perhaps thousands – of belief systems that have made similar claims. Some still expect the end of the world on some other date, while others claim not to know the exact date but are convinced it will happen soon.

A great many Americans, for instance, are convinced that at some point soon, every truly devout Protestant Christian will suddenly and mysteriously disappear from the face of the earth and go to meet Jesus in the clouds. "The Rapture," as this disappearance is called, will usher in a period of seven years called "The Tribulation," in which most of humanity will be exterminated by a succession of natural and unnatural disasters carried out by the minions of the world's last tyrant, the "Antichrist." At the end of the seven years the Antichrist and his followers will be wiped out by Jesus and the Christian faithful will rule with him over the earth for the next 1,000 years. Those who believe in this are convinced that it is predicted in the Bible and a large number of them are convinced it will happen during their lifetimes.

And they're not alone in this belief.

Many devout Muslims believe in a similar version of the future. While the Rapture doesn't appear in Muslim apocalyptic lore, the equivalent of the Antichrist, the Dajjal, is expected to be every bit as horrible and his destruction at the hands of the Mahdi, the future prophet who will lead the faithful to paradise, is just as real to Muslims as Jesus is to Christians. Plenty of orthodox Jews, in turn, wait for the appearance of the Messiah. There are many Hindus who anticipate the birth of Kalki, the next avatar of the god Vishnu, while Buddhists in Central Asia long for an appearance of the great king Rigden Jyepo, who will emerge from the city of Shambhala to vanquish the enemies of the Buddhist Dharma.

Obviously, the idea of the end of the world in the apocalypse, and the antichrist is not a new one – it's just not as old in America as it is in the rest of the world. But there's no need to worry, we have no shortage of insanity related to it.

The national faith in an imminent Second Coming (i.e., Rapture or Apocalypse) sank its root into American soil in the early part of the eighteenth century. In the years after 1720 when a minister named Jonathan Edwards kick-started the country's Great Awakening with an obviously light-hearted sermon called "Sinners in the Hands of an Angry God," most of New England was gripped with fear that the earth was going to open up beneath them as they sat in church and drop them straight into Hell. Like all subsequent religious revivals, the Great Awakening ran out of steam after a few years as the people who had run in terror to churches, hoping to hear about themselves being consigned to one colorful version of Hell after another, found other things to do with their time.

But the idea of the apocalypse stuck. Within a generation, new revivals sprang up in other places, and nearly all of them (like in the Burned-Out District) embraced the same themes of the Christian end of the world.

These outbreaks of religious mania drew heavily on a divide in American society that goes all the way back to Colonial times – the enduring cultural divide between the cities along the coast and the farm country further inland. The wealth, political and social liberalism, and the cosmopolitan attitudes of the urban cultures of the coasts have always sparked resentment from the poorer and more conservative inhabits of what we now call the "fly-over states." And the people of the cities returned that resentment with interest.

Religious revivals played to that divide, condemning the cities as modern-day Babylons that God would assuredly smite, after which the more virtuous folks of farm country would receive a suitably spiritualized version of all the things their rivals had once enjoyed.

Popular as it was, the revival phenomenon remained localized for as long as America itself was a collection of local and regional cultures, each shaped largely by its colonial heritage. In the decades after the Revolutionary War the former colonies gradually merged into a nation, and new methods of transportation and communication – like railroads and the telegraph – made it easier for people and ideas to move from one area to another.

Religious thought – and apocalyptic movements – grew accordingly. Sooner or later one of these movements was going to catch fire over a large section of the new republic and leap across the gap between the rural communities and the coastal cities.

And in the 1840s, one of them finally did.

The Millerites

The Millerites movement was birthed by one of America's first great waves of social reform. Soon after the War of 1812 many Americans began to embrace scores of liberal and radical causes including the abolition of slavery, women's rights, pacifism, temperance movements, diet and dress reforms, and many others. As has already been mentioned, most of the movements considered Christian in America at the time were anything but conservative. Most of the leading reform organizations – Anti-Slavery Societies, the Temperance League, and others – were allied with churches and staffed and supported by clergymen of all kinds. In the 1820s and 1830s, evangelical Protestantism was the counterculture movement of the day.

It was into this setting that William Miller came with news of the imminent end of the world.

Born in Pittsfield, Massachusetts in 1782, Miller grew up estranged from his Baptist upbringing, largely indifferent to religion. After serving in the army during the War of 1812, though, he began to embrace a view that was common among returning soldiers – that his survival had been divinely ordained. The man who had largely ignored religion came home with a deep interest in questions of faith and immortality.

Now convinced that the Bible was a literal record of truth, Miller undertook an obsessive study of every word, line, and letter to determine the exact date of Christ's return – a date that he believed would usher in a millennium of peace. Although only moderately educated, Miller spent the next 14 years poring over the scriptures, organizing and cross-referencing all that he found, to build an orderly blueprint of what he believed was God's plan.

He settled on a verse in the Old Testament – Daniel 8:14 – as the secret of the world's end. The verse read:

And he said unto me, Unto two thousand and three hundred days; then shall the sanctuary be cleansed.

William Miller – the man who convinced thousands the world was going to end in 1843.

According to the established biblical interpretations of the time, 2,300 days meant 2,300 years. Counting from the restoration of the Jews to the Holy Land at the end of the Babylonian captivity in 457 BCE, which meant that 1843 was the time when "the sanctuary would be cleansed." It was a metaphor – of something – but Miller believed that it indicated nothing less than the Second Coming of Christ.

This date formed only one part of a complex theory of prophecy that mapped the events of the Book of Daniel and Revelation onto more than 2,000 years of history. For Miller – and for many of his contemporaries – every major event in the history of the Christian world between the last page of the Book of Acts and the end of the world had already been foretold through prophecy – and a lot of effort had gone into figuring out just what historical kingdom or event was represented in every metaphor or symbol in the Bible. Everything, they believed, corresponded to some historical happening.

I think it goes without saying that few of these would-be prophets agreed with one another. You could multiply the number of toes on the colossal statue that Daniel talked about in an apocryphal vision by the number of theories about what the toes of gold, silver, brass, and iron meant, and still not come up with as many claims that were made about what was going to happen in the near future.

But Miller's system of prophecy adopted all the standard tools of interpretation available at the time. The other thing that made his calculations different from all the other prophets of the era was that he believed the end of times was close enough to be marked on a calendar. It was Miller's acceptance of the standard religious beliefs of the time that made his prediction so compelling to his contemporaries.

Miller had spent 14 years checking and re-checking his figures and consulting historical and scriptural authorities. He had no desire to start a cult or seek converts, and he kept his insights to himself during this time. But Miller eventually thought people might be interested and wrote a document about his findings, explaining that the world was going to end "sometime near 1843."

For several years after this he traveled the back roads of New England from one small church to another, spreading the word about the end of times. He began to gain a serious audience as one of the wandering religious speakers of the day.

He seemed an unlikely preacher, though. He had terrible stage fright in the early days but soon gained both confidence and zeal. Within a few years he was speaking to packed audiences and began to gain attention in the larger cities.

In 1838, he met Boston clergyman and publisher Joshua Vaughan Himes and quickly found himself a national phenomenon. Miller captivated people as few other preachers had done before or since.

Reverend Joshua Himes was one of the greatest spiritual leaders of 1830s Boston, a city that had become the country's center for radical religious and social movements. Himes was active in almost every imaginable reform group of the time and was an effective organizer and media manager. With Miller's blessing he took charge of publicizing and financing the message of the looming apocalypse. In 1840 Himes started the first Millerite newspaper, *Sign of the Times*, and soon followed it with a pamphlet series, *The Second Advent*, and a printed edition of Miller's lectures. Later that same year the first conference of the new movement brought hundreds of Millerites to Boston. Money poured in, the number of committed followers grew, and controversy over Miller's predications began filling newspaper columns and being spread from church pulpits across America.

One of the reasons why Miller's message enthralled so many people was because it came on the heels of a movement for social reform just when that movement was starting to falter. It offered new hope to console the repeated failures of the believers in charge. By the end of the 1830s it had become clear that the counterculture of the era had accomplished nearly all that it could – most of the proposed reforms had gone nowhere. Women still didn't have the right to vote. Saloons, breweries, and distilleries were still serving and making liquor. Two of the central causes of the time – the struggles against slavery and war – were on a collision course with each other. It had become clear that the only way to end slavery in America would likely only be obtained by violence or civil war.

But those reformers who were still so desperate for change at the beginning of the 1840s were quick to embrace an ideology that told them they would get the perfect world that they wanted handed to them by God very soon.

Miller and Himes took advantage of their vulnerability with one of the first massive media campaigns in American history. By 1843, when the movement was in full swing, more newspapers were added to the Millerite campaign, including the *Midnight Cry* in New York, the *Philadelphia Alarm*, and the *Western Midnight Cry*, printed in Cincinnati. Between newspaper editions, Millerite presses turned out tracts, pamphlets, and posters that spelled out Miller's prophecies with garish imagery. Between 300 and 400 ministers were busy spreading the message of the Second Coming, and Himes himself

For the Millerites, it was the end of the world as they knew it – and end that never happened.

was touring with what was said to be the largest tent in the country, a monster-sized pavilion that could hold as many as 4,000 people who came to hear lectures and sermons about Miller's predictions. Once, near Rochester, New York, a strong wind snapped 15 of the massive tent's chains and several inch-thick ropes and violently ripped it into the air. Amazingly no one was hurt – which just deepened the belief that Miller's message was blessed by God.

A financial depression that hit in the early 1840s, followed by several astronomical events – like a huge meteorite shower and Halley's Comet – served to only heighten the need for deliverance. To many Miller's radical predictions made it all clear – the end of the world was coming.

The excitement continued to build as Miller's calendar ticked off the dates. The Second Coming would occur sometime between March 21, 1843 and March 21, 1844. Millerite leaders, including Miller himself, tried to avoid pinning the movement down to just one date. More than 100,000 followers – along with another one million or more that had attended lectures about the prophecies – kept a watchful eye toward the predicted date with general fear. Millerites took joy in the impending doomsday and considered those who scoffed to be damned to hell. They alone, they were convinced, would be saved.

As the last year began, Millerite preachers began what they believed would be the final round of tent revivals, lectures, and media campaigns before the world ended. More than five million copies of Millerite publications saw print during the movement's history, which was a stunning number for the time and a major factor in its success.

Bad news, though – March 1844 came and went, and nothing happened.

Critics and scoffers had a field day. Miller, Himes, and their colleagues pointed out that the calculations allowed Jesus a little wriggle room and urged Millerite believers to stand fast in the certainty that they could expect the end of the world to come very soon. Himes added two new publications for believers, a theological quarterly called *Advent Shield* and a women's magazine, the *Advent Message to the Daughters of Zion*. For the first time he also began to advocate that Millerites who found themselves being ridiculed in their churches ought to leave and start new churches that focused on the Millerite doctrine.

A cartoon that circulated claiming that the Millerites put on robes and waited on rooftops for the end of the world.

It was at this point, though, that the movement suddenly spun out of the leaders' control. An obscure Millerite preacher, Reverend Samuel Snow, became convinced that he had found an error in one of the historical texts that Miller had used to create his prediction. After he corrected the problem, Snow announced that Miller's calculations pointed to an exact date for the Second Coming – October 22, 1844.

Snow's announcement caused an explosion of excitement among Millerites. Miller and Himes tried to downplay the new date but quickly found that the movement they thought they were leading was prepared to find other leaders if they didn't provide what it wanted. Miller never really signed on to the new timeline, but Himes became convinced that the rising tide of excitement could only be the work of the Holy Spirit – or so he likely said, as he kept a close eye on his bank account.

As the summer of 1844 moved toward autumn, Snow's prediction found tens of thousands of eager listeners at Millerite camp meetings and revivals. On October 6, in front of a packed house, Himes announced that the next issue of the *Advent Herald* would be the last since the Second Coming of Christ would make future issues unnecessary.

During the last week or so before October 22, many thousands of Millerites across the country gave up all but the most necessary work and devoted themselves day and night to prayer and Bible study, preparing to meet God. Many sold their possessions and gave away their money to church officials, as it was recommended to meet Judgement Day debt-free. In cities and small towns across the country, droves of followers donned white robes and gathered on hilltops with their arms outstretched.

Stories spread that Millerites ran amok, engaging in "free love," and throwing all their money into the wind, anticipating a world without wants or demands. Others were said to take the words from the scriptures that claimed none will enter the kingdom of God unless child-like so literally that adults began to regress, skipping, and hopping around, while others sucked their thumbs or stayed in bed in a fetal position.

Whether or not such stories were true remains unknown. The most embarrassing stories seem to have been concocted by critics and neighbors who laughed at the Millerites and their controversial beliefs. But even the less religious responded to the possibility of the apocalypse. They built bunkers and one safe company saw brisk sales after modifying their "fireproof chest" to accommodate food, water, and a small fan so that the owners could use it as a safe haven to ride out what might be an impending doomsday.

And then, October 22 also came and went.

When the sun rose on an unredeemed world the next morning, the Millerite movement imploded. Most of its members went back to their old churches or went on to other new religious movements. But the failure of Jesus to appear at the predicted time did not, as we might imagine, mean the end of Miller's cult. Miller believed, until the day he died five years later, that it was all a math error, and the Second Coming was still going to take place on some imminent – but undetermined – date. Miller said that "The Great Disappointment," as the fiasco came to be called, was a divine test of their faith. His adherents remained devoted to his prophetic vision long after his death in 1849.

"The Great Disappointment" delivered a crushing blow to the American apocalyptic movement, but it certainly didn't kill it off. It remained alive during the nineteenth century and endures in other forms today. Conservative Christians have continued to speak of Christ's imminent return, but very few people want to be reminded of the consequences of taking that belief seriously enough to set a date for it.

But, of course, some did it anyway.

Herbert W Armstrong, the founder of the Worldwide Church of God, predicted that the Second Coming would happen sometime in 1936. When this prediction failed, he concocted a new one – 1975. Oops.

A pastor from California, Mihran Ask, claimed that "Sometime between April 16 and 23, 1957, Armageddon will sweep the world! Millions of persons will perish in its flames, and the land will be scorched." Since you're reading this, you know that didn't happen.

During the Six-Day War in 1957, the Israeli army captured all of Jerusalem. Many conservative Christians believed that the Rapture would occur soon after – it didn't.

William Branham, a Baptist minister from Kentucky, was allegedly visited by an angel in 1946, who gave him magical powers to diagnose disease and demonic oppression, as well as the gift of prophecy. He believed that the year 1977 would bring about the Rapture. He died in 1965 more than a decade before his prediction was proven wrong.

In May 1980 televangelist and Christian Coalition founder Pat Robertson startled and alarmed many when — contrary to Matthew 24:36, which says, "No one knows about that day or hour, not even the angels in heaven..." – he informed his *700 Club* television audience that he knew when the world would end.

"I guarantee you by the end of 1982 there is going to be a judgment on the world," Robertson said. I'm not sure why but the failure of this prediction has not affected his popularity among those who will believe anything.

Arnold Murray of the Shepherd's Chapel predicted that the war of Armageddon will start on June 8, 1985, in "a valley of the Alaskan peninsula." Guess that was wrong, too.

Author Hal Lindsey predicted in his book *The Late, Great Planet Earth* that the Rapture was coming in 1988 – one generation, or 40 years, after the creation of the state of Israel. This failed prophecy did not appear to damage his reputation, either. He continues to write books of prophecy – which I would suggest you take with a grain of salt.

Edgar Whisenaut, a NASA scientist, published the book *88 Reasons Why the Rapture Will Be in 1988*. (I wonder if he knows Hal Lindsey?) It sold over 4 million copies and probably made him a multi-millionaire.

Peter Ruckman concluded from his analysis of the Bible that the Rapture would come within a few years of 1990. I think that we can safely say that this prophecy failed, as well.

And that's just a sampling. There have been a lot of others.

In recent years, though, probably the most spectacular failed prophet was Harold Camping, a Christian radio broadcaster, author, and evangelist. In 1958 he started Family Radio, a California-based radio station group that eventually was broadcast in more than 150 markets in the United States. But that's not what really made him famous – it was his predictions, which temporarily gained him a global followed and earned him millions of tax-free dollars in donations.

Camping first predicted that the Second Coming would occur on or about September 6, 1994. When it failed to happen, he revised the date to September 29 and then to October 2. Both those days passed with no sign of Jesus, but somehow, he didn't lose his audience. Like the Millerite leaders, he just changed the date again.

Next, Camping predicted the Second Coming of Christ on May 21, 2011, after which the saved would be taken up to heaven in the Rapture, and that "there would follow five months of fire, brimstone, and plagues on Earth, with millions of people dying each day, culminating on October 21, 2011, with the final destruction of the world."

Yikes.

By the time of this new prediction, it was no longer the 1990s. Social media and 24-hours news cycles had become commonplace, and his prediction for May 21, 2011 apocalypse was widely reported. Family Radio promotion went into overdrive and the cash began to pile up.

And then, nothing happened on May 21. But Camping wasn't deterred. He announced that a "spiritual judgment" had occurred on that date and that the physical Rapture would occur on October 21, 2011, simultaneously with the final destruction of the world by God.

The press didn't buy it – and neither did most of Camp's followers. This second "Great Disappointment" led to the near-collapse of Family Radio and probably was the reason for the stroke that Camping suffered in June 2011.

Believe it or not, Camping seemed to learn his lesson after that. He later admitted in a private interview that he no longer believed that anybody could know the time of the Rapture or the end of the world. He added that his attempt to predict the date of the Rapture was "sinful," and his current searches of the Bible were simply to be "more faithful." He expressed his regrets, but when he died in 2013 every obituary that was written about him talked of little but his failed predictions.

Perhaps the next prophet that comes along should see that as a warning.

Doomsday and Corn Flakes

After the death of William Miller his movement lived on. One faction of Millerites continued under the leadership of Ellen Haron, who, as a teenager in the 1840s, believed so fervently in Miller's dogma that she began to announce her own visions and prophecies of impending doom. She claimed that angels took her on an arduous journey to heaven and was sent back to start a new branch of Miller's church.

She eventually married James White, a fellow advocate of the apocalypse, and together, they gathered many new followers through preaching, claims of new visions, and their extensive writings.

They moved together to Battle Creek, Michigan, where they established many creeds regarding worship and health issues. Ellen had been a sickly child and attributed that to her working around toxic chemicals in her parent's hat business. In those days hat makers used mercury to form the crisp brims of their hats. The term "mad as a hatter" came into general use when it was discovered that mercury caused varying degrees of insanity – including visions, hallucinations, and hearing voices.

In Michigan, Ellen had visions that told her to avoid both doctors and prescription drugs – it should be noted that most prescriptions contained things like opium at the time – and instead use "God's water" for healing. Cold baths and hydrotherapy became the usually suggested remedy for ill health among Ellen's followers.

She also strongly believed in simple foods. Dr. John Kellogg took charge of the healthy foods for the sect, and he invented Corn Flakes. Sylvester Graham, interested in Ellen's visions about the evils of flour, promoted whole wheat products and invented the Graham Cracker.

Ellen's branch of the church exists today as the Seventh-Day Adventists. The seven-day part of their name means they rest on Saturday instead of Sunday, unlike most Christian groups. Adventists still believe the world faces an imminent end, but, wisely, they no longer try and nail that down to exact date.

The Seventh-Day Adventist church now has more than five million members across the country. At some point in the twentieth century they entered the mainstream of American religious life.

But it wasn't always that way. There was at least one offshoot of the sect that found itself with the kind of publicity that no church could ever want.

"The Pocasset Horror"

In the 1870s, while Ellen Haron was leading her flock to Michigan, another group of Seventh-Day Adventists set up a church in Cataumet, Massachusetts, a small village at the extreme western end of the Cape Cod peninsula, on the shores of Buzzards Bay. Among the members of the church was Charles Freeman, a local farmer who lived in the nearby town of Pocasset with his wife, Harriet, and his two daughters – six-year-old Bessie and four-year-old Edith, who was her father's favorite.

Charles was later described by the newspapers as a man of "upright life and conduct," and he was admired – perhaps even revered – by his fellow Adventists for the strength of his religious convictions. He often spoke of the need to prove his faith through sacrifice and declared that "he had given his whole family to God." None of his friends or fellow church-goers doubted his sincerity, but they had no idea that his dreadful fixation on blood sacrifice was growing stronger in him with each passing day.

It would finally erupt into madness with the murder of his daughter.

Charles F. Freeman was a man obsessed with God. Freeman's God was a cruel and jealous being, demanding much of his followers, who were expected to follow him blindly and without question. And when God demanded a sacrifice – as he did from Freeman in the spring of 1879 – his servant was expected to provide it. He knew it was the right thing to do because God had told him to do so.

On the night of April 30, 1879, Freeman attended a church gathering at the home of another fervent worshipper then returned home and tucked his daughters, Bessie and Edith, into the bed they shared. He kissed them goodnight and went to his own bed and began drifting off to sleep. He thought of his daughters as he did so, and later recalled, "They never seemed so dear to me as then."

At the darkest hour of the night he jerked awake and began to shake his wife's arm. He told her that the time had come for his sacrifice. He had been willing to offer himself up to God, but his vision told him that it was not his time to die. "The Lord has appeared to me," he whispered feverishly. "I know who the victim must be – my pet, my idol, my baby, Edith."

"No!" Harriet wailed, bursting into tears. She never believed that her husband would go through with it. She believed that God spoke to Charles, but she never believed that he would tell him to kill their daughter. She shook with horror as she made one last plea to spare the little girl's life.

But Charles would not be deterred. "The Lord has said it is necessary."

And now Harriet also believed. It was not her place to disagree with her husband, and certainly not with God. If God had willed it, then who was she to stand in the way of his wisdom. She told her husband, "If it is the Lord's will, I am ready for it."

But Charles had not needed his wife's blessing – he was doing God's work. He praised the Lord through song as he dressed and as he walked out of the house to the shed in the back yard. He opened the shed's door and stumbled inside. It was dark, but he knew what he was looking for. A large sheathed knife was hanging on the wall. He pulled the blade from the leather sheath and carried the knife back into the house.

His prayers increased in volume. He was now praying, singing, and laughing at the same time. He carried an oil lamp with him to his daughter's bedroom. His older daughter Bessie awoke, and he told her to leave the room and get into bed with her mother.

Alone with a sleeping Edith, Charles placed the lamp on the chair next to the bed, and he silently got down on his knees. He pulled aside the blankets on the bed, uncovering the sleeping little girl. He prayed that she would not wake up and he prayed that God might stay his hand at the last moment, as Abraham's hand had been stayed when he was told to sacrifice his son.

But God did not stop Charles Freeman.

Charles lifted the hand holding the knife high above his head, and, at that instant, Edith opened her eyes and looked up at her father. But this did not stop him. He drove the knife deep into the little girl's side.

"Oh Papa," she gasped – and then she died.

Charles climbed into bed next to his daughter and took the corpse into his arms. He remained there until the sun came up later that morning. He later said that a great feeling of peace – even joy – came over him. He had been tested and found worthy. He had done God's will, and he would be rewarded.

In three days, God promised, his little girl would return from the dead.

In the lurid writings that appeared about the murder, it was always mentioned that Freeman was an Adventist.

On the morning of May 1, several dozen of Charles's neighbors were summoned to his home. They all received a message that they would be given a great revelation when they arrived. The sun had been up for just a few hours when 25 people – nearly all of them Adventists – crowded into the Freemans' parlor.

They fell silent when Charles began to speak. He rambled on for nearly an hour, often pausing to fall into eerie silence or, even stranger, into bouts of weeping. He spoke about the imminent Second Coming of Christ and the overwhelming feeling that had taken control of his soul during the two weeks that had preceded this glorious morning. Then – with his sobbing wife next to him – he led the gathering into the adjoining bedroom, where a little form lay beneath a bloodstained sheet. He reached down, drew back the covering, and revealed to his neighbors the sacrifice that he had made at God's behest.

As his fellow Adventists looked on in confusion, Charles assured them that they need have no concern for Edith. In three days, the child would return from the dead. Her resurrection would be a sign that Christ had returned.

The crowd was shaken by the sight of the butchered child, but instead of immediately summoning the authorities or taking Charles into custody on their own, they praised him for his astounding act of faith. Charles had been right in what he had done, they agreed and expressed a belief that God would raise Edith up on the third day as a sign for those who did not believe.

They soon dispersed to their homes and, without mentioning the awful scene they had just witnessed to anyone outside of the sect, returned to their daily affairs. The Boston Journal would later report, "It is almost impossible to conceive of an assembly of people in such a state of mind as to attempt to conceal such an atrocious deed, but they told no one and went about their usual vocations."

What followed was a bizarre wake at the Freeman house as Charles and his fellow sect members waited for Edith to be resurrected. When nothing happened after the third day the local Adventists were genuinely astonished. Some of them even went as far as to accuse God of breaking his promise with Charles by not resurrecting Edith.

By this time, despite the silence of the sect members, word of the murder had reached the ears of the local constable. Charles and Harriet were soon under arrest and lodged at the Barnstable jail.

Meanwhile, Edith's funeral was taking place. It was widely attended. According to newspaper accounts, the Methodist Church where the services were held was packed to capacity. Hundreds were left standing outside. The Adventists were all in attendance, keeping an eye on Edith's coffin and hoping for a last-minute miracle. The tension was high between the sect and the rest of the community. After the pastor lectured the Adventists on their false beliefs, Alden P. Davis – who was leading the sect with Charles in jail – was prevented from making a speech under threat of arrest.

Undeterred, Davis managed to speak in the churchyard after the service had concluded. His speech was a ringing endorsement of Charles Freeman and his sacrifice, which stirred up the angry crowd even more. Many in the crowd threatened to kill Davis, the Freemans, and any other Adventists they could get their hands on. The sect members fled the churchyard before violence broke out.

The horrific nature of the murder – combined with the complicity of the Adventists – set off a firestorm of outrage throughout New England. Ministers gave sermons about the danger of religious fanaticism, a phenomenon that was seen as a growing social threat. The New England Adventist Association, on the defensive after the murder, quickly distanced itself from the sect members in Cataumet and Pocasset, denounced Charles' act as "red-handed wickedness, diabolical bigotry, and inexcusable religious frenzy." The newspapers spread the story with lurid headlines, ghastly illustrations, and wild editorials about the dangerous behavior of religious cults.

An editorial writer for the religious newspaper, the *New York Evangelist*, wrote, "We hope that this murderer would be treated as all murderers should be and that it will not be admitted that religious fanaticism is to justify human sacrifices. The law expressly holds that crime committed while a man is intoxicated is the same as if the man was sober; and so Mormons, Adventists, and Spiritualists should be held responsible for offenses against the law, notwithstanding their pretended revelations of a higher law. There is no safety in society if any other principle prevails."

In the hours after his arrest Charles had calmly and cheerfully greeted visitors to his cell with the assurance that he would soon be vindicated. His daughter was dead, but she'd soon be back. He told one reporter, "I can't conceive of such a thing as God failing to justify me. His power is about to be revealed in an astonishing manner to the world, and all disbelievers will be humbled in the dust at His feet." Edith, he insisted with confidence, would shortly be "restored to earth life."

But, of course, Edith did not awaken. Three days after she was slaughtered – on the very morning when she was supposed to be resurrected – the dead girl was buried in the Pocasset cemetery.

On the day after Edith's funeral, Charles and Harriet – displaying "not the slightest regret at the commission of their sacrificial act" – were brought before Justice Hopkins at Barnstable and charged with murder. They were then returned to their cells to await the action of the grand jury, which indicted Charles during its October session. Although Harriet was regarded as a willing participant in Edith's death, she was released.

At a special session of the Supreme Court in January 1880 a sanity hearing was held and, after listening to several alienists and medical specialists, the justices ruled that Charles was insane and unable to stand trial. Charles, of course, scoffed at the ruling, insisting that he was not insane. He was simply embodied with the "spirit of Truth."

He told reporters, "I represent Christ in all his parts, prophet, priest, and king. All good is represented in one person, and that person is me. I feel sure that my name will be honored above any other name except Jesus." When asked how he felt about the death of his daughter, he calmly replied, "I feel perfectly justified. I feel that I have done my duty. I would not have her back."

Nope, nothing wrong with Charles Freeman – obviously sane.

As readers will not be surprised to learn, he was promptly committed to the State Lunatic Asylum at Danvers. It took a few years, but by 1883 Charles' perspective on things had changed. Interviewed by some of Boston's leading alienists, he acknowledged that he had been an "insane man" when he murdered his daughter and regretted it as "the most dreadful act that was ever perpetrated." Having seemingly recovered from his violently delusional state he was ordered to stand trial.

The proceedings were held in Barnstable on December 3, 1883, and only lasted one day. During his testimony, Charles wept openly on the witness stand. He claimed to have recovered his senses while in the asylum. He was finished with religion, he said, and vowed never to return to the Adventists.

Harriet Freeman testified that her husband had always been kind to their children and was a good provider for the family. After his religious conversion, though, everything changed. Not only did he neglect his business and devoted himself to the cult, but he began experiencing religious visions that told him to send a message to the world. His newfound religious mania became so problematic within the family that Harriet's brother had threatened to shoot him on one occasion.

She explained that Charles' visions in which he had been told to sacrifice Edith had come after going several days without food and water. Though she admitted to agreeing with her husband that he needed to kill their daughter, she defended herself by saying that she could not believe he would ever hurt Edith. She regarded it as a test of faith – like Abraham and Isaac – and God would stop him before he went too far by causing Charles to come to his senses. His faith had been tested in the past, she said, but he had never gone so far as to endanger her or the children – until this time.

On the night Edith died, however, she was told by her husband that God has asked him to make a great sacrifice. She then saw him "leave the room, and when he came back he had the child in his arms; it was dead; he walked the room with it and prayed and wept; he took it to bed with him and kept it with him all night; the whole scene is like a terrible dream, which one remembers, but can't distinctly connect, and which when I try and think of it, seems like an awful recollection."

Several expert witnesses followed Charles and Harriet on the stand – all of whom testified to the defendant's derangement at the time of the murder – and the jury took only 10 minutes to find him not guilty by reason of insanity. He was sent back to the Danvers Lunatic Asylum, presumably for the rest of his life.

Charles' "life sentence" turned out to be just four years. By order of the governor he was pronounced "cured of his delusion and harmless" and was set free in 1887. Little is known about what happened to him after his release from the asylum, but he died in Lawrence, Michigan in 1928. Apparently, he left Massachusetts and headed west to Chicago where he owned a restaurant for a time. He later returned to farming in Michigan. The last public records of Charles Freeman are an application for his military pension from the Civil War in 1908 and his obituary on November 4, 1928.

We'll never know what happened in his life during the years after he left Danvers State, or what happened to his wife and surviving daughter. Was Charles really "cured" of his religious delusions by his stay in the asylum? I'd like to think so and perhaps if he was, he finally realized that Edith's death was not a "sacrifice to God" but the result of his own madness.

I'd like to think that he grieved, not for himself, but for a life that was ended before it had a chance to begin.

Knocking on Doors

Just as the Millerite doctrines influenced the creation of the Seventh-Day Adventists, it also had a hand in spawning another of America's most popular sects – the Jehovah's Witnesses.

In 1869, a young man named Charles Taze Russell attended a lecture given by a Millerite minister named Jonas Wendell, who had reset the day of the Second Coming for 1873. Inspired by the lecture Russell started a Bible Study Group in Pittsburgh, Pennsylvania, and began his own detailed study of biblical prophecy. After 1873 came and went without the return of the Messiah, Russell became convinced that the Second Coming had already happened – that Christ has returned, but invisibly.

In 1876, Russell met Nelson H. Barbour, another Millerite who'd come to the same conclusion, and they jointly produced a book called *Three Worlds*, which proclaimed their interpretations of prophecy to a mostly uninterested world. The book disputed many beliefs of mainstream Christianity, including immortality of the soul, hellfire, the fleshly return of Jesus Christ, and the Trinity. Russell believed that God dealt with humanity in blocks of time, each ending with a "harvest." His recent invisible return would end in 1914 when world society would be replaced by God's kingdom on earth.

Charles Taze Russell

Russell and Barbour parted ways over theological differences in 1897 and soon after Russell began publishing a magazine called *Zion's Watch Tower*. The magazine's purpose was to demonstrate that the world was in "the last days" and that a new age under the reign of Christ was imminent.

Russell organized 30 congregations to study the Bible, and during 1879 and 1880 he visited each to provide the format he recommended for conducting meetings. In 1881 Zion's Watch Tower Tract Society was presided over by William Henry Conley, and in 1884 Russell incorporated the society as a non-profit business to distribute tracts and Bibles. By 1900 he had recruited thousands of followers, appointed foreign missionaries, and established branch offices.

Thanks to his voluminous writings – in the *Watch Tower* and other places – he became the most distributed religious author in the United States. In his writings he stressed that Christ's invisible presence in the world would come to an end with an apocalyptic bang in 1914. Many of his followers saw the beginning of World War I as proof of his teachings, but when Russell himself died 1916 no further divine manifestation followed.

So, it was up to his successor to – as scores of Millerites had done in the wake of the "Great Disappointment" – retool the operation and keep the followers and their donations coming in. After a flurry of political infighting, the group's legal representative, Joseph Rutherford, took over in 1917. Russell's theories continued to be a good model, and before long the Watch Tower Society was claiming that the end of the world in 1914 had also been invisible, just as the Second Coming in 1872 had been.

Soon after taking over the leadership of the sect, Rutherford issued a posthumous release by Russell that was a compilation of his commentaries on the Bible books of Ezekiel and Revelation. It strongly criticized Catholic and Protestant clergy and Christian involvement in the Great War. The book was not well-received – to put it

An early copy of the Watchtower Magazine... you may have gotten a newer one of these magazines if you accidentally responded to a knock on your door.

lightly – and resulted in the arrest of the directors of the Watch Tower Society on charges of sedition under the Espionage Act of 1918. The arrests led to mob violence against church members, continuing until the directors' March 1919 release. Charges were eventually dropped, but the arrests, as well as disappointment over failed predictions, later led to a re-branding of the organization.

Rutherford followed up his unwise book release with some significant changes in the society's doctrine, including a 1920 announcement that Hebrew patriarchs – like Abraham and Isaac – would be resurrected from the dead in 1925, marking the start of a 1,000-year earthly kingdom of God. Because of disappointment over the changes – and a long list of unfulfilled predictions – tens of thousands of defections occurred. More than three-quarters of the members who had followed Charles Russell left the church over the next decade.

Rutherford decided to reorganize and come up with a more distinctive name for the group. On July 26, 1931, at a convention in Columbus, Ohio, Rutherford introduced the new name – Jehovah's Witnesses – which he borrowed using a turn of phrase from Isaiah 43:10. The name was meant to symbolize the instigation of new outlooks and the promotion of fresh evangelizing methods. They were all based on the idea that the world would soon be coming to an end.

Among these new outlooks was that only 144,000 Jehovah's Witnesses would survive the coming apocalypse. They were the "anointed," who would be transferred to live in heaven and rule over the earth with Christ. But that was okay because there would also a separate class of members who would live in a paradise stored on earth. Starting in 1935 all new converts to the movement were considered part of that class. When would all this start? In the 1960s Witness publications stated that it would be in 1975. As a result, membership numbers began to climb – only to drop again in the late 1970s after the Second Coming failed to happen again. The date shuffled a couple of times, but then in 1995 Witness leaders abandoned the idea that the apocalypse had to occur during the lives of the generation that was alive in 1914.

As of now, they say it's still coming. No one knows when but they'll assure you that it will be soon.

The Jehovah's Witnesses have, like the Seventh-Day Adventists, managed to slide into the edges of the mainstream of American religion, but their belief system is a little strange to the average person.

Jehovah's Witnesses are most famous for their door-to-door ministry and the Watch Tower publications that they still use today. They're also known for refusing blood transfusions, which is based on a variety of Bible scriptures regarding the sanctity of blood. Jehovah's Witnesses maintain political neutrality and refuse to vote or go to war, partly because of Jesus' exhortation in the Gospels to "be no part of the world." Early on, they had decided that saluting the national flags was a form of idolatry, which led to problems with the government, fresh out of World War I.

Jehovah's Witnesses also avoid nearly all the terminology that's common for mainstream Protestants, like "church," "hymn," or "cross." They don't celebrate Christmas, Halloween, or Easter, citing pagan origins. The same goes for birthday celebrations — partly because of the origins of the candles and wishes, but also because they see birthdays as evoked in a negative light in the Bible. They limit their contact with nonbelievers so it's rare for someone unrelated to a member to be invited over for dinner. All of this is to keep their spiritual health unstained and their standing with God intact. Worship takes place in functional buildings called Kingdom Halls, which can be found in towns all over the country.

While some parts of their doctrine have changed over the years, the big stuff remains – they still believe that the divine new world order is right around the corner, maybe even in single-digit years from now.

I had a friend who grew up as a Jehovah's Witness, and he told me that he would almost have a panic attack at school when he heard a thunderstorm or a louder-than-usual truck in the distance. This was it, he always thought.

He said that from a young age he was forced to get involved in door-to-door ministering, delivering copies of the *Watch Tower* from house to house. He said that the stated goal was "Bible education," not "conversion." They had a series of memorized lines for any kind of person you might run into – Catholic, Muslim, Atheist, whatever.

We all might be annoyed when we get the inevitable knock on the door from a passing Jehovah's Witness, but they're pretty harmless. Most of them are modest, hard-working, middle-class people, and few of them are college-educated. The Jehovah's Witnesses don't outright ban going to college, but it's not recommended. From their point of view, you don't have the time to attend meetings, nor go door-to-door, while writing your doctoral thesis.

Today the Jehovah's Witnesses have members all over the country, and they're still preaching the imminent arrival of the end of the world but, like so many others have learned, at least they're not trying to nail down the date.

The Mark of the Beast

Hopefully, someone is reading this book who perhaps grew up in a mainstream denomination of American Christianity and is beginning to understand the way that William Miller's crackpot theories have infiltrated the doctrines of even the most seemingly ordinary churches in this country. He literally made up the idea of the imminent Rapture to scare his followers, and church leaders have continued to do this as the years have gone by. Even though the Bible specifically states that "no man knows the day or hour" of Christ's return, if church-goers can be convinced that it's going to happen at any time, they're always going to be in the pews on Sunday.

Sigh.

But how did things get to that point? We've discussed how Miller's philosophies affected the fringe cults, but what about all the mainstream churches that are teaching more or less the same ideas that you'll find at your neighborhood cult meeting?

We have to blame it on a minister named John Nelson Darby, who took Miller's ideas about the coming apocalypse and gave them another twist. His main innovation was an ingenious response to the trap that caught Miller – the insistence that the entire history of the world from Christ's crucifixion to the Second Coming had to be predicted by the Bible. Darby's system of interpretation divided history into different periods, which each represent a particular way that God deals with humanity. The Bible, Darby believed, had plenty to say about the periods that occurred up to and including the crucifixion, and nearly as much about the ones that will follow once the events of the Book of Revelation begin.

What it did not discuss in detail is the period that falls between these two points. Darby called this the Church Age and said it began when the Holy Spirit descended on the apostles and would continue until the opening events of Revelation when the clock of prophecy starts to tick once again, and the apocalypse gets started.

Instead of trying to make all the world's history fit into the framework of Revelation, this new plan allowed all the events of John's vision to be set in the future and be treated in the most literal terms. It dodged the bullet of setting any dates for it and allowed preachers to claim that the end was breathing down all our necks. This was a major innovation, but it was not the only one. The second innovation turned out to be equally central to the success of Darby's new apocalyptic theology – the Rapture.

The whole thing is based on a single ambiguous verse in the New Testament – I Thessalonians 4:17, which reads, "Then we which are alive and remain shall be caught up together with them in the clouds, to meet the Lord in the air, and so shall we ever be with the Lord." The doctrine of the Rapture – taught literally in most churches in America – states that when the events of the Book of Revelation start to happen, all true Christians will suddenly vanish, body and soul, to meet Christ in the air, while everyone else on earth will be left to suffer the horrors that John of Patmos predicted for the world in its last days.

It was a brilliant idea – the notion of having a ticket to heaven, while everyone else gets to suffer seven years of torment, proved just as popular as the Millerite dreams of the skies opening up to reveal Christ to the world.

By the middle nineteenth century this new idea had begun to fill the gap left open by the Great Disappointment and allowed evangelical preachers with plenty of ammunition for scaring the bejesus out of their congregations. However, it didn't take off at first. Most of the people who would consider an idea that was outside of the mainstream had bitter memories of the Miller debacle, so Darby's followers labored on the fringes of the Christian world for years, finding most of their converts among the poor and disenfranchised. At a time of soaring optimism that had been nicknamed the "Gilded Age," most people didn't want to hear about an imminent Second Coming.

But that began to change in the early years of the twentieth century when power struggles between European empires finally exploded in the summer of 1914 and became the First World War. By that time, Miller's debacle had faded from America's collective memory and those who embraced Darby's warmed-over version of it found that the temper of their times was shifting in their favor. Marketing campaigns that borrowed heavily from media advertising methods of the time enabled the apocalyptic message to spread far and wide. A group of devout oil barons funded a series of pamphlets about this new message called *The Fundamentals* and they were distributed by the millions across America. The movement had found its name.

By the early 1920s fundamentalism was a rising force in American religion and culture and had started to form relationships with other groups on the conservative end of society. The Ku Klux Klan was among the most important of these allies. The original Klan had been a southern guerilla group opposed to Reconstruction, and it was crushed by Federal troops and the courts during President Grant's administration. It was revived in 1915 as a vehicle for racist and anti-immigration activism. It quickly gained a following in the South, the Midwest, and the West Coast. In the early 1920s, when the revived Klan was at its height, some 40,000 fundamentalist ministers were proud Klansmen, and 29 of the state lecturers that the Klan paid to promote its ideas were preachers in fundamentalist churches. Reverend E.F. Stanton, one of these ministers, saw nothing inappropriate about writing a book called *Christ and Other Klansmen, or, Lives of Love*, which was published in 1924 to rave reviews in the right-wing media.

However, an alliance with the Ku Klux Klan turned into a liability for fundamental churches when the Klan all but collapsed in a series of scandals in the late 1920s. The Great Depression also hurt the fundamentalist movement, as conservative economic policies that were backed by fundamentalist ministers failed to do anything to the economic troubles of the time other than to make them worse. It ended up taking 40 years and the cultural revolution of the 1960s to breathe new life into the surviving fundamentalist churches and give them a new platform for their apocalyptic nightmares.

Perhaps the greatest of these fundamentalist nightmares was the idea of the Antichrist – the sinister figure that would rule over the world after the Second Coming.

Much like the Rapture, the lore of which was created from a single verse in the Bible, the Antichrist seems to be more legend than anything allegedly coming from God. The word "antichrist" appears in just three passages in the Bible – in the New Testament letters known as 1 John and 2 John. It doesn't appear anywhere in the Book of Revelation, even though that's what fundamentalists have linked the idea most closely with. They believe the Antichrist is central to the apocalyptic world view that sees human history as a struggle between God and Satan for the fate of mankind.

Here's how it works in fundamentalist prophecy: Just before the Second Coming, the Antichrist will act as Satan's chief agent on earth. The Antichrist – a sort of evil twin of Jesus – will forge a one-world government through promises of peace. But when Jesus returns, he will expose the Antichrist as an impostor, defeat him in the battle of Armageddon, and reign with the Christian martyrs for 1,000 years on earth.

Most of what we know about the Antichrist comes from movies like The Omen, not from the Bible.

Most of what we know of today about the Antichrist is a mixture of fundamentalist legend, popular culture – movies like *The Omen*, and writings that date back to 950 CE. It does not come from the Bible.

According to the early writings the Antichrist would be a Jew (anti-Semitism dates back a long time, unfortunately) and he would be conceived in the usual way, rather than some diabolical equivalent of the Virgin Birth. His mother would be wickedest woman in history, possessed by demons before, during, and after the Antichrist's birth. He would grow up proud, wealthy, and famous, and would become a leader, instructing people to revel in sin and vice and to turn away from God. His career would be filled with bribery and corruption, and he would rise to the top in both the material and political worlds. As his power increased, his opponents would be tortured and killed until he had absolute power over the world – until Jesus returned, of course.

There was nothing in the lore suggesting he would be born from a jackal, could be killed by magic daggers, or would be the ambassador to England – that was a movie.

Even though there's no mention of the number "666" appearing on his head anywhere, the number did make an appearance in the Book of Revelation. Some scholars have suggested that the Antichrist would gain control of the world economy by forcing each person "to be marked on the right hand or the forehead, so that no one can buy or sell unless he has the mark, that is, the name of the beast or the number of its name . . . six hundred and sixty-six." As far as most fundamentalists are concerned the beast and the Antichrist are the same thing.

The idea that this Christian boogeyman was going to make an appearance in the End Time had been around for hundreds of years by the dawn of the twentieth century, but never before had it seemed such a clear and present danger.

For many years most fundamentalists believed that the Antichrist was none other than the Pope. This notion had been accepted without question by John Nelson Darby's original followers and stuck around even after the unification of Italy stripped the Vatican of the last of its once mighty political and military power and left the Pope the undisputed ruler of a few neighborhoods in Rome. That didn't stop the traditional evangelicals, though. After John F. Kennedy was elected in 1960 a minister named J. Dwight Pentecost dragged out the old Pope-Antichrist hype when he denounced the new president's Catholicism. A little later, Hal Lindsey predicted in *The Late Great Planet Earth* that the Papacy would return to secular power as a proponent of the international peace and prosperity schemes that he believed would form the Antichrist's platform.

Of course, that guy thought the Second Coming was going to occur in 1988, so I'm not sure how seriously we should take his thoughts on anything.

As the decades of the twentieth century passed new candidates for the role of Antichrist were clearly needed, and new prophecies appeared to fill the demand. Adolph Hitler got some attention as a potential Antichrist, especially when some wag figured out that if you assigned each English letter a three-digit number – with A=100, B=101, C=102, and so on through the alphabet, the name "Hitler" adds up to 666.

During the heyday of communism, Lenin and Stalin were also named as possible candidates, although most writers preferred to assign Russia its role as one of the two armies that would meet for the final battle of Armageddon.

The most popular candidate for the Antichrist during the years between the two World Wars was Benito Mussolini. The Italian dictator's insistence that he was restoring the Roman Empire, along with his desperate need for the spotlight, was seen by many as signs that he was the long-awaited "Beast." One evangelical writer theorized that the *fasces*, the ancient Roman emblem that Mussolini had adopted for his Fascist party, had also started appearing on U.S. dimes in the early twentieth century – a sure sign that the Antichrist's plans for world dominion were already in the works.

But things didn't work out so well for Mussolini with the war, and he was soon taken off the list. There were plenty of other options, though. Cold War maneuvering between the U.S. and the Soviet Union, followed by the energy crisis of the 1970s that created OPEC, made the Middle East a prime location for new candidates. Two successive presidents of Egypt – Gamal Abdel Nasser and Anwar el-Sadat – were discussed feverishly by the fundamentalists as possible Antichrists and, of course, Saddam Hussein, during the years when he was America's archenemy was also a hands-down favorite.

Other writers in the prophecy business looked for less obvious figures. Henry Kissinger, whose name in Hebrew adds to 111, was widely discussed as a potential Antichrist in the 1970s. The birthmark on the forehead of Mikhail Gorbachev had some comparing it to the Mark of the Beast before the Soviet Union collapsed on his watch. For the Antichrist this was not exactly promising, though, it's curious to note that the majority of political figures selected as potential Antichrists by prophecy writers in the twentieth century ended their careers with embarrassing incidents of one kind or another.

Still, these failures were balanced in the years after World War II by two events that seemed to suggest that the prophecies of an apocalypse were being fulfilled. The first was the atomic bomb that fell on Hiroshima. A great many people not otherwise looking for signs of the end of the world couldn't find many other ways to make sense of weapons that were almost literally apocalyptic in their effects. American prophecy writers were quick to jump on the atomic bandwagon, revising their predictions of global war and the coming of the Antichrist to include mushroom clouds. All during the Cold War it became nearly an article of faith among fundamentalists that the End Times would involve a nuclear war between the United States and the Soviet Union.

The second event to give the apocalypse its post-World War II boost was the founding of the modern state of Israel in 1947. To most would-be prophets, the return of the Jews to the Holy Land had long been one of the important signs of the imminent Armageddon. The establishment of a Jewish state in Palestine seemed to be both a stunning confirmation of an old prediction and a signal that the End Times were near. Most people don't like to talk about the fact that all through the first half of the twentieth century fundamentalist churches played a huge role in setting the stage for Israel's founding, advocating for Jewish settlement in Palestine, and pressing the British and American governments to support the project.

This would lead the uninformed or the naïve to believe that they did this out of their concern for the Jewish people, but that's far from the truth. The majority of fundamentalists are viciously anti-Semitic. Their goal – even today – is simply to push forward their prophecies and bring about the end of the world.

You might think that I'm exaggerating, but I'm not. Stop reading and go and take a look at what the evangelical agenda is for Israel. You'll see that I'm telling the truth. In order to fulfill their prophecies, the fundamentalists need the Jews of Israel to either be slaughtered en masse by the Antichrist or to convert to Christianity when Christ makes a reappearance. I don't think that either of these things was what the founders of Israel had in mind for their people, but that is exactly what the fundamentalists expect to happen.

As the twentieth century drew closer to its end, these trends and many others helped spark a second wave of American fundamentalism that was nearly identical to the one that rose and fell in the 1920s. The profound social changes of the 1960s shocked many former liberal Americans to the core and made many of them listen to the ministers who identified these changes as signs that this time, the end was really close at hand. The same mass marketing techniques that helped drive the first wave of fundamentalism, using new technology, created a new generation of televangelists and fundamentalist political causes.

When Ronald Reagan was elected in 1980, fundamentalist leaders found themselves welcome in Washington, D.C., thanks to the fact that their grassroots kind of church networking had garnered a lot of votes for Republican candidates. This newfound political power, though, did nothing to soften the fundamentalist message that we were living in the End Times and that the Antichrist was going to show up any time.

One of the bestselling religious writers of the time was one we have already mentioned – Hal Lindsey, a former minister who wrote the first of several wildly popular books about the end of the world. *The Late Great Planet Earth* turned the Antichrist and the Rapture into Lindsey's cash cow. His strategy with the book was to twist current events into signs that proved the Rapture, the Tribulation that followed, and the apocalypse were about to arrive.

But as political conditions changed, so did Lindsey's books. Each announced in the same shrill tones that current events – whatever they might be – proved the Second Coming was about to occur, but then each round of predictions was conveniently forgotten once it turned out to be inaccurate. *The 1980s: Countdown to Armageddon*, with its insistence that the Rapture would occur in that decade, was quietly replaced in the early 1990s with *Planet Earth – 2000 AD*, which insisted with the same amount of force that Christians could be expected to be scooped up off the planet before the turn of the millennium. Before that happened, he put out a few other books, like *Planet Earth: The Final Chapter*, hoping to make a few last bucks before everyone was gone.

Lindsey was far from the only fundamentalist author to build a lucrative career by scaring people into believing that it was the end of the world, but he was one of the worst.

And the trend hasn't stopped. More recently we've seen the rise of a sprawling series of Christian apocalyptic thriller novels, authored by long-time end of the world preacher Tim LaHaye and novelist Jerry Jenkins. They began the *Left Behind* series in 1995 and have made millions from spreading fear to a whole new generation of people.

The premise of the series was both clever and simple. After the Rapture LaHaye and Jenkins assumed that there would be some people who had previously doubted the truth of Christianity and then began to reconsider their beliefs following the mysterious disappearance of all true Christians. These new believers provided the series with its main characters, and the events of the seven years after the Rapture supplied the plotline. Unlike previous novels set in End Times – and there had been many before, dating back to 1903 – LaHaye and Jenkins kept their books fast=paced and suspenseful, so that ordinary readers might be tricked into reading the heavy doses of theology that each book contained.

These books became just one of the symptoms of the new rise of fundamentalism that began in recent years. The church of the Reagan years fell out of favor for a while, only to have a resurgence during the years of the Obama presidency, when the racism of the 1920s began to rear its ugly head again. The new fundamentalists even renewed their links with White Nationalist groups – who weren't nearly as overt as the Ku Klux Klan, but just as dangerous – and found acceptance again after the election of Donald Trump. After he took over the White House, he openly courted the televangelists and megachurch preachers, who took to the airwaves to pronounce him "chosen by God."

The more things change, as they say, the more they stay the same.

The renewed mainstreaming of fundamentalist beliefs has both thrilled and terrified the American public. There is a very large percentage of American Christians who remain convinced that sometime very soon, they will abruptly disappear from the planet, leaving the rest of us behind to fill supporting roles in a horror film with the Antichrist as a special guest star.

The Prophet and the Antichrist

As has been established, a belief in the Antichrist is nothing new. Religious zealots have been awaiting his appearance on earth for centuries, expecting him to begin wreaking the havoc that would eventually destroy the world. There have been those who have actively sought him out and some who would do anything to destroy him – like a woman named Rhoda Wakeman, a prophet and religious leader of the nineteenth century.

In fact, on the morning of December 24, 1855, Rhoda killed a man who was possessed by the Antichrist in New Haven, Connecticut. The man was a member of her sect, and he participated in his own execution, during which he was bound and beaten with a stick, had his throat cut, and was stabbed, all to prevent the Antichrist's malignant spirit from infecting Mrs. Wakeman.

It is a story of murder, prophecy, religious mania, and a death-crazed belief that the end of the world was coming soon.

The woman who murdered the Antichrist was born Rhoda Sly on November 6, 1786 in Fairfield, Connecticut. She was the first of four children fathered by Phineas Sly and his unnamed wife. Sly later married Eunice Baker, who gave birth to Rhoda's half-brother, Samuel, in 1803. At age four Samuel suffered a serious head injury that left him with brain damage. He never recovered.

Around 1800, Rhoda married a distiller named Ira Wakeman and they eventually had several children ranging from nine to as many as 15; no one knows for sure. Little is known about Rhoda's early religious beliefs, though she reportedly attended Methodist meetings and read the Bible and Milton's *Paradise Lost*.

In 1825, Ira threatened to kill her for the first time, and the prospect of death provoked some kind of crisis in Rhoda, who claimed that she prayed fervently until Jesus himself appeared to her. He showed her the sufferings of the saints and martyrs, she said, and told her, "Thou art justified forever – peace to thy soul."

This vision marked the beginning of Rhoda's "seven years of travail," where she believed that her husband might murder her at any time. According to her daughter Selina, her fears were well-founded. Ira was a heavy drinker who became angry at even the mention of Rhoda "getting religion." He once told Rhoda that if he caught her praying or reading the Bible, he would kill her on the spot. He often took a straight razor to bed with him, just in case he felt the urge to cut his wife's throat.

Ira's treatment of her left Rhoda "partially deranged." He eventually set a date for her death and told her that he had made a "league with the Devil" to commit suicide, but first he had to dispatch his wife. After that, he knew he would be executed on the gallows.

On the day of the murder he lit a small fire, put two chairs in front of it, and told Rhoda to prepare for death. She sat down in one chair, with her husband facing her in the other, and expected to feel the blade of the razor against her throat. Instead, Wakeman took a length of burning wood from the fire and thrust it into her heart. She said, "It was the last I knew of this world."

Rhoda later claimed that she found herself surrounded by a thousand little black spirits that were preparing to take her away when a white spirit appeared and chased away the black imps. The white spirit carried Rhoda thousands of miles away, to a place of bright white clouds, where she had a series of visions of Christ, angels in white robes, and a blinding image of Heaven. Then the spirit returned her to Earth, where she saw her dead body lying on the floor. After two angels spoke to her kindly, she returned to her body and was revived.

Ira shouted three times, "By God, she's raised!"

That was Rhoda's story of the event that created her beliefs and doctrines. According to other sources, Ira Wakeman didn't stab his wife with a flaming piece of wood. Instead, he gave her a brutal beating that left her unconscious. But whatever happened, Rhoda accepted the event as a revelation upon which she could found her sect of followers.

Some of her new beliefs were ordinary, while others were decidedly not. She professed a belief in the literal truth of the Bible, as well as the belief that God was the supreme ruler and that Christ came into the world to save man from his sins.

After that, things got a little skewed.

It should come as no surprise, with the husband that she had, that she decided that it should not be legal to marry. All marriages were the consequence of worldly lust. She believed that she was a messenger, sent by God, to redeem the world from sin. She would tell his followers that the Devil had power over death and whenever he chose, a sinner could die. But Rhoda also believed that God had given her the power to forgive sins so she could save those marked for death. She also believed that God had given her the power to destroy the entire world if she chose to do so, bringing on the apocalypse. God had, she claimed, also given her the power to know the thoughts of other people merely by looking into her eyes.

And if anyone didn't believe she could do all those things, the Devil would place an evil spirit upon them, marking them for an early death.

One of Rhoda's most important doctrines was gleaned from the writings of the Apostle Paul to the Thessalonians, in which he wrote:

Let no man deceive you by any means: for that day shall not come, except there come a falling away first, and that man of sin be revealed, the son of perdition.

Rhoda came to believe that the "man of sin" was the Antichrist, but that he was not a living person. Rather he was an evil spirit that moved from one person to another so that he could kill her. If Rhoda died, she explained, humanity would be damned, and the world would be destroyed.

She believed that her husband had been revealed as a vessel for the Antichrist when he had attempted to kill her. However, angels had made Rhoda immune from earthly dangers and his plot had been temporarily foiled. She wasn't pressing her luck, though, and left home to live with a daughter. Soon after she began her ministry by preaching door to door.

When she eventually visited her husband, she had several of her followers with her, and they seized Ira and tied him up. Rhoda drew a knife and began cutting and stabbing him, "including wounds of a very serious nature," one account later said. Before she could kill him, however, one of her followers got nervous and ended the attack. Ira Wakeman didn't die from the wounds he suffered that day, but they certainly hastened the end of his life. He died on March 8, 1833.

Samuel Sly – Rhoda's brain-damaged half-brother who became one of her most devoted disciples – later said about Ira: "He was not killed by any of us, he came to his end when he was 50 years of age by the termination of his league with the Devil. I understood from the revelation given to my sister that his league with Satan was that he should live in health and comfort for 50 years, and during that time, he was to work the deeds of wickedness."

But, of course, the death of Ira Wakeman would not keep Rhoda away from the deadly clutches of the Antichrist.

Little is known about Samuel's and Rhoda's activities between 1833 and 1840. On July 3, 1836 two of her future followers – Justus Matthews and Mehitable Sanford – were married. Later that same year, another disciple, Massachusetts schoolteacher Thankful Hersey started a school for children. She closed it years later in 1842 after the devoted Millerite decided to abandon everything and wait for Christ's return. At some point after the Great Disappointment, she met Rhoda and became a passionate acolyte.

Samuel Sly had been Rhoda's easiest convert. She simply interpreted passages from the Bible in the way that she wanted him to understand them, and Samuel accepted everything she told him without question. One jarring new fact that she introduced to him was that the power of the Antichrist had been transferred from Ira Wakeman to another man, Eben Gould.

This man's identity is never clear – nor do we know why Rhoda believed him to be possessed. Her daughter Sarah was married to a man named Alden Gould, and Eben may have been his father, but no one knows for sure. All that we know is that Samuel embraced Rhoda's creed with great enthusiasm, preaching to anyone who would listen to him and dropping to pray anywhere – and anytime – he felt the urge.

Before his conversion Samuel had been regarded in the neighborhood as a "very good, harmless, prayerful man," though he "acted and spoke like a child." He often worked as a farmhand but would neither slaughter livestock nor step on an insect and seems to have been regarded with the exasperation reserved for children and harmless eccentrics. But that changed once he embraced his sister's beliefs. He became less friendly and very suspicious, refusing to walk past the homes of people he believed had the "devil's power." He began to believe that his neighbors were plotting to kill him, so he was quick to agree to leave home and preach his sister's gospel across Connecticut.

And what a gospel it was – spread by a woman that many believed was a lunatic. Her daughters believed that Ira Wakeman's cruelty had left their mother unhinged, and they may have been right. She was certainly odd. She wept at the sight of people walking to churches that believe it was God who had the power of death, not the Devil. Spirits appeared to her in the night, begging her to preach. Evil enchanters – what her ancestors called witches – were everywhere, and all her relationships seemed to follow a distinct pattern.

Rhoda held people in high regard until they did or said something that was critical of her. That exposed them as wizards, possessed by an evil spirit, or it meant they were the Antichrist. A perfect example of this is her treatment of Ephraim Lane, husband of Rhoda's daughter, Caroline. In 1852, he told her that her beliefs were nothing more than a delusion and Rhoda immediately announced that Ephraim had a "bad spirit that wanted to kill the good spirit in her." Caroline herself was denounced in 1854 when the Wakeman followers were excommunicating Charles Willoughby, another of Rhoda's sons-in-law. Charles had been accused of causing winter storms and conjuring up demons to torment Samuel Sly. When Caroline expressed doubts about this, she was also accused of trying to kill Rhoda.

But Samuel remained true. Eventually he was able to save enough money that he could free his sister from the "hard bondage of weaving" that she had been doing to support herself for years and moved her into a series of rented houses in New Haven where they could hold regular meetings. The meetings were soon attracting farmers from the surrounding area, as well as workers from the various firearms factories in the town.

Rhoda's followers met every Sunday and then again during the week. Samuel later described the meetings as "prayer and singing by the faithful believers, and then my sister would select quotations from the Bible, and explain them, and then the spirit of the Almighty would descend on her, and she would reveal to us the sayings of the Deity, and guide us in our temporal as well as spiritual doings."

In 1845 two important events occurred in the happenings of Rhoda's cult. First, Mehitable Matthews' nephew, Charles Sanford, was released from the Hartford Retreat for the Insane. He began attending services and soon prayer meetings were being held for him, presumably to cure the insanity that had not really been helped by his stay at the asylum. Secondly, a 17-year-old named Amos Hunt joined the sect.

By 1850 Rhoda and Samuel were living in a small house on Ashum Street, near Yale University. They supported themselves by taking care of children and selling fruits, berries, and "syrups and herbal medicines." The medicines proved popular and Rhoda gained a reputation as a "healer," mostly for the working poor and farmers in the area, like a man named Sperry, who would go on to play an unfortunate role in Wakemanite history. She gave away almost as much medicine as she sold.

Over the next few years Rhoda and her followers were quiet about their work. Amos Hunt came to hold an honored position among them. Samuel described him as "a firm believer in our doctrines." He attended every meeting and induced many people to attend meetings and listen to the wisdom that Rhoda had to share.

But, of course, demons are notorious for harassing the devout.

In late November 1855, Amos and his wife attended a Sunday service and brought food with them to share – a pie and seven cakes, all carried in a tin pail. Samuel put the items on the kitchen table and when they all sat down to a potluck dinner Rhoda ate a piece of the pie and one of the cakes and became violently ill. Rhoda was convinced the food was poisoned, especially after Samuel and another follower also became sick. Rhoda spent two days in agony before visiting Dr. E.C. Chamberlain, who had been treating her for six years and considered her insane. She had only started seeing Dr. Chamberlain after she learned that her previous physician turned out to be an "enchanter."

Samuel reportedly took the uneaten pie to Dr. Benjamin Stillman at Yale, renowned chemist who apparently made himself available to local eccentrics.

According to Rhoda, Stillman found enough poison in each cake to kill 10 men – or he might have if Rhoda had not gone ahead and announced his findings before he even reached them. The truth, she said, had been revealed to her by God.

The cake and pie provided by the Hunts contained no ordinary poison. Rhoda was, of course, immune to common poisons like arsenic. These items contained a magical poison made from the "brains of a man, the oil of men's bones, eyes of dogs, eyes of roosters, garden basil, topaz stone, copper, zinc, platinum, and the entrails of common toads." Or it could have been a simple case of E. coli since everyone who ate it got sick. It's also been suggested that Hunt had intentionally doctored the food with *something* to see if Rhoda was "human or divine."

In the end it didn't matter. Eben Gould, the last Antichrist, had passed away, so Amos Hunt was a prime candidate to become the new archenemy of Rhoda Wakeman. It was obvious to her that Hunt was "next to take the power." Hunt had made "a league with the Devil" and to "him was given all the power that was ever on the earth for sin." Of course, this sounds crazy now, but Rhoda's followers took this seriously, and Amos knew he had been marked for death. Hoping to save his life he offered Rhoda and her followers a cash settlement of $500. It was accepted by an attorney on her behalf.

And then, naturally, the Antichrist left Amos Hunt and went seeking a new "man of sin" to inhabit – Wakemanite Justus Matthews.

By December 1855 Rhoda and Samuel were living in a small story-and-a-half house on Beaver Street in New Haven that was crowded with cult members. It was here that she announced the name of the man that was now inhabited by the spirit of the Antichrist. Matthews was an unremarkable man who worked in a pistol factory. He attended Wakemanite meetings with his wife, Mehitable, and her sister, Polly Sanford, but had little regular contact with Rhoda. There was no obvious reason why the evil spirit chose him, but its presence was revealed when Mehitable began experiencing seizures. When Rhoda also became sick, the sect became worried. In the vigilant atmosphere that followed the assassination by poison attempt, this was enough to make everyone concerned.

Matthews was baffled by the accusation, but cooperative. He didn't object when members of the sect first attempted to drive out the spirit by giving him copious amounts of tea brewed from the bark of witch hazel trees, which Rhoda believed had the power to drive off evil. The tea didn't work, and after hours of prayer Rhoda decided on a new course of action. On December 21, Matthews began a three-day fast while Samuel cut a long branch of witch hazel and put it in the cellar of the house.

On December 23, the Wakemanites gathered at the house for worship. Rhoda had about 15 followers at the time and among those gathered there were Thankful Hersey, Abigail Sables, Julie Davis – all three lived in the house with Rhoda and Samuel – and Polly and Almeron Sanford, Isiah Wooding, Betsy Keeler, and Josiah Jackson, an African American who worked as a porter at the train station.

There was a full moon in the sky, and if the traditional beliefs about the full moon are true, it might explain a lot about what happened that night.

It was generally understood that Justus Matthews was going to be there that night, and it was expected that a special effort was going to be made to drive the evil spirit from him. Samuel built a fire in the stove in the front room at around 10:00 p.m. and Matthews arrived soon after. He sat down, removed his boots, and was warming his feet by the stove when the Antichrist began tormenting Rhoda. Because the gaze of the spirit was capable of causing harm, Polly Sanford blindfolded Matthews and asked him if he was willing to be tied with a cord. He said he would. "If it would bring the millennium, or subdue evil power in him," he added, he would allow it. His wrists were tied behind his back. When the exorcism began, he was on a day bed. He later moved to a rocking chair and then was on the floor.

For the next two hours the Wakemanites alternated between the upper floor of the house and the front room, praying fervently for the Devil to be driven from Matthews. As they stood over him, they begged him to renounce the unclean spirit. He was told that his presence was killing Rhoda and that it would be better to have him die than to have Mrs. Wakeman and the whole world die. There was a general agreement that Matthews would die if the spirit couldn't be driven from him. Matthews agreed. He was willing to be killed if it would "quench the evil spirit."

While the exorcism was taking place downstairs, Rhoda was upstairs experiencing bizarre and painful torments. Around midnight she fell into great distress and was unable to breathe, then had to lie down to keep from fainting. An hour later she claimed to be dying from the creatures that were crawling around inside her. Josiah Jackson later stated, "She had three live creatures in her, which were crawling up her throat and choking her. I put my hand on her chest and stomach, and I felt them!"

Samuel, Hersey, and Wooding rushed downstairs and cried out, "He's killing the messenger, he's killing the messenger!"

Samuel, knowing that the entire world was in jeopardy if anything happened to Rhoda, knew that he had to act. He retrieved the witch hazel branch – a stick of wood about one inch in diameter and two and a half feet long—from the cellar and returned to the front room to "knock this evil spirit out of him."

As Matthew sat bound and blindfolded, Samuel drew the curtains, locked the doors, and struck the helpless man with a blow to the right temple, knocking him out of his chair and onto the floor. He hit him several more times. Then, feeling "urged on by some influence," he cut Matthews' throat with a small knife. There was a handle in the room that was used for lifting the stove lid, and he plunged the metal rod into Matthews' chest 12 times in the shape of a cross – apparently to release the evil spirit.

Matthews' brother-in-law, Almeron Sanford, heard a gurgling sound coming from the front room and began pounding the locked door. Others held him back, though. They told him, "If he's killing himself, he'll be raised." There was another gurgling sound, pounding noises, and then cries of pain. Unsure of what to do next Sanford went back upstairs to pray.

By 2:00 a.m., Rhoda felt well enough to notice strange noises coming from downstairs and told Betsy Keeler that "all was not right below."

A half-hour later Samuel unlocked the door. He went to a back room where Thankful Hersey used a basin of water to wash the blood from his clothes. The sleeves of his shirt were so sodden with blood that they were cut away and burned in the stove. The witch hazel stick with Matthews' blood and hair still stuck to it, was dropped through the hole of the outdoor privy and the knife was placed next to Matthews' body so that it would look as though he'd killed himself. Samuel wiped up most of the blood on the floor and then went upstairs to pray.

Josiah Jackson feared that the corpse could still harm Rhoda if left in the house, and he told the Sanfords to move it. But after a long night of worship, prayer, and murder, the Wakemanites were exhausted and needed sleep, so Matthews' body was left on the floor through the night.

At some point early the next morning Almeron Sanford left the house and returned with 19-year-old Willard Matthews, the oldest of the dead man's five children, who had been out looking for his father. Sanford, possibly troubled by the events of the previous night, seems to have brought his nephew to the house intentionally.

When he entered the silent house, Willard saw his father's body in the middle of the room, lying on its left side. Clotted hair and blood were on the floor around him, and several large pools of blood were soaking into the wood near his head. His throat had been cut from ear to ear, nearly severing his head from his body. Pieces of rope were next to him on the floor and there were red marks on his wrists, making it evident that he had been tied up. And yet when he saw the horrible state of Matthews' body, Willard cried out, "Oh! Dear father has killed himself!"

After recovering from his initial shock, he went to the house of a neighbor, who summoned the justice of the peace. And soon after the cult of Rhoda Wakeman began spiraling toward its inevitable end.

Sheriff Leander Parmalee arrested everyone who had been present in the house that night and convened a coroner's inquest. The jury heard evidence on Christmas Day, and it was on the following day that Samuel decided to confess. Holding a Bible, he told the entire story to the jurors, who decided to release everyone except Samuel, Thankful Hersey, Josiah Jackson, Abigail Sables, and Rhoda Wakeman. They went back to jail to await the grand jury.

The newspapers had a field day with the slaying and with the strange cult that they dismissed as "fanaticism" and one of the "frightful effects of Millerism." The Great Disappointment, they said, was bound to have a terrifying effect on the country.

As for Rhoda Wakeman, she was believed to be too deluded to be taken seriously as a threat. But reporters and the authorities forgot one thing – she had a remarkable aptitude for getting others to kill.

There was more blood going be spilled by Wakemanites in the days to come.

Charles Sanford, the nephew of Wakeman follower Mehitable Matthews, had been released from the insane asylum nearly a decade before the murder. He was an unusual character. Accounts describe him as having a protruding jaw that stuck out farther than his nose. He limped heavily as a result of a clubfoot or an accident, was chronically insane, and had an advanced case of tuberculosis. What bothered him most, though, were stomach pains. He suffered from massive cramps that he believed were inflicted on him by magic, thanks to the teachings of Rhoda Wakeman and his absorption into her cult.

Two years of relative sanity ended with the violent death of his uncle, Justus Matthew. The following night he simply snapped.

On Christmas Eve he caused a disturbance at a church in Hamden Plains, telling the minister that "he had said enough" and that he needed to stop talking so that Sanford could preach the true gospel. Despite this outburst – not to mention his history as an asylum inmate – Sanford must not have seemed dangerous to the members of the church. Even when he left his parents' house with an ax on the morning of January 1 it didn't seem out of the ordinary because he often worked as a woodcutter.

But why he carried a three-foot-long hickory club, sharpened at both ends and covered with undecipherable writing, was much harder to explain.

Two and a half miles from the Sanfords' was the home of Enoch Sperry, a 69-year-old local farmer who was known for his "integrity in business and as a natural genius for figures." On this snowy morning he was on his way to a neighbor's house to pick up a borrowed sleigh box. He had hitched a pair of sled runners to his farm horse and was walking the animal along the snow-covered road.

Sanford probably knew Sperry. The farmer's health was generally good, except for occasional "fits" and a "stroke of palsy" that left his face partially paralyzed. Sperry had reportedly visited Rhoda Wakeman for various complaints and had purchased some of her medicinal syrups. Since Sanford was one of Rhoda's followers, they had likely met many times.

At around 11:00 a.m. Sanford and Sperry met by a small brook on the way to Amity Road. Whether it was a chance encounter or Sanford deliberately chose the isolated spot to lie in wait is unknown. A few words may have been exchanged, but what they might have been is also unknown.

Instead, what we do know for sure is that Sandford struck the older man with the blunt side of the ax, first at the right temple and then just above the right ear. Sperry's skull was immediately shattered. When he fell Sanford swung again, this time with the ax's blade, and it hit his neck just under his chin. His head was nearly severed.

Sanford fled the scene in one direction, and Sperry's horse went the other. It tramped on toward Amity Road, where it entered the stable at the Clinton Hotel and halted. One of Sperry's neighbors, Samuel F. Perkins, recognized the horse as belonging to Sperry and, assuming he'd had one of his "fits," resolved to check on him later that day.

Meanwhile Sanford was not finished with his bloodbath. His flight through the woods led him to the farm of Ichabod Umberfield. Between 2:00 and 3:00 p.m., he entered the house, placed the ax and the club in the hall, and found the housekeeper, Lucy Deming, washing the kitchen floor. Slipping an arm around her waist, Sanford pulled Lucy into the hallway, but she turned and slapped him, and Sanford ducked away from her. He grabbed his ax and entered another room where he came face-to-face with Eliza Deming. The 10-year-old recognized him and locked herself into a bedroom with her mother. Thinking quickly, Eliza opened a window and called to her father outside, "Charles Sanford is in the house with an ax, and he is crazy – you must come in!"

When Umberfield entered the house, he found Sanford seated by the stove. Believing that he could reason with him, he pulled up a chair and tried to engage Sanford in conversation. But he refused to speak. He sat there, staring at the fire for a few minutes, and then gathered his club and his ax and limped toward the door.

This took him behind Umberfield's chair, where he paused and brought the ax down on the man's head.

Umberfield pitched forward onto the floor. He groaned and Sanford hit him again, splintering his skull. Lucy Deming rushed into the room just in time to see a third blow strike her employer in the neck. Blood sprayed wildly in the kitchen. Eliza had also entered the room and she began to scream, which annoyed Sanford. He lunged toward her and she ran. As he followed, he screamed at her, "Stop your noise or you'll get your head chopped off!"

Finally, he gave up and went outside to clean the blood off his ax in the snow. Someone locked the door behind him, and he headed back into the woods.

While this was happening, Samuel Perkins was on his way to the Sperry farm. While on the road near the stream he was startled to find his neighbor's mutilated body in a ditch. He summoned help and the body was carried to the Sperry farm, where two doctors examined the remains and sent a message to New Haven to inform the farmer's sons of his death.

The police and some of the neighbors began looking for his killer. Following his trail through the snow was not difficult, even though it was near dark when Officer Lucius Doolittle and a posse of seven men, armed with clubs and farm tools, started in pursuit. They soon caught up with Sanford near the junction of Brooks and Downs Road, near the Umberfield house.

Sanford fought like a cornered animal. He attacked them all at once and managed to land a blow on Officer Doolittle's shoulder with the ax. A man named Peck cornered Sanford with a pitchfork and distracted him while a Mr. Gorham knocked him down with a cudgel. He was hauled away to jail --- and interrupted from continuing the day's slaughter.

Two inquests were held that evening, both of which decided that Charles Sanford had committed the murders of Enoch Sperry and Ichabod Umberfield. The motive for the crimes was unknown, but it was suggested that Sanford had heard about the murder of his uncle, Justus Matthews, and wanted to copy it. Sanford claimed that he had killed the men in self-defense – he had a cramp in his stomach and if he had not murdered the two men, the cramp would have killed him.

After confessing to the murders Sanford was put on trial, convicted of both crimes, and was sentenced to hang. However, he never did. He had, as one reporter noted, "every appearance of being far gone with consumption." Six months after the murders, he died.

While Charles Sanford was committing murders, "God's Messenger" was in jail awaiting trial. Thankful Hersey and Rhoda Wakeman shared a cell at the New Haven County Jail, and though Rhoda was often sick in bed, she managed to compose a document to the "ministers of the world." It cataloged all the misdeeds of the Antichrist, along with all of her suffering, and was interspersed with threats, pleas, and an exposition of mankind's collective guilt with regard to her situation. In other words, it was everyone else's fault that she was in jail. If she didn't get out soon, she said, the world would be doomed.

In another letter she complained about the unfaithful among her followers who lied and claimed that they would never leave or forsake her – that they would have their heads taken off before they did it. This suggests that the three murders of Matthews, Sperry, and Umberfield – all of whom were, or nearly were, decapitated – may have been inspired by some aspect of Rhoda's teachings.

Who knows what might have happened next if Sanford had not been caught?

On January 17 Samuel, Thankful, and Rhoda were back in court when the grand jury returned a true bill of murder against Samuel and indicted Thankful and Rhoda as accessories. Josiah Jackson and Abigail Sables were released from prison.

Rhoda wept when she learned that she had to remain behind bars. Thankful pointed a finger at her as she sobbed beneath heavy black veils and announced to the court, "They little know what they are about shutting up that person."

Rhoda declared that the world would end before they were tried – but added that she would allow everyone to live a little longer if she was released on probation. Otherwise, she would bring judgment day when she was ready to do so.

Three months later, on Wednesday, April 16, Judges Hinman and Waldo were presiding over the Wakemanites' trial in New Haven. District Attorney E.K. Foster and John D. Candee represented the state of Connecticut, while Joseph Sheldon, Jr. and Henry Dutton defended the prisoners.

The courtroom was packed with people – every seat was taken, and the standing room was filled – and the proceedings began with a plea of "not guilty." Dutton didn't dispute the fact that Samuel killed Matthews, or that the two women were accessories to the crime, but said: "the defense would give conclusive evidence that those persons, at the time the murder was committed, were laboring under an insane delusion."

As for the state, they claimed that a more conventional motive for murder was at the heart of the crime than the fact that the defendants believed Matthews was the Antichrist. The prosecutors cited jealousy, revenge, and greed. It was their contention that Matthews had borrowed $200 from a bank, loaned the money to Rhoda, and was killed so that it did not have to be repaid.

The defendants disputed the claim. According to Rhoda she had never gotten anything from the victim except, "a few vegetables, a few apples, and a small piece or two of salt pork." Samuel claimed that Matthews actually owed him money for clothes, but that "I have never made a claim against him, for I loved him very much and wished him to be freed from sin." No one seemed to know what Matthews did with the $200 – or what happened to the $500 settlement from Amos Hunt. Rhoda claimed that she was so poor that she "was obliged to sell my best feather bed to get money to pay the rent." Even then, testified Ephraim Lane, "she would always give away everything she had."

The first day of the trial was spent establishing the facts of the case. Jurors saw a floor plan of the house where Matthews was murdered, heard his injuries described, and heard the Wakemanites testify about the night of the slaying. Sheriff Parmalee related the details of Samuel's confession and displayed the physical evidence, including the knife, the club, and the bloody clothing. The state rested its case that afternoon, and the remainder of the day was dedicated to testimony about the strange beliefs and behaviors of the defendants.

Witnesses included Phoebe Beckwith, a former Wakemanite who was declared a nonbeliever after Rhoda "began to talk so much about this enchantment which I could not believe." When Phoebe had last visited the sect, Samuel had shut himself in a closet because he was so afraid of her.

The trial resumed the following day with more witnesses who spoke about the cult, including a baker who told how the Wakemanites "had an idea that my bread was enchanted and that anyone who ate it would die." Friends and relatives also took the stand, followed by experts who evaluated the defendants' mental conditions. Five different doctors – including E.C. Chamberlain, Rhoda's personal physician – had some differences of opinion, but none of them believed the defendants were competent to stand trial. Samuel was considered a "weak-minded imbecile, possibly suffering from dementia." One doctor, Worthington Hooker, thought that when Samuel killed Matthews, "there was an intense excitement in the house, and I think if he had any consciousness that he was doing a wrong act, the consciousness was very slight." Thankful Hersey's mind, though strong, was wholly given over to Rhoda and she'd had two relatives who went insane. Dr. Jerome Smith believed that Rhoda was insane, or nearly so. Dr. Pliny Jewett doubted the sincerity of Mrs. Wakeman's beliefs, but this was a minority view – none of the others questioned the depths of her convictions, no matter how strange they might be.

As Ephraim Lane put it, "You might as well try to move the West Rock [a local mountain ridge] as to reason her out of her delusions. I have heard ministers speak with her about them, and they said it was no use to talk to her." He also noted that he had "no doubt but that the old lady got her mind so wrought up that it really did hurt her when a person came whom she thought had a bad spirit."

At the end of day two, Henry Dutton asked District Attorney Foster if he would seek a verdict other than not guilty on the grounds of insanity. The prosecutor replied that he did not feel authorized by the evidence to claim any other because "the case had assumed an aspect not contemplated by him at its commencement." In other words, he had no idea just how crazy the defendants were when the case got started.

After agreeing to let the case go to the jury as it was – without any closing arguments – Judge Hinman told the jurors to retire and "bring in such a verdict as they thought was right."

The jury deliberated for only 10 minutes.

Between Samuel's mental limitations, Thankful's fanaticism, and their utter faith in an unbalanced woman, the defendants were found not guilty by reason of insanity. Rhoda and Samuel wept when they heard the verdict, while Thankful seemed troubled by the fact that she was considered insane. The prisoners were then ordered returned to jail until further orders were given by the court.

The destination for Samuel and Rhoda was the Hartford Retreat, which was then Connecticut's only asylum for the destitute insane. Thankful Hersey was more fortunate. During the trial the court had received several depositions testifying to her excellent character. A man named Samuel Foote paid a bond for the protection of the community and hired her to work in his home. She lived there, doing sewing and light housework, until her death in 1857.

Samuel remained in the asylum for the next 10 years and in that time came to believe that he was the prophet Elijah. Eventually he refused to eat or drink and died of starvation on July 14, 1865.

By then his sister, the prophet, had been dead for six years. She had died from natural causes – making her second trip to heaven – in 1859.

Blinded By Science

What if all our health ailments could be cured by the power of the mind? What if sickness was merely an illusion, brought about by our lack of faith? Could not praying hard enough actually fail to save our lives? Doctors, hospitals, and vaccinations, it was believed, might save our physical lives, but doom our souls.

It seems difficult to believe in our modern times that this radical system of religious beliefs once attracted hundreds of thousands of people to follow it. But the early popularity of Christian Science was tied directly to the promise of healing. The overwhelming majority of those attracted to the movement came to be healed or came because a husband, wife, child, relative or friend needed healing. The claims of Christian Science were so compelling that people often stayed in the movement, whether they found healing or not. They simply blamed themselves – and not the church's teachings – for any failures.

The teachings were radically simple. The founder of the church, Mary Baker Eddy, taught that disease wasn't real because the human body, along with the rest of the entire material world, was merely an illusion of the gullible. They were a waking dream. Those who awoke and knew the "Truth" could be instantaneously healed.

What was the "Truth?" The so-called "Scientific Statement of Being" assured believers that "there is no life, truth, intelligence, nor substance in matter." Eddy's definition of man was even starker: "Man is not matter; he is not made up of brain, blood, bones, and other material elements." Followers were instructed to repeat that philosophy as needed for whatever ailment came along, from headaches to cancer. The trick lay in the application – allow no hint of doubt, neither aspirin nor vitamin. It was a dogma so dire it was taken to absurd lengths – and caused scores of deaths.

How did it get to the point that a religious movement – founded with the best of intentions – became such a menace that it is literally killing off its remaining members?

Mary Baker was born in a farmhouse in New Hampshire on July 16, 1821. She was the youngest of six children born to Mark Baker, a farmer, and his wife, Abigail. Mark Baker was a strongly religious man from a Protestant Congregationalist background and a firm believer in the final judgment and eternal damnation. He had a reputation for his terrible temper, which his children inherited from him. Mary was lucky enough to inherit her mother's beauty and was known as the loveliest girl in the village.

Life on the farm was spartan and repetitive, and Mark Baker was a harsh taskmaster. He and Mary did not get along and she was often harshly punished, even though her mother intervened as often as possible. As a result, Mary experienced periods of sudden illness – perhaps to control her father – and would suddenly fall to the floor, writhing and screaming, or silent and apparently unconscious, sometimes for hours. This sent the family into a state of panic and Mary would often be sent to the home of the village doctor.

Years later Mary downplayed these hysterical incidents and said that she suffered from an eating disorder as a child. She wrote that she suffered from chronic indigestion and was nearly an invalid due to weakness from hunger and pain. She claimed that her parents tried all kinds of treatments – from homeopathy to electricity and hydropathy – but nothing helped.

By her mid-thirties she had gone through two marriages. Her first husband died of yellow fever only six months after their wedding, leaving her pregnant and penniless. She divorced her second husband, a dentist, for suspected philandering. Through all of this her ailments remained, and she became desperate to not feel sick and lethargic all the time.

This led her to seek out a different sort of doctor – a clockmaker named Phineas P. Quimby, who believed that the mind brought on most sickness and that if channeled properly, it could restore a person's health.

In the 1830s, Quimby had become an advocate of mesmerism and began using its methods to further his ideas about health. He began touring New England in the 1840s with a 17-year-old boy named Lucius Burkmar, whom Quimby placed in a trance state. Under the spell of mesmerism, he diagnosed and prescribed folk cures for diseases. Stories spread about Burkmar's abilities, but Quimby eventually became convinced that it was neither the boy's powers to mentally scan the human body nor his herbal tea remedies that were curing people – it was the Burkmar's ability to change their beliefs about their illnesses. The mind itself was where the illness was, and it was the mind that was curing people of their problems.

By 1859 Quimby had developed a philosophy of "mental healing," and he began using it to treat patients himself, without the trance and the clairvoyant. When a man was sick, he explained, "I affirm that the disease is in his belief and his belief is in error." While Quimby focused primarily on the mind's curative abilities, he increasingly came to view the subconscious as an extension of the Divine power, through which a person could, with training and understanding, create an external result.

Quimby's ideas quickly gained followers among metaphysical writers and the pioneers of the "New Age" in America. They helped to spread his ideas beyond New England, but in 1862 he met the woman that would become his greatest apostle – Mary Patterson, who would marry again to become Mary Baker Eddy.

Eddy became an extraordinary, if troublesome, proponent of spiritual healing. Far and above any of Quimby's other patients, she built a theology around the "doctor's" core ideals. She called it *Christian Science* – a term that Quimby himself had used. Eddy's philosophy would overlap with Quimby's and then sharply diverge from it. Rather than embracing the virtues of the human mind, she believed in the need for its eradication. The "mortal mind," steeped in malevolence and illusions, needed to be overcome by the universal "divine mind," the one true and absolute reality. Eddy denied the reality of disease, evil, and physical matter as human perversions, or "an illusion of the material sense."

After Quimby died in 1866 – at the age of only 64, so I guess healing himself was out of the question – Eddy, whose own health had been suffering, briefly looked for a new mentor. Finding none that fit with her beliefs she decided to build her own spiritual healing religion, with herself in charge. She started writing a book that would become the backbone of the new First Church of Christ, Scientist called *Science and Health with Key to the Scriptures.*

She would later claim that her inspiration to write the book followed a bad fall that she took on an icy sidewalk. She stated that she had cured herself to a state of superior health, almost instantaneously, through the power of her mind and intense prayer.

History tells a slightly different version of the story, though. It seems that Mary's recovery was not quite as quick as she later claimed. Records show that she filed a claim for money from the city of Lynn, Massachusetts for her injury because she was "still

Mary Baker Eddy

suffering from the effects of that fall." She later withdrew the lawsuit – likely when she found she could put her recovery from the fall to better use. Eddy went on to state that it was a debilitating injury but her attending physician, a homeopath named Alvin M. Cushing, stated that he "did not at any time declare, or believe, that there was no hope for her recovery, or that she was in critical condition."

He may have been the last doctor that she ever saw, though, because she soon began offering the controversial advice that, "no true Christian Science member should ever go to a doctor, hospital, or take any kind of medicine, for to do so is to deny Divine Science." Disease, she believed, like all physical reality, was imaginary.

As the movement began to grow Eddy took hands-on control of building a headquarters in Boston, dubbed the Mother Church, and had zero tolerance for disloyalty, real or imagined. A disagreement, contradiction, or interruption while she spoke was met with ferocity.

The movement attracted thousands of new members and flush with cash, Eddy purchased properties on which she built enormous, stately churches. The metaphysical movement fit in nicely with the nation's orthodox Christian congregations at first, but Christian Science tolerated no individual experimentation, nor did it seek to move with the times. To guard against future problems Eddy began forbidding sermons in her churches in 1895, and instead began requiring that weekly passages from Scripture and *Science and Health* be uniformly recited from the pulpit each morning by rotating "readers."

Even so, the movement continued to grow, and there was good reason for its success. Throughout the late nineteenth century the nation had no standard system of medical licensing, and some doctors persisted in prescribing dangerous and painful treatments like bloodletting and the ingestion of mercury. For many Americans, Eddy's message of spiritual healing represented a gentler, safer alternative.

But those alternatives came at a price.

The consequences of Eddy's instructions to her followers – she demanded "radical reliance" on her methodology to the exclusion of all else – quickly caused havoc. Newspapers and prosecutors noticed the casualties, especially children dying of unreported cases of diphtheria and appendicitis. This began to touch off battles with the American Medical Association, which tried to have Christian Science healers, or "practitioners" as they called themselves, arrested for practicing medicine without a license. But, since practitioners did nothing but pray, their activities were protected by law. Reacting with righteous zeal, Church leaders continued their efforts for decades, quietly slipping protections into the law and encouraging insurance companies to cover Christian Science "treatment." Since it cost very little the companies cynically complied.

As a result by the 1970s – the highest point of the church's political power, with many Christian Scientists serving in Nixon's White House and federal agencies – the church was well on its way to accumulating an incredible array of legal rights and privileges across the country, including broad-based religious exemptions from childhood immunizations in 47 states, as well as exemptions from routine screening tests and procedures given to newborns in hospitals. The exemptions had terrible consequences, resulting in modern-day outbreaks of diphtheria, polio, and measles in Christian Science schools and communities.

In many states Christian Scientists were exempt from charges of child abuse, neglect, and endangerment, as well as from failure to report such crimes. Practitioners – who receive religious indoctrination but no medical training – were recognized as health providers, and in some states were required to report contagious illnesses, even though their religion demanded that they deny that illnesses exist. Practitioners, of course, have no way of recognizing the symptoms of an illness, even if they believe it exists, which they don't.

A whole system of Christian Science "nursing" was created in unlicensed Christian Science nursing homes, which catered to patients with open wounds and suffering from cancer. There, no medical treatment could interfere with prayer. Assigned only the most basic duties – feeding and cleaning patients – Christian Science "nurses" are not registered and have no medical training. Instead, they engage in bizarre practices such as leaving food on the mouths of patients who cannot eat. They provide no assistance for those who are having trouble breathing, administer no painkillers, and react to no emergencies.

"Do Not Resuscitate" is basically their default setting.

Thankfully, though, the days of the movement seem to be numbered. The decline of the faith may be among the most dramatic contractions in the history of American religion. It has simply become irrelevant.

Eddy forbade counting the faithful, but in 1961 the number of branch churches worldwide reached a high of 3,273. By the mid-1980s, the number in the U.S. had dropped to 1,997. Between 1987 and late 2018, 1,070 more closed while only 83 opened, leaving around 1,000 in the United States.

The number of practitioners fell to an all-time low of 1,126 in 2018, and during the last decade the church's *Sentinel* magazine has lost more than half its subscribers.

The *Christian Science Monitor*, the public face of the Church, laid off 30% of its staff in 2016. It is now available as a five-days-a-week emailed newsletter or a thin print weekly that continues to lose subscribers.

Principia College, the Christian Science educational institution in Elsah, Illinois, has lost so many students that its future is in question. Its enrollment was down to 435 in 2018, while its school had 400 students, with just eight in the first-grade class.

But church officials were oblivious to the crisis. In 2005 Nathan Talbot and J. Thomas Black, longtime church leaders who had promoted recklessly irresponsible policies encouraging the medical neglect of children, endorsed ambitious plans for raising the dead. Black argued that Eddy wanted to keep alive the possibility of defeating mortality, saying, "What would set us apart as a denomination more than raising the dead?"

It should be noted that Black died in December 2011 and didn't come back.

Another church document envisioned a scenario in which an "intergalactic" Christian Science reading room would be established on the Mir space station by 2009. That, too, was a fantasy. But real estate has pulled them back from the financial brink. In 2014 the board announced that it had sold closed churches and land parcels to balance budgets.

By 2010 signs of the church's own impending mortality had become so unmistakable that officials took a previously inconceivable step – they renounced Mary Baker Eddy. A century after the death of their "beloved founder and leader," the directors took her precious principle of radical reliance – requiring Scientists to hew solely to prayer – and tried to seek a truce with modern medicine. In a newspaper article Philip Davis, then manager for the Committees on Publication, made an admission so fundamentally at odds with church theology that it would later be described by one of the faithful as "truly jaw-dropping." Davis said: "We are a church on a slow curve of diminishment, in good part because of what people see as our stridency." Practitioners would now be less "judgmental," he promised, offering Christian Science treatment to everyone, including hospitalized patients accepting medical care.

Davis's remarks ignored the scores of bodies that have been left in the church's wake. No one will ever know how many – the church does not allow statistics to be kept – but there have been many that have made headlines.

There was Ian Lundman, who died in Minnesota at age 11 in May 1989 of juvenile-onset diabetes. He spent days vomiting while "cared for" by a Christian Science "nurse." She treated him by dribbling water between his lips and wrapping his scrotum in a plastic bag and a washcloth to prevent his urine from wetting the bed. The nurse, the boy's mother and stepfather, the Christian Science practitioner, Church officials, and the Church itself were eventually found to be negligent in a civil trial brought by Ian's father.

There was also two-year-old Robyn Twitchell, whose bowel obstruction and perforation caused him to vomit excrement before he died in 1986. And there was Ashley King, who lay in bed for months with a tumor on her leg that grew to 40 inches in circumference before she died in June 1988.

Speaking of the more than 50 Christian Science parents or practitioners who had been charged with crimes for allowing children to suffer or die of treatable conditions, Davis promised that "the church of today would not let that happen." The church claimed that it would be pulling back on aggressive state lobbying and start taking a neutral position on religious shield laws, but this did nothing to make up for the century of suffering and death caused by the church.

It seemed to be at least a small step in the right direction, but many in the congregation resisted. They wanted things to stay as they were – a position that would inevitably lead to more unnecessary deaths.

One writer called Christian Science "Jonestown in slow motion" – a reference to the apocalyptic cult where more than 900 people died in a mass suicide in 1978. And he was right. The church is slowly dying out, and, in my opinion, it deserves to.

But even so, it could disappear today or tomorrow or years from now, however its beliefs and the religious exemptions it created in laws all across the U.S. will leave a disaster in its wake, causing lives to be ruined, creating suffering and death, and leaving us with legislation that allows every crackpot cult and anti-vaccination zealot to essentially kill their children.

That is the legacy that Mary Baker Eddy and the Christian Scientist church leaves behind. You might be able to find a more dangerous mainstream movement in American history, but it would be difficult.

A Life Meant to Be Simple

I have two weaknesses when it comes to food. Okay, likely more than two, but these are big ones – fried chicken and fresh-baked bread. Because of these weaknesses, I have had quite a bit of contact with people of the Amish faith, who are, of course, known for their cooking and baking skills.

Also, I grew up in Central Illinois where we had quite a large contingent of the Amish around the towns of Arcola and Arthur. There was even a sort of Amish "theme park" called Rockome Gardens nearby, which offered food, buggy rides, log-splitting, and even a tour of a "typical" Amish home. To most people this probably sounds a little strange but when you grew up nearby it just seemed like a part of everyday life, just like the plain black, horse-drawn buggies that you'd see clipping along the side of the highway.

I admit that, as a kid, I never gave much thought to the Amish. The bearded men in their black suits and hats and the women in their long, dark dresses and caps were just part of where I grew up. I knew their lifestyle wasn't one for me, but I respected the way that they stuck to it. They were quiet, peaceful, and kind, and my interactions with them were always pleasant.

Of course, I had no idea then just how complicated their "simple" lives really were or how many rules they had to live by, depending on where they lived, what sect within a sect they belonged to, or what their lifestyles truly consisted of.

So, if you didn't know much about the Amish before you started reading this chapter, you're not alone. Even though they have had a presence in my life for many years, I didn't really know much about them before I started writing it.

Several different factions make up the modern Amish and Mennonite churches in America, but they all got their start with the Anabaptists, who date back to 1525 and Zurich, Switzerland. It was started by George Blaurock, who was baptized as an adult on January 21 of that year. He had already been baptized as a baby but had launched a movement that rejected infant baptism in favor of a believer's baptism when an adult decides to join a church in a declaration of faith and free will.

At the time this was a very radical idea. Waiting until adulthood to be baptized was dangerous since infant mortality rates were so high. Dying unbaptized was believed to condemn a baby, child, or young person to certain Hell. Like many of those who joined his movement, Blaurock was considered a heretic and was eventually burned at the stake.

The movement became another part of the Protestant Reformation, and the Anabaptists also rejected idolatry and the Catholic Mass. They called for a separation of church and state and insisted on following a literal translation of the Bible. To that end, they believed that baptisms should be performed in the way that Paul suggested in the Book of Acts – after the believer found Jesus Christ. Their name "Anabaptist" means "re-baptizer" and was initially meant as an insult. But the followers adopted the name.

Like their founder, the Anabaptists were persecuted throughout Europe and expelled from Switzerland, Germany, Holland, Poland, and Russia. At the invitation of Quaker William Penn, many Anabaptists migrated to Pennsylvania in the early eighteenth century where they finally found religious freedom. There were – and are – many similarities between the Quakers and the Anabaptists. Both believe in peace and pacifism, they don't allow weapons, and refuse to perform military service.

The Anabaptists believed in peace, but they didn't always agree with one another. They have suffered many schisms over beliefs and practices over the years. The followers of Menno Simon branched off to become the Mennonites, while those who supported the ideas of Jakob Hutter became the Hutterites. Then, a Mennonite named Jacob Amman became unhappy with the apparent lack of discipline in his church, so he initiated a much stricter sect, who became the Amish.

America has a deep fascination with the Amish. Their name conjures up images of buggies, green fields, fresh-baked goods, and smiling children in cute costumes. They symbolize peace, piety, and purity and are known for their kindness and humility. While Americans have often demanded that immigrants assimilate to mainstream culture, the Amish are preferred as a time capsule of early America.

The Amish have become an industry of cookbooks, natural foods, and handmade furniture. They represent a simpler era, far removed from the hectic speed of modern life. Their simple lifestyle, driven by religious beliefs, is often placed side-by-side with our worries about the environment, sustainability, and reducing our carbon footprint.

To those who admire them, the Amish seem to have found their utopia. However, their lives are not all handmade quilts and milking the cows. Traditionally a closed society, increased contact with mainstream society has revealed many controversies. *Rumspringa* is the rite of passage before joining the church where young people experience the outside world – and often end up in serious trouble. If they join the church and break the rules or leave, they will be shunned by friends and family. Shockingly, many cases of incest and physical abuse have emerged from their communities. Education is discouraged and women are oppressed. Farmers have been accused of illegal health practices and cruelty to animals. The considerable differences between the Anabaptists and modern society often result in serious cultural clashes.

But what does it mean to live within the isolated communities of the Anabaptists? The stereotypical members of the movement are the Old Order Amish of Lancaster County, Pennsylvania – who are basically the same sect of Amish that I lived near while growing up. The Pennsylvania Dutch, who earned the nickname because they spoke German or *deutsch*, is the oldest of the settlements in the country. Anabaptist groups all fall somewhere on the scale between traditional and modern. Modern Mennonites are at one end of the scale and are little more than Protestants. The more traditional Anabaptists wear beards and bonnets, but the rules and regulations even among the various traditional groups, vary widely. The most conservative don't permit the use of electricity, gas, or indoor plumbing, while others are allowed to drive cars and use cell phones.

There is no central Amish or Mennonite church. Instead, there are thousands of different districts across the country comprised of dozens of families. These districts seem to continuously splinter because no single congregation can agree on all the rules. Agreement is important because these rules govern nearly every detail of their lives. The acceptable length of a man's beard and the style of a woman's underwear become religious decisions. Not only that, but the rules can be wildly inconsistent. Some churches prohibit their members from riding bikes, but they can use roller skates. Some can't own televisions, but they can watch television. Some can't own cars but are allowed to ride in them.

These rules are known as the *Ordnung*, meaning "order." These strict regulations determine what is permissible and what isn't and are designed to keep the community together while keeping the modern world away. They are intended to guard against pride, laziness, dishonesty, and envy – all sins that can erode the community. The Ordnung is created by the adults of the church district and may have little in common with the rules of another district nearby.

But all the rules are interwoven with religion and based – according to their interpretation – on scripture. If a rule is violated, that person is given a reprimand. Further defiance leads to excommunication from the church. Each community believes that God does not exist outside of their own order, so banishment condemns the former member to damnation. Sometimes members will leave on their own. It's not sin that often divides the community. Church districts become divided over how long a shirt hem should be, or how one should sing hymns in church on Sunday. A disgruntled member might join another settlement, choosing a new one that is less strict or may simply decide to start their own.

The conservative Amish refuse to conform to the outside world. Their motto is a paraphrase of the biblical verse of Romans 12:2, to be "in this world, but not of this

The Amish, often known as the "Plain People," try to live a simple life but it isn't always possible.

world." They keep separate to preserve their culture. They don't vote, they shun modern technology, they live close to the land, and they wear distinctive clothing, and speak in a German dialect that is unique to the Amish. They call Americans who are not part of their community "English," in reference to the language we speak.

The Amish are often known as the "Plain People" in the sense that they lead simple lives, and they value honesty and humility. Leading a simple life maintains equality among community members because while they live separate from the outside world, their own community is closely knit. Community support is vital to their existence, whether for barn-raising, for quilting, shucking corn, canning fruit and vegetables or helping a fellow member affected by illness or disaster. They believe in social solidarity, where the needs of the group are prioritized over the needs of the individual. A core value of the Amish is *gelassenheit* – to give themselves up to God, the church, and the will of others. To maintain harmony in the community, the Ordnung forbids lying, stealing, smoking, drinking, swearing, gambling, and the use of illegal drugs.

Their homes are practical in both function and style. The furnishings are clean lines and minimalist in quantity. Technology is forbidden or at least kept to a minimum because it distracts from family life. Some orders allow radios or forbid televisions and phones. The kind of technology allowed in a home is dependent on the Ordnung of the district, which controls the design of a home right down to the color of the paint. Some orders only use candles and lanterns for lighting and have outhouses instead of indoor toilets. Some don't allow indoor telephones but allow outdoor telephone shanties.

More progressive groups allow new technology for business or practical reasons, but nothing designed for entertainment. They believe that material possessions promote vanity, and by extension lead to discontent that leads to sin. For new technology to be allowed it must pass rigorous examination. It needs to have a low social impact and cannot rely on secular society. It will be rejected if it introduces questionable values.

However, some technology must be used, whether it defies the Ordnung or not. Some things are even more powerful than Amish rules—like the Food and Drug Administration. If a farmer wants to sell milk commercially, this can't be done using the simple method of a milk pail and a stool. There have been many issues surrounding Amish farmers selling unpasteurized milk to the public. Natural food advocates promote "raw milk" as being healthier, but it's also much riskier. Pasteurization kills harmful bacteria and prevents the spread of milk-transmitted diseases like typhoid and diphtheria. No matter how conservative, Amish dairy farmers must have the latest pasteurizing equipment, even if it's powered by diesel or gas generators.

Travel can be interesting for the Amish, depending on the strictness of their particular district. They may travel by boat or by train, but usually not by airplane. Some communities permit the use of bicycles, motorcycles, and roller skates, others ban them. Cars are usually banned. Although some orders allow their members to ride in them as passengers. The "English" locals who provide rides for them are often referred to as the "Amish taxi." Some Mennonite groups are more liberal and own and drive their own vehicles. Some groups make a clear distinction between ownership and usage. In this way, some orders allow their members to watch television or listen to music in a non-Amish home, to rent a car while traveling, or to use a computer at work, but they are not allowed to own any of these things at home.

Of course, the preferred method of transportation is the horse-drawn buggy. The use of the buggy is to keep Amish lives moving at a slow pace, to place less reliance on mainstream society, and to limit travel so that they spend more time with their families.

Amish parents avoid sending their children to public school, preferring to school them within the community. Usually, children of all ages are taught together in a single classroom and only attend until the eighth grade, which is the minimum requirement by state law. Higher education is normally banned by the Ordnung.

When children leave school around age 14, they will begin to learn practical skills on the farm or in an apprenticeship. Young women often become teachers since no special training is required. The schools don't teach any art or science, usually just reading, writing, basic math, and religion.

The modern world has changed the work prospects for the Amish. Farming is on the decline these days because of the cost of real estate. A few have made unexpected money by selling their farms and moving to cheaper areas or by sell oiling and gas drilling rights on their land. Beyond farming, many of the men work construction or factory jobs, while others have become renowned for their cottage industries. The men make craftsman furniture, cabinets, and leather goods, while the women make jams, bakery items, and quilts that are painstakingly handmade – and fetch high prices. They don't like to deal with the general public and so they often sell their wares through small shops and resellers.

Those who stick with farming might grow cash crops of popular "English" foods, such as popcorn or hot peppers. To earn extra money, many Amish open their communities to the public, offering tours of farms and homes, complete with buggy rides. However, they don't allow their photographs to be taken. The Ordnung doesn't permit "graven images," which they believe is noted in Exodus 20:4. Besides, posing for photographs is a kind of pride. This rule can sometimes be circumvented if the subject doesn't look at the camera. This rule doesn't apply to unbaptized children and teenagers.

At the end of the day Amish families sit down to a large, home-cooked meal. Amish fare is generally hearty and may include dishes like chicken and dumplings, meatloaf or butter noodles, with sides of mashed potatoes, carrots, and beans. A traditional dish is called *pon haus*, or scrapple, which is kind of an Amish ham loaf made from pieces of the pig not suitable for anything else.

An Amish favorite for Sunday after church is peanut butter spread blended with marshmallow, honey or molasses, added to pickles, meat, and cheese and turned into a sandwich.

The Amish are also celebrated bakers, and an Amish meal always includes homemade pie, cookies, and cakes. Shoofly pie is a specialty. It's a molasses pie that gets its name from the flies that it attracts that must be shooed away.

We think of the Amish as preferring healthy, wholesome food, but, once again, the modern world has intruded into their lives and they have developed a fondness for fast food and snacks. It's not uncommon to see their buggies parked outside McDonald's or to see teenagers eating candy bars and drinking soda.

And those children will just keep arriving, possibly creating even deeper connections with mainstream society. The Amish typically have large families, often with seven or more children. This is helped along by the Ordnung, which bans all forms of birth control. The Amish population doubles every 20 years by way of birth rates, not evangelism. Marriage is probably the most important milestone in one's life, and members typically marry at a young age after they have decided to become baptized in the church. Divorce is forbidden and homosexuality is simply denied or is viewed as a sin that can be "cured" through confession and prayer.

Of course, dating as a young Amish person is nothing like it is in the modern world. The Amish are always reminded that they must "keep pure," although some orders have customs for dating couples that even most modern parents would not allow. They allow courting couples to go on dates, but this is not like going to a movie or the school dance. Instead, they practice "bed courtship." The young man visits the girl when she is already in bed, and he asks if he may stay the night. If she accepts, he takes off his hat, jacket, and shoes and gets into bed with her. They lay side by side in her bed all night. While the temptation is there, they are only allowed to *schmunzle*, to hug and to kiss, and that's all. Of course, some go further than that, which simply results in a faster marriage.

The Amish marry other Amish and only within their own order. As a result, there are a lot of common names in every community. Marriage to second cousins is common. Centuries of intermarriage and genetic isolation have led to rare inherited disorders in some communities. These include problems with the liver, a type of dwarfism, and Maple Syrup urine disease that is named for the sweet odor of a sick child's urine. Some diseases are unique to Amish communities, like Troyer Syndrome, which causes learning disorders and paralysis of the limbs. Infants suffering from Amish lethal microcephaly are born with a small head and underdeveloped brain and usually only live for a few months. This condition only occurs within orders in Pennsylvania. These communities also have a much higher incidence of muscular dystrophy, cystic fibrosis, and deafness.

One of the few matters not regulated by the Ordnung is healthcare. The Amish pay their taxes but don't accept welfare or Medicare. They rarely have healthcare because it is expensive and "not trusting in God." An Amish dentist is usually a farmer with a pair of pliers. They often have a distrust of modern medicine, so patients turn to prayer as a remedy, or resign themselves to illness as God's will.

Instead of conventional medicine many communities place their trust in alternative therapies, like homeopathy, herbal medicine, or folk remedies. A few men and women practice as healers for the community and for stubborn sickness will try what are called pow-wowing ceremonies, where the healthy will try to extract the pain from a sick person.

One thing that almost everyone who has any knowledge of the Amish thinks of first is their appearance. They all wear plain dress to keep them separated from modern society. All clothing must be modest. Typically, the men wear a black suit and white shirt to church. On workdays they wear a blue shirt with black trousers held up by suspenders. Shirts must be tucked in, and t-shirts can only be worn under other clothes. Outside pockets are not allowed because having a pocket means that you would want something to put into it, which is a sign of greed. Male members of the church don't wear underwear. Their shirts are long and double as nightshirts, so underwear is unnecessary.

These clothes are handmade and every stitch is regulated by the Ordnung. It dictates the precise design and measurements of seams, collars, cuffs, and colors. Any infractions must be corrected, or the member could be excommunicated. For some groups even the order in which a man gets dressed is dictated by the Ordnung, meaning that shirts must be buttoned from top to bottom.

The men wear beards, but mustaches are not allowed because they were traditionally associated with military men, and the Amish don't believe in war. Beards also have matrimonial significance. In most orders a man only grows a beard after he is married. A beard confirms that a man is spoken for in place of a wedding ring because a ring can be taken off.

The Ordnung doesn't permit the "painting or powdering of face," so Amish women are not allowed to wear makeup – or lipstick, jewelry, or clothing other than plain dress because such things invoke vanity. These things are banned because of a biblical passage in I Peter 3: 1-7, which states, "Your beauty shall not come from outward adornment, such as elaborate hairstyles and the wearing of gold jewelry or fine

clothes." Instead, women wear long, plain dresses and sweaters in solid dark browns, blues, greys, and greens with sensible shoes and stockings. Women in most orders do not wear underclothes as we know them, but that's not as risqué as it sounds. The Ordnung doesn't allow elastic, so dresses are overlaid with an apron that covers the bodice for modesty. Button, hook, and eye fasteners or straight pins are used instead of zippers (also forbidden) so instead of standard bras and underwear they wear long, loose undergarments. They are not allowed to be tight because they might be sexually arousing to the woman wearing them.

As already mentioned, conservative orders don't have indoor plumbing, so without running water in the home for showers, baths are usually taken once a week. Women are not allowed to wear perfume or deodorant and are not allowed to shave their legs or under their arms. They don't use tampons or sanitary pads; instead, they use rags that are washed and reused, and often shared by all the women in the family.

Amish women also keep their heads covered in public at all times. The women wear a white prayer cap, while young girls wear a black hood. The head coverings are worn in obedience to Corinthians 11: 1-16, which says, "But every woman that prayeth or prophesieth with her head uncovered dishonoureth her head: for that is even all one as if she were shaven. For if the woman be not covered, let her also be shorn: but if it be a shame for a woman to be shorn or shaven, let her be covered." For this same reason, women grow their hair long and never cut it. They wind it up into a bun held in place by pins – hair clips are not allowed – and cover their hair with a cap when in public. Because of all the admonitions about covering their head when they pray some women had come to fear praying or even thinking about prayer when they're not wearing a cap. Some are so scared of violating this rule that they wear their caps to bed and even when they bathe.

Men wear straw hats during work and wide-brimmed black felt hats to church, but always remove them during the service. The same passage in Corinthians that tells women to cover their heads states that men bring shame to themselves if they pray while having their heads covered.

It becomes difficult to even imagine how hard it must be to remember all these rules and regulations, but I suppose if it's your entire way of life you learn to adapt.

As you can see, the "simple" life of the Amish is not all that simple. Also, it's not always pleasant. There is a downside to this lifestyle, even if those who are embedded in it don't always see it that way.

The Amish community – like most strict religious groups – is a patriarchal one. Although the goal of social equality is sought through plain clothing and simple living, some of the members of the community are more equal than others. Corinthians also teaches that "the head of every man is Christ, and the head of the woman is man." The Ordnung states that "the man should be the head of the house," while the women should be "a help-meet for her husband." Men and women are not unequal – they simply have different purposes. Women are mothers and homemakers. They handle the domestic tasks of cooking, cleaning, and making clothes, which are all made more difficult by the lack of modern conveniences. Men are the heads of the family, community, and church – women are taught to be submissive and obedient to men.

And how they grow to assume those roles is a part of the strangest and most controversial tradition of the Amish. The Anabaptists practice believer's baptism instead of infant baptism, and so children may be called "Amish" as a label but are not truly considered members of the church until they have been baptized. Baptism is only performed on a person who has made a free and informed decision to join the church and community.

So, how is that decision made? Amish groups have a tradition called *Rumspringa*, a period when adolescent Amish, usually from ages 16 to early 20s, must make the decision about whether to join the church or not. As they are not yet under the authority of the church they are allowed to experiment with the outside world and do the things that the Ordnung doesn't allow the baptized to do. They can wear modern clothing and hairstyle, watch television and movies, listen to music, dance, drive cars, and generally anything that they will no longer be allowed to do if they join the church. And like most people of that age, they are likely to experiment with sex, drugs, and alcohol. Rumspringa is technically not a license to go wild – such behavior is not so much allowed as it is unpunished.

Rumspringa had been sensationalized by the media as a lurid, non-stop spring break for Amish youths, but that's not necessarily accurate. It's usually mild rather than wild and is really just a chance to sow a few wild oats and decide what Amish young people want their futures to look like. If they decide to return to the community and be baptized, they have to relinquish their cell phones and televisions and go back to the life in which they were raised. The girls tend to return sooner than the boys, while the boys usually come back because they have fallen in love with an Amish girl who has declared her intentions to be baptized. Most Amish come home and between 85-90 percent become baptized in the church. There are reasons for this high retention rate.

Rumspringa releases these teenagers into a world with which they have no experience. They are naïve and unprepared, and the shock of modern life is designed to drive them back home to safety. It is too difficult for them to make the transition into such a harsh world alone. They are citizens of the United States, but they have no social security numbers, no money, or real-world experience. They have an eighth-grade education that only qualifies them to be Amish.

There is also something waiting for them if they choose not to return and be baptized – they are shunned by their family and friends for the rest of their lives. This social avoidance of members is known as *Meidung*, which means "avoidance." In other words, if you leave, you can never come home. That's enough to convince most Rumspringa youths to return home, whether they really want to or not.

And there are certainly reasons – aside from plain living and the absence of indoor bathrooms – to make a life among the Amish a difficult one.

The Amish attempt to detach themselves from modern society, but the outside world often imposes on their simple life through hazing and hate crimes. The Amish often find themselves the victims of verbal and physical assault, property damage, and robberies. Attacks on horses and buggies are common. Bullies will scare the horses with firecrackers, spray water on the drivers and passengers and throw rocks, eggs, water balloons, and worse at them. Aggressive drivers swerve at the buggies, cover them in a cloud of dust, or force them off the road. The Amish are easy targets – they turn the other cheek and don't fight back – and as the Ordnung teaches, they are not supposed to get angry or seek revenge.

One horrific attack occurred in Pennsylvania on October 2, 2006, when a man named Charles Carl Roberts entered an Amish school armed with firearms and other weapons. He rounded up the female students who were aged six to 13, while he freed the teacher and the boys. He called his wife from the scene and confessed that he had previously molested two young girls and was tempted to rape more. After holding his victims hostage for two hours, he shot 10 of the girls, five of whom died. And then he shot himself.

There have also been occasions when hate crimes have come from *within* the community. A few years ago, a series of attacks were reported from Ohio about an Amish man named Sam Mullet, a bishop and father of 18. Using scissors and battery-powered shavers, Mullet and his gang of fellow Amish men went on a beard-cutting spree of rival community members. They also cut the long hair off the men's wives. Mullet kidnapped the men and imprisoned them in chicken coops, while he forced their wives to live with him in his commune.

And this is a crazy story that we know about. Most of the stories we will never hear. Amish communities are shrouded in secrecy, but in recent years some of these communities have been revealed as oppressive, abusive environments for women and children. Startling cases of child abuse, incest, and physical and sexual abuse have emerged from within some communities. One case is the story of a woman named Mary Byler, whose childhood and adolescence were filled with physical attacks and molestation. Her stepfather beat her with shovels, farm tools, and his fists, all in the name of discipline. When she was six-years-old, her 12-year-old brother began raping her. Soon, two other brothers started molesting her, too. They trapped her in the outhouse, the dairy, or her bedroom and raped her repeatedly. Amish women are not provided with any kind of sex education, so Mary couldn't even explain what had happened to her – only that it was "bad."

The worst thing about the way that Amish communities deal with crime is that they don't. They often don't report offenders to the authorities. The church condemns civil lawsuits, and by extension, prefers not to involve the law at all. They resolve disputes internally. This often means that they close ranks after a crime has been committed. A man named David Yoder became an "Amish whistleblower" in St. Lawrence County, New York after a tragic crime was covered up by the community. His sister murdered her child within days of the birth, probably as a result of severe postnatal depression. When she confessed the crime to an Amish bishop, she was told that her confession could never leave the room "for the betterment of the community."

Alternatively, the Amish believe that a perpetrator's confession and repentance are enough. The Ordnung says to "have a forgiving spirit." A sin is forgiven and forgotten. The slate is wiped clean and it is as if the crime never happened. The public and the press marveled at the Amish community's forgiveness of the Pennsylvania shooter and the compassion for his family, for whom they set up a charitable fund. But within the community there is no assistance for victims, and they have no advocates. The Amish protect the abusers, not the abused. When Mary Byler told her mother what had happened to her, she was told: "You don't fight hard enough and you don't pray hard enough."

The Amish don't know how to deal with these problems, and mainstream society doesn't know how to deal with these Amish problems either. When the Amish do try and get the authorities involved, they are often reluctant to intervene. The crimes are often misconstrued or dismissed as religious customs, which makes the involvement of the authorities seem like an infringement of religious freedom. Modern society, as we discussed earlier, seems more concerned about protecting religious rights than human rights. Amish justice is either too lenient or too severe. Punishments may involve a public confession and apology. At worst, an offender might be expelled from the church for a few weeks. According to their system, someone who drinks to the point of intoxication receives the same punishment as a child molester.

When Mary Byler's four-year-old sister approached her and told her that her brothers were doing something "bad" to her, Mary knew she needed to seek outside help. Her brothers eventually confessed in church and apologized, but this wasn't enough. When she sought legal help, her mother accused her of being "unforgiving." She believed that her sons had already been punished. To the Amish their records were already clear, but that was not the case according to the law. Her stepfather and brothers were all charged with crimes and were sent to jail or placed on probation. Even her mother was charged with failing to protect her daughters.

Mary eventually left the Amish, but her experience was an uncommon one. Wives are discouraged from speaking out about abuse. They are trapped in their marriages because divorce means excommunication. Patriarchal societies devalue and dehumanize women, making abuse easier. The Amish see patriarchy as the natural social order, but in the eyes of modern society, the women in these communities are seen as second-class citizens.

The Ordnung ensures that the Amish lifestyle remains oppressive. By overseeing trivial issues like the design of underwear, and interpreting violations as sins punishing by excommunication, these communities become little more than a cult. The Ordnung is not the word of God, it's the word of Amish bishops and leaders. The rules are subjective, not divine, as the Bible is strangely silent about cars and cell phones. Community members are forced to rely on their leaders' interpretation of the Bible. Yet they are unquestioning, and often don't even understand why some practices are not allowed. When rules are justified by archaic Bible passages as an explanation for why they exist, they mean little other than an example of the dangers of blind faith.

Growing up near Amish country, I am as guilty as other Americans when it comes to how we romanticize the Amish and related sects. No one wants to see their "simple life" destroyed and so the Amish have many apologists. Of course, they are only human and have problems like everyone else. Despite their desire for separation, the Amish still have an unavoidable dependence on mainstream society. For this reason, they must be treated the same way that everyone else is supposed to be treated. They can live by the Bible, but they also need to follow the biblical instructions to "obey the law of the land." The community of the country is much larger than the small community they have created for themselves.

The Amish, whether they like it or not, are in this world – and of this world, as well.

Signs and Wonders
Pentecostals in America

I've already given you a taste of Pentecostalism in the opening section of this book, but my anecdotes are far from the whole story of this religious sect, which is an offshoot of mainstream fundamental Christianity. As noted, Pentecostalism places special emphasis on a direct experience of God through the spiritual baptism of the Holy Spirit. After the crucifixion and resurrection of Jesus, the Bible tells of what happened to his followers on the first day of Pentecost, a date that is seven days after Passover in the Jewish calendar. While gathered together, the apostles were possessed by the Holy Spirit. The Book of Acts described how small flames appeared above their heads and how each of them spoke aloud in languages that were previously unknown to them.

The idea of "speaking in tongues" became a basic tenet of the Pentecostal movement, and it is still widely practiced today. There are quite a few different types of Pentecostals but the most conservative are members of the Apostolic branch, who are separated from other "charismatic" churches. Apostolics believe that possession by the Holy Spirit is essential to salvation. They also believe that women should only wear skirts and dresses, should never cut their hair, should not wear makeup or jewelry, and should be subservient to their husbands. They can find biblical passages that can be interpreted to instruct believers in all these things. For the men, their hair should always be short. They should not have facial hair and should always wear long pants, which cover the skin. Shorts are never acceptable. Apostolics believe in what is called the "Oneness" doctrine. This means that they only accept baptisms, healings, and prayers that are in the name of "Jesus" only – not "in the name of the Father, Son, and Holy Ghost," as is common in most churches.

One thing about Apostolic churches – they are never boring. Services are lively, putting great emphasis on testifying, praise, fiery sermons, and beat-heavy, hypnotic music. It is during the music and praise sessions that members of the congregation become possessed by the spirit, which results in speaking in tongues, dancing, jumping up and down, running up and down the aisles of the church, shouting, crying, falling on the ground, and even fainting. These services can be bizarre to the uninitiated – and a little frightening, too.

In extreme cases, divine spirit possession leads some to handle snakes and to drink poison – because God says they can. These sects – offshoots of offshoots, most commonly – also draw their inspiration from the Bible's book of Mark: "And these signs shall follow them that believe; In my name shall they cast out devils; they shall speak with new tongues; They shall take up serpents; and if they drink any deadly thing, it shall not hurt them; they shall lay hands on the sick, and they shall recover."

My thought on this is that just because the Bible says you can do something doesn't necessarily mean you should.

The Pentecostal sect traces its beginnings back to the years shortly after the death of Jesus Christ. It was now up to his Apostles to preach the Gospel. This was a difficult job without the Messiah and his miracles to prove they had been sent by God. So, when Jesus was resurrected, he promised to send the Holy Spirit to help the Apostles with their task of building a church. These were the gifts of speaking in tongues, raising the dead, predicting the future, and performing miracles and wonders. These are gifts – the Pentecostals believe – still with them today.

The Holy Spirit arrived "like a mighty wind" at the place where the Apostles were celebrating Pentecost with about 100 followers. The "tongues of fire" appeared and landed on everyone in the group, filling them with the Spirit. The people gathered that morning were from all over the known world – Judea, Egypt, Asia, and Rome – and they all spoke different languages. However, after the Holy Spirit descended on them, they all heard everyone speaking in their native tongue.

By now a crowd had gathered and those who were speaking in tongues were accused of being drunk. But Peter, who had been Jesus's right-hand man, told the crowd they were not drunk – it was only 9:00 a.m. He followed this up with a sermon about Jesus, making the crowd ashamed for the role they had played in his crucifixion. Remorsefully, they asked Peter what they should do and according to the Book of Acts 2:38, he had an answer for them that would come to define the Apostolic faith: "Repent, and be baptized every one of you in the name of Jesus Christ for the remission of sins, and ye shall receive the gift of the Holy Ghost."

It was recorded that more than 3,000 people converted to Christianity that day, and Pentecost became known as the start of the Church. The Apostles, filled with the Holy Spirit, went on to perform many "signs, wonders, and miracles."

The Holy Spirit waited for almost 2,000 years before appearing again in Topeka, Kansas (obviously), creating the modern-day Pentecostal church. There were actually several events that occurred around the turn of the twentieth century that led to the church's formation, but the first was in 1901. It happened during a class at Charles Fox Parham's Bethel Bible College. Parham, formerly a Methodist minister, had decided that speaking in tongues was "evidence" of possession by the Holy Spirit. He cited the experience of the gathered disciples of Jesus on the day of Pentecost – as well as instructions given by Peter in the Book of Acts – as justification for his new doctrine. Parham and his class prayed over a woman named Agnes Ozman one day and after laying hands on her, she suddenly began speaking in tongues. There was no mighty wind, or tongues of flame, but a halo that appeared around her face as she began to speak in Chinese. Soon, Parham and the other students began speaking in tongues, too.

After seeing his doctrine in action, he left Topeka and took his show on the road, so to speak, traveling the country with a tent revival meeting ministry. Along the way he gained a student, an African-American man named William J. Seymour. They met during one of Parham's meetings in Houston, Texas, but since Seymour was black, he was forced to sit outside of the meeting to hear Parham speak. Despite the racial segregation of the Jim Crow era, the Apostolic movement was largely accepting of African-Americans and welcomed them into the church. This is significant because it would be Seymour who soon became the central figure in the Pentecostal movement's most important event.

Speaking in tongues was already occurring in churches across the country by 1906, but the Azusa Street Revival would be the event that would make the movement known across the country.

In early April of that year, in a run-down warehouse district in Los Angeles, there were rumors of strange religious happenings. William Seymour had started a ragtag congregation in a former livery stable at 312 Azusa Street. The quiet, unassuming man had transformed overnight into an electrifying speaker who encouraged everyone to be filled with the power of the Holy Spirit. In this makeshift church, Seymour sat on a shoeshine box and put his head inside of another box while he prayed. Suddenly, he jumped up, inspired, energized, and well, seemingly possessed. He touched people

The Azusa Street Mission Building in Los Angeles, the birthplace of the modern Pentecostal movement

and they fell to the floor, while others danced, shook, and trembled, calling out religious-sounding gibberish, often in a trance-like state that sometimes continued for hours.

The day after the *Los Angeles Times* ran an article about Seymour – with headlines that read "Weird Babel of Tongues, New Sect of fanatics is breaking loose, Wild scene last night on Azusa Street, gurgle of wordless talk by a sister" – an earthquake virtually destroyed the city of San Francisco. Soon after, Seymour found 1,500 people of all races crammed into his makeshift mission church, looking for spiritual revival. The church was later organized as the Apostolic Faith Mission and became known around the country. Today, almost every Pentecostal denomination can trace its historical roots back to Azusa Street.

At least the mainstream versions of the sect can do so. Like any other religious movement, Pentecostalism has given birth to branches, separatists, and even cults. They use the same biblical references as a starting point but wildly vary after that. It is a faith that is outside the norm, and even its inception ran counter to the racial culture of the times. Record numbers of African-Americans and women, both black and white, were the initial leaders. As the Azusa Street Revival began to wane, doctrinal differences, as well as pressure from the social, cultural, and political climate of the time, took their toll on the membership.

As a result, there were major divisions that occurred, with many groups becoming even more extreme. Not wishing to affiliate with the Assemblies of God – which formed in 1914 and also used the baptism of the Holy Spirit as the way to salvation, but left out the strictness of dress, hair, and culture – a group of ministers from predominantly white churches formed the United Pentecostal Church in 1919.

But even these churches vary somewhat in their standards. Like the Amish with their various communities, there are dozens of splinter groups that, while they are Apostolic, are not part of the United Pentecostal Church. It is another American movement that had a lot of moving pieces.

Denim Skirts and Tennis Shoes

All my experience with Pentecostals is associated with Apostolics. You have, whether you realize it or not, encountered members of this faith in your day-to-day life. The women are the easiest to spot, thanks to their long hair, dresses and skirts, and lack of jewelry and makeup. Before we tackle the clothing, though, we should cover the basic belief systems of the Pentecostals, before we get to their raucous church services.

Every belief that is held by Pentecostals begins with that verse from the Book of Acts where Peter tells the assembled crowd that if they are baptized in the name of Jesus, they will receive the Holy Spirit. This is their go-to verse for pretty much everything. It starts with repenting, moves on to baptism in the name of Jesus – and not in the name of the "Father, Son, and Holy Ghost" because they don't believe that's biblically correct – and is followed by speaking in tongues, as evidence of your conversion.

They believe that the Trinity – which is basic in most churches – is incorrect. They follow what they call the "Oneness" doctrine, which means there is only one God, not the Trinitarian belief that there are three separate beings who are God – the Father, his son Jesus, and the Holy Spirit. Trinitarians believe that these three coexist and

are equal but are separate. For example, they say that the Father is not the Son or the Holy Spirit, the Son is not the Holy Spirit or the Father, and the Holy Spirit is not the Father or the Son; yet separately the Father is God, the Son is God, and the Holy Spirit is God.

Confused? Yeah, so were the Apostolics who put this together. They believe there is one God who manifested as Father, Son, and Holy Spirit. That God is all these things – and they have a lot of Bible verses they believe backs this up. Of course, I have discovered that you can find a Bible verse that, if presented a certain way, can back up about anything, but I digress.

They have arguments for Bible verses that seem to say the opposite. For example, in Matthew 28:19, it says, "Go ye therefore, and teach all nations, baptizing them in the name of the Father, and of the Son, and of the Holy Ghost." That seems to say the opposite of what they believe, but they focus on the word "name" in its singularity. And well, since God and Holy Spirit aren't really names, but Jesus is, then that must be the name that Matthew is talking about. This is why, at an Apostolic baptism, that they only use the name Jesus.

What it all boils down to is that they believe that God is not three beings but one God who has three manifestations. They will state that the Trinity is never mentioned in the Bible, so it must not be real. It is accurate that the Trinity doctrine was created by the Council of Nicaea about 300 years after the death of Christ, but it was supposed to make the concept of God as three beings understandable by all people – not confuse them even more.

But the Pentecostals are stuck on "Jesus" and nothing else. Of course, there is a small issue with this – his name was never "Jesus" at all. Controversial? Yes, but it turns out that the name we all know came from a mistranslation.

Neither English not Spanish were around in modern form when Jesus was actually alive, or even when the New Testament was written. Jesus and his followers were Jewish, so they had Hebrew names, even though they like spoke Aramaic. The "J" sound used to pronounce Jesus' name does not exist in Hebrew or Aramaic, so he was obviously called something else during his lifetime.

Most scholars believe that his name was "Yeshua," a fairly common name around the time Jesus was alive. There were a lot of men named "Yeshua" around in this time, so why did the name "Jesus" become unique?

Since not every language shares the same sounds, people have historically adapted their names so they can be pronounced in various languages. Even in modern languages, there are different ways to pronounce Jesus. In English, the name is pronounced with a hard "J," while in Spanish, even though the spelling is the same, the name is pronounced with what would be an "H" in English.

It was this kind of transliteration that has evolved "Yeshua" into the modern "Jesus." The New Testament was originally written in Greek, which not only uses a different alphabet than Hebrew, but also lacks the "sh" sound in "Yeshua." The New Testament authors decided to use the Greek "s" sound in place of the "sh" in Yeshua and then added a final "s" to the end of the name to make it masculine in their language. Later, when the Bible was translated into Latin, the translators changed the name to "Iesus."

In the Book of John 19:20, the disciple wrote that the Romans nailed a sign on Jesus' cross that read "The King of the Jews," and states that "it was written in Hebrew, and Greek, and Latin." The inscription has appeared in most depictions of the crucifixion for centuries as "INRI," an abbreviation for the Latin *Iesus Nazarenus Rex Iudaeorum*, or "Jesus the Nazarene King of the Jews."

Since Latin was the preferred language of the Church, the Latin version of "Yeshua" was the name for Christ across Europe. In the 1611 publication of the King James Bible, the "Iesus" spelling was being used.

No one knows for sure where the "Jesus" spelling came from, but many historians speculate that it started in Switzerland. Since the Swiss pronounce the "J" more like an English "Y," or the Latin "Ie" as in "Iesus." When the Catholic Queen Mary I took the English throne in 1553, Protestant scholars fled the country, and many found refuge in Geneva. It's thought that they created the Geneva Bible, which began using "Jesus" in Swiss spelling and popularized the spelling.

The Geneva Bible became an enormously popular translation and was the version of the Bible quoted by Shakespeare and Milton. Eventually, it came to the New World and by 1769, most English versions of the Bible used the "Jesus" spelling popularized by the Geneva Bible.

And it was the name that became such an important part of the Pentecostal tradition – even though it's incorrect.

But this is not the only tradition that causes Pentecostal followers to stand out from other faiths. While their overall beliefs are quite a bit different, Pentecostals actually have more in common with the Anabaptist Amish than they would probably care to admit. A lot of those similarities can be found in their traditions and rules. A lot of the things that Pentecostals do is to set themselves apart from mainstream society, especially when it comes to hair and dress. Also, many of those standards vary by the church, pastor, and personal convictions. In other words, the rules for dress and daily life may be different in one part of the country when compared to another.

But one thing that is always the same is the women's hair. Most Apostolic churches – but not all – have a strict no-cutting policy for women's hair. Some allow them to trim their hair if it's a small amount and the hair stays long, but that's rare. They have biblical reasons for this – including the same verse that the Amish use to justify women wearing prayer caps – which essentially boil down to maintaining the difference between men and women with the length of their hair, covering a woman's head in prayer, and separating themselves from mainstream society by the length of their hair. They can also cite verses from the Bible about times when women cut their hair and were "humiliated" or were "haughty" and "wanton" because they cut their hair. Those women ended up in sackcloth, rejected, forsaken, and shamed.

This is a vintage photograph of a group of Pentecostal women from the early 1900s – but not a lot has changed when it comes to hairstyles and clothing.

As I think we have already shown, by digging into the Bible deep enough, you can find verses that will justify just about every kind of rule that you want to set for your sect or movement. Church leaders can give you a reason for all the Pentecostal traditions, which they will then turn into individual "convictions" for their followers. Every rule is easier to follow when you think it's your own idea – and when you are shamed into it through peer pressure, of course.

Pentecostals used the word "modest" to describe their dress code, slightly different than the Amish use of the word "plain." Women always wear dresses or skirts, with no exceptions, and the length varies from below the knee to ankle length. It doesn't matter what activities you're taking part in – a skirt is required, hence the "denim skirts and tennis shoes" title of this section. Men are also required to keep their legs covered in public, which means no shorts are allowed.

They've dug up a verse from Deuteronomy to explain the fashion, which roughly says that women and men are supposed to wear the clothing that matches their sex – women in dresses and men in pants. Otherwise, it's an "abomination to the Lord." They also refer to the coverings that Adam and Eve used after getting expelled from the Garden of Eden as a reason to be modest. After their eviction, God made them "coats" of animal skin, when in ancient Greece was an outfit that covered the wearer from the elbows to the knees, which is why Pentecostals insist that this area of the body is always covered.

In public women do not wear shirts that show any kind of cleavage or stomach, and both men and women must always have shirts with sleeves. The length of that sleeve depends on the pastor of the church.

Men and women never wear any unnecessary jewelry, and piercings are strictly forbidden. In I Timothy, women are told to adorn themselves in modest apparel and not wear "gold, pearls, or costly array." Another widely cited reason is that during biblical times Jewish men and women who were slaves were forced to wear earrings to show the world that they were property.

Women are also never allowed to wear anything but clear fingernail polish and are never allowed to wear makeup. Is that in the Bible? No, but Pentecostals believe that since every woman in the Bible who "paints their face" was labeled a "harlot," no woman should wear makeup. In other words, if you're a woman reading this and you're wearing makeup, all Pentecostals believe that you're a whore. Nothing judgmental there at all, right?

All these rules and traditions are about being modest. Pentecostals believe that they should never wear clothing that will distract the opposite sex from their walk with God. Women are taught that if one of their "brothers in Christ" struggles or falls because they dressed immodestly, it is their fault. If only they had dressed more modestly, they're told, they could have prevented it.

Speaking in Tongues

A Pentecostal service can be like a rock concert, as I have already described earlier in the book. Worship is typically led by a band, although everyone sings along, shouts, claps, and testifies. Just like in the days of the Azusa Street Mission, people enter into "spiritual drunkenness," where they shake, twitch, jerk, gyrate, jump up and down, fall on the floor, run around in circles, and so on.

Pentecostals are known for their church service yelling, crying, and shouting, but they are most popularly known for speaking in tongues. This is believed to be a heavenly or angelic language, which is spoken when one is seized by the Holy Spirit. This is a staple practice for Pentecostals. It is perceived as evidence that you have been baptized by the Holy Spirit, and you really only qualify as a Pentecostal if you do.

But, boy, there are a lot of problems when it comes to speaking in tongues.

The practice today is a modern interpretation of the story from the Book of Acts. The "speaking in tongues" that was done by the Apostles was understood by speakers of foreign languages. Therefore, the original speaking in tongues was a form of xenoglossia – the spontaneous speaking of unlearned foreign languages. When cases of xenoglossia are genuine, they are usually the result of a brain trauma known as bilingual aphasia. This occurs when a bilingual person suffers a stroke or accident, which causes them to temporarily or permanently lose one of their languages.

When Agnes Ozman was speaking in tongues at the Bethel Bible College, it was reported that she spoke "Chinese." This would be consistent with the Bible story in

A Pentecostal church service is more like a rock concert than what most Americans are used to experiencing in their neighborhood church.

Acts – that is if her audience actually spoke Chinese, but none of them did. Ozman also produced some samples of "Chinese writing." Both her written and spoken "Chinese" could not be authenticated by linguists. Similarly, when Charles Parham began speaking in tongues, he believed that he could speak "Swedish." He couldn't. Instead, Ozman's pseudo-Chinese and Parham's pseudo-Swedish are more consistent with a phenomenon known as glossolalia.

Glossolalia is uttering a stream of sounds that mimic a foreign language. However, it isn't a language because it is without words, grammar, and structural features that make it a language. Speaking in tongues is – and trust me on this because I have heard it hundreds of times – usually, nothing more than ecstatic gibberish, babbling that is more like jazz scatting than speech. Speaking in tongues is a social phenomenon, not a linguistic or spiritual one.

Congregations are socialized into the practice. They are taught to speak in tongues and encouraged to imitate others. There is a pious peer pressure to speak in tongues, and worshippers are made to feel guilty if they can't do it. I can tell you that first-hand.

The problem is that most of those who speak in tongues are merely jabbering in a manner that resembles a known foreign language (like the Swedish Chef on *The Muppet Show*), and they can easily pass as such for anyone who is not actually conversant in those languages. But this does not make it real. Some will argue that this is an "unknown tongue" – which gets mentioned in I Corinthians as the "tongue of angels" – or some supernatural language.

But that's not what it's talking about in the Book of Acts, which specifically states that other people could understand it. What is conveniently forgotten at most Apostolic tongue-speaking services is that there is supposed to be someone present who can interpret the messages. Why bother to have messages from the Holy Spirit if they're just gibberish that no one can understand? That's what Paul asked the people in Corinth in his letters. So, why follow one part of the doctrine – in the same biblical book, for pete's sake – if you're not going to follow the other?

It would be nice to say that the "gift" of speaking in tongues was some sort of evidence of the miraculous or the supernatural, but we can't. It really seems to be little more than a nonsensical kind of utterance that – depending on the motives of the speaker – falls somewhere between devious deception and religious self-delusion.

Taking Up Serpents

"He that believeth and is baptized shall be saved; but he that believeth not shall be damned. And these signs shall follow them that believe; In my name they shall cast out devils; they shall speak with new tongues; they shall take up serpents; and if they drink any deadly thing, it shall not hurt them; they shall lay hands on the sick, and they shall recover."
Mark 16: 16-18

That's a biblical passage that seems to offer a lot of benefits to the believer, but unfortunately, it is also one of the most widely interpreted verses that you're going to find. As I said earlier, just because you believe the Bible tells you that you can do something, that doesn't always mean that it's a good idea.

Especially, in my opinion, when it has anything to do with snakes.

The founders of the early Church – Peter, Paul, and that bunch – didn't leave any records behind to say that they went around drinking poison or handling snakes as a popular pastime. My guess is that they just wanted people to know that believing in the teachings of Jesus would allow them to do great, even terrifying things. And yet, somehow, in the early days of the Pentecostal movement, one offshoot of the main church came to believe that their faith would protect them from serpents and other harmful things in the same way that they now could speak in tongues.

Snake-handling seems to have started in 1910 by George Went Hensley, an illiterate preacher who was in his late twenties at the time. He had been doing a lot of thinking about that curious passage in the Book of Mark and, like most members of the Pentecostal churches of the time, he was inclined to take whatever he read in the Bible very literally. If speaking in tongues was part of a service, then why not also take up serpents?

The following Sunday he was preaching a sermon about that passage from Mark at an outdoor service near Cleveland, Tennessee and reached into a box of rattlesnakes that had been conveniently left next to his pulpit. He grabbed one of the serpents and held it up in the air over his head, to the wonder and amazement of the people who had gathered to watch. With a snake in one hand and the other hand

George Went Hensley, snakes in hand

pounding on the pulpit, he challenged his congregation to handle snakes, too. If they didn't, well, they just might be "doomed to eternal hell."

A new and spectacular tradition had been born and Hensley became known as the "original prophet of snake-handling."

Hensley spent the next few years traveling around Tennessee, holding services where snakes were one of the main attractions. It wasn't long before he had built a small following. Again, taking a cue from Mark, he also pioneered the practice of drinking poison – creating a mixture of strychnine and water he called a "salvation cocktail."

Skeptics often came to his services and brought snakes with them. During one of Hensley's services, a box of copperheads, cottonmouths, and rattlesnakes was dumped on the floor by a group of unbelievers. According to a witness Hensley picked them up "like a boy would gather stove wood in his arms to carry to the house."

He also spawned many imitators. In 1912 a former Baptist names James Miller starts his own snake-handling cult and spread the tradition through Alabama and Georgia.

As word spread Hensley's activities came to the attention of A.J. Tomlinson, a former Bible salesman who founded the fundamentalist Church of God in 1903. He invited Hensley to come and speak at one of his churches – with his snakes, of course – and was so impressed that he immediately ordained him as a pastor. Snake-handling then spread quickly through the Church of God, but enthusiasm waned a bit in 1918 after one preacher was bitten and took several weeks to recover. That same year an Alabama man named Jim Wiley Reece became the church's first recorded casualty.

Snake handling churches became popular, mostly in the South, starting in the 1920s and continuing for several decades

Hensley himself even strayed from snake-handling for a time. After going through some marital problems, he became what he'd later call a "backslider," coining another fundamentalist title. For the next few years, he made moonshine and spent some time in jail. He came roaring back in 1922 though, with a new wife and a new excitement about dancing around with snakes in his hands. He brought the practice to Kentucky and popularized it there.

Snake handlers got their first real publicity in 1938 when a farmer who didn't like the idea of his wife handling snakes brought a lawsuit against three members of the Church of God in Pine Mountain, Kentucky. They were acquitted but the trial got the attention of a St. Louis newspaper, which dispatched a reporter and photographer to cover the story. They found 75 worshippers crammed into an old wooden church in the woods, singing hymns, speaking in tongues, and pounding out a religious rhythm with their hands, feet, drums, and tambourines. Their bodies shook and jerked – and they loudly praised the Lord – as they passed snakes back and forth to each other. Everyone present took part – except for the reporter and photographer, I'm sure. Even a baby was seen touching one of the snakes. Some of the men also took part in "fire handling," which usually involves putting your hands into an open flame from a lamp or torch.

In 1943 snake-handling came back to the hills of Eastern Tennessee when a preacher and disciple of Hensley's named Raymond Hayes started his own church. The building, with dirt floors and rough-hewn wood walls, was given the name the Dolly Pond Church of God With Signs Following. Another preacher, Tom Harden, offered services on Saturday and Sunday nights that always included a bevy of poisonous snakes. It was at this church in 1945 that a truck driver named Lewis Ford was bitten by a snake and died. His funeral was attended by more than 2,500 people, and at the service, snakes were handled over his coffin.

Two weeks later Tom Harden, George Hensley, and other members of the congregation went to Chattanooga and started holding tent revival meetings on the outskirts of town. When the crowds became so big that traffic was disrupted, the police arrested Harden and Hensley. They were charged with disorderly conduct and fined $50 each, but they refused to pay. They did some time on a road gang, but the charges were eventually dismissed.

In February 1947, after a number of deaths, the state of Tennessee outlawed snake-handling. But, of course, the handlers refused to follow the "laws of man" and kept holding their meetings. At one point the entire congregation of the Dolly Pond church was arrested. They laughed, sang, and praised the Lord as they were hauled off to jail. They were later released but the snakes didn't do so well – they were confiscated and killed by the authorities.

Faced with persecution in Tennessee, snake handlers moved to Virginia and North Carolina where the tradition was just catching on.

In North Carolina, the movement was centered around the Zion Tabernacle in Durham and its self-appointed leader Reverend Colonel Hartmann Bunn. In October 1948 Bunn was charged with violating a city council ordinance that banned handling snakes in public. He was defiant of the laws though and announced that he was planning a three-day, multi-state, snake-handling conference later that month. Snake handlers from surrounding states converged on Durham on October 15. On the first evening, the police raided the Zion Tabernacle and confiscated four copperheads and a rattlesnake. Bunn jokingly offered his help in catching them, but the police declined – they had brought along a large pair of forceps for the task.

The following night the police didn't appear during the service, even though Bunn brandished a half-dozen snakes and hung them around his neck while he preached.

On Sunday the meeting – which promised to be a humdinger – was moved to outside city limits and local police jurisdiction. Bunn told his audience that he had a particularly large snake that he didn't want the police to get, but the real reason was that some news photographers had asked to see snake-handling in a more "rural" setting – in other words, so the crowd looked like hillbillies – and Bunn wanted the publicity. And he got it. He and his fellow snake handlers put on an enthusiastic performance from the back of a pickup truck as photographers and newsreel cameras captured the whole thing.

One snake handler apologized to a reporter, explaining that his usual specialty was poison drinking, but he had not had enough time to purchase any strychnine.

Why do snake handlers do it? That's a good question. In every case, snake handlers are linked to fundamentalist Pentecostal, or Holiness, churches where speaking in tongues, fainting, prophesying, and healing are all pretty standard. Snake-handling and poison drinking are simply slightly more dramatic ways of affirming a person's faith in the Lord.

An anthropologist who studied snake handlers in the 1950s, Weston La Barre, noted that snakes can be found in the mythologies of every culture around the world. They are often connected to the concept of immortality in that a common folk belief is that snakes can endlessly regenerate themselves by sloughing off their dead skins. In the Bible, God punished Adam and Eve for being tempted by a serpent.

Snakes appear in many forms in the Bible. They are often symbols of evil or death – the Devil is compared to a serpent – but they also represent knowledge and wisdom. In the Book of Numbers, the Jews began questioning God and Moses after the Exodus and god punished them by sending fiery serpents to bite and kill them.

Based on this the only surprising thing is that people didn't start taking up serpents earlier. My guess is that it took the emergence of the Pentecostal movement to encourage worshippers to take things even further. The first snake handlers were fiercely conservative rural folks who distrusted city people and were always on the lookout for signs of evil. They were farmers and miners; many of the older members were uneducated or even illiterate. They didn't smoke tobacco or drink alcohol; the women wore their hair long and always wore dresses. Taking medicine for an illness was seen as a sign of insufficient faith and many who needed glasses refused to wear them. They lived and died by God's will and, when the spirit moved them, they handled snakes.

Through the 1950s snake handlers remained in the headlines, thanks to a steady stream of deaths. Victims included a woman named Ruthie Craig, who held services in her Alabama home, and Reece Ramsey, who was bitten three times by a rattler during an outdoor service in Georgia. After he was bitten, he fell to the ground and died just as the choir was singing "I'm Getting Ready to Leave this World." Ready or not, Reece certainly left it.

Then, at a Florida service on July 24, 1955, the "prophet of snake-handling" George Hensley was putting a rattlesnake in its box when it turned and bit him on the wrist. His arm swelled up and turned black but – as most snake handlers do – he refused medical treatment. Hensley had once boasted that he had been bitten 400 times, but this turned out to be the last time. He died while vomiting up blood the next morning.

The tradition of snake-handling has risen and fallen in terms of popularity over the years, but it has never died out. No major Pentecostal denomination endorses snake-handling today but there are rural congregations that continue the practice, most in Appalachia. Many laws have been passed against it over the years, but most have either been overturned – or are ignored by law enforcement – based on religious freedom. Even so, it's not widespread today and is usually branded as "backward." It is estimated that there are about 100 small congregations still practicing the tradition, mostly in the southeastern part of the country, with about 2,000 people regularly handling snakes.

At those churches, the members have retained the strict morality and customs of the original snake handlers and most belong to families that have been involved in the tradition for generations. The churches are unaffiliated but many of them know each other and intermarry. The most prominent preachers travel around, taking part in each other's services.

The services last for three hours or longer, building in emotion and intensity, and snake-handling is the culmination of an evening of preaching, singing, testifying, faith healing, speaking in tongues, and an occasional drink from a Mason jar allegedly filled with strychnine-laced water. If a worshipper is not clapping their hands and raising their arms, they will pick one of the snakes and dance with it.

The snakes used in such services are highly venomous, including rattlesnakes, copperheads, cottonmouths, and water moccasins. The snakes are usually raised in captivity and may be somewhat used to all the noise and activity, but there are no tricks involved – aside from preachers who will sometimes "milk" most of the venom from the snakes before the service.

Snake bites are common. To some believers, a bite might signify a weakness of faith, as would seeking medical attention afterward. Some worshippers talk about a state of "perfect anointing" in which the handler becomes so filled with the Holy Spirit that he can't be bitten, but it doesn't often happen. Most say that the Bible never says they can't be bitten and expect it to happen. Some older snake handlers have been bitten so many times that their hands are deformed and they're missing fingers. But they all believe in Jesus instead of anti-venom, which can lead to days recuperating from a bite and occasionally, result in death.

There are over 100 documented deaths resulting from snake-handling during the history of the tradition, from young children who were also allowed to take part in the worship, to old-timers who had been handling snakes for decades. Although given the large number of people who have handled snakes over the years that's a pretty small number. Sure, snakes can be "milked" of most of their venom – but never all of it. Nor can snakes be hypnotized or trained not to bite.

But what about those who do die? Snake handlers have various explanations for this. They say that perhaps the person wasn't in the right spirit, or was a "backslider," or maybe God just decided it was their time to go.

In truth though, what happens after someone picks up a serpent doesn't matter. The command to take up serpents and drink deadly things is clear and in black and white to believers. In fact, according to Mark, these were the last things that Jesus said before he left the earth. Since fundamentalists believe that every word in the Bible is true, they must follow all the rules – no matter how insane they might be.

Don't believe it?

On October 3, 1998, Reverend John Wayne "Punkin" Brown was preaching at a revival meeting at Rock House Holiness Church in Alabama. During the snake-handling portion of the service, a four-foot-long rattlesnake bit him on the middle finger of his left hand. Brown was a highly-regarded evangelist who had been taking up serpents for 17 years. He was even known to wipe the sweat from his brow during a heated service with a rattler. He had been bitten 22 times before so he figured this time wouldn't be any different. He kept on preaching for another 15 minutes – and then dropped dead.

It gets worse. Brown's wife, Melinda, had died from a snake bite three years earlier. They left five children behind.

Con Artists for the Lord

The faithful – whether they are part of an Apostolic church or believe in handling snakes or drinking poison – believe in what they are doing without question. Outside of the movement, it's seen with suspicion and often, outright disdain. Mainstream Christians believe that signs, wonders, and miracles ceased with the deaths of the Apostles in the First Century. They say that Pentecostal beliefs and practices are unscriptural or even that so-called gifts of prophecy, healing, and speaking in tongues are occult practices and the work of Satan, not God.

Personally, I don't think any of it is that simple. Most of the Apostolics that I have met over the years are honest people who believe in the truth of their faith. Deluded? Maybe, in some cases, but not all. I think this is a faith of personal experience. Some are so desperate to have an experience that they exaggerate their "gifts" or convince themselves that what they experience is real.

And then, of course, there are those who are so desperate for other people to have an experience that they are willing to fake them. The motives for this are many and range from gullibility to greed.

One of the gifts that is said to be given to Pentecostals is prophecy. This is when someone receives a direct revelation from the Holy Spirit in the form of a vision, dream, or "word of knowledge." In some churches, anyone can receive such a message. They testify about them during the service, and a typical revelation might be a text from the Bible, a prayer, a personal experience, advice, or an idea.

In other churches only a select few people have this gift of prophecy and the rest of the congregation is supposed to "discern" the messages and figure out what they mean.

Of course, there's a fine line between a prophet and a fortuneteller. Some believe the messages from God are intended for good and must comfort, encourage, or inspire. If the message creates fear, negativity, or conflict, then it's believed to be from the Devil or at least from someone with an agenda.

The Bible has a simple test for determining if a prophet is legitimate. In Deuteronomy it says, "When a prophet speaks in the name of the Lord, and if the word does not come to pass or come true, that is a word that the Lord has not spoken." In the Old Testament, the penalty for false prophecy was death but in the New Testament false prophets were merely blinded or thrown in a lake of fire and brimstone and tormented for all eternity.

Luckily an evangelist named Bob Jones received a message directly from God that told him that modern prophets only have to be accurate 66 percent of the time. Whew.

Most readers will not be surprised to learn that phony prophets exist right alongside phony psychics – and they pretty much use all the same tricks. Parishioners line up in their churches for ambiguous predictions about their career, health, and relationships using the "cold read" method used by psychics, where the person uses generalizations and personal cues to provide a convincing reading. Before anyone can contradict or ask the pastor questions, they are "struck in the name of the Holy Spirit," and they fall backward into the arms of catchers. Many evangelists also use the age-old trick of gathering information about the congregation and make "predictions" that are suspiciously accurate.

Most of the time, though, evangelists will stick to vague forecasts about the economy or politics, or safe predictions of common natural disasters, like earthquakes and hurricanes. If they don't pan out, they just haven't happened yet, or the date gets moved. When disasters do occur, they are interpreted as God's punishments for our sins. Pat Robertson blamed Hurricane Katrina on abortion, while John Hagee said it was divine retribution for all the homosexuality that exists in New Orleans. Collectively, of course, they are "signs of the end times."

The main problem with specific prophecies is that they can be proven false when they don't occur. Regardless, evangelists specialize in failed doomsday predictions. Billy Graham predicted the end of the world in 1952. Pat Robertson said it would happen in 1982. And Harold Camping just kept changing the date until he died.

The founder of the Church Universal and Triumphant, Elizabeth Clare Prophet, predicted that the world would end in a nuclear holocaust on April 23, 1990 – and on at least four other dates. She and her followers holed themselves up on her Montana ranch where they built fallout shelters, stockpiled weapons, and prepared for the apocalypse. The reason she kept getting the date wrong? According to a local resident it was because her followers prayed so hard that it wouldn't happen, doomsday was postponed.

The Holy Spirit really gives bad information to evangelist and faith healer Benny Hinn (more about him in a moment) who predicted the end of the world in both 1992 and 1999. He also missed the death date of Fidel Castro by about 16 years. In 1989 he prophesized, "The Lord tells me to tell you in the mid-'90s, about '94-'95, no later than that, God will destroy the homosexual community of America. But he will not destroy it with what many minds have thought, he will destroy it with fire. And many will turn and be saved, and many will rebel and be destroyed."

Benny Hinn didn't even score to the 66 percent accurate mark on that one.

Faith healing is probably the most popular gift bestowed on believers by the Holy Spirit. This kind of supernatural healing can supposedly cure just about anything with a prayer or a touch.

What we are dealing with in this section should not be confused with the kind of faith-based prayers for healing that are common in most churches, whether they be mainstream or fringe. A sincere prayer for healing can be beneficial to the sick or dying, providing comfort and even true healing. There are more cases than can be easily counted of patients healed by prayer – or what some might call, the "power of positive thinking." Even if you don't believe that this kind of healing is divine, it's okay to admit that the mind has a powerful influence over physical health. If you truly believe in healing, it's possible that your body can heal itself. The facts are out there, and some believe that this positive thought is provided by God.

In Pentecostal churches, faith healing will sometimes be done in groups. The sick person is anointed with oil and there are calls for the Holy Spirit's intervention. It usually involves the biblical cure of "laying on of hands." The leader will place his left hand on the person's shoulder and his right hand on their head. The minister then leads the prayer and petitions the Holy Spirit for healing. Everyone else places a hand on the person as they pray and possibly speak in tongues. At the climax of the ritual the subject falls backward into the arms of the group. They believe this is the power of the Holy Spirit, but it's more likely the power of social pressure.

As mentioned, most churches have some belief in faith healing. The Catholic Church is even famous for it, but it's usually the Virgin Mary who does the healing. Saints are also petitioned for cures and healings have even been attributed to "weeping" religious statues. Miraculous cures were reported during alleged instances when the Virgin Mary appeared at places like Lourdes or Guadalupe – and also on windows, trees, and grilled cheese sandwiches. Millions of miracle seekers make the pilgrimages to blessed places to bathe in blessed waters, drink from magical springs, or light a candle at mysterious walls. Often there are numerous abandoned crutches (but no prosthetic limbs) left behind at such places as testimonies of the inexplicable healings that have occurred.

Although it frequently happens in churches all across the country, faith healing has come to be closely associated with tent preachers and television evangelists. They promise to heal people in their audiences and viewers at home if they touch their television screens. At these circus-like events, individuals from the crowd faint as they are "healed" by the invisible touch of the Holy Spirit, or they line up to receive a physical touch on the forehead from the evangelist, which sends them flying back into the arms of his waiting assistants. They may even writhe about on the floor in convulsions, requiring the disease-causing demons to be cast out in the name of Jesus. There's a long list of evangelists who have made a profession from faith healing, including Kenneth Copeland, Robert Tilton, Pat Robertson, and my two personal favorites – Peter Popoff and Benny Hinn. Like fraudulent psychics and prophets, the healers use cold reads and other deceptive practices to give the appearance that they have supernatural gifts. Over the years, *all* have been revealed to be charlatans – and that's not a misprint, *they have all turned out to be frauds.*

But none of them are as spectacularly phony as Peter Popoff and Benny Hinn.

Popoff originally gained fame because of the amazingly accurate information that he came up with – information that was a little too accurate. He knew the exact names of people in his audience and described their ailments precisely. Of course, he claimed that information came directly from God.

In 1986, working with magician James Randi, crime-scene analyst Alexander Jason attended one of Popoff's healing events and rigged up a surveillance device to detect any secret audio communication. Before long he heard "God" speaking to Popoff. He said, "Hello Petey!" in a voice that sounded just like Popoff's wife, Elizabeth. She continued, "Can you hear me? Because if you can't, you're in trouble."

Evangelist Peter Popoff putting out his "healing hands" ... probably looking for your wallet.

Throughout the event, she provided Popoff with names, addresses, personal information, and seat numbers – all of which were collected from the audience before the show. She guided her husband to the unwitting rubes who were astonished at his "revelations."

After collecting hours of proof at different events across the country, James Randi exposed Popoff on Johnny Carson's *Tonight Show*. Popoff initially denied the accusations and then admitted his deceit, defending his actions by comparing his ministry to a television game show. The scandal bankrupted him and that should have been the end of his career, but he managed to resurrect his act a short time later and went on to even greater fame.

There is, as the saying goes, a sucker born every minute.

And many of those suckers find their way into the orbit of Benny Hinn, either at his live events or tuning into his shenanigans on television. Hinn's healing technique can actually be quite effective – not for the results but for the methods he uses. Instead of the sick being invited on stage to be healed, the evangelist starts with mood music and, in time, announces that healing miracles are taking place. For example, he declares that someone is "healed of witchcraft," that others were having the "demon of suicide" driven out, while others were being cured of cancer.

Then, only individuals who self-select – emotional and receptive people who believe they have been healed – are invited to come forward. As they gather near the stage Hinn's cronies look for those who tell the most interesting stories with the most enthusiasm. They are the ones chosen to come onstage. After their performance or sobbing testimonial, Hinn offers a brief prayer or other response, and then his catchers

Benny Hinn, who attempted a mass raising of the dead through television sets in 1999. Spoiler alert: it didn't work.

move into place to grab those who topple over backward after being "slain in the spirit."

It seems like a simple, harmless sideshow act, but it should be obvious that convincing people they are cured when they are not is anything but harmless. The deceived often forsake medical assistance that could bring them relief or even save their life. On one occasion, Hinn prayed for a boy dying from a brain tumor. The boy's parents pledged a monthly sum to the Benny Hinn Ministries, but he died anyway.

On October 19, 1999, Hinn attempted a mass raising of the dead. He told viewers of the show *Praise the Lord* to cancel funeral services and place their recently deceased in front of their television set for 24 hours.

And no, I am not making this up.

Hinn predicted, "I see rows of caskets lining up in front of this TV set and I see them bringing them closer to the TV set and as people are coming closer I see actual loved ones picking up the hands of the dead and letting them touch the screen and people are getting raised as their hands are touching that screen."

There would be thousands of people raised from the dead during that time, Hinn promised. Would you like to guess how many people came back from the dead thanks to Benny Hinn's healing powers?

None.

According to the Bible, Jesus and his Apostles performed many miraculous healings to prove to unbelievers that they were from God. They allegedly cured people of blindness, paralysis, birth defects, diseases, and even – unlike Benny Hinn – raised the dead.

Unlike these biblical stories, we don't see today's faith healers attempting to heal skeptics to prove their abilities. They preach to the choir, so to speak. They allege that they have replicated these miracles, but their claims have never been authenticated. All that exists are testimonies that can be exaggerated, misrepresented, mistaken, or faked. They don't minister to people in hospitals or visit funeral parlors and accident scenes and perform miracles because they can't. They use techniques perfected by fake psychics and plant people in their audiences who can toss away their crutches because they've been "healed." They avoid patients with visible conditions and prefer disabilities or diseases that can't be seen.

The modern Holy Spirit seems to be able to cure anything, as long as it's no more serious than a headache or hemorrhoids. Some people do experience temporary pain relief induced by euphoria, or they are relieved of psychosomatic conditions. They are not "healed" by the Holy Spirit; they're used helped by the power of the placebo effect.

Again, that's not to say that spontaneous recoveries never occur. Sometimes they are revealed to be cases of coincidental remission or mistaken diagnoses, but not always. Sometimes recovery occurs as a result of concurrent medical treatment, although the faithful prefer to give credit to God instead of a doctor. And, as I have already stated, I believe there is a lot to be said by the power of mind over body.

What's tragic is when the faithful are led to believe that their illness has not been cured because of unconfessed sins or a lack of faith. I once knew of an evangelist who would force people out of their wheelchairs and pray over them, and when they were unable to stand, he'd scold them by saying, "You don't have the faith!" It couldn't be his fault – it was their lack of belief in his abilities.

Of all the sections in this book, this might have been the toughest one to write. My own personal contact with people of the Pentecostal faith left a deep impression on me. And while most of those I knew were kind and sincere, the movement probably did more to make me skeptical about religion than anything I have ever experienced in my life.

None of us have all the answers but my brief time involved with this church led me to believe there have to be other answers out there that don't involve strange rules based on obscure Bible verses and shaming people into believing that imitating gibberish is the only real way to have a connection to God.

The Cult of Personality

Fringe sects and alternative religions are often built around the beliefs of a single person – as we'll see many examples of in the second part of this book – but it can happen in what many consider "mainstream" religions, too. Or I suppose we should call them "mainstream" for the purposes of this book. This is, as you have undoubtedly realized, *not* a book about Baptists, Methodists, Catholics, and Lutherans. We are a little further off the beaten path with this one. Even so, the first part of this book has dealt with the less bizarre sects and movements in American history.

The second part is going to really get weird.

But we're not quite there yet. Before we do get there, I wanted to take a look at a few of the movements that were generally deemed "acceptable" during the height of their popularity. They were certainly off-kilter but, for the most part, were not regarded as frightening and overtly weird – that weirdness was saved for what went on behind the scenes.

God's Messenger
The Story of Father Divine

He sprang onto the national scene in 1931, after being convicted of disturbing the peace in the otherwise quiet town of Sayville, Long Island. Reverend Major Jealous Divine, as he was calling himself at the time, was already a familiar sight in the black neighborhoods of Harlem and Brooklyn and as the host of a weekly feast that was held at his mansion in Sayville, where he lived with two dozen followers who called him "Father." They referred to the feasts as "Holy Communion," and they enjoyed them every day. On Sundays, Divine and his followers threw open their doors and welcomed anyone in need of a meal.

In 1931, in the early years of the Great Depression, this was a lot of people. The crowds created a lot of traffic through the neighborhood. The cars were bad enough, but for some local residents, the passengers were far worse – a motley crowd, dark in color, and arriving from the city's poorest blocks, expecting a free meal and words of wisdom from the man who offered this weekly event.

Sayville's patience eventually ran out, resulting in Divine's arrest and eventual conviction. Three days after sentencing Father Divine to a year in prison Judge Lewis J. Smith dropped dead. Reached for comment in his cell Father Divine's only words were, "I hated to do it." Celebrity status in Harlem, which became his principal residence, was guaranteed.

Father Divine went on to become a national sensation. During his lifetime African Americans acknowledged him – many of them begrudgingly – as one of the more important civil rights leaders in the first half of twentieth-century America. And yet Divine's rise to stunning wealth and fame – and his decades of work on behalf of racial equality – are not well recorded in the annals of the civil rights movement. It would be fair to say that Father Divine has, for the most part, been written out of that history because of his strange theology, his unappealing blend of communistic lifestyle and politics, his movement's disavowal of racial identity, and most of all because of Divine himself – a squat, bald man whose followers called him God and their Redeemer.

His origins have remained a mystery, and he did all that he could to frustrate those who tried to determine his birthplace. He once claimed to have "combusted" in New York and for all that we can prove, it's possible that he did.

There isn't much that we know about Father Divine's early life – we don't even know his real name. He never kept many records and declined several offers to write his biography saying that the history of God would not be useful in mortal terms. He also refused to talk about his family or where he was from but newspapers in the 1930s did dig up his likely name – George Baker. The FBI had their own file on him, which recorded his name as George Baker, alias "God."

In 1936 a woman named Eliza Mayfield appeared on the scene and claimed to be Divine's mother. She stated that his real name was Frederick Edwards, he was from Hendersonville, North Carolina, and that he had abandoned his wife and five children. But Mayfield offered no proof and said that she was unable to remember his father's name. Father Divine gave only a brief statement about Mayfield's claims – "God has no mother."

More recently author Jill Watts discovered evidence in old census records suggesting that Divine was George Baker, Jr., who was born in Rockville, Maryland. If her research is correct, then Divine's mother was a former slave named Nancy Baker who died in May 1897. However, notoriously poor records were kept in this era for African Americans who had once been slaves, so the puzzle is probably never going to be solved. One thing was sure, Father Divine was no help in solving the mystery.

What we do know is that Father Divine – possibly using the name George Baker – worked as a groundskeeper in Baltimore around the turn of the last century. His mother had raised him in the Methodist Church, but Divine preferred attending the many storefront churches that thrived in the city at the time. The enthusiasm of the self-proclaimed ministers was infectious, and he soon began calling himself a preacher. But Divine's ministry would be different than anything he was hearing in the many churches he attended in the Baltimore area and even across the South, which he toured in 1902.

Divine had become familiar with the ideas of Charles Fillmore and the New Thought Movement, a philosophy of positive thinking that would inform his later doctrines. Fillmore taught that anyone – male, female, black, or white – could enter into spiritual communication with the Divine Consciousness that others called God and could attune his or her consciousness to its wisdom. It also asserted that negative thoughts led to poverty and unhappiness, while positive thinking allowed the believer to achieve a life of abundance. This was pretty conventional New Thought material – and not much different than the modern "Prosperity Gospel" – but Fillmore also taught his followers to abstain from sex. He believed that sex was physically depleting and competed with spiritual development.

By examining the addresses of the publishing houses for New Thought material that were circulating, Divine learned that New Thought was most popular in the West. He put together enough money for a sojourn to California and while there paid a visit to William Seymour's Azusa Street revival, where he not only witnessed other people speaking in tongues but experienced it for himself.

Eventually, he returned home and brought even more new ideas with him. He soon met an itinerant preacher named Samuel Morris, who had come to Baltimore because he believed that the Bible had literally told him to do so. God had, he believed, returned in physical form, and he needed to spread that news. He adopted the name Father Jehovia and quickly got used to being forcibly kicked out of the churches he visited. He had a habit of standing up during the middle of services to declare his divinity – or worse, he dared to announce that God had disavowed the existence of racial differences.

Divine was in attendance for one of these services. Whether out of pity or belief in his message, he invited Morris back to the boarding house that he shared with landlady, Anna Snowden. Jehovia wasted no time in converting the pair and they became Jehovia's first and second followers. Divine adopted a pseudonym, "The Messenger" – the Christ figure to Morris's God the Father. Divine and Father Jehovia were later joined by John A. Hickerson, who called himself Reverend Bishop Saint John

Father Divine, soon after achieving fame in the 1930s

the Vine. John the Vine shared the Messenger's excellent speaking ability and his interest in New Thought.

In 1912 the three-madman ministry collapsed when John the Vine decided to deny Father Jehovia's monopoly on godhood, citing 1 John 4:15 to mean God was in everyone: "Whoever shall confess that Jesus is the Son of God, God dwells in him and he in God." This was an assertion backed by the general drift of New Thought teachings but Jehovia violently disagreed. He counted on the Messenger to come down on his side, but Baker instead declared himself as the receptacle of God's spirit.

After the odd trio parted ways Father Divine traveled south to Georgia, where he began preaching in local churches. Most of the small African American congregations that he appeared in front of weren't receptive to his New Thought platitudes and his "God in the Body" ideas, but he did garner interest in the banquets he threw wherever he was invited to speak. Although he refused to accept donations, he did accept contributions – usually, the dishes that made up his communal feasts. He presided over the potlucks by blessing the food and referring to them as Holy Communion. He slowly amassed a small following of hungry people.

Leading souls away from their congregations was bound to get him into trouble sooner or later. In Savannah local ministers managed to have the Messenger arrested and put on a chain gang. Rather than be embarrassed about his arrest, he took pride in it and even claimed responsibility when state prison inspectors were injured during his confinement.

In Valdosta, he was immediately disinvited from a church where he was speaking after he began preaching about the imminent arrival of a black messiah. But Valdosta was not easily rid of the preacher. Divine had stolen the racial ideas of his old mentor, Jehovia, and started talking about equality and the power of women. He attracted attention from more than a few women from the local churches and they invited him into their homes where he spoke about the necessity of celibacy. One of the ladies brought the Messenger home to live with her and several other women joined them at the household turned commune.

Unfortunately, many of Divine's new followers were married, and when they joined the commune, they took with them their housework and, sometimes, their income. Valdosta husbands afflicted by the mass conversion to celibate communism believed they were unjustly deprived of the sexual attentions that were their right. These disgruntled men were angry enough that they managed to get Divine arrested on charges of insanity that rose to the level of a public nuisance. When the police came to haul him away the women formed a human shield around him. After this failed to stop his arrest, they followed the police back to the Valdosta jail where they publicly worshipped him as God. The jailed man, who refused to give his legal name, was booked as "John Doe, alias God."

Being in jail managed to enhance Divine's reputation. His claims of divinity brought religious seekers and the curious to his cell. Some came to speak in tongues, but others were New Thought devotees who read about his teachings in the newspapers. To the surprise of the jail guards many of these visitors were white.

At trial a local holiness minister testified on his behalf, recounting services where believers possessed by the Holy Spirit spoke in tongues yet were never punished for insanity. The jury was unmoved by the defense and instead focused on the testimony that claimed that Divine had some sort of hypnotic control over his brood of women. They found that Divine was undoubtedly of "unsound mind" but spared him confinement in the state asylum, as long as he left Valdosta without delay. He did – and he took many of his followers with him.

After some more time in the South, mostly being rejected by audiences, the Messenger returned north and ended up in Brooklyn in 1914. One of the devoted followers who accompanied him there was Joseph Gabriel, a minister who'd had his own church in Georgia. He allowed the Messenger to preach at his church after witnessing Divine perform a miracle by walking across wet concrete without leaving a single footprint.

Divine rented a flat on Myrtle Avenue and paid the rent by leasing out his faithful followers as domestic workers and day laborers. Worship was held over communal meals in the evening, a continuation of the method that Divine had used in Georgia to bring the poor and hungry into his fold.

The residents of the Myrtle Avenue flat were a ragtag lot – divorcees, victims of domestic abuse, and housewives that had never held a job. But Divine had an uncanny knack for finding jobs for his followers. Members came and went, but the commune slowly grew. By economizing on shared food, housing, and even clothing, the sect saved enough money to purchase a home in Sayville on Long Island. Ironically, it was racism that allowed the community of celibate African Americans to move into the all-

At one of Father Divine's weekly dinners, he can be seen standing at the head of the table with Peninnah, the first "Mother Divine."

white seaside town. A German American resident, angered by the prejudice he'd endured in Sayville during World War I, advertised his home for sale in the black newspapers that the Messenger scanned for job listings. The man had stated his preference for a "colored" buyer to spite his neighbors.

When the Messenger signed the deed for the house he did so as Major Jealous Devine. He later altered the spelling to "Divine" and while he used the honorific "Reverend" for a time – so that his white neighbors wouldn't wonder why he lived with a dozen adults who called him "Father" – he eventually became "Father Divine" for the rest of his life.

Cosigning the deed with Divine was a woman named Peninnah, a hefty matron whom the others considered to be the Messenger's wife. She had been a member of Joseph Gabriel's church but had pledged allegiance to Divine after he cured her of crippling rheumatism. She became Divine's most trusted follower and he could not have managed without her. She became known as "Mother Divine" and served the important role of defusing rumors of impropriety about Divine and his female followers. However, they always asserted that their marriage was never physically consummated.

In Sayville, the movement thrived. Divine played the part of the kindly preacher to get rid of any suspicions about his unusual household. He made certain to be seen around town, making large purchases for the commune, taking care to patronize local businesses. He continued to advertise "reliable colored help" in Long Island newspapers and became well known as a trusted source for good domestic employees. The sect began making so much money that Divine purchased himself a Cadillac.

As the next decade passed in peace, the movement grew. He began holding his weekly banquets for the public and began attracting many new followers, including white ones. And it was then that he began to upset his neighbors. Members of the community looked at his integrated commune house and spread rumors that he was keeping a large harem there and engaging in scandalous sex, although the Suffolk County district attorney's office found the claims baseless. To try to please his neighbors Divine had a sign posted at his driveway that warned guests, "NOTICE—Smoking—Intoxicating Liquors—Profane Language—Strictly Prohibited." Divine's followers claimed that singing was prohibited at the house after 8:00 p.m. and all windows and blinds had to be closed by 10:00 p.m. Nonetheless, the neighbors continued to complain.

The police began to ticket illegally parked cars of those who came to his weekly feasts, but Divine responded by converting a large section of his lawn into a parking lot. More resourceful neighbors, suspicious of the wealth that Father Divine seemed to now have, attempted to get him charged with racketeering or mail fraud by sending him cash and checks. Divine widely canceled the checks and returned the cash to senders whenever possible.

And then on May 8, 1931, a Sayville deputy arrested and charged Father Divine with disturbing the peace because of the crowds that had gathered for one of the weekly Holy Communion dinners. Mother Divine and a flock of followers appeared with Divine in court, where he was represented by Ellee Lovelace, a black lawyer who became a believer after Divine cured his debilitating arthritis. Mother Divine produced $1,000 in cash from her purse to pay his bail on the spot.

The trial, not as speedy as the neighbors wanted, was scheduled for late fall, allowing Father Divine's popularity to grow throughout the entire Sayville vacation season. The black press took up his cause, calling his persecution racist. Tempers simmered over the summer as Divine's banquets drew more than 3,000 people, stretching late into the

The house in Sayville where Divine lived with his followers and held loud meetings that disturbed the neighbors.

evening to accommodate the crowds. Petitions demanded Divine's removal were presented to the authorities. Some Sayville residents were less polite, dumping litter and garbage on his lawn. This did nothing to slow down the dinners – or calm down the neighbors.

On Sunday, November 15 at 12:15 a.m. a police officer was called to Father Divine's property. By the time state troopers, deputies, and prison buses were called in to arrest everyone, a mob of neighbors had surrounded the compound. Afraid that a riot might occur, the police informed Father Divine and his followers that they had 15 minutes to disperse. Divine had them wait in silence for 10 minutes, and then they filed into police custody. In all there were 78 worshippers booked at the county jail, including Divine – 15 of them were white.

The initial booking took until 3:00 a.m. Frustrated clerks were forced to deal with followers who often refused to give them legal names, stubbornly offering the "inspired" names they had adopted in the movement. The arraignment took all night. Two-thirds of the flock offered a guilty plea and were fined $5 each. The remaining members were ordered to appear in court for trial the following Friday. Father Divine was clapped with an additional charge of maintaining a public nuisance. He paid all the fines with a $500 bill, which the court clerk was embarrassingly unable to make change from.

Father Divine's arrest and the movement's doctrines were sensationally reported. The frenzy surrounding the event made it the most famous moment of Father Divine's life. Although they were mostly inaccurate, new articles about Father Divine made him even more popular. By December his followers began renting buildings in New York City for Father Divine to speak in. Soon he often had several engagements on a single night. On December 20 he spoke to an estimated 10,000 in Harlem's Rockland Palace, a spacious former basketball venue. By the spring of 1932 meetings were regularly held at the Rockland and throughout New York and New Jersey. His popularity grew and he attracted followers in other states who heard about him in the *New Thought* magazine, which was published in Seattle. Curiously, although the movement was predominantly African American, most of his followers outside of the New York area were middle-class whites. In this period of expansion several branch communes were opened, and Divine's followers named the movement – the Peace Mission.

Father Divine's trial concerning the November 1931 incident was finally held on May 24, 1932. His legal team had requested the trial be moved outside of Suffolk County due to potential jury bias – but this turned out to be a mistake. It was moved to the Nassau County Supreme Court and to the courtroom of Justice Lewis Smith, a conservative white judge who was known for his zealous sentencing of offenders. The prosecution called a parade of angry neighbors before the court and Judge Smith listened to them with obvious apathy.

The defense wanted to establish Father Divine's legitimacy as a faith leader, but this proved to be an uphill battle in Smith's courtroom. As an important witness they chose Eugene Del Mar, a former banker and stockbroker who became a leader in the New Thought Movement. He had traveled to Long Island to investigate the stories he'd heard about Father Divine and by 1931 was a faithful follower.

As one of Divine's educated white followers, he could not be easily dismissed as a nut or ignorant dupe. Unfortunately, though, what he had to say didn't help the defense. He confirmed that Divine's followers considered their leader a deity with "unusual powers." Many of them, he told Judge Smith, addressed him as God, or believed that he was the second coming of the Messiah. He connected this belief to Divine's miraculous ability to feed the masses, as Christ had done, adding that some of the group members claimed to have seen Divine "multiply the food before their very eyes." Del Mar didn't believe that testifying to miracles and healings by a black minister was absurd, but he wasn't making arguments that were suitable in a courtroom ruled by a white Presbyterian judge.

Other witnesses at the trial affirmed that Father Divine did not accept donations or possess a bank account, inflaming Judge Smith's already cynical view of the case. At one point, he intervened in the proceedings to bully a witness who refused to identify their race. After the closing arguments Smith instructed the jury to ignore all the statements made by witnesses who were not present on the night of the raid. This order invalidated most of the testimony in Divine's favor and crippled the defense. The jury found Divine guilty on June 5 but asked for leniency on his behalf. Ignoring this request, Smith lectured the courtroom about Father Divine being a fraud and a "menace to society" before issuing the maximum sentence for disturbing the peace: one year in prison and a $500 fine.

And then things got weird.

Judge Smith died a few days later on June 5 from a heart attack. Father Divine was widely reported to have commented on the death, "I hated to do it." In fact, he wrote to his followers, "I did not desire Judge Smith to die.... I did desire that MY spirit would touch his heart and change his mind that he might repent and believe and be saved from the grave."

The impression that Smith's death was "divine retribution" – so to speak – was perpetrated by the press, ignoring the judge's previous heart problems and implying that his death was more unexpected that it was. Never let the truth get in the way of a good story, it's often been said.

The Messenger was released on bail two weeks later and Father Divine permanently relocated to Harlem where he had gained a significant following within the black community. Members, rather than Father Divine himself, held most deeds for the movement, but they contributed toward Father Divine's comfortable lifestyle. Purchasing several hotels, which they called "Heavens," members could live and seek jobs inexpensively. Father Divine, and the Peace Mission, were the largest property owners in Harlem for years. The movement also opened several budget enterprises, including restaurants and clothing shops, that sold cheaply by cutting overhead. These proved very successful during the Depression. Economical, cash-only businesses were what made Father Divine wealthy and kept the movement well-fed while others were standing in bread lines and eating in soup kitchens.

By 1934 branches had opened in Los Angeles and Seattle and gatherings had occurred in France, Switzerland, Canada, and Australia. However, membership totals were overstated in the press. *Time* magazine estimated nearly two million followers, but the true figure was likely in the tens of thousands, inflated by the number of people who attended his gatherings out of curiosity.

Nonetheless, Father Divine was increasingly called upon to offer political endorsements. For example, New York mayoral candidates John P. O'Brien and Fiorello H. LaGuardia each sought his endorsement in 1933, but Father Divine wasn't interested at the time. That changed after the Harlem Riot of 1935. The riot was caused by a rumor claiming that the police had killed a black teenager. It wasn't true, but it left four dead and caused over $1 million in property damage in Father Divine's neighborhood. Divine's outrage at this and other racial injustices fueled a keener interest in politics. In January 1939 the movement would organize the first-ever "Divine Righteous Government Convention," which crafted political platforms incorporating the so-called "Doctrine of Father Divine."

But before that, at the height of Father Divine's influence, the movement began to suffer a series of setbacks that were much worse than mere arrests for disturbing the peace.

In 1935 Father Divine had started expanding the Peace Mission outside of the city. He turned his attention to the rural areas of New York, particularly to the fertile farmlands of the Hudson Valley. As the Depression wore on, forcing rural property owners to sell out, Divine seized the opportunity to advance his self-sufficiency empire by purchasing farms where his followers could produce food for sale at a discount to his city businesses.

With bags filled with cash, trusted followers bought up land in Ulster County and started the first Peace Mission extension there in 1935. Land was purchased in New Paltz, and Marbletown and about 125 followers traveled upriver to Poughkeepsie and proceeded by bus and car to the new farms. The place in Marbletown – which they dubbed Stone Ridge Farm – became Divine's favorite. He preferred the house on the property whenever he stayed overnight in the county and often spoke there. It was a historic home and dear to Divine for symbolic reasons – local lore claimed it was the base of operations for the Ku Klux Klan years before.

The movement added several more farms in Ulster County in 1935 and 1936, including properties in and around the town of Saugerties, where the Peace Mission established a hotel, restaurant, candy store, and gas station. In nearby Kingston they purchased another hotel that became the Peace Mission's upstate headquarters. This property was managed by Miss Satisfied Love and her assistant, Miss Lamb. The idea of two black women running a hotel that integrated its rooms by race but separated the sexes by floor was not something that local residents found easy to swallow. Unlike the farms, the hotel was a very visible example of what Father Divine was trying to achieve, and he wanted to publicize it.

In August 1936 he chartered a steamer up the Hudson to ferry 1,877 of his followers – at least 50 of them white – to march in a parade through the village. Dressed all in white, the group filled the streets of the small town, led by Father and Mother Divine in a blue Rolls-Royce convertible.

The police arrived just in time to rain on the parade. A man named Harry Whitney had gotten upset about a flag that he'd seen waving at the parade and called the

Father Divine's Peace Mission in Ulster County

authorities to lodge a complaint. The responding officer demanded that the group hand over the red, white, and blue banner that stated simply – "Peace, Father Divine is God." The banner mysteriously vanished for a time and then was finally handed over. The police then informed reporters that it would be destroyed. Divine's fame was such that the affair was reported on the front page of the *New York Times*. Reached for comment, one of Divine's lawyers replied to the absurd harassment by promising that Ulster County would soon be home to more than 2,000 Divine settlers – and he was right. A short time later members of the sect bought the Hotel Delmont in High Falls and began cooperative efforts in several businesses, including a department store, candy factory, bakery, gas shop, and a dress shop that was run by Mother Divine, who took up residency in a small cottage behind the hotel.

Over the next few months, the Peace Mission continued to buy up property in Ulster County. The identities of the buyers were usually concealed, or white members of the group served as fronts for the riskier purchases. They purchased a resort called Greenkill Park, the Divine Lodge, a former resort for Broadway actors, and the Hope Farm, managed by Simon Peter, a white doctor who had converted to the Peace Mission after burning down his practice for the insurance money.

In time around 2,300 followers came to live in the Ulster County colonies. Their relocation took a lot of courage during the Depression because wealth in the hands of formerly poor blacks living in the mostly white Hudson Valley provoked a lot of animosity. A cross was burned in front of the Hotel Belmont and two more were burned near Stone Ridge Farm in 1937, the same year that one of Divine's properties, a lodge east of New Paltz, mysteriously caught fire in the night. Greenkill Park, which had been suggested as a possible future headquarters for the Harlem-based movement, also burned down that same year.

The authorities conveniently never determined that the cause of any of the fires was arson, but a large number of properties belonging to the same group suggests that the fires were deliberately set.

Because Father Divine didn't carry any insurance the movement lost about $25,000 on the night of the Greenkill Park fire alone. Newspapers speculated that the Ku Klux Klan might have been responsible, but the local sheriff declared the fires all accidents.

The Ulster County fires were dramatic setbacks for Father Divine, but he had other things to worry about in 1937. He had been released from jail just one day before the Greenkill Park fire. On April 20 he had been arrested in connection with a stabbing that occurred in Harlem. Paul Camora, an officer of the court, had gone to the Peace Mission building on 115th Street to serve an order for Father Divine to return money given to him by a plaintiff, Jessie Birdsall, who claimed that Divine owed her $2,000. Camora arrived with a friend, Harry Green, who was curious to see what the place was like. According to Green the two men arrived just as Divine finished a rousing sermon to about 1,500 of his followers. When he learned that the two men intended to serve him with a summons, Divine told the crowd to "go get him." This allegation was denied by Divine, as well as by his co-defendants and a reporter who was on the scene. None admitted seeing a weapon but before he escaped the building Green was stabbed in the stomach with an icepick.

A warrant was issued for Divine's arrest, but he had gone on the run.

During his absence, one of Divine's most prominent followers, a former homeless prostitute named Viola Wilson, who now went by the name Faithful Mary, defected and took control of a large commune, which was technically in her name.

Mary had been born in Dublin, Georgia in 1892. Her father was an alcoholic and abusive Baptist minister, and she grew up in a crowded shack with her parents and her 15 brothers and sisters. Tired of her drunken father, she left home at 14 and started working in the cotton fields. She married young, separated from her husband, and ended up a single teenage mother. Unsure of what to do, she gave away her child to an older married couple who agreed to take him off her hands. She married again a few years later but her second husband got sick and died.

Nearly 30, widowed, and poor, she went north after World War I and ended up in Newark in 1920. Not long after her arrival she claimed to receive a recipe for a curative for rheumatism in a dream. She prepared the tonic, found that it worked, and started a thriving business making the medicine. After being ruined by a cheating business partner, Mary then took a job as a matron on the Pennsylvania Railroad where she turned to drink. She became an alcoholic, lost that job and all that followed, and by 1928 she was homeless and sleeping with men to survive.

After learning that her sister was in desperate circumstances, one of Mary's siblings, who lived in Buffalo, New York, tracked her down, cleaned her up, and tried to get her involved in her church, but it didn't stick. Mary went back to the bottle and prostitution. Then, one morning when she awakened in a pool hall after a night of drinking, she felt a light wash over her and she became convinced that God had healed her. She soon learned about the Peace Mission extension in Newark and became actively involved in the movement.

She started out running the extension house in Newark, and then Divine put her in charge of other properties. Faithful Mary – transforming from a gutter drunk prostitute to a celibate businesswoman – made Divine seem capable of working real miracles.

But Divine's disappearance proved too big of a temptation for Mary. The newspapers stated that she and Divine had "quarreled" before the stabbing incident, but no details were known. According to Mary's version of events, Divine had reproached her for criticizing his leadership and threatened to demote her to the kitchens of one of the farms in Ulster County.

Father Divine and Viola Wilson, who became better known as "Faithful Mary."

Faithful Mary's tiny empire hardly rivaled Divine's but she had enough influence that Divine's reprimand served to provoke her into action. While Divine was on the lam, Mary announced that her properties were no longer under Divine's control and were now part of her own Universal Light movement. It was a short-lived rebellion. Aside from another defector, who called himself Son Peter, the Universal Light movement failed to attract anyone from the Peace Mission.

To make matters worse Mary had miscalculated the degree of difficulty that was faced by Father Divine because of the stabbing. In May Divine had been tracked down and was found hiding behind a furnace at a Peace Mission extension in New Milford, Connecticut. He appeared in court three times before he was finally cleared of all charges. He followed the dismissal of the case with a 10-course victory dinner that lasted from "midnight to dawn."

One of Divine's first orders of business was to crush Mary's rebellion, ordering his followers to shun her businesses. They obeyed and Mary was soon on the brink of ruin. Looking for revenge, she and Son Peter joined forces with another former Peace Mission member, Verinda Brown. She had sued Divine and was seeking allies among his enemies. Faithful Mary and Son Peter became star witnesses in Brown's lawsuit, offering unlikely testimony about how Divine's followers in the Hudson Valley were going hungry and were being used as slave labor.

In the lawsuit Brown claimed that she had entrusted her life savings to Divine. She and her husband had joined the movement in 1931 but, four years later, decided that they wanted to live as husband and wife again and decided to leave. They requested that Divine return their investment in his mission, but he refused, stating that the money had been invested in real estate. Thanks to their evidence, and testimony from Faithful Mary and others critical of the movement, the court ordered repayment of the money. However, this opened up an enormous potential liability from all ex-followers, so Father Divine resisted and appealed the judgment.

Meanwhile, Faithful Mary was still looking for retribution. She self-published a tell-all memoir about her time in the Peace Mission, alleging that rampant homosexuality was taking place in the movement and that Father Divine collaborated with the upper echelons of the missing to cover up the deaths of more than 200 followers.

By this time, though, Mary posed little threat to Divine. She had been forced to sell all her properties to cover her debt and began drinking again. By the end of the year she was begging for Divine's forgiveness, which he granted, after publicly humiliating her by forcing her to make a public confession during with she admitted that she had lied about her charges against the movement.

She was absorbed back into the Newark extension, but her recovery was only temporary – Faithful Mary died from an overdose of sleeping pills after ending her days poor, drunk, and destitute in Los Angeles.

Wayward follower John Wuest Hunt, also known as "John the Revelator"

And those weren't the only problems that Divine was dealing with. The most embarrassing one was a case involving John Wuest Hunt, a wealthy white follower who had taken the name John the Revelator. He had run an advertising agency in Los Angeles, spent far too much time in the red-light districts of Mexican border towns, and lived across the street from actor Lionel Barrymore in Beverly Hills in a house where he was known for throwing boozy wife-swapping parties and showing lewd films. However, after depression pushed him to the brink of suicide, Hunt began seeking help in various L.A. churches. He stumbled on a Peace Mission extension, was struck by the faith of its members, and became one of the largest backers of Father Divine's movement in the Los Angeles area.

As we'll see in later chapters, Los Angeles is no stranger to unusual religions, but the holy-rolling ruckus that was coming from Hunt's home so angered the neighbors, including Barrymore, that the police were called to the scene. Hunt, his brother Warner – now called John the Baptist – and their secretary were all arrested.

But an arrest for disturbing the peace didn't slow Hunt down. Divine led John the Revelator to believe that he could receive powers equal to those of Father Divine if he was able to secure a $100,000 donation to the Peace Mission. Whether this was the reason or not, by 1937 Hunt became convinced that he was Jesus Christ.

Things just got worse from there.

While visiting a mission commune in Denver, Hunt became smitten with a 17-year-old follower named Delight Jewett. He invited the young woman, and several others, for a ride in his Packard and after some rousing Peace Mission hymns, Delight began speaking in tongues. Declaring her consecrated in the movement, the Revelator gave her a new name – Mary Dove.

"Cult victim" – as the newspapers called her – Delight Jewett

Hunt went back to Los Angeles, and he took Mary Dove with him. It's unknown whether her parents gave consent to this trip but regardless, it didn't look good. In L.A. Hunt convinced the girl that she was the Virgin Mary and announced that she was going to give birth to a "New Redeemer" by "immaculate conception" in Hawaii. Hunt just thought he'd help things along by having sex with her. The two did not return to Denver as expected but drove to New York City instead. When Father Divine learned about what had been going on, he separated the holy lovers and chastised Hunt for violating the celibacy rule.

Meanwhile, Delight's parents had followed their daughter and the Revelator to New York and demanded an audience with Divine. They wanted the new Virgin Mary to return home with them to Colorado, but Divine pacified Mr. Jewett with a job offer to run one of the farms in the Hudson Valley.

Her mother, Elizabeth, was not so easily managed. She began demanding money for damages. Hoping to convince her to let things go, Divine released the girl but that wasn't enough. When the Jewetts failed to get the money they wanted, they sold their story to William Randolph Hearst's *New York Evening Journal,* which had always been critical of the movement. The paper dragged the whole sordid story before the public and a warrant was issued for John the Revelator's arrest. The subsequent manhunt and Hunt's indictment on charges of violating the Mann Act – a law that prevented women from being taken across state lines for the purposes of sex—provided days of lurid headlines. The papers printed every strange detail of the case and Hunt was eventually sentenced to three years in prison. There, he adopted a new name – the Prodigal Son.

Surprising many of his followers, Father Divine publicly endorsed the conviction of John the Revelator. Many of them had hoped he might "smite" another judge. But Divine wanted it over with. The incident had caused a lot of bad publicity for the movement. Every news story implied that followers of the Peace Mission were gullible and possibly dangerous.

By the late 1930s the New Deal had alleviated some of the worst effects of the Depression, which tarnished the appeal of the Peace Mission. Although the Peace Mission never kept membership records, it had become clear that movement had entered a slow decline.

The courts eventually ruled in favor of Verinda Brown, ordering Divine to pay a judgment of $5,000. He appealed the ruling but finally lost the case in 1942. At this point in his life money meant almost nothing. Although he held no property or bank accounts in his name, the Peace Mission controlled millions – money protected by the fact that the movement was officially a tax-exempt religious organization.

But Divine was personally liable for the result of the Brown lawsuit, which he refused to pay because it was evidence of the "corruption of earthly authorities." Even though his followers would have lined up to pay the judgment on his behalf, Divine decided to avoid arrest by moving his headquarters to Philadelphia. Since New York state law prohibited serving subpoenas on Sunday he often returned on the Sabbath to speak in Harlem or Ulster County.

Mother Divine never made it to Philadelphia. She had been spending most of her time at the upstate farms when her health began to fail. She suffered from heart and kidney problems, which forced her into the hospital on two occasions. Her second stay lasted for months. Her status was meant to be a secret, but reporters discovered her whereabouts after her absence became obvious. Divine never visited his wife in the hospital. Initially he might have avoided her because he didn't want to draw attention to her illness but in hindsight, it's apparent that if Divine truly believed that impurity of thought was the cause of illness and death then Mother Divine was as corrupt as the many others whose deaths he had blamed on their own mental failings.

Mother Divine recovered and was spotted at meetings in Kingston and High Falls as late as 1938. Her last known appearance was at a 1942 Holy Communion banquet in New York. By the following year, though, she had disappeared. It's believed that she died at some point that year, but no one knows for sure. Father Divine never talked about it or even acknowledged her death, but it must have rattled him, making him aware of his own mortality. He realized – as did many of his followers – that the movement might not make one immortal, as he had asserted for so long, at least not in the flesh.

On April 29, 1946 Father Divine married again. His new bride was a 21-year-old white Canadian woman named Edna Rose Ritchings. The ceremony was kept secret from most of Divine's followers until Edna's travel visa expired. Critics of the Peace Mission believed that Divine's seemingly scandalous marriage would destroy the movement, but instead followers celebrated the marriage and their anniversary became a lauded yearly event.

Divine claimed that Edna, who became known as Mother S.A. Divine, was the reincarnation of his first wife, Peninnah. Although reincarnation had never been a part of the movement's doctrine, followers believed that Peninnah was an exceptional case and they viewed her "return" as a miracle.

By the 1950s, the movement was entering its decline, and the newspapers rarely covered Divine. When they did it was no longer as a cult leader but as an amusing relic. They ran light-hearted stories when Divine pronounced Philadelphia as the capital of the world and when he claimed to inspire the invention of the hydrogen bomb. However, they tended to ignore his work for civil rights. In 1951 he advocated for reparations to be paid to the descendants of slaves. He also argued in favor of integrated neighborhoods. However, he did not participate in the growing civil rights movement – something that continues to plague his reputation. His lack of participation had a lot to do with his declining health but even more important to him was his dislike of racial labels. He had always denied that he was black.

The new "Mother Divine" – a 21-year-old Canadian woman who "contained" the spirit of the first Mother Divine. She carried on Divine's work until her death at age 82

In 1953, one of Divine's still devoted followers gifted him with a hilltop estate in Gladwyne outside of Philadelphia called Woodmont. The French gothic manor became his home and the site of his increasingly infrequent Holy Communion banquets in the late 1950s.

After 1960, Divine's health forced him out of the public eye. Periods of serious illness related to diabetes led to secret hospital stays. Otherwise he rarely left the grounds of Woodmont.

It was there, while living at Woodmont, that Father Divine met a man who would become one of his most important admirers. This white minister from Indiana, who had started the first integrated congregation in Indianapolis, had come to see for himself how Father Divine had created his movement. The mister left deeply impressed by the Divine methods of living according to apostolic socialism and became resolved to implement in his own church.

The minister's name was Jim Jones.

On September 10, 1965 Father Divine died of natural causes at the Woodmont estate. His widow, who became the spiritual leader of the movement, and his remaining followers still insist that his spirit is alive today and always refer to Father Divine in the present tense. To this day the furnishings in his personal rooms at Woodmont are kept just as they were when he was still in physical form.

He has, as far as they are concerned, never left them.

My guess is that few people reading this book are familiar with Father Divine. He is, in many ways, a relic of bygone days. His movement came to life at a time of terrible economic depression in America, and no matter what you might think of his doctrine he gave hope to a lot of people who didn't have any. Despite his claims of immortality Divine's declining health made it impossible for him to change with the times and adapt his message to reach new people as the Depression came to an end and the needs of his target audience began to change. In time he was dismissed, ignored, and mostly forgotten.

Believe it or not, though, Father Divine's message lives on in a way that you might never imagine – through song. Legend has it that singer and songwriter Johnny Mercer came to hear one of Divine's sermons in 1944. The subject of the sermon was to "accentuate the positive and eliminate the negative" – a pretty standard part of the Peace Mission's objective.

Mercer was struck by the phrase and when he went back to Hollywood, he got together with songwriter Harold Arlen – who wrote a tune you might know called "Over the Rainbow" – and together they wrote "Ac-cent-tchu-ate The Positive." It became a smash hit for Bing Crosby and the Andrews Sisters in 1945.

Look it up and listen. It's one you'll know.

And then realize that you've channeled a lit bit of Father Divine.

Sister Aimee

While Father Divine was thriving in the east, there were scores of religious movements that were springing up in the west. No state has witnessed more of a tidal wave of churches, cults, and communes in the way that California has. In the early 1900s Los Angeles was home to more alternative religious movements that anywhere else in the world. They ranged from the Theosophical Society to the Church of I Am, which was based on the worship of the questionable deity, St. Germaine, who supposedly gave off a violet ray of supernatural power.

According to novelist Nathaniel West, who used the dark side of L.A. for atmosphere in several of his books and stories, some of the local churches included the "Church Invisible," where fortunes were told; the "Tabernacle of the Third Coming," where a woman who dressed as a man preached the Crusade Against Salt; and the "Temple Moderne," where 'Brain-Breathing, the Secret of the Aztecs" was taught. In 1917 the *Los Angeles Times* referred to some of the early communes as "spookeries" or "fairy farms" and did anything it could to undermine the success that all of them seemed to be enjoying.

While the crackpots and weirdoes were trying to appeal to the stranger side of the local populace, one evangelist was working to present a kinder, gentler message of peace, love, and understanding. She did so with flamboyant presentations that were right out of a Hollywood musical and, in fact, the regular appearance of movie stars at her services was one of her claims to fame. The evangelist's name was Aimee Semple McPherson, and the Pentecostal church that she founded, the International Church of the Foursquare Gospel, still exists today.

But, as for Sister Aimee herself, it would all come crashing down in 1926.

"Sister Aimee," as her thousands of followers would someday call her, was born Aimee Kennedy on a farm in rural Ontario on October 9, 1890. Her mother, Mildred, said that her baby was an answer to her prayers. She had been forced to give up her active life in the Salvation Army, in which her father was a captain, for a joyless marriage to a farmer that was 35 years her senior. She had asked God to give her a daughter who could spread the gospel in her place. The answer she received was Aimee.

Or so the story – later printed in publicity ads – was often told.

Minnie planned to keep her end of the bargain with God. When Aimee was only three weeks old, she bundled her up and took her to a Salvation Army worship service and formally dedicated the child to Christian service. As she grew up Aimee thrived in the Salvation Army, with its military-style organization and devotion to relieving misery through "soap, soup, and salvation." She loved the uniforms, marches, and pageantry in the name of religion and would do so for the rest of her life.

Aimee became something of a religious child prodigy. By age five she could recite just about any Bible story by request. Other parts of her education suffered, though. When she started school, she knew none of her letters. However, thanks to her quick intelligence and good-natured eagerness to please, she quickly caught up and became an excellent student.

She broadened her religious horizons as she got older. She still did Salvation Army work with her mother, but she also started attending a local Methodist church and enrolled in a Sunday school. She was so respected at the school that she began to get invitations to speak at churches from many different denominations. Before she reached her teens, she won a gold medal in a public speaking contest sponsored by the Women's Christian Temperance Union.

Aimee began to drift when she entered high school. She started reading novels, going to movies, and attending school dances – all to her mother's stern disapproval. Things took another turn when she began studying Charles Darwin's theories in school and began doubting the accuracy of the scriptures that she had been accepting as truth for her entire life. She even began questioning the existence of God. She demanded answers from her mother and even a local minister, challenging their basic religious beliefs. Minnie began to wonder aloud how she had failed as a mother.

Then, one afternoon in 1907, she and her father were driving down the street and Aimee saw a sign in a window announcing a Pentecostal mission with meetings every night and all day on Sunday. Curious about the meetings – she'd heard the

Robert and Aimee Semple in 1910

stories of people jumping, dancing, and falling down under the power – she asked her father if she could go to one. He agreed, and they went the next night.

It was a spur of the moment decision that changed Aimee's life.

Aimee Kennedy, only 17-years-old, was initially amused at the antics of the Pentecostals at the meeting. When a man she knew, the local milkman, was struck by the spirit and fell to the floor, praising the Lord as he rolled around, she couldn't stifle her laughter. She later recalled, "I giggled foolishly, not understanding it and thinking it very laughable."

But when Robert Semple got up to speak Aimee's attitude changed. He was a handsome man, but that wasn't the attraction. As he began to speak, she was captivated. The sermon – about the baptism of the Holy Spirit and one he'd likely given a dozen times – was eye-opening for Aimee, and she always said that it changed her life. She quit the play that she was supposed to appear in and then burned her dance shoes, her ragtime sheet music, and her novels. She told Robert Semple of her conversion and began coming to the mission every day, even skipping school in her determination to achieve her own spirit baptism. Her grades suffered and her mother began hearing complaints, not only from the school principal but from Minnie's Salvation Army associates, who worried that Aimee was getting involved with "fanatics."

A short time later Ontario was hit with a powerful blizzard that knocked down power and telephone lines and closed the roads and railroad lines. Aimee used the time to pray at the home of one of her Pentecostal "sisters," hoping to bring on her spirit baptism. Finally, after several days of almost non-stop prayer, she was rewarded with visions, convulsions, and speaking in tongues.

Aimee had been transformed in her faith and in her personal life, too. She had been corresponding with Robert Semple ever since he'd left the area and moved on to hold mission meetings in another town. He returned as soon as he heard the news of Aimee's baptism. One evening, as they were reading the Bible together, he told her of his dream of traveling to China as a missionary. Then he shocked her by asking her to marry him and go with him on his mission. He insisted that they pray together before she gave her answer, but Aimee had already decided: "I rose and said yes to God and yes to Robert."

They were married on August 12, 1908 and Aimee began her life as the wife of a nomadic Pentecostal preacher. They moved to various towns in Ontario before going to Chicago to work and study at various missions and camps. During this time Aimee earned a reputation as a tongue-speaker and interpreter and was loosely "ordained" to speak as someone who had experienced a divine calling.

By early 1910 Robert was ready to depart for their long-anticipated mission to China. Unlike missionaries from more established Protestant denominations, the Semples would make the trip with no guarantees in place – no living expenses, no home, no local support – nothing but a conviction that the Lord would provide.

Unfortunately, in this case, he didn't.

The mission was a disaster. For weeks Robert succeeded in winning Chinese souls for Jesus, but the living conditions were dangerous and unsanitary. Aimee, who had learned on the voyage to the Far East that she was pregnant, contracted malaria soon after they arrived. Then Robert came down with dysentery, complicated by his own case of malaria. He grew steadily worse until, as Aimee lay sick in another hospital room, he died on August 19, only six weeks after they had arrived in China. He was only 29-years-old. One month later Aimee gave birth to their daughter, who she named Roberta, after her late husband.

Aimee was now alone and penniless in China with a newborn infant. For a time, she considered staying to continue Robert's work – or so she claimed – but when a return ticket arrived from her mother she went home.

Instead of Ontario, though, she met her mother in New York. Minnie Kennedy had come to believe that her religious calling would not be found on a drab, rural farm but with Salvation Army work in Manhattan. Aimee and the baby moved into Minnie's apartment on 14th Street and Aimee went to work at the Salvation Army Rescue Mission while she decided what to do with the rest of her life. Minnie encouraged her to stay with the Salvation Army, but Aimee felt a different calling. She wanted to carry on her husband's work of saving souls, but she wasn't quite sure how to do it – not yet anyway.

Aimee grieved for her husband and took care of Roberta, who was a sickly child, for nearly a year. She traveled back and forth to Canada and visited her Pentecostal community in Chicago. Sometime in 1911, when she was back in New York, she met a man named Harold McPherson, a cashier at a fashionable Midtown restaurant, who had seen Aimee one day when she was collecting Salvation Army donations. He walked her home and the two began dating. McPherson, although religious in his own way, was conventional and worldly and Minnie disapproved of him as a match for her widowed daughter. But Aimee knew that she and Roberta needed stability in their lives and so she accepted his marriage proposal in late 1911.

McPherson was a kind man who provided her with a good home with him and his mother in Providence, Rhode Island. She had money and comfort, but she did not have happiness. She became miserable and depressed and not even the birth of another child – a boy named Rolf – could lift her out of her funk. In the winter of 1912, she was hospitalized for several surgeries, including a hysterectomy, and claimed to be close to death in the recovery room. She believed that God had forsaken her because she had turned his back on him when she married Harold.

Harold McPherson was just about to lose out to God.

Aimee soon decided that she was going to return to her calling as a traveling evangelist, a decision that Harold and his mother strongly objected to. So, Aimee took matters into her own hands. One night in June 1915 when McPherson was away, she packed her things, got into a taxi with her children, and bought one-way train tickets

Aimee Semple and her second husband Harold McPherson. For a time, Harold traveled with his wife Aimee in the "Gospel Car" as an itinerant preacher.

to Ontario. Her mother – who had returned to the family farm – agreed to care for the children while Aimee went on the road.

Harold was, not surprisingly, unhappy to see his family disappear in the dead of night. Over the next week he sent letters and telegrams to Aimee, demanding that she come back to Providence and "wash the dishes," "take care of the house," and "act like other women." But that was one thing that Aimee wasn't – she wasn't like other women.

Leaving the children with her parents, Aimee traveled to Kitchener, Ontario to attend a Pentecostal camp meeting in July. From there she went to London, Mount Forest, and other towns after receiving invitations to speak. It was in Mount Forest that Aimee truly came into her own as an evangelist.

Unable to attract more than a handful of people to her gatherings, she decided to try an old Salvation Army trick. She took a chair out to the town's main road, stood on it, closed her eyes, and lifted her hands in the air to God. She didn't speak and didn't make a sound. Minutes passed, and people began to gather around her motionless form, curious about a woman who was apparently pretending to be a statue. When she had a crowd around her, she suddenly opened her eyes. "People!" she cried. "Follow me, quickly!" She jumped down from the chair and then ran down the street to the mission. The crowd followed her and when they were all inside, she ordered the door to be locked and kept locked until she was finished.

Aimee preached for the next 40 minutes and excited by what they heard most of the crowd returned the next night and for many nights to come. And they brought people with them. The crowds just kept getting larger.

That was the last time that Sister Aimee ever had to work to get a crowd.

For the next three years Aimee preached at Pentecostal camps, revivals, and missions whenever she could. She was a natural – warm, charismatic, inspiring, and effective. She made scores of converts wherever she spoke. Dozens at every meeting were baptized by the Holy Spirit, falling to the ground or running around the halls and auditoriums where she preached. Speaking in tongues and shouts of "Hallelujah!" and "Praise the Lord!" erupted everywhere. She also conducted healing services, praying with the sick until, in many cases, they stood up and threw away their crutches, claiming to be cured. Even those who were not spirit-struck or healed were fascinated with the spectacle of her services. They came back to see her again and again and brought friends and family with them.

Even Harold McPherson – when he finally caught up with his wife – fell under her spell. On the night he arrived in Canada he stood at the back of one of her meetings with a suitcase in his hand, openmouthed and stunned by what he was seeing. He immediately realized that Aimee would not be coming back with him – he would be following her. That first night, under Aimee's guidance, he was baptized by the Holy Spirit and began speaking in tongues. He decided on the spot to join her mission and help glorify God.

That such things were being accomplished by a woman – and a young, attractive one at that – added to the mission's allure. As Aimee knew, a female evangelist was a novelty in 1915, and she faced criticism from most conservative clergymen. She didn't let this discourage her. Instead she used it to her advantage, bringing in the curious who had never seen a woman preacher before.

Initially Aimee confined her travels to southern Canada, then expanded into New England using the McPherson house in Providence as a base. But she wanted to go farther. Harold quit his job, the couple sold their furniture, and they set out in a new Packard, "Gospel Car," staging tent revivals and saving souls all along the eastern seaboard. They spent the summer in the tourist spots like Cape Cod, but when the weather turned cold, they packed up the tent and went south. Minnie cared for the sickly Roberta and Aimee and Harold took baby Rolf on the road with them. They preached during the day – under a tent or in a local mission or church – and camped at night, turning the reversible front seats of the Gospel Car into comfortable sleeping quarters in tourist camps or on the side of the road.

Aimee drew audiences wherever they went. Skeptics were won over, the lame and sick were healed, and souls were saved for Jesus. Her fame as an evangelist continued to spread at first by word of mouth or personal connections, but soon through magazines and print articles.

At the same time, her following was growing there was one soul that she lost – Harold. Perhaps tired of playing second fiddle to his charismatic wife, he spent more and more time away from the crusade. At first, he tried starting his own career as an evangelist, but eventually he went back to work at an everyday job. He and Aimee quietly divorced in 1921 and he gradually vanished from the lives of his ex-wife and children.

Aimee continued to travel with Rolf as her only companion. They lived day by day on the donations given by those who came to hear her preach, but life wasn't easy. She often had to skip meals, pitch tents in the rail, and survive on the verge of physical and mental collapse. When she finally reached her limit, she telegraphed her mother for help. James Kennedy had died some time earlier, so Minnie was free to leave the farm and travel south to find Aimee with Roberta in tow. Together they became a three-generation evangelical traveling show. Minnie took care of the children and worked as Aimee's business manager while Aimee drove the Gospel Car and mesmerized the crowds.

In the fall of 1918 during a revival in New Rochelle, New York Aimee became ill with the Spanish Influenza that was sweeping the nation. Her case was not too serious and despite chills and fever, preached at all but one of the services that she had scheduled. But one night she returned to the rooms where the family was staying and found that Roberta was sick with the flu and was near death. Terrified, Aimee stayed up all night and prayed over the feverish, unconscious little girl and had a vision that would change her life once again. According to Aimee she saw God himself, who told her that Roberta would live and that she would take her family to California and start a new life in the sunshine.

Aimee readily followed her new calling. Roberta recovered, and the family sold the Packard and bought a roomier and more reliable Oldsmobile. They packed up the car and made plans for a cross-country trip to their new home in Los Angeles.

They left New York on October 24, 1918 accompanied by secretary Mabel Bingham, and spent the next two months driving, handing out religious tracts, and spending nights in the homes of Pentecostal brothers and sisters along the way. Arrangements had been made in advance for Aimee to preach at a few revivals in Indianapolis, Tulsa, Oklahoma City, and other places. Many cities had banned public gatherings because of the Spanish Flu epidemic, but restrictions always seemed to be miraculously lifted just in time for Aimee to speak.

In December they made it to Los Angeles – and Sister Aimee was finally home.

As will become obvious in many of the chapters to come, California has always been a fertile ground for alternative religious movements and beliefs that are outside the norm. When Aimee arrived in the 1910s, she found the region ripe for the picking. Despite the decade's influx of godless movie people and their entourage of hangers-on, the city was a magnet for aging health-seekers, middle-class seekers of warmer weather, and retirees from the Midwest. They were an uprooted population with a lot of time on their hands, and for those who were looking for a religious movement that was not too far outside the norm, they became a natural audience for Sister Aimee.

But she had to start modestly. Her first revival was at Victoria Hall, a small Pentecostal mission downtown. Though the auditorium had seating for 1,000, services had been attracting less than 50 people – well, that was before Aimee got to town. By the end of her first week, Aimee was filling every seat in the auditorium and packing the aisles with a standing-room-only row in the back. On weekends the demand for seats was so great that she was forced to move the show to the 3,500-seat Temple Auditorium on Pershing Square. The city's Pentecostal community, which had become driftless since the closing of the Azusa Street Revival, was instantly reenergized as word of Aimee's gifts spread across the city.

One Sunday evening after Aimee arrived in the city a woman stood up and announced that she had a plot of land that she wanted to give to the Sister to build a home for her children. A man then stood up and offered to donate the lumber to build the house. Soon people were popping up throughout the audience, offering furniture, beds, rugs, and a completely furnished home. As she later told the story, there were even spontaneous offers of a canary and a rosebush, the two things her children had wanted the most.

Three months later the family had a home of their own – built almost entirely from donated materials and by volunteer labor – on a quiet street in Culver City. For the first time in her adult life Aimee had a real, permanent home.

But for the next four years she didn't stay there often. She frequently left the children with her mother as she traveled, building her following with revival after revival. She always imagined herself as a traveling evangelist but, in time, Los Angeles would change that. As she watched her children thrive in the stable environment of a home, she realized that she didn't need to search for followers – they could come and find her. In a city filled with movie stars, Aimee Semple McPherson would, at least for a time, become the greatest celebrity of all.

For Los Angeles to become a permanent location for her followers Aimee knew that she would have to build a

Aimee became one of the first evangelists with a need for publicity photos. Her ministry fit in perfectly into the show business world of Hollywood.

center for her evangelism. As she traveled and preached, she began talking about her vision for the place, where believers of all creeds could gather for the greater glory of God. To raise money to build the center she sold $1 photos of herself and little bags of cement for $5. For $25 a donor could receive a miniature chair, representing a seat in the temple that would always be reserved for them. Eventually she sold thousands of those chairs – and just hoped that all the chairholders would never show up all at once.

At first her plans for the evangelical center were modest. Her initial idea was to build a plain wooden church. It would be a simple but permanent structure that would be dedicated to religious services, not an auditorium that might be offering boxing tournaments or shows a few nights each week. But as the months of revivals continued and her following grew larger, she began to expand on her original concept. In mid-1922, as donations kept pouring in, the simple wooden church in her mind became a much grander temple.

When she was finally ready to start construction, the contractor asked her how much she had to start with, and Aimee replied that she had $5,000. He incredulously told her that would be about enough money to just dig a hole. "By the time you dig the hole, I expect to have enough money for the foundation," Amy replied – and she was right.

Even the location itself seemed blessed by God. In the summer of 1920 Aimee and her mother had been driving around Echo Park, and Aimee had been impressed by the neighborhood. She found the perfect location for her church, a large lot on Glendale Boulevard overlooking Echo Lake and the surrounding park. She was determined that it would be the site of what she was going to call Angelus Temple.

The only problem was that the lot wasn't for sale. The elderly owner had already turned down dozens of offers, but Aimee interpreted that news as that God had been saving it for her. When Aimee inquired about the property the owner changed his mind and sold it to her for a "splendid price."

Soon after the groundbreaking Aimee doubled her fundraising efforts, determined to pay all the construction bills as they came in. She continued to spread her message in every way possible, even throwing tracts from an airplane as it flew over neighborhoods populated by recent arrivals to the area. Soon, however, Aimee didn't have to drum up crowds. The newspapers and word of mouth were doing it for her. She was packing standing-room-only crowds in the largest venues in every town.

Aimee didn't chastise her audiences about their sins and unworthiness. She offered a bright vision of God, served with charm and charisma. There would be parodies of popular songs using religious lyrics and plenty of wholesome fun. And there would be a message that would be easily understood and relatable to everyone.

But what really drew the crowds were the astounding reports of Aimee's faith healing. Sick people swarmed her revivals, desperate for her healing touch. Accounts of these sessions – even from skeptical, cynical journalists – sound miraculous. Aimee touched the ears of the deaf and they could hear. She massaged the limbs of children, crippled since birth, and they could walk.

Naturally many outsiders were skeptical about what was allegedly happening. Some claimed the sick and disabled at the services were frauds or victims of hysterical illnesses that were "cured" by the emotional impact of Aimee's larger-than-life personality. Others pointed to healings that turned out to be only temporary, lasting only as long as the sick were under the influence of their religious hysteria. But many turned out to be legitimately convinced, despite their initial suspicions. As one Presbyterian minister wrote, "I cannot blame anyone for not believing things that can and will be told of these meetings, for I probably would not believe them myself had I not seen them, but I have seen them."

In August 1921 members of the American Medical Association secretly sent spies to the healing sessions at one of Aimee's revivals. After witnessing several sessions and examining those who claimed to be healed, they issued a report approving of Aimee's work and declaring her healings to be "genuine, beneficial, and wonderful."

It's hard to know exactly what to think about that.

Whatever was happening to the people throwing away their crutches and wheelchairs, Sister Aimee's acts of healing were an effective fundraising tool. The

Aimee's Angelus Temple opened in Los Angeles in 1923

money was continuing to pour in, and she was many steps closer to having that magnificent temple to serve as her home base.

Angelus Temple opened to the public on New Year's Day, 1923. Thousands of people descended on the scene. They traveled to Los Angeles from all over the country and across the world. When Aimee climbed onto the platform on that first day every one of the 3,500 seats in the building were filled and many thousands more filled the lawn of the temple, the nearby park, and the surrounding streets.

The temple itself was an expansive wedge-shaped auditorium with a curved, columned façade, modern theater marquee, and as one writer put it, "half like a Roman Coliseum, half like a Parisian Opera House." Rising above the façade was a huge dome, sparkling because crushed seashells had been added to the cement. Inside it was just as opulent. Two balconies overlooked the stage on which stood the altar and pulpit. The interior walls were hung with heavy burgundy curtains. One of these curtains could be pulled back to reveal a baptismal pool, fed by an artificial stream and framed by a painted backdrop of the river Jordan. The magnificent pipes of the Kimball organ loomed above the choir loft, and, above it all, the underside of the dome had been painted with azure blue skies and white fluffy clouds. The motto of the church could be seen there, too: "Jesus Christ, the Same Yesterday, Today, and Forever."

An interior view of the extravagant Angelus Temple

It was the largest religious building ever constructed in Los Angeles. It cost more than $1.5 million to build and every penny had been raised through donations.

In the weeks and months after it opened, the Angelus Temple became an institution in the city, as much a part of L.A.'s cultural life as the Hollywood Bowl, Exposition Park, and the University of Southern California. Aimee initially intended it to be the hub of her worldwide ministry, devoted to the saving of souls and the training of new evangelists. She never intended it to be a neighborhood church with a weekly schedule of weddings, funerals, and Sunday school classes. But it soon became that and so much more.

The original plan was for the temple to be open four days each week, but that didn't work from the very beginning. People often came on off-days and camped on the lawn, sidewalks, and neighboring park, waiting to gain admission when the doors opened again. Aimee responded by opening the temple every day of the week. But even services every night and three times on Sunday didn't satisfy the crowds. Every seat in the theater and every standing space in the aisles and hallways were filled for every service, every prayer meeting, and every healing session. Sometimes hundreds – even thousands – were turned away. Aimee began offering additional services in the city, with regular sessions at the county jail, the general hospital, the local Ford factory, and other places of business.

And still, people kept coming.

Besides entertaining and preaching, Aimee was also an avid organizer. She began coordinating with some 250 affiliated churches, started a rescue mission, a publications division, and an orchestra; creating a massive organization that is only rivaled by today's mega-churches. She also composed 180 hymns and several musical pageants. In keeping with her Salvation Army background, she designed uniforms for herself and her female bodyguards.

Shortly after the temple had opened Aimee started the prayer tower – a room where volunteers would come to pray around the clock. They worked in two-hour shifts and took telephone calls from anyone with a sick relative or who needed divine intervention. She also opened a training institute for evangelists in a small building next to the temple. More than 50 students joined initially, but as more enrolled the school had to be moved into a much larger space inside of the temple. There were also youth group meetings, special services for children, choir performances, sisters who sewed baby clothing for poor local mothers, brothers who helped recently released prisoners find jobs, and more.

A souvenir postcard of the Angelus Temple shows the radio towers that were connected to the building. Aimee was one of the first mass media ministers

When broadcast radio became popular in the early 1920s, she raised $25,000 to start a 500-watt station and hired a man named Kenneth Ormiston to build it. In February 1924 – just a few years after the first federally licensed radio station began broadcasting in Pittsburgh – Aimee's own station went on air with hymns, testimonies from converts, organ recitals, Bible readings, and live broadcasts of Sunday services. One of the station's most popular shows was the "Sunshine Hour," which Aimee hosted at 7:00 a.m. every morning when she was in town. Her warm, enthusiastic persona was perfect for the new medium of radio and her voice became a welcome one in homes throughout Southern California and the West.

Perhaps the most beloved – and best-attended – nights at the Angelus Temple were Aimee's "Illustrated Sermons" on Sunday nights. On those evenings she entertained the faithful and curious alike with often bizarre stage shows that borrowed heavily from the Hollywood studios just up the road. She sometimes even competed with the studios to rent costumes, lighting equipment, and animal extras. Shows featured a USC football player making a touchdown for Jesus and an LAPD motorcycle cop riding in to arrest sin. The crowds were thrilled and even Hollywood stars were impressed by her showmanship. Charlie Chaplin once told her, "Whether you like it or not, you're an actress."

Aimee's "illustrated sermons" proved to be very popular with audiences, offering a sermon and a stage show

And she was. She also had a spontaneous sense of humor. Once she borrowed a macaw from a local circus for a Garden of Eden tableau and ran into trouble with the bird. It proved to be capable of only saying one thing – "Oh, go to hell!" The first time he said it a horrified silence settled in over the audience. But Aimee laughed and worked his scandalous line into her sermon as a running gag – treating it like the voice of the Devil, causing Adam and Eve to be evicted from paradise.

Some of Aimee's critics said that her performances exuded a sexual undercurrent at odds with their wholesome subject matter. Although Aimee was no Hollywood bombshell, she was an attractive, vibrant, and charismatic young woman, and there are a lot of reports from the 1920s about men swooning in her audience from something other than religious fervor. This was especially true after 1925 when, against her mother's wishes, she cut her hair short in a flapper's bob and began to wear more stylish clothing. And there was evidence in her history – confirmed by her mother and ex-husband, who complained about her "wildcat habits" in private – of her impulsiveness and hot temper that often-caused friction with those who were closest to her.

This was something that eventually led to her downfall.

But Aimee never lost sight of the bottom line. She was a one-woman powerhouse with a talent for raising money that supported not only the church but also her home near the MGM Studios in Culver City, her wardrobe of expensive clothes, and fine automobile. She was never shy in her appeals for contributions. At collection time she would often tell her followers from the stage, "Sister has a headache tonight. Only quiet money, please."

In other words, paper money, not coins.

By the middle 1920s the Angelus Temple could claim a regular congregation of 10,000 members, allegedly making it the largest single Christian congregation in the world. So many people came each Sunday that the city's streetcar line had to build a special siding at Echo Park so that extra cars could be put on to carry church-goers to and from the Sunday and larger weeknight gatherings.

A large part of the church's growth was attributed to the inclusiveness of Aimee's message. People of all backgrounds and denominations responded to what she called the Foursquare Gospel – a fourfold vision of Christ as savior, healer, sanctifier, and king. Aimee taught that Jesus Christ was an active, living, everyday presence in life rather than a God to be catered to only on Sunday mornings or the occasional religious holiday.

Also, unlike the leaders of most other Christian denominations of the 1920s, Aimee made an effort to reach out to Latino and African American communities. Although she steered clear of challenging racial divides in the city, she encouraged the formation of black and Mexican Foursquare branches churches in the region and used her radio broadcasts to bring her message to these communities. Occasionally, when contingents of the Ku Klux Klan showed up at her services in full white-hooded regalia, she would cautiously urge them to lead lives "that would stand the full light of day." She promised them prayers as long as they "stood for righteousness" and "defended the defenseless."

Roberta Semple Salter, Aimee's daughter, later told a story about one of her mother's services in 1924 when hundreds of KKK members appeared at a Sunday evening service. Aimee told them a parable about Jesus appearing to an elderly black man who had been refused admittance to an all-white church. Jesus said to him, "Don't feel sad, brother. I, too, have been trying to get into that church for many, many years." Aimee then stared at the Klan members in silence until, one by one, they left their seats and exited the temple. After a time, they all returned – minus their white robes. Park attendants supposedly found the robes the next morning, stashed in bushes all around Echo Lake.

That's not to say that all went perfectly for Sister Aimee. Despite her success – or more likely, because of it – she began facing staunch opposition from competing religious organizations and other elements of the Los Angeles community.

The earliest complaints came from Pentecostal groups, who felt that Aimee was watering down their message. After coming to L.A. Aimee had started discouraging the more extreme manifestations of religious mania. There was no more screaming, rolling on the floor, and running around, things that had characterized her early tent revivals – and which were, of course, staples of the Pentecostal movement. She had angered the Apostolics by becoming more palatable to the Methodists, Episcopalians, and Lutherans.

But she didn't fare much better with them. Practices that were too tame for the Pentecostals were far too wild for the traditional churches, who had started to lose members to the Foursquare Gospel. The mainstream clergy, which had been

Aimee with her mother, Minnie Kennedy

supportive of her traveling evangelism, became much more critical after Aimee settled down as a resident pastor and started drawing worshippers by the thousands every week. Fundamentalist organizations, like the Moody Bible Institute, began to object to practices like healing and speaking in tongues and accused Aimee of using the Gospel just to draw attention to herself.

Aimee's most vocal critic was her main competitor in Los Angeles, Robert "Fighting Bob" Shuler, pastor of Trinity Methodist Church downtown. A sharp-tongued, troublemaker with a folksy phoniness, Shuler hailed from the coal-mining areas of West Virginia and had arrived in L.A. a year or so before Aimee did. His rise to prominence – mostly appealing to the rural, uneducated pilgrims who left their farms to come west – was almost as fast as Aimee's was. He quickly established a sizable local following while also establishing himself across the country by publishing a magazine and then starting his own radio station, two years after Aimee started hers.

But large congregations and radio stations were where the similarities ended between them.

While Aimee's message was upbeat and inclusive, Shuler's was relentlessly negative and confrontational. His sermons bristled with attacks on Jews, Catholics,

African Americans, Hollywood studio moguls, newspaper publishers, public school officials, and liberal politicians.

He was, essentially, what we think of as a conservative talk show host today.

Fighting Bob saved many of his harshest criticism for Sister Aimee. He complained that most of her converts were stolen from traditional churches and that her flamboyant persona trivialized the gospel ministry. He claimed that her followers didn't worship Christ, they worshipped Aimee. He gathered his complaints into a series of sermons that he called "McPhersonism" and accused her of commercializing religion, playing fast and loose with her contributions, and engaging in all kinds of dishonesty and scandal.

Of course, Aimee's response was to invite Shuler to come and speak at the Angelus Temple's anniversary celebration – an invitation he chose to ignore.

Aimee's biggest problems weren't caused by idiots like Fighting Bob, though. Someone closer to home posed the greatest threat to her ministry – her opinionated and difficult mother, Minnie Kennedy. As the temple's business manager, Minnie received and paid out thousands of dollars each week, with no oversight. Noting that Minnie and Aimee held title to the temple in their own names, some members wondered where all the money from the overflowing collection plates was going. Minnie was holding onto it – very tightly. Within months of the temple's opening, staff members were already complaining about her spendthrift, dictatorial ways. For instance, she forbade the use of the temple switchboard and made them spend their own nickels to use the payphone in the lobby, even for business-related calls.

Minnie also named herself as the temple's unofficial sergeant-at-arms. She made no secret of the fact that she considered many of Aimee's followers to be "nuts," and she did her best to weed them out of the congregation. In August 1923 a faction of the congregation (calling itself the Committee) tried to stage a revolt. They lodged a formal complaint against Minnie, questioning her lack of accountability in the temple's financial matters and even threatening to take their complaint to the district attorney. Minnie responded by excommunicating the entire Committee, tearing up their membership cards without ever consulting her daughter.

Two years later the Santa Ana branch of the Foursquare Church faced a similar situation. When Minnie's behavior caused the church to break away from the main congregation, she secretly sent a moving crew to strip the Santa Ana temple of all its furnishings while no one was there. The conflict eventually became so bad that Minnie began traveling with a volunteer bodyguard.

Faced with these disputes Aimee tended to back her mother, at least at this point in their relationship. She was concerned about the spiritual side of the church, not the day-to-day business. And someone, after all, had to keep people from taking advantage of Aimee's overly trusting nature.

Plus, Minnie wasn't wrong about the increasing number of "nuts" drawn to Aimee as her celebrity grew. In September 1925 two separate women had to be arrested for threatening to harm Aimee – Mrs. Marion Evans Ray, who plotted to kidnap her for ransom, and Mrs. Mercie Stannard, who came to the temple with a pistol to kill Aimee for setting up a radio broadcasting in the Stannard home so that the family's secrets could be revealed to the world.

Not all of Aimee's enemies could be dismissed as crackpots, either. She was also making enemies among the city's growing criminal underworld of bootleggers, drug dealers, and gambling parlor owners. She was vocal in her opposition to them and was active in city anticrime initiatives. More to the point, she used her radio station to undermine their criminal activities, calling out the addresses of speakeasies and gambling halls over the airwaves. She even occasionally broadcast the names of local criminals and their associates. It was a dangerous game, and she was often warned that her boldness could get her into serious trouble.

Aimee's radio station manager – and possible lover – Kenneth Ormiston

Aimee was riding high on a great gospel wave of success until May 1926 – when her glory days came to an abrupt and scandalous end.

The trouble began the previous year, or so Minnie Kennedy believed. That was when Aimee's success had given her an excuse to be as headstrong and imprudent as she wished. She had once listened to her mother's advice, even when she didn't like it, but Aimee had now started pouting like a willful child when Minnie tried to warn her away from some poor choice or bad behavior – then went ahead and did whatever she liked.

And, Minnie was convinced, the trouble started with Kenneth Ormiston, who oversaw the broadcast services on Aimee's radio station. Aimee had installed a telephone next to her pulpit that was connected to the temple's radio booth, high up in the building's dome. Aimee had developed a habit of talking on it during choir performances and Bible readings, giggling like a schoolgirl. During these frequent "sound checks," Ormiston, who was not a church member or even particularly religious, liked to offer droll observations about what was going on in the temple, while he and Aimee bantered back and forth in a way that could only be described as flirtatious. A group of church members had even written a note of complaint to Minnie about these exchanges. Thanks to the excellent acoustics in the temple, every word that Aimee said to Ormiston – who was married and had a small child at home – could be heard in the auditorium.

Ormiston had become a particular point of contention between Minnie and Aimee. Ken was an attractive and witty man, and he treated Aimee not as some kind of prophet but as a woman to be teased and flirted with. Aimee responded in kind. Ormiston's wife had already made her displeasure known, even hinting that her husband's relationship with Aimee might go beyond flirting. If any suggestion of that was made public, it would be disastrous. The L.A. press had already turned against the Angelus Temple following the defection of the Santa Ana church in the summer of 1925, so this made Minnie, Aimee, and the church all vulnerable. An adultery scandal would do more damage than any of them could afford.

Minnie decided that she would try and make things as uncomfortable for Ormiston as she could, hoping that he'd quit since she knew Aimee would never allow him to be fired. In December 1925 her plan worked. Ormiston resigned, which led to Aimee becoming moody and depressed and clashing with her mother over everything from how she wore her hair to how much money she spent on clothing.

One of Aimee's more ardent followers, choir director Rudolf Dunbar, noticed her moodiness and distraction and suggested that she take a well-deserved break. He knew a Chicago-based evangelist who could fill in for her and she could take a vacation. Aimee liked the idea and began planning a trip to Europe and the Holy Land with her daughter, Roberta, who was now 15. They left Los Angeles on January 11, 1926 with thousands gathered at the train station to bid Aimee a lively farewell. Their first destination would be England and Ireland and from there, they'd go on to Europe and the Middle East.

But even thousands of miles from L.A., Aimee couldn't stay out of trouble.

Soon after her departure Mrs. Ormiston contacted Minnie to report that her husband was missing. She hinted that she might divorce him and name Aimee as the co-respondent. Then a temple staff member came to Minnie with rumors that a Hollywood scandal sheet was getting ready to print a report claiming that Kenneth Ormiston was traveling with Sister Aimee in Europe.

Frantic, Minnie sent a wire to the travel agency for the tour and instructed them to assign a guard to keep an eye on Aimee around the clock. She also sent a telegram to her daughter, informing her of the rumors and urging her to behave herself.

The telegram caught up with Aimee in Italy, where she had gone after leaving Roberta with relatives of her late husband, Robert, in Ireland. Whether she had a traveling companion or not, the telegram had the desired effect and Aimee returned to Ireland, fetched Roberta, and took her to the Holy Land without further delay. They visited Nazareth, Jericho, and Cairo before returning to London so that Aimee could preach at the Royal Albert Hall. Then, rested or not, they went home.

When Aimee landed in Los Angeles on April 24 – again to a reception of thousands – the immediate crisis had passed. Some weeks earlier Ormiston had called the temple radio station as if unaware that anyone was looking for him. Minnie insisted that he appear on the air to prove that he was in Los Angeles – not in Europe with Aimee. But Minnie remained suspicious, especially because Aimee seemed more willful than ever after her return from vacation. She was sarcastic and demanding and insisted that her mother raise her monthly allowance, refusing to say why. Minnie resisted, but then, realizing that she was in danger of damaging their relationship further, finally agreed to turn over the cash collected during the first Sunday service of every month, uncounted. This seemed to satisfy Aimee, though she never revealed why she needed the money.

Aimee had already thrown herself back into her usual whirlwind of activity at the temple. She directed prayer meetings, delivered radio sermons, hosted Bible study classes, and conducted daily worship services. She was also caught up on a political issue. The beach resort community of Venice had petitioned the city to create a special "amusement zone" that would be exempt from Sunday blue laws that prohibited dancing on Sunday. The issue was coming up for a vote in the citywide elections and Sister Aimee was encouraging her congregation and radio listeners to vote the issue down. During this campaign she made the bold statement, "I would rather see my children dead than in a dance hall." She lost the crusade but managed to make more enemies with her opposition.

On May 18, 1926 an exhausted Aimee decided to take a day off and enjoy the beach. She took along her secretary, Emma Schaeffer, for company. The two women drove to Ocean Park Beach in Santa Monica, purchased some waffles and popcorn for a snack, and rented an umbrella tent from the Ocean View Hotel to set up near the water.

For the next few hours Aimee, wearing a pea-green bathing suit, worked on notes for her Sunday sermon, occasionally stopping for a dip in the Pacific as a fully dressed Emma read a book nearby. Aimee was also thinking about her children's program for that evening and decided on some changes. She wrote up some notes about the musical program and then asked Emma to go to a nearby drugstore and telephone the temple with her last-minute instructions. She told her that she was going to have another swim while Emma was gone.

When the secretary returned to the beach tent a short time later, carrying a cup of orange juice that she'd bought for Aimee, she saw – or thought she saw – the evangelist swimming far out in the water. She watched the figure of a few anxious moments and then realized that it wasn't Aimee. She scanned the other bathers in the water but saw no one who resembled her. Frantic, Emma ran up and down the shoreline, looking for the green swimming suit – but she was gone. After about an hour of fruitless searching she notified the lifeguards.

It was nearly 5:00 p.m. when Frank Langdon, the manager of the Ocean View Hotel, called Minnie and told her that her daughter was missing. That night, before a packed audience that had come to the service, Minnie made a shocking announcement.

"Sister is gone," she told them. "We know she is with Jesus."

By noon the following day one of the largest maritime searches in California history was underway. Lifeguards searched the beach area, fishermen dragged their nets along the shore, and airplanes scoured the coastline. More than 10,000 congregants from the Angelus Temple and Foursquare branch churches gathered on the beach to weep, pray, and sing hymns as divers searched the water. One diver stayed down too long and died of exposure, and one of Aimee's more devoted followers became so distraught that she threw herself off a pier and drowned.

But no trace of Sister Aimee was discovered.

Dozens of newspaper reporters and photographers swarmed the beach, Angelus Temple, and Aimee's home, hoping to get some sort of scoop about the biggest story of the year. Rumors and speculation were rampant. Most newspapers and their readers first assumed that Aimee had drowned, but as days passed with no trace of a body other explanations emerged. Some suspected foul play, others thought suicide. One writer suggested that she might be wandering in the canyons with a case of

AIMEE M'PHERSON DROWNED, BELIEF

Wet Leads for Senate in Pennsylvania Vote

FAMOUS PASTOR VANISHES WHILE BATHING IN SEA

amnesia. A former mayor of Venice surmised that she had fallen victim to a six-finned sea monster that had been recently sighted off the amusement pier at Venice Beach. One poetic theory was that the hard-working evangelist had simply disappeared, hoping for freedom from her endless responsibilities, and returned in secret to the Holy Land.

The theories turned uglier a week later though, when the Los Angeles Times broke the story that Kenneth Ormiston had also gone missing and that his wife had taken their child and returned home to Australia. The rumors of an affair between the evangelist and the radio engineer were suddenly back in the news and were given extra life by alleged "Aimee sightings" that were pouring into the temple and the district attorney's office from places as far away as Denver and Mexico. With these numerous reports pouring in – one day Aimee was

(Top) One of the many newspaper stories printed when it was believed that Aimee was dead

(Bottom) Crowds on the beach, looking for Aimee's body

"seen" in 16 different places – and with no corpse to be found, the L.A. County coroner's office refused to issue a death certificate. Minnie Kennedy offered a $25,000 reward for information or the return of her daughter, although she still stubbornly believed that Aimee had drowned.

Things became more complicated after two different ransom demands arrived at the temple asking for money for Aimee's return. In one letter Minnie was told to be at the Palace Hotel in San Francisco where she would be given further instructions. She believed the note was a hoax and gave it to L.A. police captain Herman Cline who was in charge of the case. He also believed it to be a hoax but asked the San Francisco police to send two plainclothes detectives to the hotel to see if anyone showed up. None one did, but strangely, the ransom letter later disappeared from police files – the first of many strange things that happened in the investigation in the months to come.

The second ransom demand instructed a Long Beach attorney to bring $25,000 to a meeting for Aimee's return. The deadline came and went with no further contact from the alleged kidnappers, and this demand was also dismissed as a hoax.

The case took an interesting turn when Kenneth Ormiston turned up at the ongoing temple vigil at Ocean Park beach on May 27. Confronted by the police he explained that he had purposely dropped out of sight earlier in the spring, traveling under several different false names. He implied that an extramarital affair was the reason for this but denied knowing anything about Aimee's disappearance. He offered to help the investigation any way that he could, but since he seemed to have no relevant information he was released. He then vanished again with no explanation.

Minnie Kennedy – despite the many sightings and weird kidnapping claims – remained convinced that Aimee had drowned. She started planning a huge memorial service for her at the Angelus Temple. That kind of event, she hoped, would quiet the speculation and allow Aimee's followers to experience some sense of closure about her fate. The service was held on June 20 and Minnie tried her best, consoling the crowd with the belief that she didn't believe Aimee's body would ever be found because it was "just too precious to Jesus." The congregation's response was overwhelming. A collection taken at the service raised nearly $35,000. The money was going to be used to support the ongoing mission of the temple and, perhaps, to build a monument to the lost evangelist.

And then things took another, completely unexpected turn.

On June 23 Minnie received a long-distance telephone call from a hospital in Douglas, Arizona. She immediately recognized Aimee's voice on the other end of the line, hurriedly telling her mother than she had been held by kidnappers in a shack somewhere in Mexico. Minnie, knowing that police captain Herman Cline was listening in on the call, interrupted Aimee: "Don't talk!"

It was great advice. Aimee was alive, but that didn't mean she wasn't in trouble.

But Aimee, as usual, didn't listen to her mother. By the time that Minnie, Captain Cline, Deputy D.A. Joseph Ryan, and a herd of L.A. newsmen arrived in her hospital in Douglas, Aimee had been telling her wild and unlikely story to anyone who would listen. She told it again after the group from L.A. arrived, speaking for three hours from her hospital bed as every word was recorded by a stenographer borrowed from a nearby military post.

According to Aimee's story she had been lured out of the water at the beach by a couple who told her that they needed her to pray for their dying baby. Of course, there was no baby. They led Aimee to a parked car where a man waited with the engine running. She was pushed into the backseat and rendered unconscious by a cloth that smelled like chloroform. When she woke up later the three kidnappers informed her that they were holding her for a half-million-dollar ransom. Several weeks passed as they tried to figure out how to make Minnie Kennedy believe that Aimee was alive and that the kidnapping was not a hoax. They threatened to send Minnie one of Aimee's fingers as proof.

Then, a few days later, she was awakened in the middle of the night and was taken to a two-room shack somewhere in the desert. They remained there – "where no one can find you" – for several days, sleeping on army cots and eating meals from cans. One day the two men left, and Aimee remained a captive of the woman, who needed to go into town for supplies. She tied Aimee's hand and feet, pushed her onto a cot, and left in the kidnapper's second car. Aimee managed to get one of the cans they'd been eating out of and cut her ropes with a jagged edge. Once free, she climbed out of a window and ran away into the desert.

For the entire next day, she wandered, dazed and confused in the heat. After nightfall she saw the lights of a town that turned out to be Agua Prieta, Mexico. She collapsed in the yard of the first respectable home that she saw, and the owners found her and nursed her back to consciousness. The put her in a taxi to take her over the border – first to the police station in Douglas and then to the hospital. There she was tested for alcohol on her breath and when it became clear that she wasn't drunk she was put to bed. She had been there ever since, anxious to get the ordeal behind her and go home.

When Aimee finished this true crime adventure, right out of a Hollywood movie, it was clear that Cline and Ryan found her story difficult to believe. Aside from the preposterous nature of it, there were some obvious issues that shed doubt on the account. Captain Cline noted that Aimee's shoes were barely scuffed and worn, as they would be after wandering in the desert for a day. She wasn't dehydrated or sunburned, and there was little sign of perspiration on her clothing. She was also wearing a watch, one report claimed, that she had not taken with her to the beach on May 18. Also, despite an exhaustive search of the surrounding area, she was never able to locate the shack in which she had been supposedly held.

True or not, Aimee's story made for great newspaper copy and the national press responded with one of the biggest media frenzies of the decade. Journalists dissected every bit of Aimee's story and millions of people across the country who had never heard of the evangelist before her disappearance were now eager to read every word that was printed about her. In Los Angeles, where she was a household name, coverage of her ordeal would remain on the front pages for weeks and months to come.

While the authorities and the newspapers responded to Aimee's alleged kidnapping with doubt, her most devoted followers accepted it unconditionally. The

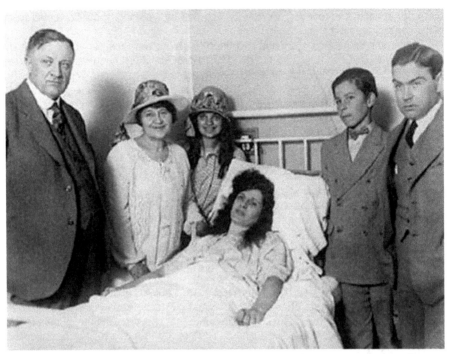

Aimee Semple McPherson (center) convalesces in a Douglas, Arizona, hospital. From left to right are District Attorney Asa Keyes; her mother, Minnie; her daughter, Roberta; son, Rolf; and Deputy District Attorney Joseph Ryan.

story was, one church spokesman said, simply too unbelievable to have been made up. She returned to Los Angeles on June 26 and a carpet of roses was spread on the platform when she disembarked from the train. More than 100,000 people lined the streets and cheered as she drove by.

But many were convinced that nothing was what it seemed.

Much of the coverage of the kidnapping story had been openly skeptical of Aimee's story. Upton Sinclair went as far as to compose a poem in which Sister Aimee asks God to forgive her "one little lie." Worried that she was turning the city into a laughingstock, the Chamber of Commerce pressured District Attorney Asa Keyes to get to the bottom of the situation. Kenneth Ormiston was still missing, and a report published in one paper in late May claimed that several witnesses had seen Ormiston and a woman resembling Aimee at a holiday cottage in Carmel, a few hundred miles up the coast. There were suspicions that the abduction had been a ruse to conceal an affair between the married radio operator and the evangelist. Keyes convinced a grand jury to order an investigation. It was assumed the investigation was to find and indict the kidnappers, but in truth it was to unearth the real story behind Aimee's disappearance. Aimee was, of course, subpoenaed, and her mother and attorney both begged her to ignore the summons and let the matter drop, but Aimee didn't listen.

She had nothing to hide, she told them.

At the hearing, Aimee, the supposed victim of the crime, was instead questioned as though she were the defendant. Keyes drilled her mercilessly, implying that she had invented the abduction story as publicity for her ministry or for some other unseemly reason. Aimee – who had come to the hearing surrounded by a "purity brigade" of seven young women in white dresses and blue capes – stood firm under his questioning, repeating her same story again and again. She didn't need publicity, she said, and would not have risked her ministry for the kind of sinful activity that was being reported in the newspapers.

But not everyone was convinced. After hearing other witnesses over the next week, the grand jury voted on July 20 that there was insufficient evidence to issue indictments for any kidnappers, named or unnamed. Out of 17 jurors, 14 of them did not believe that any kidnapping had occurred.

The investigation continued. Keyes believed that he had evidence for a different set of charges – perjury and fraud with Aimee and Minnie as the two main defendants. Responding to pressure from the grand jury, the Chamber of Commerce, and Fighting Bob Shuler – who was determined to use the scandal to destroy his rival, Keyes aggressively pursued the Kenneth Ormiston angle. He sent his Deputy Joseph Ryan to Carmel to interview the witnesses who claimed to have seen Aimee and Ormiston at the cottage. Within days Ryan had what he believed was irrefutable evidence that the evangelist and radio engineer had spent 10 days there in May, shortly after Aimee's disappearance. Evidence that included eyewitness accounts and a grocery list found at the cottage that was in Aimee's handwriting.

Stories of the "love nest by the sea" soon filled the papers. Over the next week an estimated 75,000 curiosity-seekers came to Carmel to see the notorious bungalow. Fighting Bob continued to fire away at Aimee from the pulpit of his church, over the airwaves, and at a Sunday afternoon rally that drew several thousand people. He attacked her character and complained about city officials and about the snail's pace of the investigation. Somehow, he tracked down Harold McPherson and had him on the air for four straight broadcasts, airing all of Aimee's dirty laundry.

Aimee refused to fight back. "A dog may bark at the queen," she said, "but the queen doesn't necessarily have to bark back."

But the case against Aimee hit a snag when a woman named Lorraine Wiseman-Sielaff announced that it was she, not Aimee, who had been at the cottage in Carmel with Kenneth Ormiston. Her story came under intense scrutiny by both the newspapers and D.A. Keyes, which is when it fell apart. It was soon discovered that Lorraine was wanted on check fraud charges, and she was arrested. She tried to get bail money from Aimee and Minnie but when they turned her down, she changed her story. She had been lying before, she said, because Aimee and Minnie had paid her $5,000 to say she had been at the cottage and draw attention away from the evangelist. This new story – true or not – sold a lot of newspapers.

With this new evidence of fraud in hand, Keyes felt that he finally had enough to file charges. On September 16 he had arrest warrants issued for Aimee, Minnie, the already locked up Wiseman-Sielaff, and the still missing Kenneth Ormiston, on charges of obstruction of justice, perjury, and conspiracy to manufacture false evidence. Aimee suffered a nervous breakdown before she was arrested, which delayed things for a few days, but she was recovered enough by September 27 to appear in court for her preliminary hearing.

The hearing lasted for six weeks and generated more than 3,500 pages of transcripts as Asa Keyes tried to prove his case. The sheer volume of evidence promised a major trial to follow, longer and more expensive than anything in L.A. history at the time – although many of the costs, it later was revealed, would have been helpfully paid for by two of the city's largest newspapers.

But as the weeks of testimony dragged on it became clear that the prosecution's case was not exactly airtight. Several of the key witnesses who had seen Ormiston's companion at the Carmel cottage now denied that the woman they saw was Sister Aimee when they saw her sitting in the courtroom. Others admitted that they'd never seen Aimee before and had made the connection only after Deputy D.A. Ryan showed them her picture.

The defense produced affidavits from people in Douglas who stated that Aimee had been more much disheveled and exhausted from her alleged desert walk than Ryan and others had claimed. Several Douglas locals even insisted that they had followed a woman's footprints out into the desert and found a rundown adobe shack that could have been the place where she was held captive.

Also, Lorraine Wiseman-Sielaff's accusations could hardly be considered rock-solid, given that she had already changed her story several times and had once – according to a certified document from a psychiatric hospital in Utah – been incarcerated for "ungovernable lying."

But the evidence was strong enough for the judge to deem it sufficient for the case to go forward. On November 3, 1926 Aimee and Minnie were officially charged with three counts of criminal conspiracy and obstruction of justice, which could have sent them to prison for as long as 42 years. Aimee would be free on bail until the trial began after the first of the year.

And Aimee planned to make the most of that time.

During the six weeks of the preliminary hearing she had been on the radio every night, talking about the day's court proceedings and making a case for her innocence. While out on bail she intensified her efforts, turning the scandal into a struggle between true believers and "those who are opposed to the old-time religion." She put together elaborate sermons that compared her to Joan of Arc, William Jennings Bryan (who'd recently lost the Scopes Monkey Trial), and other persecuted Christians. One Sunday she promised a sermon called "The Biggest Liar in Los Angeles." Congregants were left to wonder who it might be about – the Judge? Asa Keyes? Fighting Bob Shuler? But Aimee revealed it to be (rather disappointingly) the Devil himself.

Aimee was putting on a brave face, but the truth was she was being badly hurt by the terrible press. It was true that she didn't lack for followers – the temple was booming – and many L.A. people were rooting for her out of sympathy because they didn't like the way the prosecutor was treating her, but far too many were lined up against her. The Los Angeles city establishment had lost their taste for her antics and

rivals like Robert Shuler and the L.A. Church Federation were hoping to sink her. She was losing most of the goodwill that she had built up over seven years of her ministry in the city. For many people, Sister Aimee had become an embarrassment, a scandal, and a dirty joke.

Soon after the new year, Asa Keyes' case fell apart. His star witness, Lorraine Wiseman-Sielaff, changed her story again, saying that Aimee and Minnie had never paid her. Without her, Keyes decided that any attempt to convict a person of Aimee's tremendous popularity would be foolhardy. On January 10, 1927 he announced that the trial would not be going forward, and he was dropping all charges against mother and daughter. He insisted that he still believed Aimee was guilty but the confusing and contradictory evidence had made his prosecution impossible. As he told reporters, "Let her be judged in the court of public opinion."

And public opinion didn't spare Aimee from further pain. She and her mother were free, and Aimee quickly spread the news. But Minnie insisted that the lack of resolution in the case was hardly anything to celebrate. It had left her daughter "in a dirty hole," as she put it, where suspicion about her guilt would never go away.

She was right, but Aimee refused to see it that way. Disregarding the advice from her mother and church members, Aimee refused to adopt a lower profile after the charges were dismissed. Minnie told her to "get off the front pages," but Aimee wanted to take a "vindication tour" to celebrate her triumph. She hired a new publicity manager and went on tour, doing a one-woman traveling show called "The Story of My Life" – a theatrical extravaganza that climaxed with her kidnapping and victory over the enemies of old-time religion.

All grandstanding aside, what Sister Aimee represented for Los Angeles was never the same again. For one thing, she had changed. Under the influence of her new publicity manager and her new handlers she changed her hair, wore heavier makeup, and abandoned her uniforms for stylish clothing. Many of the more conservative members of her church objected, claiming that the God of the Gospels had been replaced at Angelus Temple with the God of materialism." Many ended their association with the temple, and hundreds more followed.

The city that had once embraced the warm and irrepressible celebrity evangelist would never see her the same way again – but Aimee Semple McPherson was not quite finished yet.

The 1926 kidnapping drama had turned Aimee into a national curiosity. More people came to see her revivals for the novelty of them than came to save their souls. Movie studios reached out to try and make a deal for the story of her life, but all the deals fell through. Aimee then decided to start her own movie company, Angelus Productions, to film and distribute her sermons and to produce a feature called *Clay in the Potter's Hands,* based on her life. But this project never happened – even though Aimee lost 40 pounds to prepare for the part and, according to rumor, had a facelift. Undeterred, she soldiered on and even launched a religious vaudeville act that ran for a week at the Capitol Theater on Broadway in the fall of 1933.

Aimee's name was still in the newspapers, but now she was facing dissension in the church she had created. Her new worldliness had unsettled even more of her most

Aimee worked hard to remain relevant in the years after her "disappearance" but she often struggled and eventually, the church she created moved on without her

devoted followers, especially after her surprise 1931 elopement with David Hutton, an opera singer who was 11 years her junior. Since her divorced husband, Harold McPherson, was still alive, many conservative followers regarded the new relationship as adultery. And, years before, Aimee would have agreed. Now, though, she met the news of defections with defiance. "Let them walk out of the temple," she said. "I'll fill it up again."

Aimee and Minnie went through a terrible split in 1929, Minnie had never forgiven her for the "kidnapping" episode, and they continued to argue about money. Minnie told reporters: "The situation has become nearly intolerable when it has reached the point that I can talk to my daughter only through an attorney." She left L.A. for the Pacific Northwest, where she established her own ministry. But given the co-dependent relationship that existed between Aimee and her mother there were more reconciliations and disagreements over the years.

There were also many projects – including a Foursquare resort in Lake Tahoe and a Foursquare cemetery in Burbank – which were never completed. All of them left a trail of messy lawsuits in their wake. Even Aimee's marriage to David Hutton ended with an embarrassing divorce. "It's just a comic strip, this life of ours," Minnie said when her own rushed marriage collapsed after a bigamy charge against her husband of several months.

And many of the temple's former followers would agree.

Aimee, who was frequently ill in the late 1930s, eventually managed to fall out with everyone close to her – her mother, her husband, her substitute preacher, her longtime confidantes, and even her daughter, Roberta, who ended up suing her mother's lawyer for slander. The L.A. newspapers became so tired of Aimee's drama that they ended up declaring a moratorium on any news that had to do with her. "The first time was a sensation," one editor wrote." The second time it was still good. But now it's like the ninth life of a cat, about worn out."

None of this, however, could wipe away the legitimate good that Aimee still tried to do for people. When the Depression hit Los Angeles, the temple started a soup kitchen to feed anyone who needed help. It ran 24-hours-a-day, seven-days-a-week, and offered an employment office and a first aid station. Actor Anthony Quinn, who played in the temple band and sometimes served as Aimee's translator, later recalled, "She literally kept most of that Mexican community alive, and for that, I'm eternally grateful." Though her need for drama never went away she continued to do valuable work into the 1940s, selling bonds for the war effort during World War II.

Because of her nervous condition and anxiety, Aimee was given a prescription for Seconal, and on September 7, 1944 she died in San Francisco from an accidental overdose. Rumors of suicide followed but those still close to her attributed the accident to a combination of a broken heart and exhaustion from her endless struggle to restore her name, popularity, and influence. Her funeral was held at the Angelus Temple, where more than 40,000 mourners passed by her casket to bid farewell. A predictable family scuffle over her estate occurred after her death but the church was left in the more reliable – but much less colorful hands – of her son, Rolf. He led it through decades of growth and today the International Church of the Foursquare Gospel has over 6 million members across the globe.

But would it be the story of Sister Aimee without at least a little more drama?

It seems that a weird rumor followed Aimee to the grave. When she was buried at Forest Lawn Cemetery in a huge tomb with an iron gate guarded by two kneeling marble angels, it was said that a direct telephone line to the Angelus Temple was buried with her. That way when she returned – as her most devout followers believed she would – she would be able to alert someone to come to the cemetery and let her out of the tomb.

Was it true? No idea – but if this isn't true, it should be.

The Man with the Golden Plates
Mormons in America

Legend had it that Mountain Meadows, located at the southern edge of the Wasatch Mountain foothills of Utah, were created by God as a resting place for weary travelers who were trekking across the country to California in the middle nineteenth century. Mountain Meadows, about 300 miles from Salt Lake City, was a valley five miles long and only a few hundred yards wide. Fed by mountain streams that caused the grass to grow tall and green and the trees to stand thickly on the slopes of the rounded hills that overlooked it, it was a place of calm restfulness and a respite from the hot, dusty hardships of the trail. Before they reached Mountain Meadows the settlers in their creaking wagons traveled across miles of rocky wasteland. After the meadow they faced the rigors of the Mojave Desert. But for a few brief days at the meadows, while their livestock were watered and fed and their children played in the waving grass, it was as if they were given a taste of what awaited them in California.

It was a peaceful place – except on the morning of September 11, 1857.

It was on that day that one of the worst civilian massacres in American history took place – a crime of religious fanaticism that a special report to Congress would call "a hellish atrocity."

The massacre claimed the lives of 120 men, women, and children from a wagon train that had camped in Mountain Meadows. To make matters more shocking, the murderers were members of the Mormon Church, a mysterious religious movement that would go on to become one of the most mainstream cults in American religious circles.

And, unfortunately, Mountain Meadows was not the end of the story. There have been many more incidents of murder, violence, rape, and worse in the story of the Mormons – or the Church of Jesus Christ of the Latter-Day Saints, as they are known today. The story of the movement is one of invention, infamy, scandal, success, and blood – a lot of blood. And perhaps, for this reason, it is the most famous of all of America's homegrown religions.

The story of the Mormons began with the birth of the movement's founder, Joseph Smith, who was born in Vermont in 1805. When he was 15 his family – which included his parents and eight siblings – moved to Western New York. His father was a farmer, and Smith grew up in the "Burned-Over District." He would eventually become one of the most influential religious leaders to spring forth from it. Raised on the folklore of the region he used his cleverness and claims of extraordinary visions to establish one of the largest religious groups in the modern world.

As a teenage boy living in Palmyra in the 1820s, Joseph was locally-known as a clairvoyant who could track down hidden treasure using a "seer stone" – a smooth rock, that might be opaque or marked with magic symbols. He would place the stone in his hat and gaze into it so that he could gain the power of second sight. Treasure hunters who lived in the area valued his scrying talents. In the Western and Central New York region of the early nineteenth century many believed that ancient artifacts were hidden away in Indian mounds or in secret chambers under the local hills and hollows. Legends of the region told of buried ruins that belonged to a civilization older than the Indians.

The Smith household was immersed in magic and myth. The family owned magical charms, dowsing rods, amulets, a ceremonial dagger inscribed with astrological symbols, and parchments marked with occults signs and cryptograms that were popular in early nineteenth-century American lore. In an 1845 memoir the family matriarch, Lucy Mack Smith, recalled the Smiths' interest in the "faculty of Abrac" – a Gnostic term for God that also served as a magical incantation. It forms the root of a magic word that is known to every child: *abracadabra*.

Joseph Smith was enthralled with the powers of the planet Jupiter, which was prominent in his astrological birth chart. Smith's first wife, Emma, reported that until the day he died Smith carried an amulet that was composed of a dove and an olive branch, plus the astrological sign of Jupiter. Smith's occult interests were simply a part of everyday life in Central New York. Later in life he would suggest the existence of a male-female God, an idea that he likely lifted from the teachings of Mother Ann Lee or from the Universal Friend. He was also fascinated with the temple rites and symbols of Freemasonry, a movement of tremendous influence – and controversy – in the Burned-Over District.

Founder of the Mormon faith, Joseph Smith

The rebellious and spiritually adventuresome Smith began reporting divine visitations in the 1820s, although these claims were not that much different from other such reports in the region. What made Smith's claims different was that they involved an angel named Moroni directing him to the location of a buried book made of golden plates that had been hidden in a hill called Cumorah near his home. The hill was a spot where local legends claimed a great civilization – some believed it to be the lost tribe of Israel – made its last stand against marauding Indians. This story would become an important part of Smith's later theology.

Like Smith, many men of the time took seriously the existence of a highly-developed civilization in the area that pre-dated the Native Americans. Those who studied the history of the Iroquois found esoteric fraternities among them, which some considered a form of "ancient Freemasonry." These speculations were heightened when Seneca leader Red Jacket and other New York-area Indians were seen wearing Freemason-style medals in the shape of the square and compass of the order.

All the area myths – from the lost civilization, the use of peep stones, and the lure of ancient treasure – seeped into Smith's expanding worldview. They intertwined into the narrative found on the golden plates that Smith discovered at Cumorah, which had conveniently been written in "reformed Egyptian hieroglyphics." Naturally, no one could read them except for Smith, and he had to do so by using the pair of ancient seer stones that were the equivalent of magic spectacles. In 1830 he revealed that the words on the tablets were the Book of Mormon, which traced a vast alternate history involving a tribe of Israel fleeing from the Holy Land for the American continent. They were later visited directly by Christ and then defeated at "a great and tremendous battle at Cumorah... until they were all destroyed." The scale and scope of the Book of Mormon, no matter what one thought of its dubious origins, was seen by his followers as evidence of the truth of local folklore, rather than Smith's obvious pilfering of it.

Before the publication of his book and while Smith was still only dreaming about the golden plates his family was facing financial hardship due in part to the death of his oldest brother, Alvin. Family members supplemented their income from their farm by hiring out for odd jobs and, of course, working as treasure seekers. Despite the reputation Joseph had for "second sight," he failed many times to find buried treasure on the land of a wealthy farmer in Chenango County and in 1826 was brought before a judge for fraud.

During his travels he boarded at the Hale home in Harmony, Pennsylvania and began courting Emma Hale, who would become his first wife. When Smith first proposed, Emma's father, Isaac, objected because he didn't believe that Smith would ever have the money to support his daughter. So, the two eloped and were married on January 18, 1827. Later that year, when Smith promised to abandon treasure hunting, Isaac Hale offered to let the couple live on his property in Harmony and help Smith get started in business.

But Smith had a better idea of what he wanted to do with his life.

On September 22, 1827 Smith made his last visit to Cumorah and took Emma with him. This time the angel apparently allowed him to retrieve his magic plates – but commanded him not to show them to anyone else. Smith was only supposed to translate them and then publish what they said.

Smith went to work and transcribed some of the characters that he said were engraved on the plates. He dictated their translation to Emma. It was slow going and Smith turned to a friend and neighbor named Martin Harris for help. Harris took a sample of the lettering on the plates to a few prominent scholars including Charles Anthon, a respected creator of books for schools and colleges. Anthon was said to have first authenticated the letters and their translation, but then retracted his opinion after learning that Smith claimed to have received the plates from an angel. Anthon stated that he tried to convince Harris that he was the victim of a fraud. But Harris refused to believe it and returned to work with Smith on the translation.

But his belief in Smith – who claimed to read the plates in secret and then provided Harris with the text – didn't last. By June 1828 he was having doubts about the project, mostly because his wife was so skeptical of it. Harris convinced Smith to let him take 116 existing pages of manuscript to show a few family members, including his wife – and then he lost them. There was no other copy.

As punishment for losing the manuscript, Smith said that Moroni returned and took away the plates and revoked his ability to translate. During this time Smith attended Methodist meetings with his wife until one of the church members objecting to having a "practicing necromancer" in the congregation.

Luckily for Smith the angel returned the plates in September 1828. Harris was replaced as his scribe by a man named Oliver Cowdery who dictated everything Smith told him. The two men worked full time on the manuscript between April and early June 1829. That was when they realized they needed help to finish. They recruited a friend of Cowdery's named Peter Whitmer and moved into his home to continue the writing. When the narrative described a church as an institution and a requirement of baptism, Smith and Cowdery baptized each other.

Mormon tradition states that Smith dictated the writing on the golden plates into the Book of Mormon, by peering into a hat with a moonstone, the same method he often used when seeking buried treasure in upstate New York.

The dictation from the plates was finally finished on July 1, 1829. During the writing Smith had refused to show the plates to anyone, but now he told Martin Harris, Oliver Cowdery, and David Whitmer that they would be allowed to look at them. The men – who became known in Mormon lore as the "Three Witnesses" – signed a statement that they were shown the golden plates by an angel and that the "voice of God" had confirmed the truth of their translation. Later, a group of "Eight Witnesses" — all male members of the Whitmer and Smith families — issued a statement that they had also been shown the golden plates by Smith.

Skeptical? Naturally, but they all swore the plates were genuine and contained the text of the Book of Mormon, an alternate testament of Jesus Christ. All that is needed to prove the authenticity of all the claims made by the Mormon Church is one look at the golden plates, right?

One small problem – according to Smith, the angel Moroni took the plates away after Smith was finished transcribing them.

The completed work, titled the Book of Mormon, was published in Palmyra, New York on March 26, 1830. Soon after on April 6, Smith and his followers formally organized the Church of Christ and small branches were established in Palmyra and two other New York towns, Fayette, and Colesville.

When the contents of the book were revealed, some of Smith's former treasure hunting associates believed that Smith had double-crossed them and had not shared the golden plates with them as partners. They ransacked several possible hiding places for the golden tablets but, of course, found nothing.

Smith's Book of Mormon was slow to gain notoriety, but word of mouth eventually spread. Perhaps unsurprisingly in a region known for bizarre religious movements, Smith's fantastical tales of angels, golden plates, and magic spectacles eventually found a receptive audience, and the ranks of followers began to swell. Just as unsurprisingly, Smith and his followers began to meet resistance and persecution for their unorthodox beliefs. After Cowdery baptized several new church members, the Mormons received threats of mob violence. Before Smith could confirm the new members, he was arrested and brought to trial as a "disorderly person." He was acquitted but he and Cowdery had to sneak out of town to escape a gathering mob. Their escape even provided him with a new idea. He announced that Peter, James, and John had appeared to him in the night and had ordained him and Cowdery as members of a higher priesthood.

The new Mormon Church was having trouble with the "Gentiles," as non-believers are still called, but not everything was going smoothly within the ranks either. Smith's authority was undermined when Oliver Cowdery, Hiram Page, and a few other church members also claimed to receive revelations from God. In response Smith dictated a new revelation of his own that clarified his role as a prophet and an apostle, and which declared that only he held the ability to give doctrine and scripture for the entire church. Effectively dealing with the troublemakers, Smith sent most of them on a mission to recruit Native Americans to the church. Cowdery was assigned the task of locating the site of the church's Promised Land, which he called "New Jerusalem."

Opposition continued to grow in New York. Most in the region considered Smith nothing more than a former "peep stoner," peddling himself as a prophet. Like a mythical lost tribe of Israel, he would need to make a journey to achieve what he believed was his destiny. He soon offered another revelation stating that Kirtland, Ohio was the eastern boundary of his New Jerusalem. It was there that his followers must gather.

Smith was leaving the Burned-Over District, but he managed to take part of it with him. The ideas that he developed in Central New York soon had profound consequences for the lives of Smith and the small band of followers that followed him out of the region.

When studying Mormon ceremonies and rituals, it becomes obvious that Smith was fascinated with Freemasonry. Many of the rituals practiced by the order eventually seeped into the practices that are now part of the inner workings of the Mormon Church. Freemasonry has strong roots in American history, and it was especially prevalent in the Burned-Over District. Freemasonry drew upon arcane codes for personal and spiritual development. As members rose through the fraternity's ranks their achievements were noted on ceremonial aprons as rising suns, glowing eyeballs, pentagrams, and pyramids. This practice created one of the greatest symbols of Freemasonry – the all-seeing eye and the unfinished pyramid of the Great Seal of the United States, which any reader can find on the back of a $1 bill.

But Freemasonry did not last as long as it should have in the murky mysticism of the Burned-Over District. It ran into trouble, thanks to a scandal that nearly threatened its existence in America. It began in the 1820s, sparked by an incident that occurred not far from the home of Joseph Smith, and it would affect not only his life but his death, as well.

In 1826 William Morgan was a disgruntled Freemason living in Batavia, New York. He was threatening to expose all the order's secret rites in a manuscript that he was preparing to publish. When word spread of his plans, Morgan began to suffer from a variety of misfortunes, ranging from his arrest on false charges to the attempted arson of the print shop that planned to release his book. He was eventually kidnapped and never seen again. He was possibly murdered at the hands of Freemason zealots – or at least that's what many residents of the Burned-Over District believed.

The presumed homicide and the failed investigation that followed raised suspicions about the influence that the Freemasons had over the law and courts. The incident began a wave of anti-Masonic feeling, first in the Burned-Over District, and soon throughout the country, spread by a general mood of discontent over corruption in high places. In time 52 anti-Masonic newspapers started in America, and dozens of anti-Masonic politicians were sent to state legislatures. Things soon calmed but Freemasonry would never again command the same level of respect in American life.

But the order's influence still managed to seep into Mormonism, and the way that it did was rather unexpected.

William Morgan, the disgruntled former Freemason who vanished, left behind an attractive widow named Lucinda. She eventually remarried a man named George Harris with whom she traveled west as part of a new religious order – Mormonism. But Lucinda was no ordinary convert to Joseph Smith's new faith. Around 1836, the blond, blue-eyed young woman, though since remarried, became one of many "spiritual wives" of the prophet Joseph Smith. As a younger man Smith had been swept up in the region's wave of anti-Masonry, but when he was older, he became secretly fascinated with the society that had allegedly widowed his new bride and borrowed many parts of the order's rituals for his own use.

Mormonism was not the first religious movement to take root in Kirtland. A restorationist church was already living there under the influence of a man named Sidney Rigdon. The restorationists believed that Christianity needed to be restored along the lines of what is known about the early apostolic church, which they believed was a purer and more ancient form of the religion.

When Smith arrived in Kirtland, along the southern shores of Lake Erie, he was looking for a place to build a Mormon community that would be a paradise on earth that could be duplicated in heaven. He found a religious culture there that included a belief in demonstrations of spiritual gifts like fits and trances, rolling on the ground, and speaking in tongues. Smith took over the Kirtland community and put a stop to these outbursts. Rigdon's followers had also been practicing a form of communal living, which Smith adopted, calling it the United Order. Smith had promised church elders that in Kirtland they would receive an endowment of heavenly power, so he introduced the greater authority of a High ("Melchizedek") Priesthood to the church. This, he hoped, would keep some of the possibly rebellious early converts in line.

As word of the movement spread new followers poured into Kirtland. By the summer of 1835 there were 1,500 to 2,000 Mormons in the area, many of them expecting Smith to lead them to the New Jerusalem very soon. Though his mission to convert Native Americans had been a failure, Oliver Cowdery reported that he had found the site for Smith's New Jerusalem in Jackson County, Missouri. Smith visited there in July 1831 and agreed. He called the small frontier town of Independence the "center place" of Zion.

Sidney Rigdon, who had converted to Mormons with the rest of his followers, didn't believe that Zion could be anywhere other than Kirtland, Ohio. Because of this for most of the 1830s the church remained divided between Ohio and Missouri. Smith continued to live in Ohio but visited Missouri again in early 1832 to prove that he was not ignoring the Missouri settlement.

But that was not the main reason for the trip. Some of the non-Mormon residents of the Kirtland area had become unhappy with the United Order and with Smith's growing political power. With such a large number of followers in the region he could control a huge number of votes. An angry mob gathered one night, beat Smith and Rigdon unconscious, tarred and feathered them, and left them for dead. Both survived but believed leaving the area for a time was in their best interests.

Honestly, though, things weren't going much better in Missouri.

Politics and religion were angering non-Mormons in Jackson County, too. Tensions increased until July 1833 when a group of Mormons was forcibly evicted from their property and their homes were destroyed. Smith advised them to accept the violence patiently until they were attacked multiple times, after which they could fight back. The settlers returned fire on their attackers and killed two anti-Mormon assailants. The Mormons were overwhelmed and brutally expelled from the county.

Back in Ohio Smith ended his experiment with the United Order. Peaceful communal living couldn't fight back against violence. He changed the name of the movement to the "Church of the Latter-Day Saints" and formed a small military expedition – dubbed Zion's Camp – to go to the aid of the Mormons in Missouri. As a military campaign the expedition failed because the men were outnumbered and struck with cholera, but Zion's camp transformed the Mormons, and many future church leaders came from among the Zion's Camp participants.

It also proved to the Mormons that turning the cheek was not always the answer. Sometimes violence – or even the threat of violence – had to be answered with blood.

After the expedition returned to Ohio, Smith chose leaders for the five governing bodies of the church from among the men of Zion's Camp. The five bodies were originally of equal authority so that they could check one another. Among these five groups was a quorum of twelve apostles. Smith told them of a revelation he had received stating that in order to redeem Zion his followers would have to receive an endowment in the Kirtland Temple, the first physical religious structure built by the Mormon Church. The temple was dedicated in March 1836 and participants in the promised endowment saw visions of angels, spoke in tongues, and prophesied.

But time was running out for the Mormons in Kirtland. Smith, a handsome, charismatic man, began to spread a philosophy of polygamy, although he called it "celestial marriage" and justified it by pointing to the great characters of the Bible who all had many wives. Polygamy became a source of conflict both in and out of the Mormon Church, especially in a frontier community where the men greatly outnumbered the women. The general public was horrified – and fascinated – with the practice, and it would plague the church for many decades to come.

A rift formed between Smith and Oliver Cowdery over the practice. Cowdery suspected Smith had engaged in a sexual relationship with a teenage servant in his home, Fanny Alger. Smith never denied the relationship but insisted it was not adulterous, presumably because he had taken Fanny as an additional wife.

In April 1841 Smith wed Louisa Beaman. During the next two-and-a-half years he married – or was sealed to, as the Mormons call it – about 30 additional women. At least 10 of them were already married to other men. Some of these marriages were done with the consent of the first husbands, and some plural marriages may have been considered "eternity-only" sealings, which meant that the marriage would not take effect until after death. Of all of Smith's plural wives, 10 of them were between the ages of 14 and 20 and others were over 50.

The practice caused a rift between Smith and his first wife, Emma. In 1843, she temporarily accepted Smith's marriage to four women and allowed them to live in the Smith household. She soon regretted her decision, though, and demanded that the other wives leave. In July 1843 Smith dictated a revelation directing Emma to accept plural marriage, but a few months passed before she finally accepted this command from "God."

In the early years of the church there was an attempt to keep polygamy secret from most members of the church – and certainly from all non-Mormons – but word naturally leaked out. However, it wasn't polygamy that finally drove the Mormons out of Ohio – it was money.

In January 1837, Smith and other church leaders had created a stock company called the Kirtland Safety Society Anti-Banking Company to act as a sort-of bank. The company issued banknotes that were backed in part by real estate. Smith encouraged the Mormons to buy the notes and he invested in them heavily himself. As the bank panic of 1837 hit the United States the company failed, leaving useless paper currency spread around the area. Building the temple had left the church deeply in debt and Smith and the rest of the Saints in Kirtland were hounded by creditors and debt collectors.

Smith was outed as responsible for the company's failure and there were widespread defections from the church, including many men who had been Smith's closest advisors. After a warrant was issued for Smith's arrest for bank fraud in January 1838, he and Sidney Rigdon fled Kirtland in the middle of the night for Missouri.

In Jackson County Smith made plans to start over again. They would begin to build their Zion and would construct a new temple. In the weeks and months that followed, thousands of Latter-Day Saints followed them from Kirtland.

It was during this time that Smith began to have trouble with some of the same familiar faces – the "dissenters," he called them – who had caused problems in the past. A church council expelled John Whitmer, David Whitmer, W.W. Phelps, and Oliver Cowdery and Smith hoped the difficult times would be behind him.

But that was not the case. Familiar problems of politics and religion sprang up between the old Missourians and the newly-arriving Mormon settlers, creating new tension between the two factions. By this time Smith's experiences with mob violence led him to believe that his church's survival required greater military strength. Around June 1838, Smith created an armed militia that he called the Army of God. The 2,000 troops were a quarter of the size of the standing U.S. Army at the time.

In addition, a recent convert named Sampson Avard formed a covert organization called the Sons of Dan, or the Danites. Taking their name from the biblical prophet Daniel, they were created to intimidate Mormon dissenters and deal out vengeance in the form of "blood atonement" to anti-Mormons who wronged Smith or the church. Though it is unclear how much Smith knew of the Danites' activities, he clearly approved of those which he did know about. After Sidney Rigdon delivered a sermon that implied that rebellious Mormons had no place in the community, the Danites forcibly expelled every person that he directed them towards.

Rigdon followed the sermon with a political speech on July 4, declaring that Mormons would no longer tolerate persecution by Missourians and made vague references to a "war of extermination" if Mormons continued to be attacked. Smith endorsed his speech – he probably helped write it – and many Gentiles understood it as a thinly-veiled threat. A flood of anti-Mormon rhetoric flooded the newspapers and was heard frequently during the 1838 election campaigns.

The rhetoric was followed by more violence. On August 6, 1838, men in Gallatin tried to keep Mormons from voting. The election day incidents started what became known as the "Mormon War." Vigilantes raised and burned Mormon farms and the Mormons retaliated with violence of their own. The Danites burned homes, pillaged towns, and executed men they believed were the worst offenders among the Gentiles. At the Battle of Crooked River, a group of Mormons attacked the Missouri state militia, mistakenly believing them to be anti-Mormon vigilantes. Governor Lilburn Boggs stated publicly, "Mormons are the common enemies of mankind and ought to be exterminated or driven from the state."

Many agreed. A band of vigilantes attacked a Mormon settlement at Haun's Mill on October 30 and killed 17 Mormons. They gunned down an entire family, including a 10-year-old boy, in cold blood. "Nits grow lice," one of the men reportedly said before he put a bullet in the boy's head.

The following day the Latter-Day Saints surrendered to 2,500 state troops and agreed to forfeit their property and leave the state. Joseph Smith was arrested and hauled before a military court. He was accused of treason and sentenced to be executed the next morning. However, Missouri state militia Brigadier General Alexander Doniphan refused to carry out the order. Smith was then sent to state court for a preliminary hearing where several former allies testified against him. Smith and five others, including Sidney Rigdon, were charged with "overt acts of treason" and were locked up in the jail in Liberty, Missouri, to await their trials.

Months passed behind bars. In close quarters with a sick and unlikable Sidney Rigdon put considerable strain on the two men's relationship. Aside from that, Smith caused little disturbance during his imprisonment. He even urged his followers to moderate their antagonism toward the Gentiles. On April 6, 1839, he and the others testified before a grand jury and then, later that night, escaped from custody and disappeared. It remains a mystery as to who aided them in their escape.

Smith fled toward Illinois, where Brigham Young, the president of the Quorum of Twelve, had moved nearly 14,000 Mormon refugees. Many in Illinois, and in other states, had been critical of Missouri for the Haun's Mill Massacre and the expulsion of the Latter-Day Saints, so an agreement was reached for their resettlement. Initially the Mormons were welcome as "potential taxpayers and voters at a time of slow economic growth in the state." They purchased land in Hancock County, which was little more than mud, swamp, and malaria, and carved out a settlement there.

In addition to refugees from Ohio and Missouri, Smith also attracted a few wealthy and influential converts to the ranks of the Saints. One of them was John C. Bennett, the Illinois Quartermaster General, who used his contacts in the Illinois legislature to obtain an unusually liberal charter for Smith's settlement of "Nauvoo," a Hebrew word meaning "to be beautiful." The charter granted the city full right of self-government, authorized a university, and granted the city *habeas corpus* power, which allowed Smith to fend off extradition to Missouri. Though Mormon authorities controlled the city's government, Nauvoo promised a guarantee of religious freedom. The charter also authorized the Nauvoo Legion, a militia whose actions were only limited by state and federal laws. "Lieutenant General" Smith and "Major General" Bennett became its commanders, controlling the largest body of armed men in Illinois. John Bennett also became Nauvoo's first mayor.

Within a few years, Nauvoo was the largest community in the state, with more than 11,000 residents. Thousands of Mormons and new Mormon converts arrived in the city from the eastern United States, Canada, and England.

Smith had many civic concerns with the new community, but he also worried about things moving forward with the church. One of the first things he organized in the settlement was a Masonic Lodge. Smith had come to believe that the priestly rites of Freemasonry represented a degraded version of the lost rituals of Hebrew priests, and since Mormon lore dated back to the Lost Tribes of Israel it was natural for the Mormons to embrace them. Such rites, he believed, were the link to the ancient temple of the Hebrews. He was determined to take that link, mix it with the divine revelations of his own, and restore the old ceremonies.

He soon introduced the Masonic symbols of the rising sun, the square and compass, and the beehive into Mormonism. He created his own versions of Freemasonic rites – which included ritually bathing new members, dressing them in temple garments, giving them new spiritual names, and instructing in secret handgrips and passwords – and conducted initiation ceremonies in a makeshift temple over a store he owned in Nauvoo. Smith also studied Hebrew and possibly elements of the Kabbalah – the ancient Jewish tradition of mystical interpretation of the Bible – with a Jewish scholar and Mormon convert named Alexander Neibaur. It was a period of wild innovation within the burgeoning religious movement and, had Smith survived Illinois, the LDS church might be a very different thing today.

Going along with other radical additions he was making to Mormon doctrine, he also began revealing the idea of plural marriage to a few of his closest male associates, including John Bennett, who used it as a way to seduce numerous women. This was not what Smith had in mind. When embarrassing rumors of what Bennett had been

Joseph Smith's home in Nauvoo, Illinois

doing got back to him, he forced Bennett's resignation as Nauvoo's mayor. In retaliation Bennett left the church and wrote "lurid exposés of life in Nauvoo."

More innovation followed. Smith introduced the idea of "baptism for the dead," which is still used today and is a religious ritual that baptizes a person on behalf of one who is dead. In 1841 construction began on the Nauvoo Temple, but it would not be completed until after Smith's death.

In 1841, Smith received further revelations that caused him to revise the washing and anointing rituals as part of the new Nauvoo "endowment." At first the endowment was open only to men, who were initiated into a special group called the Anointed Quorum. For women Smith introduced the Relief Society, a service club and sorority within which Smith offered women "the keys of the kingdom."

The endowment – which was obviously inspired by the rituals of Freemasonry – is a ceremony designed to prepare participants to become rulers and gods in the next life. As part of the ceremony participants take part in a reenactment of the Biblical fall of Adam and Eve. The ceremony includes a symbolic washing and anointing, the receiving of a "new name," which they are not to reveal to others except at a certain part in the ceremony, and the gift of the temple garment, which Mormons then are expected to wear under their clothing day and night throughout their life. Some refer to these garments sarcastically as "magic underwear."

When the washings and anointings were first designed men and women were taken to separate rooms where they disrobed and, when called for, passed through a canvas curtain to enter a tub where they were washed from head to foot while words of blessing were recited over them. Then oil from a horn was poured over their head while more incantations were spoken over them. There were now ordained to become kings and queens in the afterlife. Men performed the ritual for men, and women performed the ritual for women.

For decades this ceremony was conducted in the nude, but, starting in the twentieth century, participants were given a white, poncho-like cover to wear during the washing and anointing. Since 2005 anything close to nudity has been banned and the application of oil and water is just on the participant's head. The washing is only symbolic in nature today.

It was also during this time in the early 1840s that Smith began to talk more openly about his plans for a millennial kingdom. He no longer envisioned the building of Zion in Nauvoo – he believed that the Mormons would someday rule the entire earth.

It didn't take long for things to sour in Illinois.

In November 1840 former attorney Thomas Coke Sharp had become a co-owner and editor of the *Warsaw World* newspaper, published in Warsaw, Illinois, located a little south of Nauvoo. Sharp renamed the paper the *Warsaw Signal* and began publishing stories and editorials that were critical of the Mormons. He kept his readers informed about Mormon activities and carefully agitated for action about Smith and his followers.

Sharp, like many long-time residents of the county, resented the growing power of the Mormons, who were starting to influence local and regional elections because they voted in a block, which was directed by Smith. Sharp also called for the creation of an anti-Mormon political party in 1841. Tensions escalated a year later when John C. Bennett split from Smith and started spreading the word about how the Mormons were practicing polygamy.

He likely forgot to mention that he was the worst offender of the practice.

In May 1842, an unknown assailant shot and wounded Missouri governor Lilburn Boggs and critics of the Mormons spread rumors that the assailant had been Porter Rockwell, one of Joseph Smith's personal bodyguards. Though the evidence of this was weak, Boggs ordered Smith's extradition. Certain that he would be killed if he ever returned to Missouri, Smith went into hiding twice over the next five months. Eventually a U.S. district attorney for Illinois argued that Smith's extradition would be unconstitutional, and the demands were dropped. Porter Rockwell was later tried for the crime and acquitted.

But Smith's enemies were not finished trying to get him back to Missouri. In June 1843 powerful adversaries convinced reluctant Illinois Governor Thomas Ford to extradite Smith to Missouri on the old charges of treason. Smith was arrested by two Missouri lawmen while riding outside of Nauvoo but were intercepted by several Danites with a writ of *habeas corpus* from the Nauvoo municipal court.

The arrest was a sign that legal and political pressure on the Mormons was increasing, and Smith reacted. The city council soon passed a law authorizing the mayor, who happened to be Joseph Smith, to review any "foreign" legal paperwork issued from outside of the city and decide whether to honor it. Smith had essentially set up his own little kingdom inside of Illinois.

And it got worse. In December 1843 Smith petitioned Congress to make Nauvoo an independent territory with the right to call out federal troops in its defense. He then wrote letters to leading presidential candidates and asked each what they planned to do to protect the Mormons. After receiving noncommittal or negative responses, Smith announced his own independent candidacy for President of the United States. He used his followers as political missionaries to further his cause. In March 1844 — after a dispute with a federal bureaucrat — Smith organized the secret Council of Fifty. Smith stated that the Council had the authority to decide which national or state laws Mormons should obey. They were also tasked with selecting a new site for a Mormon settlement in Texas, California, or Oregon, where Mormons could live under laws that were defined by a religious authority, not by the U.S. government.

Smith was making grandiose plans but should have been watching what was happening closer to home. In June 1844 a group of men established the *Nauvoo Expositor*, a newspaper with a clear anti-Mormon agenda. The paper stated that its mission was to expose the "abominations and whoredoms" of the religious movement established by Smith and show that the Mormons were not following the teachings of Jesus Christ and his apostles. The newspaper also claimed that Smith was using religion as a pretext to bring innocent women to Nauvoo, where they became part of the "growing harems of Mormon wives."

Immediately after the first issue of the newspaper was published the city council met to discuss the threat that it posed to the community. Smith persuaded the council to declare the newspaper a public nuisance and to destroy its printing press. Later that same day Smith ordered the city marshal to have the militia carry out the order.

This was the biggest mistake that Smith could have made. The destruction of the printing press incited anti-Mormon sentiment throughout the entire region, inviting criticism from newspapers all over the state. Some took it further than others. In his paper Thomas Sharp wrote that he and other anti-Mormon factions were ready to "exterminate, utterly exterminate, the wicked and abominable Mormon leaders," and called for an attack on the city of Nauvoo. Some of Smith's enemies acted with a bit more subtlety. Legal charges were filed, claiming that Smith and other Mormon leaders had promoted a riot. A constable was sent to Nauvoo from the county seat of Carthage to arrest Smith, but he refused to leave with him. In response anti-Mormon factions sent out messengers to surrounding communities and asked for armed men to come to Carthage and see that Smith was taken into custody.

Faced with what seemed to be an armed action against the Mormons, Smith declared Nauvoo under martial law and called out the militia. This action later resulted in his enemies filing charges of treason against him. On June 21 Governor Ford learned of the impending conflict and traveled to Carthage to try and defuse the situation. He asked Smith to submit evidence justifying his actions against the *Expositor*, the newspaper he had destroyed. After reviewing the documents Governor Ford wrote to Smith and told him that his actions had been illegal and demanded that he turn himself over to authorities in Carthage. He told Smith that if he did not comply, he feared an attack on Nauvoo.

Smith sent a letter in reply. He feared for his life if he left Nauvoo, he wrote, and wouldn't feel safe until the armed mobs in Carthage were dispersed. Soon after, fearing that the situation was out of control, Smith and his brother, Hyrum, fled across the Mississippi to Iowa. He wrote to his first wife, Emma, asking her to bring his other wives and his children and join him. Together, they would escape out west.

The letter alarmed Smith's followers in Nauvoo, many of whom felt he was abandoning the church at the time they needed him most. Several church leaders persuaded Emma to write him a letter that urged him to return. Stung by the criticism, Smith and his brother returned to Nauvoo and agreed to surrender to the authorities in Carthage. Despite

The jail in Carthage where Smith and his brother were killed

assurances from Governor Ford that he would be safe, Smith told his followers before he left, "I go as a lamb to the slaughter."

When they arrived in Carthage on June 24, Joseph and Hyrum Smith spent the night at the Hamilton House, the same hotel where the governor was staying. The next day, the Smiths surrendered to the constable and were incarcerated in the prisoner's quarters on the second floor of the jail, a two-story stone building on the north side of town. They were ordered held without bail until June 29, when a material witness would be able to appear.

Confined on the jail's upper floor, the brothers found themselves without the protection Governor Ford had promised. The days turned tense as armed men began arriving in town. During the early evening hours of June 27, a mob – which included some of the Illinois militia soldiers who were supposed to be guarding Smith but had smeared soot on their faces as a "disguise" – stormed the jail. Hearing the commotion and shots being fired, the Smiths attempted to barricade the door. As Hyrum Smith blocked it with his body, shots were fired through the wooden barrier and struck him in the face. He was instantly killed. Enraged, Joseph, who had been smuggled a small pistol by a sympathizer, flung open the door and began firing into the crowd. After emptying the gun, he ran to the window where he was spotted by men outside.

Legend says that when he appeared in the window, he issued the Masonic distress signal, which meant lifting his arms in the symbol of the square. He shouted, "Oh

Lord, my God, is there no help for the widow's son?" just before he was shot. It was a code used by Freemasons looking for help – but it didn't save Smith.

The men outside opened fire. Smith was struck four times: twice in the back, once in the right collarbone, and once in the chest. Mortally wounded, he fell from the second-story window. According to several eyewitnesses he was still alive after he fell and apparently "raised himself up against the wall curb, drew up one leg and stretched out the other and died immediately."

With Smith dead, the mob quickly dispersed. When the news of the murder reached Artois Hamilton, proprietor of the Hamilton House in Carthage, he drove a wagon to the jail to secure the bodies of Smith and his brother, which he hid away at his hotel. The next day they were taken to Nauvoo, where they were eventually buried.

The murder of Joseph Smith marked the beginning of the end for the Mormon settlement in Illinois. In the aftermath Mormon leaders bickered over the issue of secession, causing a deep divide within the church that caused it to splinter into several alternate movements.

In August of the following year, the ruling council chose Brigham Young as their new leader. He was a dynamic speaker and natural leader, but he knew the Mormons could not stay in Illinois and prosper. He still needed to create the new Zion that Joseph Smith has espoused, and Young knew it needed to be far to the west in an unpopulated territory. With that decision made, Young led his people on a terrible journey in 1847 and settled them in the arid country around the Great Salt Lake in present-day Utah. It was not the biblical paradise that Smith had envisioned, but Young insisted that they begin irrigating the country on the day they arrived and gradually, Salt Lake City began to grow.

Brigham Young was born on June 1, 1801, the eighth child of John and Abigail Young, a farming family in Whitingham, Vermont. When he was three his family moved to what would become the Burned-Over District of upstate New York. The family moved twice more, and Brigham's mother died from tuberculosis when he was 14. Two years later his father forced him to leave home. He first worked odd jobs and then became a builder's apprentice, working as a carpenter, joiner, glazer, and painter.

In 1824 Young joined the Reformed Methodist Church. This was after a period of intense Bible study that led to his belief that baptism should be carried out by immersion instead of the normal practice of sprinkling. He also married that same year and he and his new wife, Miriam, moved into a small house in Port Byron, New York, next to a paint factory where Young worked. Four years later, after the birth of their first daughter, the family moved to Oswego, New York, and then to Mendon where most of Young's siblings also lived. He became friends with a man named Heber Kimball who got him work as a carpenter and then at a sawmill he operated. In 1832 Miriam died and Young and his two small daughters moved into the home of Kimball and his wife, Vilate.

Disillusioned, Young had by then left the Reformed Methodist Church. He became a seeker, looking for a church with the true authority of Jesus Christ. Around 1830 Young was given a copy of the Book of Mormon by his brother, and soon after five Latter-Day Saints missionaries arrived in Mendon to preach. Young was drawn to the new church and officially joined in April 1832. A branch of the church was organized in Mendon and Young became one of the regular preachers. He began traveling around the area, spreading the word about the Mormon Church. During one incident in the Burned-Over District Young witnessed another Mormon speak in tongues. To his surprise Young replied to him in an unknown language. In November 1832 Young traveled with Kimball to Kirtland, Ohio where he met Joseph Smith for the first time. He now truly believed that he had found the religious movement that he had been seeking.

Brigham Young

Over the next several months, he continued his mission work in New York and Canada. Then, in the summer of 1833, Young moved to Kirtland, Ohio where he soon met Mary Ann Angell. The two of them were married in February 1834. In Kirtland Young continued to preach, which was how Mary Ann first met him. He also resumed the work of building houses and was responsible for directing much of the carpentry work for the Kirtland Temple. In May Young became a member of Zion's Camp and was part of the failed campaign to protect Mormon settlers in Missouri. Mary Ann remained in Ohio caring for Young's two daughters while pregnant with their son, Joseph.

In May 1835, Young was ordained as a member of the original Quorum of Twelve Apostles, which would soon issue a testimony in support of the divine origin of the Doctrine and Covenants, a book of scripture that contained revelations from God to Joseph Smith. During this time Young was also traveling to the Northeast and to England, recruiting new followers for the church. He was back in Kirtland when the Mormons were forced to flee the city and he accompanied Smith to Missouri. Young would organize the Mormon exodus from Missouri while Smith was in jail in Liberty.

Young served faithfully alongside Smith until 1844 when the Prophet was killed in Carthage by the armed mob. There were several claimants to Smith's role of church president and a succession crisis ensued. Things turned ugly and several factions abandoned Nauvoo. Even those who stayed suffered through contentious meetings and debates. Sidney Rigdon, the senior surviving church member, argued that there could be no successor to Smith – whoever took over should be made the "Protector" of the church only. Young opposed this reasoning. Smith had earlier recorded a revelation which stated the Quorum of the Twelve was "equal in authority and power," so Young claimed that the leadership of the church fell to the Twelve Apostles. The majority in attendance were persuaded that the Quorum of the Twelve was to lead the church, with Young as the quorum's president. Sidney Rigdon left the church as a result and started a new movement based in Pittsburgh.

Years later many of Young's followers would claim that when Young spoke during the meeting, he was transformed by God to look and sound exactly like Joseph Smith. They attributed this to the ease in which he made his case to the people.

Young was ordained as president of the Latter-Day Saints in December 1847, more than three years after Smith's death. He would go on to rule the church with authority and an iron hand. He knew the Mormons could not remain in Illinois and continue to prosper, so he began making plans for a new journey. The Mormons would have the Zion that Smith had promised them, even if they had to spill blood to do it.

Legend claims that after Young was ordained as president, he told Danite soldier John D. Lee, "By the eternal Heavens I have unsheathed my sword, and I will never return it until the blood of the Prophet Joseph Smith is avenged."

On July 24, 1847 – now celebrated as Pioneer Day in Utah – a wagon traveled out of a canyon and gave Brigham Young his first look at the Great Salt Lake Valley. That wilderness would become the new Zion for the Mormons. "If the people of the United States will let us alone for 10 years," he would later recall saying that day, "we will ask no odds of them."

Young wasn't wrong to ask for such a thing. By now some Latter-Day Saints had been driven from their homes four times. They wanted a place to call their own, free from the burden of the Gentile government. The Mormons had fled Nauvoo, camped in Winter Quarters, Nebraska, and then continued their journey to the Salt Lake Valley. The Mormon journey became one of the largest and best-organized westward treks in American history. The Saints were ready to lay down roots. In fact, just 29 days after they arrived, Young organized the Mormon Tabernacle Choir.

When the Mormons left Illinois most of what would become the American Southwest belonged to Mexico. However, Young believed that Mexico's control over its northern frontier was so loose that the Mormons could settle there without interference. In the spring of 1847, he led an advance party of 147 Saints from Nebraska to the Salt Lake Valley, arriving in July. Over the next two decades more than 70,000 Mormons would follow.

In February 1848, Mexico was forced to surrender what is now California, Nevada, Texas, Arizona, New Mexico, Colorado, Wyoming, and Utah, to the United States after losing the Mexican-American War. Just six months after arriving in Zion, the Treaty of Guadalupe Hidalgo placed the Mormons back under the authority of the U.S. government.

To preserve self-rule, church leaders quickly sought official status. They petitioned Congress in 1849 for territorial status and then asked for statehood. The land they wanted was vast, stretching from the Rockies to the Sierra Nevada and from the new Mexican border to present-day Oregon. Congress, caught between pro- and anti-slavery forces, created the Utah Territory, but not before reducing the size of it to present-day Utah, Nevada, western Colorado, and southwestern Wyoming.

Territorial status gave the federal government more authority over Utah affairs than it would have as a state, but President Millard Fillmore softened the blow by naming Brigham Young as the new territory's governor in 1850. It was a decision that one of his successors would come to regret.

GREAT SALT LAKE CITY. (From the North.)

The Mormons built roads and bridges and laid out the streets in Salt Lake City — and later communities — in a numbered grid system that made everything easy to find.

Under Young's direction the Mormons built roads, bridges, forts, irrigation projects, and established a form of public welfare. They also made war, then peace, with Native Americans in the region and established an efficient mail service. Young was one of the first to subscribe to Union Pacific stock for the construction of the First Transcontinental Railroad, and he also organized the first legislature. He helped to establish the University of Deseret in the Salt Lake Valley in February 1850. Its name was eventually changed to the University of Utah.

Since Young ran the Utah Territory about the same way that Joseph Smith ran Nauvoo, conflicts between the religious and secular authorities soon began. The Mormon leaders were suspicious of both the character and intentions of federal appointees, like a judge who was found to have abandoned his family in Illinois and brought a prostitute to Utah. And over the next seven years a long line of federal officers — from judges to Indian agents — came to Utah only to find that the governor would reverse or ignore their decisions.

Indian agent Jacob Holeman wrote to his superiors in Washington, D.C. to complain about Young in 1851. He wrote that Young "has been so much in the habit of exercising his will which is supreme here that no one will dare oppose anything he may say or do." Surveyor General David Burr reported that Young told him that federal surveyors "shall not be suffered to trespass" on Mormon land. Throughout the 1850s, federal appointees returned east frustrated, intimidated, or both by the Mormons. Some of them wrote books and articles about their harsh experiences and anti-Mormon sentiment began to spread – again.

But things got really heated when reports started to surface about polygamy.

By the time the Mormons arrived in Utah, plural marriage was no longer just confined to Joseph Smith's inner circle. Word of it had spread, thanks to Gentiles who passed through Utah on their way to Oregon and California.

The Mormon's embrace of plural marriage was based on a revelation that Smith claimed to have received years before. He stated that the possession of more than one wife was not only permissible but actually necessary for complete salvation.

Brigham Young, who took a second wife in 1842 after 18 years of monogamy, always maintained that he had been a reluctant convert. He wrote, "I was not desirous of shrinking from any duty, nor of failing in the least to do as I was commanded, but it was the first time in my life that I had desired the grave." By the time he died at age 76 in 1877, he had taken 55 wives but allegedly shared no "earthly life" with 30 of them. Even so, that's a lot of wives for a man who claimed he'd rather be dead than be a polygamist.

For years Young and other church leaders had dismissed all allegations of polygamy in their ranks as rumors spread by their enemies, but by the early 1850s there was no denying what was happening. On August 29, 1852, the church publicly acknowledged plural marriage for the first time. Orson Pratt, a member of the Quorum of the Twelve Apostles, delivered a lengthy speech, inviting the Latter-Day Saints to "look upon Abraham's blessings as your own, for the Lord blessed him with a promise of seed as numerous as the sand upon the seashore." After Pratt finished, Young read aloud Smith's revelation on plural marriage.

The admission of polygamy was widely reported outside the church, and it destroyed any hope that the Utah Territory would become a state under Young's leadership. Soon conflicts between Young's roles as governor of the territory and president of the church would become even more complicated.

In April 1855 Young called on some 160 men to leave behind their homes, farms, and families and go out into the wilderness of Utah and establish missions among the Native Americans that lived there.

This might be a good time to explain the importance of the Native Americans in Mormon lore:

The Book of Mormon was the most complex of Joseph Smith's revelations. How he wrote it – translating the mysterious golden plates – has already been discussed, but more detail is needed to understand what was happening with it. The Book of Mormon tells the story of a lost tribe of Israel that came to the Americas many hundreds of years ago. These first Americans built a flourishing and advanced civilization, but one branch, the Lamanites, killed their righteous relatives, the Nephites. For this – and their rejection of Christ's teachings – God cursed the Lamanites with dark skin and a degraded existence. Their descendants were the Native Americans, who now lived in a primitive state. The book taught that the Lamanites would not regain white skin and a civilized way of life until they accepted

Christ's teachings. Thus, the golden plates instructed Smith not only to restore the true Christian church but also to bring salvation to Native Americans.

But wait – if they were living in the Americas how did they know about Christ? Apparently, after Jesus was crucified and resurrected in Jerusalem he dropped in on the Americans, where he repeated the Sermon on the Mount, blessed children, and appointed 12 more disciples.

The early Mormons understood the book to be a religious history of the indigenous peoples of the Americas, but Latter-Day Saints today view it as a companion to the Bible and an additional testament of Christ.

So, it was a big deal to the Mormons to convert as many Native Americans to Mormonism as possible – they were saving their souls and rescuing them from a life as sub-humans, after all – and church officials said that they were undertaking the missions to convert the tribes on their borders to their faith and to improve their welfare. But Garland Hunt, who recently arrived in Utah as an Indian agent, was suspicious about their true motives. In a confidential letter he wrote to the head of the Bureau of Indian Affairs in Washington, Hunt claimed that the missions were actually intended to teach the Native Americans how to distinguish between "Mormons" and "Americans" – a distinction, he noted, that would be "prejudicial to the interests of the latter."

The first of the missionaries left Salt Lake City in May 1855. Three bands of men rode out hundreds of miles to what is now Idaho, New Mexico, and Moab, Utah. In August Young wrote to the missionaries in New Mexico, working with the Paiute Indians, and congratulated them on the "prosperity and the success which has thus far attended your efforts" and pushed them to baptize as many of the natives as possible, making them feel by their acts that "we are their real friends." The missionaries baptized scores of people, but what the Indians thought of the bizarre ritual was never recorded.

In a letter written on October 1, 1855, John Steele, an interpreter at the New Mexico mission wrote to a friend: "If the Lord blesses us as he has done, we can have one thousand brave warriors on hand in a short time to help to quell any eruption that might take place in the principalities."

The following summer Young suggested to another church leader, John Taylor – who later became Young's successor as president of the church – that "missionaries to the Indians and their success is a subject avoided in our discourse."

It was becoming obvious that the Mormons were secretly building an army of Native Americans to help them if there was a clash with U.S. military forces. By 1857 their plans had leaked. Newspapers across the country began reporting that the Mormons were forming alliances with the Indians against the rest of the country. Some accounts were based on briefings from government officials who had returned to Washington, while others were merely gossip, ramping up the terror as much as possible. In April 1857 one Washington newspaper estimated the number of Native Americans who would fight on behalf of the Mormons at 300,000 – even though the total Native American population in the Utah Territory was no more than 20,000 at most. Brigham Young characterized all the press coverage written about the Saints as "a prolonged howl of base slander."

In truth, it was a mixture of fact and fiction.

As it turned out, though, none of the missions lasted. The southeast mission collapsed within four months after a skirmish with the Utes. The New Mexico mission followed after it and shifted its focus from converting souls to mining lead, and the northern mission closed down in March 1858. But before that happened, however, the Mormons had bigger problems on their hands.

James Buchanan, a Democrat, had defeated the Republican John Fremont, and Millard Fillmore of the Know-Nothings Party in the 1856 election. He was sworn in as President in March 1857, preoccupied with the fight over whether Kansas would enter the Union as a free or a slave state. He soon had other concerns, all coming from Utah. By the time he took office every government official had either fled or had been run out of the state. Their reports did not paint a pretty picture of the chaos that was occurring out west.

Buchanan knew that he was inheriting a problem that had also plagued his predecessor. The Mormons had been in control over every route, river, trail, and mountain pass that went in, out, and through the Utah Territory since gold had been discovered in California in 1849. Young had created a kingdom that he believed was beyond the control of the federal government. Surveying parties had been attacked and massacred because the Mormons didn't want the government measuring their land. Federal judges were murdered. A settler who foolishly courted one of Young's daughters was butchered. But was it the Mormons who carried out these crimes? Not according to the Mormons. In every case the murders were carried out by Native Americans – or so it seemed. The victims were scalped and mutilated in what was presumed to be methods perpetrated by Indians, and witnesses even stated that they had seen painted warriors fleeing the scenes of the crimes.

Brigham Young's term as the territorial governor had expired in 1854, but he had continued to serve. Buchanan, whose cabinet saw the reports from Utah as a territory spinning out of federal control, decided to replace Young with Alfred Cumming, a former mayor from Georgia who was now serving as the Indian Affairs superintendent based in St. Louis. The President ordered troops to accompany the new governor out west and to enforce the federal rule in Utah – but, for some reason, he didn't contact Young and tell him he was going to be replaced.

Young found out in July 1857 – a month that was filled with bad news for the Mormons. The *Deseret News* reported that a Mormon named Parley Pratt had been killed in Arkansas by the estranged husband of a woman that Pratt had just taken as his twelfth wife.

There were also rumors circulating that federal troops were on their way to Utah, which prompted Apostle Heber C. Kimball to declare, "I will fight until there is not a drop of blood in my veins. Good, God! I have wives enough to whip out the United States."

The rumors turned out to be true. Mormons traveling from the Kansas-Missouri area confirmed that soldiers were on their way to Salt Lake City.

And then, six weeks later, an unsuspecting wagon train crossed over the border into Utah. They were emigrants – men, women, and children – heading for California, with no interest in politics, Mormon lands, or Utah's conflict with the federal government.

They were in the wrong place at the wrong time – and paid for it with their lives.

The wagon train was led by a man named Alexander Fancher, and it had originated in Harrison County, Arkansas. On March 29, 1857 the group of settlers left their home bound for California, where Fancher's brother, John, had started a ranch. Fancher, age 43, was the epitome of the Western pioneer. Sober, industrious, a Mexican-American War veteran, and a born leader, he had already led one wagon train to California and had returned to form another group made up of friends and neighbors to take with him to the rich lands of the west.

Many had begged to go with Fancher, and he was able to choose whom to take with him. The final group was made up of people like himself, 20 to 30 close-knit families who had an optimistic outlook and excitement about starting new lives in California. They were a wealthy party, many of them having converted their life savings into gold which they hid under the floorboards of their wagons and inside of featherbeds. Historians believe that the Fancher party may have been traveling with nearly $100,000 in gold coins.

The wagon train numbered roughly 200 men, women, and children when it left Arkansas. A party of that size rarely ran into trouble with Native Americans. Even so, Fancher made sure that all the men were well armed and schooled in the use of their weapons. They were not expecting problems, nor were they – as was later claimed by Mormon disinformation – wild and boisterous, "swearing and boasting... that Buchanan's whole army was coming right behind them and would kill every damn Mormon in Utah." They were, in truth, a group of ordinary families seeking a fresh start in a new place.

But there turned out to be nothing ordinary about their journey. As the Fancher party approached Salt Lake City rumors were flying throughout the Mormon community that a force of U.S. soldiers was coming to forcibly remove Brigham Young from his position as territorial governor. In reality Buchanan's army was coming, but it would not arrive in Utah until months later.

The Fancher party arrived in the Great Salt Lake basin in early August and found themselves greeted with hostility. No amount of money could purchase supplies, and so a planned weeklong rest was shortened to only two days and then the wagon train moved out again.

At that time there were two routes from Utah to California – a northern one, the California Trail through Salt Lake City and Nevada, and the old Spanish Trail, a southern route through the Mojave Desert. The Fancher Train had planned on taking the northern route but were convinced by a Mormon named Charles Rich – who rode into their camp near Salt Lake City and gave them orders to leave the area the next day – that the southern trail was safer. He claimed there were fewer Native Americans and there was more feed along the way, especially in a little valley called Mountain Meadows.

Danite John D. Lee, the mastermind behind what became known as the Mountain Meadows Massacre — the greatest stain on the history of the Mormon Church

As the Fancher party headed south their deaths had already been planned. On September 1, Brigham Young met with Paiute Indian leaders in Salt Lake City. Using his son as a translator he told the tribal leaders that all the cattle on the Spanish Trail were theirs for the taking – a clear reference to the large and valuable herd that accompanied the Fancher wagon train. The next day the Paiutes left Salt Lake City and headed for southern Utah.

While this meeting was taking place the Fancher party was passing near Cedar City, about 35 miles from Mountain Meadows. On September 4 they were refused food and feed for their cattle but were directed to the meadows as a place where they could rest and graze their livestock. Unknown to the members of the Fancher party, Danite John D. Lee had already arrived at Mountain Meadows with a mixed force of Paiute and Mormons, the latter of whom had painted their faces to look like Native Americans. They observed the Fancher party enter the valley and make camp on September 6. When darkness fell Lee and his men crept down from the hills and concealed themselves in the rocks and brush at the edge of the valley.

The morning of September 7, 1857 broke bright and clear. The travelers built up their cook fires and began making coffee and preparing their breakfast. They sat chatting near the fires and then as one of the survivors recalled, "While eating a breakfast of rabbit and quail, a shot rang out and one of the children toppled over." A second volley of shots struck between 10 and 15 of those gathered in the camp. Seven of them were immediately killed. Others, including Alexander Fancher, were mortally wounded.

Although taken by surprise, the well-trained men and women of the Fancher party took immediate action. They circled the wagons, dug ditches behind them, both as firing trenches and to offer protection for the children, and returned fire on the attackers. They assumed they were being attacked by Native Americans since they heard horrible cries in the woods and saw dark-skinned men in war paint darting through the trees and brush but were bewildered as to the cause of the attack. According to Fancher, who had traveled in the region before, the Paiutes were normally peaceful and owned relatively few firearms. The men who attacked the camp, though, were armed to the teeth and well stocked with ammunition.

But the settlers did not go down without a fight. The initial return fire killed three Paiutes. The Mormons and their allies now realized that wiping out the Fancher party

Harper's Weekly illustration of the Mountain Meadows Massacre. The Mormons had tried to keep the news from spreading beyond the Utah Territory but failed

was not going to be easy. In fact, the Paiutes called off the attack. They told John Lee that this kind of bloodshed was more than they bargained for and abandoned the Mormons in the hills. Lee knew he needed more reinforcements and so he rode to nearby Cedar City to recruit more men. According to Lee he received three wagonloads of "well-armed men" under the command of Major John Higbee. Higbee told Lee that their mission was no longer to simply frighten or harass the Fancher party, or to rob them of their belongings. Higbee told him, "It is the orders of the President [Brigham Young] that all emigrants must be put out of the way... none who are old enough to talk are to be spared."

During the time that Lee had been away gathering more men the settlers had remained under siege. Despite their bravery they were at a considerable disadvantage. They had not set up their camp near the stream that ran through the meadows because it was too swampy, so they had to travel more than 100 yards under fire to get water. As the days wore on the little water they had ran out and they began to suffer from thirst. Desperate, two little girls dressed in "spotless white" ran to the stream with pails for water but this appeal to the humanity of the Mormons did no good – the two little girls were shot to death.

By Wednesday, Lee had returned with his reinforcements and now even more men were raining bullets down on the Fancher camp. More people were killed and the bodies of the slain lay stinking and swelling in the sun. In another desperate move, two men snuck out of the camp in the night hoping to find another wagon train passing nearby that could help them. They slipped away from their attackers and rode until they saw a small campfire with three men sitting around it. Thinking they might be travelers, one of the men spilled their story of being attacked in Mountain Meadows. But the men around the campfire were Mormons – Danites, in fact – and one of the men from the Fancher party was gunned down in cold blood. The other man managed to get away and made it back to the wagon train. He told them what had happened. Any doubt that the Fancher party had about the identity of their attackers was now gone.

But when John D. Lee rode into their camp under a white flag on Friday, September 11, they had no choice but to trust him. They were nearly out of ammunition and their water was gone. Lee told them that he was a major in the Mormon militia and that the Native Americans had gone wild and attacked them. Lee promised to try to save the settlers by taking them to Cedar City under his protection. All they had to do, he explained, was give up their guns and ammunition so they didn't incite the Paiute any further. Despite their suspicions of the Mormons, there was nothing else the settlers could do. They had perhaps 20 rounds of ammunition between them and many wounded who needed care. Alexander Fancher was dying, and his nephew Matt was placed in charge of the party. He told his uncle what was taking place and Fancher gasped out weakly, "Good God, no, Matt!" They had no choice, though, and the remaining men in the Fancher party laid down their weapons.

Lee then organized the party into three groups. The wagons of the wounded were loaded first, followed by the women and children, and then the men, walking in a single file line about 10 feet apart, each accompanied by a Mormon guard. They were led by Major Higbee, astride his horse. After about a mile he stopped his horse near an open area surrounded by scrub oak and ordered the column to halt. He then fired his pistol in the air and called out, "Do your duty!"

And each Mormon turned and shot the man he was guarding.

Chaos erupted in the meadow as the settlers attempted to flee, only to be gunned down by their captors. Among the Fancher party were several so-called "apostate Mormons," who had once been members of the church but had given up the faith. They were singled out for the special treatment of "blood atonement."

In 1856 Brigham Young had preached, "There are sins that men commit for which they cannot receive atonement in this world, or in that which is to come."

The atonement of Jesus having shed his blood for them would not apply. These were people, Young and other Mormons believed, who needed to be dealt with by the practice of blood atonement. They were not merely killed but were slaughtered by the practice of "having their blood literally spilled on the ground." In other words, their throats would be cut. During the massacre Higbee sliced the throats of the former Mormons in the Fancher party.

When the shooting started the women and children began to panic. Lee then gave the order to kill them all. Sallie Baker, a child who survived, later wrote, "From the survivors went up such a piercing, heart-rending scream – such a shriek of blank despair" that everyone who heard it remembered it always. Sallie also recalled how one Mormon gunman ran up to the wagon where the women and children had been placed and said, "Lord my God, receive their spirits. It is for Thy Kingdom that I do this!" He then began firing wildly into the wagon. Another man shot two badly wounded settlers who were huddled together on the ground. A 14-year-old boy was clubbed to death with a rifle butt to conserve ammunition.

Two teenaged girls, Rachel and Ruth Dunlap, ran into a cluster of trees where witnesses said they were raped by Mormons and shot by Lee himself as they begged for mercy and promised to "love him forever" if he spared their lives. Much of the killing was done by sword and knife, and the Mormons, crazed by bloodlust, were soon covered with gore. One young girl fell to her knees in front of a teenage Mormon boy, begging him to spare her. He said he would, but his father – which some reports claim was Lee – stabbed her to death in the boy's arms.

More than 50 years later, a woman who was a four-year-old child at the time remembered seeing her mother shot in the forehead and fall dead. Other witnesses saw "children clinging around the knees of their murderers, begging for mercy and offering themselves as slaves for life could they be spared. But their throats were cut from ear to ear in answer to their appeal." A survivor of the massacre who told her story many years later was asked how she could remember everything that happened in such detail since she was just a little girl at the time. She replied, "You don't forget the horror. And you wouldn't forget it either, if you saw your own mother topple over in the wagon beside you, with a big red blotch getting bigger and bigger on the front of her calico dress."

When the killing ended the Mormons were left with the problem of what to do with the children who were considered to be of "innocent blood," which was generally under the age of eight. Since the children had not attained the age of reason the Mormons saw them as being innocent of whatever "crimes" their parents had committed. In the eyes of God, they believed, these children should be spared. However, it appears that the older children among the group (those nearer the age of eight) were the last to be killed that day because it was feared that they would carry the tale of the massacre with them.

The rest of the children, mostly age seven and under, were taken from the massacre site by wagon to a Mormon farming community called Hamblin a few miles away, just east of Mountain Meadows. The screaming and wailing of the children, most of whom were soaked in their parents' blood, was nearly unbearable to hear. The children were left in Hamblin until they could be parceled out to Mormon families – in some cases, to the families of the men who had killed their parents and older siblings.

By 1859, though, the federal government had managed to track down these children and sent them back to Arkansas to be reunited with relatives. Amazingly, the Mormons tried to demand money from the government for taking care of the children for two years.

The next day at Mountain Meadows the Mormons returned to the stiff and twisted corpses of the Fancher party, tearing clothing and jewelry from the bodies and ransacking the wagons for gold and anything useful they could steal. Afterward they made a half-hearted effort to bury the bodies by dumping them in a ditch and throwing some dirt over them. The remains of the Fancher Train were left to the wolves, the buzzards, and the elements.

John D. Lee was the only Mormon brought to trial for his role in the massacre. He was taken to Mountain Meadows and executed by firing squad. He can be seen on the far left, sitting on his coffin before his execution

The killers swore a blood oath to keep silent about the massacre, but it wouldn't last. The enormity of what had befallen the Fancher party, once the bloodlust had left them, began to weigh on many of the men involved in their deaths. Higbee and his immediate superiors felt no shame, though. They blamed the massacre on the Paiutes, although since Mormons were in possession of the Fancher supplies, cattle, gold, and surviving children, their story seemed difficult to believe. A few days after the massacre Brigham Young wrote a letter, which he dated before the slaughter, ordering Mormons not to harass the settlers – an obvious attempt to whitewash his involvement in the affair.

Whispers and rumors of the massacre spread, and subsequent wagon trains stumbled on the remains of the Fancher party. Reports from travelers reached the California newspapers and then spread to Washington. The American public demanded an investigation. Eventually the Army sent Major James Carleton to investigate and to find the surviving children. Even as late as 1859 Carleton found the scene of the massacre "horrible to look upon." He collected baskets filled with women's hair, which were lying "in detached locks and masses" throughout the site. Bones and skulls were scattered about, as well as pieces of rotted clothing, leather, and bits of metal. A pathologist who accompanied Carleton noted that, "many of the skulls bore marks of violence, being pierced with bullet holes, or shattered by heavy blows... or firearms disclosed close to the head."

This ended the lie spread by the Mormons that the victims had been killed by Indian arrows. Unfortunately, though, despite his best efforts, Carleton's report was not damning enough with which to prosecute the men who committed the massacre.

The Latter-Day Saints were simply too powerful and Utah residents – Mormon or otherwise – were too scared to talk. It would be 20 years after the massacre before the federal authorities brought murder charges against John D. Lee and four others, including Major Higbee. Lee was the only one brought to trial. Most were convinced that he was a convenient scapegoat to protect Brigham Young. He was convicted and was taken to Mountain Meadows, where he was executed by a firing squad.

The Mormon Church desperately wanted this to be the end of the matter. But the Mountain Meadows Massacre has never been truly forgotten and has always left a stain on the relationship between the Latter-day Saints and the rest of the country.

It would not be until 2007, long after the church distanced itself from polygamy and other controversial practices of the past, that the Mormons formally expressed regret about its part in the massacre. Even so, the LDS church still refuses to admit that Brigham Young ordered or had prior knowledge of the killings, as historians believe that he did.

As far as the Mormons are concerned that chapter in history is forever closed.

The Mountain Meadows Massacre has remained a stain on the history of the LDS church, but it's far from the only event that few want to talk about today. Mormon leaders also like to ignore the fact that Utah actually went to war with the U.S. government in the months after the massacre.

When the attack on the Fancher train was taking place, the new governor, Alfred Cumming, and about 1,500 federal troops were a month away from reaching Fort Bridger, which was about 100 miles northeast of Salt Lake City. Brigham Young, desperately needing time to evacuate the city, called up the Utah militia to delay the army. Over the next several weeks the militia raised the troops' supplies, burned the grass needed to feed their horses, mules, and cattle, and even burned Fort Bridger. November snowstorms made things worse for the military, and, running out of supplies, the army commander Colonel Albert Sidney Johnston, decided to spend the winter at what was left of the fort. The Mormons, he wrote, have "placed themselves in rebellion against the Union, and entertain the insane design of establishing a form of government thoroughly despotic, and utterly repugnant to our institutions."

By the time spring arrived in 1858 Johnston was prepared to receive reinforcements that would raise his troop levels to almost 5,000 – one-third of the entire U.S. Army. A short time before Young began what became known as the "Move South," an exodus of about 30,000 people from the settlements in northern Utah. Before leaving Salt Lake City Mormons buried the foundation of their Temple and planted wheat to hide it from the eyes of the invaders. A few men stayed behind, ready to burn homes, barns, and orchards to keep them out of the soldiers' hands. Once again, the Mormons were being driven from their homes – although this time, it was because of their own actions.

Help arrived in the form of Thomas Kane, an attorney, abolitionist, philanthropist, and military officer who had been influential in the western migration of the Latter-Day Saints and in getting Young appointed as the territorial governor years before. After meeting Mormon leaders at an 1846 conference in Philadelphia, Kane offered to help in their conflicts with the U.S. government as they tried to migrate west.

Mormon family of the 1870s — The patriarch and his wives with their sons and daughters and those sons with their wives and children. And on and on...

Over the winter of 1857-58 Kane set out for Utah to try to mediate what was being called "the Mormon crisis." Kane arrived in Salt Lake City in February 1858. By April, in exchange for peace, he had secured Young's agreement to allow the new governor to take office. To the public Buchanan's failure to notify Young about the new governor and the Army's delayed arrival in Utah, the expedition was starting to look like an expensive blunder that took place just as a financial panic was doing damage to the nation's economy. Buchanan, seeing a chance to end his embarrassment quickly, sent a peace commission west with the offer of a pardon for Utah citizens who would submit to federal laws. Young accepted the offer.

That same month Johnston and his troops finally arrived in an abandoned Salt Lake City — then kept marching past it 40 miles south to establish Camp Floyd, in present-day Fairfield, Utah. With the military no longer a threat the Mormons returned to their homes and began a long and uncomfortable accommodation to secular rule under a series of non-Mormon governors.

The next four decades were difficult ones for the LDS church. Federal laws against polygamy targeted Mormon property and power through the 1870s and 1880s until finally, in 1890, Wilford Woodruff, the church's fourth President, issued a formal renunciation of plural marriage. But renouncing polygamy was not done as a matter of faith — it was a political necessity, as was evidenced by Utah becoming a state in 1896.

Polygamy — as we'll soon see — continues to haunt the region today.

The Church of Jesus Christ of the Latter-Day Saints has gone on to become the largest home-grown religion in American history, now numbering nearly 14 million members, including prominent Americans like former Senators Harry Reid and Orrin Hatch and former Massachusetts Governor and Senator Mitt Romney. At the same time, a wariness of Mormons remains. When Romney was running for president as a Republican he declared, like the Catholic John F. Kennedy had done before him: "I am an American running for president. I do not define my candidacy by my religion." In a poll taken after Romney's speech, 17 percent of respondents said they would never vote for a Mormon. It was almost the same number of people who said that exact thing in 1968 when Romney's father, Michigan Governor George Romney, ran for president in 1968.

The movement created by Joseph Smith still holds an ominous place in the minds of many Americans, especially in light of the stories of Mormons and polygamy that have been in the news in recent years. LDS leaders will tell you that those people have nothing to do with the official church, but it's hard for many of us to make the separation – especially when we know the history of how the official church began.

America's Only "King" was a Mormon

"I am eager, and mankind is frail. I shall act in time to come for my own benefit," wrote the only man ever crowned king within the continental United States, James Jesse Strang – religious leader, politician, and a self-proclaimed monarch who founded a faction of the Mormon Church in the 1840s. His attempt to seize power from Brigham Young eventually led to his ejection from the church and the creation of his own sect. While serving as prophet, seer, and revelator of his church – which he claimed to be the sole legitimate continuation of the Mormon Church started by Joseph Smith – he established a kingdom on Michigan's Beaver Island and built an organization that he hoped would rival Young's in Utah. Strang even had his own mysterious tablets, just like the ones allegedly found by Joseph Smith, which came to be accepted as his sect's teachings.

He not only ran his own church – and his own kingdom – but he also managed to get himself elected to the Michigan House of Representatives and worked at various times as an attorney, teacher, temperance lecturer, and newspaper editor. But Strang's abrasive personality and strange beliefs made him many enemies inside of the church and out of it, contributing to his own demise. His weird adventure as a church leader and king would eventually lead to his assassination on a remote island in Lake Michigan.

James Jesse Strang was born March 21, 1813 in Cayuga County, New York – another son of the Burned-Over District. He was the second of three children and his parents had a good reputation in their community. In a brief autobiography that Strang later wrote he stated that he attended school until the age of 12 and missed many months of teaching because of his ill health. But this did not mean that Strang was illiterate or uneducated. He read widely and learned about a wide array of topics. As a youth Strang kept a rather profound personal diary, written partly in a secret code that was not deciphered for more than 100 years. The journal contained Strang's thoughts on many things including his burning desire to "rival Caesar or Napoleon"

James Jesse Strang

and his regret that by age 19 he had not yet become a general or member of the state legislature, which he saw as being essential by that point in his life if he was going to be famous. However, Strang's diary equally reveals a sincere desire to be of service to his fellow man, together with agonized frustration at not knowing how he might do so as a penniless, unknown youth from upstate New York.

At age 12, Strang joined the Baptist Church. He did not want to follow in his father's footsteps as a farmer, so he began studying law. He was admitted to the New York state bar at 23. He also became the county postmaster and edited a local newspaper. Strang was no longer the philosopher and free-thinker that he'd once believed himself to be.

In 1843, Strang moved his family west to Burlington, Wisconsin. In a new place he began to think about the dreams he'd had as a child and about the religious movements that had been so plentiful in the region where he'd grown up. He was seeking something that would make his life complete, and that was how he discovered the Mormons. Eventually Strang met Joseph Smith, who was so impressed by his fellow dreamer from the Burned-Over District that he baptized him into the Latter-Day Saints personally and conferred the status of church elder on his. Strang's meeting with Smith changed his life.

He moved to Ohio to be close to Smith and then followed him to Missouri and Illinois. He was with him in Nauvoo during the turbulent times that preceded the Prophet's death. Just before the murder Strang had been dispatched to Wisconsin to establish a Mormon stake called Voree, the Garden of Peace. (The Mormon Church is split up into stakes, and stakes are split up into congregations called wards.) Smith's murder occurred less than a week after Strang had left Illinois. In the days that followed chaos ruled the Mormon Church as several men claimed the right of leadership including Brigham Young, Sidney Rigdon, and James Strang.

A power struggle followed and Young eventually led most of Smith's followers to Utah, while Rigdon took his people to Pennsylvania. As a newcomer to the faith Strang did not have the name recognition that was enjoyed by his rivals and so he faced a difficult battle in his quest to be recognized as the heir to Smith's office. Strang was eventually excommunicated by the official church, even though he insisted that he did not receive a fair trial. Besides, he complained, the men of Brigham Young's group had no right to sit in judgment of him because he was the lawful president of the church.

To back his claim, Strang produced a "Letter of Appointment" allegedly from Smith, carrying a Nauvoo postmark and dated June 18, 1844. He further claimed that an angel had appointed him as Smith's successor at the time of the Prophet's. Although the postmark on the letter appeared genuine, many claimed that Smith's signature on the third page was a forgery. Others ignored the criticisms and accepted Strang's claims – at first, anyway. His claim seemed so strong that some of the early adherents to his faction of the church included many of Smith's family members.

Around 12,000 Mormons ultimately accepted Strang's leadership. However, not all of them followed him to Beaver Island in Lake Michigan, where Strang went in 1848. Most of his initial followers left Strang's church before its demise. Many of them accused Strang of dictatorial tendencies and creating a hierarchy of secret orders, which – although most didn't know it – had been Joseph Smith's plan for the future of the church.

Most defections, however, were due to Strang's seemingly abrupt reversal about polygamy. Vehemently opposed to the practice at first, Strang reversed course in 1849 to become one of its strongest advocates, marrying five wives and fathering 14 children. Strang's first wife was Mary Perce, whom he had married in 1836. They were separated in 1851, though they remained legally married until Strang's death. His second wife was 19-year-old Elvira Eliza Field, who he married before publicly announcing his reversal on polygamy. To hide her identity, he dressed the buxom young woman in men's clothing and introduced her as "Charlie Douglas," his nephew and secretary. Strang's third wife was 31-year-old Betsy McNutt, whom he married in 1852. His fourth was 19-year-old Sarah Adelia Wright, whom he married in July 1855. Strang's last wife was 18-year-old Phoebe Wright, cousin to Sarah. Strang married her in October 1855, less than one year before his murder.

The reader may have noticed that the ages of most of his additional wives make them teenagers. I'm not convinced that his desire to marry them had anything to do with a "divine principle."

Like Joseph Smith, Strang claimed to have numerous visions, and he also unearthed his own divinely created tablets. He found his ancient tablets in Wisconsin where he planned to create his new Zion on a hill. When he took a group of his elders to witness the excavation, they uncovered a blue clay box that contained three copper tablets. The tablets bore mysterious markings that only Strang could decipher. Strang published his translation of these plates as the "Voree Record," purporting to be the last testament of one "Rajah Manchou of Vorito," who had lived in the area centuries earlier and wished to leave a brief statement for posterity. The Voree Plates conveniently disappeared around 1900 and have never been found. They did serve their purpose, however, buoyed by this discovery the group baptized many new converts and settled the area.

Strang received several other revelations, which, while never formally added to his church's official doctrines, were accepted as scripture by his followers. These concerned, among other things, the building of a temple in Voree, the standing of Sidney Rigdon and Brigham Young, and an invitation for Joseph Smith III, eldest son of Joseph Smith, Jr., to take a position as a counselor in Strang's First Presidency.

"Young Joseph" never accepted this calling and refused to have anything to do with Strang's organization.

Some of Strang's teachings were much different from those of other Latter-Day Saint leaders, including Joseph Smith. For instance, Strang rejected the traditional Christian doctrines of the Virgin Birth of Jesus, as well as the Mormon doctrine of "plurality of gods." He believed there was only one God and that Jesus Christ was the natural-born son of Mary and Joseph, who was chosen to be the savior of mankind, but who had to be born as an ordinary mortal of human parents to fulfill his destiny. Also, Strang denied that God could do all things. He also introduced animal sacrifice – not as an atonement for sin, but as a part of the church's celebration rituals. Alcohol, tobacco, coffee, and tea were prohibited, as in most Latter-Day Saint factions, and polygamy was widely practiced. Also, unlike Brigham Young's branch of the church, he allowed women to join the priesthood and even welcomed African Americans into the church.

In time Strang moved his flock to remote Beaver Island on northern Lake Michigan. It was here that he began to claim that he was supposed to occupy the office of king, according to the teachings of Joseph Smith. Strang was accordingly crowned in 1850 by his counselor and prime minister, an actor named George J. Adams. About 300 people witnessed his coronation for which he wore a bright red flannel robe topped by a white collar with black speckles. His tin crown was described in one account as "a shiny metal ring with a cluster of glass stars in the front." Strang also sported a breastplate and carried a wooden scepter.

The common fishing folks who lived on the island didn't appreciate the Mormon invasion and did everything they could to discourage them from staying. Strang's followers were often beaten and threatened and some of their homes were robbed. On July 4, 1850 a drunken mob of fishermen vowed to kill the Mormons or drive them out. They were only slowed down by Strange firing a cannon over the heads. Competition for business and jobs added to tensions on the island, as did the increasing Mormon monopoly on local government.

As a result of the "coronation," together with lurid tales spread by George Adams – who had been excommunicated by Strang a few months after the ceremony – Strang was accused of treason, counterfeiting, trespass on government land, and theft, among other crimes. He was brought to trial in Detroit, Michigan after President Millard Fillmore ordered U.S. District Attorney George Bates to investigate the rumors about Strang and his colony. Strang successfully defended himself, which won him a lot of favorable press and helped him to run for – and win – a seat in the Michigan state legislature. During the 1853 legislative session, Strang introduced 10 bills, five of which passed. He was reelected in 1855 and helped to organize the upper portion of Michigan's Lower Peninsula into counties and townships. He also fought hard against the illegal practice of trading liquor to local Native American tribes, which made him a lot of enemies on Beaver and nearby Mackinac Island among those who profited from the illicit liquor trade.

Strang made a lot of enemies within his own people, too. One of them, Thomas Bedford, had been flogged for adultery on Strang's orders and had a lot of resentment against the "king." Another, Dr. H.D. McCulloch, had been excommunicated for drunkenness and other alleged misdeeds after previously enjoying Strang's favor and several high offices in local government. These two men began conspiring against Strang with Alexander Wentworth and Dr. J. Atkyn, who had allegedly tried to blackmail some of Strang's closest followers into paying some of their bad debts. A "royal" decree that all women were required to wear bloomers only added fuel to the fire for Bedford and the others. They obtained pistols and spent several days at target practice while finalizing the details of their plans.

Although Strang apparently knew that someone was planning to kill him, he never took any of the threats seriously. He refused to employ a bodyguard or to carry a firearm or any other weapon with which to protect himself.

Around 7:00 p.m., on Monday, June 16, 1856, Strang was ambushed by Wentworth and Bedford on the dock at the harbor of St. James, the largest city on Beaver Island. Strang was hit three times: one bullet grazed his head, another lodged in his cheek, and a third in his spine. One of the assassins then beat him with a pistol before the two men ducked on board a nearby ship, *U.S.S. Michigan*, where they claimed sanctuary. Some accused Captain McBlair of the *Michigan* of complicity in, or at least knowledge of, the murder, but no hard evidence of this was ever discovered.

The "king" languished for several weeks, long enough for two of his wives – four of them were pregnant – to get him off the island and return him to Voree. He died on July 9, 1856, at the age of 43. After refusing to deliver Bedford and Wentworth to the local sheriff, Captain McBlair transported them to Mackinac Island, where they were tried, fined $1.25, and then released.

While Strang lingered on his deathbed in Voree his enemies in Michigan were determined to remove his followers from Beaver Island. On July 5, 1856, four days before Strang finally died, a mob of Gentiles forcibly evicted every Mormon from the island. Strang's 2,600 subjects on the island were herded onto hastily-commandeered steamers – after being robbed of their money and other personal possessions – and unceremoniously dumped onto docks along the shores of Lake Michigan. A few moved back to Voree while the rest scattered across the country.

Strang never appointed a successor. He told his people to care for their families as best they could and await divine intervention from an angel that was supposed to appear. Lorenzo Dow Hickey, the last of Strang's apostles, emerged as an ad-hoc leader until his death in 1900, followed by Wingfield W. Watson, a high priest in the organization. He died in 1922. Left without the prophet to guide them most of Strang's members (including all his wives) left his church within a year after his murder. Most of them later joined the Reorganized Church of Jesus Christ of Latter-Day Saints, which was established in 1860.

A few of Strang's followers—the "Strangites" as they are called, numbering between 50 and 300 people – still hang on today, attempting to carry on his tradition as best they can.

The Kirtland Cult

James Strang was not the only follower of Joseph Smith who went his own way after the death of the Prophet in Nauvoo. One of the splinter sects that chose not to

Jeffrey Lundgren

follow Brigham Young became the Reorganized Church of Jesus Christ of the Latter-Day Saints and remained behind in Missouri. Most Mormons believed that Brigham Young was the Prophet chosen to lead them to Zion, but the RLDS believed that the Prophet was still to come.

Jeffrey Lundgren was born into the RLDS, and his name would become a great source of shame for the otherwise faithful members of the sect. He is, as far as I know, the only Mormon to ever be executed by lethal injection.

But there is no question that he deserved it.

Jeffrey Lundgren was born on May 3, 1950, in Independence, Missouri, the son of Don Lundgren, an RLDS elder and ex-Navy man. Neither he nor his wife, Lois, were interested in children. In fact, Lundgren later alleged that he was severely abused by his father and his mother did nothing to stop it. He grew up into a moody loner with few friends but an affinity for hunting and guns.

Lundgren enrolled at Central Missouri State University and spent time at a house that had been built for RLDS youth. While there he became friends with Alice Keeler and Keith Johnson. Alice, who had also been abused by her father, grew close with Lundgren, and they began dating. A deeply religious girl, she was thrilled when an RLDS prophet at her church prophesied that she would marry a man who would "do much good unto the children of man" and "bring forth a marvelous work and wonder." She became pregnant by Lundgren in 1969 and they were married the following year. Their first child, a boy, was born on December 2, 1970.

Faced with the draft, Lundgren joined the Navy. His ship was involved in action in Vietnam, coming under fire several times, but it was never hot. Lundgren believed that God had saved his life for some special purpose, and he immersed himself even deeper into the Mormon scriptures.

By 1974, Alice was pregnant for the second time, and Lundgren was honorably discharged from the Navy. After his second son was born the family settled in San Diego for a short time. Facing financial problems, though, they returned to Missouri. They would eventually have four children, but their marriage was a very troubled one. People close to the couple later claimed that Lundgren was always frustrated by the family's money problems. He rarely had a job and they were always in debt. They survived on the generosity of their parents and friends, and when that failed Lundgren wrote bad checks. His interest in the scriptures was matched only by his obsession with pornography. He forced some extreme sexual practices on Alice, who always went along because she believed what the church taught her – that men were the masters over women.

Lundgren could also be abusive, and according to hospital records, Alice was once hospitalized for a ruptured spleen which may have been caused by Lundgren pushing her into a closet door handle.

No matter what was happening at home Lundgren always wore another face as an elder in the RLDS church. He impressed many with his knowledge of the scriptures, but his interpretations were from the perspective of a rigid fundamentalist which was at odds with the liberalism that was then part of the RLDS. For a short period, he taught a Sunday scripture class, until his views became so unorthodox that the church ended it. After that he held classes in his home. Among the regular attendees were two couples, Dennis and Tonya Patrick who were old friends from the university, and Dennis and Cheryl Avery. The Averys were a backward, socially awkward pair, devoted to the RLDS but dismayed by the recent liberal reforms, especially the 1984 decision to allow women priests. Lundgren thought Avery was a weakling who let his wife push him around. He mocked them behind their backs, but so desperate for followers he encouraged them to keep coming back to hear his teachings.

The Kirtland Temple in Ohio

Then Lundgren received a revelation from God telling him to go to Kirtland, Ohio, where Joseph Smith had built his first Temple and gathered a sizable number of followers. As luck would have it a job opened for a tour guide at the Temple and Lundgren successfully applied for it. It was unpaid work, but a rent-free house came with it, so Lundgren gathered his family – and as many of his followers that would go with him – and moved to Kirtland.

Lundgren became an enthusiastic guide at the Kirtland Temple. The ornate interior of the building was packed with obscure symbolism, and he eagerly learned to interpret it – in his own special way. He was also put in charge of adding up the donations left at the Temple by visitors. Oddly, even though the number of people taking tours was on the rise, the temple's income began to drop.

It was during this time that Lundgren began to teach the radical concept of "dividing the word," – known as "chiastic interpretation" or "chiasmus" – to interpret scriptures. Lundgren claimed to have created chiastic interpretation – he didn't, but he did take it to the extreme. The idea behind it involved looking for repetitions. He became convinced that God always spoke using repetitions, and if that was not immediately apparent to the reader, that was because only God – or one of his prophets – could understand them. Of course, if Lundgren didn't find repetitions in a passage of scripture, that meant that it was not the direct word of God and could be ignored. What he really did was take someone else's idea and turn it into a foolproof system of interpreting scripture in any way that he liked.

Lundgren also began claiming new revelations on an almost daily basis. One night he raced home to tell Alice that he had seen a vision of Joseph Smith himself in the Temple. The Mormon founder had smiled at him – a smile of relief – because Smith had finally found the right person to carry on his work. Alice was always thrilled to hear about such visions, often more desperate for Lundgren to be a prophet than he was. If she was doing God's work by supporting her husband then perhaps that could justify the horrible life that she was trapped in.

Lundgren also began teaching scripture classes again and became a hero to Kirtland's fundamentalists, while also becoming involved in an ongoing battle with the RLDS local president, Dale Luffman, a liberal. His teaching of scriptural interpretations attracted followers. Some of them knew Lundgren from Missouri, while others were attracted to him after being exposed to his teachings in Ohio. Among them were Kevin Currie, Richard Brand, Greg Winship, Sharon Bluntschly, Daniel Kraft, Debbie Olivarez, Ronald and Susan Luff, Dennis and Tonya Patrick, and Dennis and Cheryl Avery. Lundgren still despised the Averys, but after hearing that Dennis had inherited some money, he persuaded them to move to Ohio with him. There were other followers, too, but their names were never made public during the criminal investigation that was still to come.

Lundgren's skimming off the Temple income was eventually noticed by church administrators – it was later estimated that he'd skimmed about $20,000 – and he was forced to resign. Of course, he told his followers that he had been forced out by his beliefs and proposed that they start a commune.

In 1987, Lundgren rented a two-story, five-bedroom farmhouse and barn on 15 acres of land that had once been an apple orchard. Most of his followers moved to the farm, while some of the couples maintained their own homes nearby. They all turned over their incomes to Lundgren, or to "Dad" and "Mom," as Jeffrey and Alice liked to be called.

While living at the farmhouse Lundgren's teachings continued and he began to practice methods of "mind control." For example, cult members were not allowed to talk amongst themselves. If they did it was a sin that Lundgren called "murmuring." He also eavesdropped on his followers and then repeated their conversations, causing them to believe that he could read their minds.

Deep down Lundgren was a bitter, insecure man. He brooded over the fact that he had lost his job as a temple guide. Reading over a passage that had been written by Joseph Smith, Jr. he realized that God had given him an order. He and his followers

The farm that Lundgren rented for his family and followers, where they began making plans to "cleanse Kirtland of its wickedness"

were supposed to take over the Kirtland Temple – by force – and cleanse it of its wickedness.

Lundgren had already been buying food, guns, and ammunition in preparation for Armageddon and the return of Christ, so it was easy to switch gears and start planning for the raid. Beginning in January 1988 he began hammering his followers with the most violent passages from the Bible and from Mormon writings, and he made them watch films like *Apocalypse Now* and *First Blood*. They trained with weapons, and Lundgren built a model of the Temple and surrounding buildings for them to study. His revelation told him that everyone within a one-block radius of the Temple was to be killed. He also planned to kidnap Dale Luffman, his wife, and his three children and bring them into the Temple, where Lundgren would behead them. Two days later, he explained, a mountain would rise from the ground beneath the Temple, an earthquake would destroy the rest of Kirtland and Christ would appear.

One problem, though – well, obviously there's more than one problem here, but you understand what I mean – God told Lundgren that the raid was supposed to take place on May 1, but he didn't tell him what year it was supposed to happen.

As planning and training continued, a woman who lived near the farmhouse called the police on April 23, 1988 and told them that she suspected that a cult was living next door. Apparently, one of Lundgren's sons had told her children that on May 1 the earth was going to open up and demons were going to be let loose on the world. The police officer who took the call laughed and said he'd look into it. He never did.

Lundgren had made it clear to his followers that not all of them would survive the raid. Kevin Currie, whose spirituality was doubted by Lundgren, learned that he was on the shortlist to die. Wisely, he decided to run. But before he did, he called the nearest FBI office and told the agent who took the call about the sect's plan to take over the Temple and commit mass murder.

The agent didn't believe a word he said.

So, Currie made one more call – this time to the Kirtland Chief of Police Dennis Yarborough. Here, he found a more receptive audience. Yarborough knew enough about Lundgren to take the warning seriously. With May 1 quickly approaching, he contacted Lundgren and asked him to stop by the station. When Lundgren came in Yarborough didn't mention the Temple but said that people had seen military training and heard gunfire at the farm. Lundgren said that he didn't know anything about it but would keep an eye out. He was clearly rattled when he left.

Lundgren didn't return to the farm right away. Instead he went to a mountain – really, more of a hill – where he often talked to God. He wanted to know if the raid was supposed to take place in a few days. When he returned to the farm he seemed angry. He told them that the raid had been called off because of the sinfulness of his followers. He never mentioned his conversation with the police.

Now, he explained, God had told him that they would not have to take over the Temple after all. Instead, killing many wicked people in a "blood atonement" sacrifice would endow him with the necessary power to take them all to see God.

He just needed to look through the scriptures and see who the victims should be.

Chief Yarborough and his men staked out the farm during the first few nights in May, but, of course, nothing happened. He continued to monitor Lundgren's sect throughout the summer, though.

Then in September 1988, a woman named Shar Olsen also defected from the group. Yarborough interviewed her and found that her story matched the one told by Kevin Currie in the spring. The chief put his new informant in contact with the ATF and with the FBI, who were now ready to believe the story. They began a domestic terrorism investigation of Lundgren's cult.

Dale Luffman also spoke to Shar Olsen and learned of the plans to take over the Temple and to behead him. He had Lundgren excommunicated from the RLDS and delivered the excommunication notice himself on October 10, 1988. After Luffman left, there was a thunderstorm and when the sun returned a large rainbow appeared east of town. Lundgren told his followers that the rainbow signified the opening of the first of the "Seven Seals" that, according to the Book of Revelation, must be opened before Christ can return. He told the others that the human sacrifice would open the second seal. When that had been completed, they would journey into the wilderness where he would learn how to open the remaining seals.

Further study of the scriptures revealed to Lundgren that the wicked people that he was supposed to sacrifice needed to come from his "own house." The slaughter would be a "pruning of the vineyard" that would allow the rest of the crop to thrive.

He chose the Averys to die.

On April 10, 1989 Lundgren ordered two of his followers to dig a pit in the barn in anticipation of buying the Averys' bodies there. The entire family needed to die – Dennis and Cheryl, along with their three children.

On April 17, a small group of followers, including the Averys, were invited to dinner at the farmhouse. After dinner Alice took her three youngest children shopping in preparation for their wilderness journey. Lundgren called Ron Luff, Richard Brand, Danny Kraft, Greg Winship, and Damon – his oldest son, into his bedroom. Dennis Avery was not invited to the meeting. He questioned each of them as to their purpose in what they were about to do. All the men assured Lundgren they were prepared to make the sacrifice.

Ron Luff, who had become Lundgren's second-in-command, told Dennis Avery that the Prophet wanted to see him in the barn. When Dennis entered Luff pulled a stun gun from his pocket and jabbed Avery with it. He fought back, but Luff overpowered him. Wrapping duct tape around his hands, feet, and mouth, Luff dragged Avery to the pit at the back of the barn. Greg

The pit in the barn where the bodies of the Avery family were buried – and found by the police

Winship was outside, and he started a chainsaw that would mask the sound of gunfire. Avery was shoved into the pit and Lundgren stood over him with a .45 pistol in his hand. He shot him twice in the back, killing him almost instantly. When he lowered the weapon, he called the other men over to "Come and see what death is."

Luff brought Cheryl Avery to the barn next. He told her that her husband needed help. She was gagged and taped up and shot three times, twice in the breasts and once in the abdomen. Their 15-year-old daughter, Trina, was shot twice in the head. The first shot entered but ricocheted off of her skull, missing her brain, but the second killed her instantly. Luff gave Karen Avery, age 6, a piggyback ride into the barn, where she was shot in the chest and the head. Rebecca, lured in by the prospect of seeing horses, was the only one to put up a struggle. She was quickly subdued and shot twice.

As Lundgren killed each of them, he experimented with different guns and bullets. He even shot them in different places – like with Karen, who he shot through the top of her skull. God had told him through the scriptures that he would have to kill again. He wanted to be good at it.

The bodies of the Averys were sprinkled with lime, the pit was filled in, and the area was covered with rubbish and debris to hide the freshly turned earth.

On April 18, 1989, the day after the murders, police officers, accompanied by FBI agents, coincidentally came to Lundgren's farm to talk to him. They questioned everyone and Lundgren showed them some of their legally purchased guns. The authorities had come without a search warrant and couldn't find anything illegal. They left, frustrated, planning to return.

As soon as the police and FBI left Lundgren's followers began to pack for their trip into the wilderness. Lundgren was shaken and paranoid about the visit and they left quickly. They left Ohio and moved south into West Virginia. A few days later they gathered in an isolated valley in the Appalachians where they set up camp. They now numbered 24 men, women, and children, including Lundgren's old college friend, Keith Johnson, and his wife, Kathy. They had joined the sect a month before – just in time for Keith to help dig the pit in the barn.

While his followers waited in their tents Lundgren climbed another mountain – an actual mountain, this time – and came back with exciting news. God was pleased with their sacrifice and he had bestowed a new title on him – "The God of the Whole Earth." Lundgren was also, he told them, now immortal.

The only member of the sect who seemed to be bothered by the slaughters of the Averys was Dennis Patrick, who fell into a deep depression. Lundgren became infuriated with him, accusing him of refusing to accept God's laws. He threatened to kill Dennis but then changed his mind. Dennis would be spared, he said, but his wife, Tonya, and his daughter, Molly, had to move into Lundgren's tent and become his spiritual wives. Alice objected to the idea, but she was told that God had been clear about what Lundgren had to do. As usual, Alice relented.

But Lundgren got tired of Tonya almost immediately. He accused her of sinfulness. In fact, he said, the sinfulness of the women in the group was the main problem they faced. But he knew how to fix this problem, too. All of the women could relinquish their sins by stripping off their clothes and dancing for him. While they did this, he would masturbate and finish by ejaculating into their panties. As far as God was concerned, Lundgren said, semen was the same as blood, so it would be the equivalent of Christ shedding his blood on the cross.

Over the next two days the women all stripped for him in his tent, dancing to tapes of his favorite songs, while Alice sat next to him. Having seen them all perform and, of course, removed all their sins, Lundgren decided that he was mistaken about Tonya being his wife. He chose another woman instead – a woman that Alice disliked. She left the cult and fled to the home of her parents. But Alice being Alice, she soon returned and put up with Jeffrey's other wives.

The group was now coming apart. Richard Brand and Greg Winship left. The arrival of winter forced the remaining members to abandon the woods and move into a barn that was owned by Ron Luff's brother, Rick. When Rick found out that Lundgren was a polygamist, he ordered him to leave. Lundgren didn't care. He had become disillusioned with those who were left. He and his family moved to California, leaving the rest of his followers behind in West Virginia.

With Lundgren gone the others scattered. One by one they lost faith in him as their Prophet. They knew they were all guilty of the murders but knew that if they didn't say something Lundgren would surely kill again.

Keith Johnson was the first to break ranks. On January 3, 1990 he led police back to the long-abandoned farm where the bodies of the Avery family were exhumed. With their faces plastered on newspapers and on televisions screens, the Lundgrens became fugitives. The police began trying to track the cult members and the FBI joined the hunt. Eventually, Lundgren's abandoned followers were found back east. Thirteen of them were arrested in early 1990 and they helped the police track down Lundgren. He and Alice were arrested in San Diego a short time later.

Alice, who was tried first, used "battered wife syndrome" as a defense. She said she didn't know that the Averys were going to be killed. Alice was certainly abused, but the jury didn't believe that she had no knowledge of what was happening within the sect. She was found guilty of conspiring to commit aggravated murder and sentenced to five life sentences – 150 years – in prison.

Damon Lundgren was sentenced to 120 years. Ronald Luff, the key planner of the murders with Lundgren, was sentenced to 170 years to life. Daniel Kraft was sentenced to 50 years to life. Five of the cult members were released in 2010 or early 2011 after roughly 20 years behind bars. In their original plea agreements, it was said that the five were to be eligible for release "at the earliest possible time," but the Ohio State Parole Board repeatedly denied earlier requests for parole by Richard Brand and Greg Winship, as well as Sharon Bluntschly, Debbie Olivarez, and Susan Luff. Lundgren followers Kathryn Johnson, Tonya Patrick, and Dennis Patrick were determined not to have been involved in the murders and each received a one-year sentence for obstruction of justice. Dennis and Tonya's sentences were suspended.

At his trial Jeffrey Lundgren addressed the jury for five hours before his sentencing. He went through the scriptures and defended all his actions. He explained, "Prophets have been asked by the Lord to go forth and kill since the beginning of time." He hadn't done anything wrong.

The jury sentenced him to death.

Lundgren spent his years on death row studying the scriptures and launching various appeals. On October 17, 2006, a stay of execution was granted after he claimed that because he had become so obese in prison death by lethal injection would be cruel and unusual punishment. It was rejected by the appeals court and an order was issued allowing the execution to go forward. The U.S. Supreme Court refused a last-minute request to stop his execution and Ohio Governor Bob Taft denied clemency.

And God didn't step in to save him.

Jeffrey Lundgren's story was finally over. On October 24, 2006, he was executed at the Southern Ohio Correctional Facility in Lucasville.

"How Many is Too Many?"

When I was living in Utah operating a rare and used bookstore for a while, I often got calls from people to come out to their homes to appraise their collection or, more commonly, to buy up book collections after the owners had died. One afternoon, I got a call from the wife of a book collector who lived in Provo. Her husband had passed away and she asked if I would be interested in possibly purchasing his books. I went to their home, located in an average neighborhood in town, and knocked on the front door.

It was opened by a middle-aged woman and I explained who I was and said that I had spoken to her on the telephone. "Oh, that wasn't me," she said, "but I knew you were coming. Come on inside. My husband had a lot of books."

I followed her into the house and down to the basement where the book collection was stored. A few moments later, I was joined by another woman. "Hello," she said and introduced herself. "I'm the one who spoke to you on the phone. Please take a look around. As you can see, my husband had a lot of books."

Wait a minute, I thought to myself, I thought he was *her* husband. Just how many of you are there?

As it turned out, there were three – three wives, eight children between all of them, and one husband.

This was 30 years ago, and I didn't know much about polygamy back then, although only because I hadn't lived in Utah for long when I met this family. As I would soon discover, polygamists are not as rare as many in Utah would like you to believe. Many of them are hiding, just like this family, in plain sight. They didn't dress in prairie clothing, like the compound wives on *Big Love*, or do anything else to draw attention to their lives.

Plural marriage didn't vanish when Utah became a state – it just went another direction.

When is a Mormon not really a Mormon? It's when that Mormon is a Fundamentalist Mormon. Or least that's what members of the Church of Jesus Christ of the Latter-Day Saints will tell you. There are dozens of breakaway groups – in Utah and elsewhere that, like James Strang of the Michigan kingdom – who trace their bloodline back to the religion founded by Joseph Smith. Members of the official LDS church are quick to say that these splinter movements are not *real* Mormons, but Fundamentalist Mormons will reply that they are the *only* real Mormons.

What a mess.

Even without all the Fundamentalist offshoots, Mormons remain controversial. Simply put, they're a cult with sacred underwear, baptisms for the dead, and their belief that they can become kings, queens, and gods in the afterlife. A Mormon marriage isn't merely "from death do us part." Couples are sealed in the Temple and they're stuck with each other in an everlasting covenant known as an "eternal marriage." These sealings can even be performed posthumously between a living person and a dead spouse. In every other regard their views on marriage are conservative. They don't believe in gay marriage. All marriage "should be between a man and a woman," their rules say.

Well, they say that now. It used to be that the church allowed marriage between a man and however many women that he wanted to have as his wife.

We have already covered Joseph Smith's revelations about polygamy and the alleged reluctance that Brigham Young had about making that doctrine an official one for the church. In 1853 he announced, "The only men who become Gods, even the sons of God, are those who enter into polygamy." After that it was openly taught and

The typical Fundamentalist Mormon dress code for women

practiced, although still troubling for some. Many early Mormons were unwilling to enter into plural marriages, but, well, since God told them do, they decided they'd better do it.

But God would turn out to be as uncertain about plural marriage as some of them were. He told Joseph Smith and Brigham Young that polygamy was a condition for entry into heaven. He reaffirmed that decision in a revelation to the third Mormon President John Taylor in 1866. It was an "everlasting law," he said, that he would never revoke. Even so, it seems God couldn't make up his mind. He started issuing conflicting revelations to different people. At this time polygamy was a felony in the United States, and hundreds of polygamists were arrested for violating the law. Others went underground, determined to keep marrying multiple women because God wanted them to do so.

Right?

Well, not so fast. At just the time when Utah was being considered for statehood, Wilford Woodruff receiving the conveniently timed revelation that polygamy was now immoral, and he issued the "1890 Manifesto" to announce the change. Apparently, God was now agreeing with the United States over the Mormons.

Or was he? Apparently, God told Woodruff that it would be okay to keep practicing polygamy in secret, and he said the same thing to his successors, Lorenzo Snow and Joseph F. Smith. But then he changed his mind again and told Smith that he had decided, once and for all, that the practice was no longer required to enter the Celestial Kingdom. In 1904 Smith issued the "Second Manifesto," in which the church renounced polygamy (again) and stopped performing any new plural marriages.

Maybe. Or maybe not.

God was, it seems, still undecided. He told some people that his 1904 decision was the last word, while he told others that his 1866 decision was what he really meant. The latter receivers of his revelations believed that the LDS church was bowing to political pressure, and they wanted no part of it. This led to the creation of separate factions that all seem to have a penchant for lengthy names, such as the True and Living Church of Jesus Christ of Saints of the Last Days, the Church of Jesus Christ of Latter-Day Saints and the Kingdom of God, and, of course, the now infamous Fundamentalist Church of Jesus Christ of the Latter-Day Saints. All these separate Mormon sects believe in keeping alive the traditions of the original, early church – which means they still practice polygamy.

These groups are not affiliated with the mainstream LDS church, who prefer not to call them by their mouthful of names and simply dismiss them as "polygamists." However, the LDS just can't shake the polygamy stereotype. Polygamy is strictly prohibited by mainstream Mormons and is considered a violation of the law of the land and the church. But fundamentalists still consider themselves Mormons who practice plural marriage. They don't believe they are a new church – they think the mainstream church is "out of order" about polygamy and hope it will rediscover the true path someday.

The LDS church has about 14 million members worldwide. Some sources say that there about 30,000-60,000 Fundamentalist Mormons in North America and Mexico. There is no central authority because so many smaller groups split off the mainstream church. Many of those sects have since become defunct. Others are very small, with 100 members or less, while others – like the Apostolic United Brethren and the Fundamentalist Church of Jesus Christ of the Latter-Day Saints – have managed to thrive.

Besides polygamy, fundamentalist Mormons have other controversial traditions. They segregate themselves from the public and live in closed communities and compounds in remote towns. The FLDS, the largest sect, established compounds in Texas, Missouri, Montana, Colorado, Arizona, South Dakota, and Utah. In order to purchase large parcels of land without causing suspicion, they often claimed that the property would be used for a "hunting retreat." In most cases, though, to sell property in such isolated areas, the realtors didn't ask too many questions.

The FLDS built a sizable treasury – usually estimated at over $100 million – called the United Effort Plan, which was funded by tithing. This adhered to another early Mormon doctrine called the United Order, which was meant to create a community bank, although, in reality, the leaders always controlled the money.

Fundamentalist families live in large houses or in multiple, interconnected homes or trailers, but they don't own the land on which they are built. All property is owned by the church and followers must remain in good standing to keep their homes. Those who are excommunicated – labeled as "Apostates" – are evicted from the property. In some cases, the FLDS owned entire towns, including the administration and police departments.

The church also, of course, runs the schools. In more conservative sects, children are homeschooled, or taken out of school after sixth grade so that they can help around the home or work in construction or farming. Young people who escaped from the FLDS were found to have inadequate educations with history rewritten in their textbooks. They were taught that the leader of their sect was also the President of the United States. Science simply isn't taught and most believe the moon landing never happened. FLDS teachers placed emphasis on religious studies and on proverbs spoken by Warren Jeffs, such as "When you disobey, there must, and always will be, punishment."

Behind the walls of their rural compounds, fundamentalists are isolated even further with a ban on television, radios, and the internet. Many have strict rules about clothing and members must dress modestly. Girls and women wear long prairie-style dresses, usually in pastel colors, while boys and men wear long-sleeved shirts and pants. No cosmetics, tattoos, or piercings are allowed. Women are not allowed to cut their hair, just like other sects mentioned previously in these pages.

Each community has a kind of church government called the Priesthood, which dictates all these rules. Members of the Priesthood, of course, receive revelations directly from God to guide their decisions, no matter how repulsive. All adult male members of the community are ordained into the Priesthood. Women are not eligible, nor are African Americans – if by some bizarre chance a black person would want to be associated with these people. African Americans are considered to be "descendants of Ham" and afflicted with the "curse of Cain," which comes from Genesis, chapter 4. Warren Jeffs once said that Cain was "cursed with black skin and he is the father of the Negro people. He has great power, can appear and disappear. He is used by the Devil, as a mortal man, to do great evils." This fundamentalist policy also excludes black people from participating in ceremonies in temples, too, which I'm sure is a huge loss to African Americans everywhere.

By the way, it should be noted that this racist doctrine originated with the mainstream LDS church, who didn't rescind the policy until 1978.

As with the mainstream Mormons, leaders of the fundamentalist communities claim to be modern-day Prophets. The Prophet talks to God, and God replies with visions and dreams. Every Prophet claims to be the "true prophet," leading to power struggles and the creation of even more splinter factions. In most sects the Prophet had complete power over the community and obedience to him is necessary for salvation. The Prophet is only accountable to God so, as far as he is concerned, he is accountable to no one on earth – church authorities, the federal government, or the law.

The "Principle" and Child Brides

Fundamentalist sects broke away from the LDS church to practice polygamy – or as they like to call is "celestial marriage" or "The Principle." Simply put, the only way that you'll make it to the Celestial Kingdom – the highest version of Mormon heaven, where you can become a god and rule over your own planet, and no, I'm not kidding – is to have multiple wives.

Many fundamentalist Mormon marriages are arranged. Some more permissive sects will allow young people to date and marry, but that's not common. Usually men and women are placed together and expected to learn to love each other. Joseph Smith had a unique way of getting women to marry him. All his proposals were divine revelations. He told a woman that he had received a message from God that they were supposed to be married and that marrying him would ensure salvation for her and her family. Usually the offer was only good for one day. It was a kind of "marry me, or else" situation.

In the 1940s, the FLDS came up with what was called a Placement Marriage. The Priesthood or the Prophet received a message from God, deciding who was married to whom. When a young man or woman was ready to marry, they would go to the leaders and ask for a spouse. Men and women were assigned to each other. There was no test for compatibility or engagement period – often they were married that same day.

And that first marriage, of course, was not the last. Men were soon approached to marry other women. Allegedly this was not for sexual gratification but for spiritual gratification. Three wives were the magical number to enter the Celestial Kingdom and this became an average number for fundamentalist men. However, it sure seems like God wants the Prophets to have a lot more wives than that. Many church leaders have boasted literal harems of women. Brigham Young had 55 wives who bore him 57 children – which was a lot of "spiritual" gratification. Warren Jeffs from the FLDS church had 79 confirmed wives, although some sources claimed he had as many as 180.

And the mention of Jeffs leads up to another big issue with the fundamentalist sects. Many of them don't wait for girls to be "ready to marry." Some of the sects force teenage girls – or younger – to marry much older men. Both Joseph Smith and Brigham Young had wives that were under the age of 20, but what is considered marriageable age to fundamentalists is viewed as statutory rape by the rest of society. When he was 54, fundamentalist Mormon Tom Green was convicted of child rape for marrying and impregnating a 13-year-old. In his late eighties, FLDS leader Rulon Jeffs married a woman who was 70 years younger. His son, Warren Jeffs, had 24 wives under the age of 17. There was such a demand for child brides that the FLDS has been suspected of trafficking young girls across the Canadian border into the United States for this kind of sexual slavery, several of whom were thought to have been married to Jeffs.

Taking on additional wives was supposed to be by consent of the wife or wives. But Joseph Smith's first wife, Emma, was opposed to the practice, so he withheld the "endowment" ceremony that would grant her eternal salvation until she gave in. Even so, Emma was never happy about Smith's philandering under the guise of marriage and he kept most of his marriages a secret from her – because, you know, God told him to. Rulon Jeff's first wife, Zola, a great-granddaughter of Brigham Young, refused to accept a second wife and she divorced him.

In some sects the husband and wife have no choice but to accept another wife. The union had been set up by God and additional wives are presented as a "blessing." Other men would simply never refuse a pretty young bride and the more wives a man has the greater his standing in the community. Most importantly, the more wives a man has, the more children he can produce. Children are very important in the mainstream LDS church and among the fundamentalists. They believe that spirit children are waiting to be born and this means that more souls can be brought into existence and set on the path to eternity. Wives are expected to bear and raise children and are encouraged to have babies once a year. In the Celestial Kingdom it is believed that wives will be perpetually pregnant to populate their husband's planet.

In a polygamist home, wives are expected to live with insecurity, jealousy, and resentment because these are negative emotions that are sent as a test from God. Sister wives compete for the attention of their husband. He has sex with his wives on a schedule, usually planned around their ovulation cycles. Many plural wives form deep bonds, though, working as a team to raise their many children and run their enormous households.

But the husband never has to worry about such petty things. He is the leader of the family, another kind of Prophet who receives divine revelations over his family. Like fundamentalist groups of every kind, Mormon communities are patriarchal societies. Women and children obey their husbands and fathers. A man has complete control over his wives, and his children and women are taught to always be subservient to men.

A key phrase that has been used on women in fundamentalist sects for decades is "Keep Sweet." It can be found on signs around their communities, in their newsletters, and cross-stitched in wall hangings in their homes. It is a mantra for women to keep their feelings under control, they swallow their emotions, to suffer in silence, and to be "immune to gloom." Women are constantly reminded of this and thanks to this constant indoctrination they become numb to the life that most of them were born into.

Modern life does not always make having multiple wives and numerous children an easy way to live. With so many mouths to feed many large families suffer terrible hardships. There are stories of polygamist wives scavenging through dumpsters to feed their children. In response, many fundamentalist communities have become welfare societies that rely on financial assistance and food stamps. They call this "bleeding the beast." Many leaders of sects, especially the FLDS, teach that the government is evil and encourage their followers to leech off the system. Legally, the first wife is the only wife, so all the sister wives are presented as single mothers. When they collect welfare and food stamps while all the money is turned over to the family's general fund – a fund that is naturally controlled by the community Priesthood.

A practice like this seems legally questionable, but fundamentalists don't care when their entire existence is on the border between legal and illegal. Polygamy is illegal in the United States, as it was when the LDS church renounced it in 1890, and again in 1904. (Although, as of this writing, the Utah legislature is considering a law that would no longer prosecute polygamists) Fundamentalist Mormons argue that ant-polygamy laws violate their religious freedoms. They can usually get around the law by claiming that other marriages are "spiritual marriages" if they don't live with their additional wives. Joseph Smith never cohabited with his additional wives – he just had sex with them. But modern fundamentalists usually do live together and that makes it bigamy. Bigamy then turns them into outlaws, but they believe that it's worth breaking the laws of men because of the glory they have waiting for them in the afterlife.

For the most part, though, the authorities tend to ignore polygamy. Individuals are occasionally prosecuted, but the police simply don't have the time and manpower to deal with such cases – unless they are accompanied by more serious crimes like underage marriage, statutory rape, child trafficking, welfare fraud, or tax evasion.

And sometimes, things are much worse than that.

The Church of the Lamb of God

Ervil LeBaron was a Fundamentalist Mormon of the purest kind: he believed in polygamy, and he believed in the vengeful God of the Old Testament. The word of the Lord was law and those that broke God's laws deserved to die.

LeBaron was quick to cite scripture to back up all his arguments, but many refused to see things his way. So, he decided that people had to die. His brother – and his rival for religious leadership – was the first casualty. Later his pregnant daughter was also slain. And even after his death in a Utah prison cell many others would be murdered on the orders of Ervil LeBaron.

After the LDS church decided to renounce polygamy for the final time in 1904, many once faithful Mormons split away from the church to continue practicing "The Principle," believing that God wanted them to do so. Among them was a devout Mormon named Dayer LeBaron who lived with his wife, Maud, and their eight children in the small town of La Verkin, Utah. Dayer and Maud were not yet polygamists, but they had been contemplating plural marriage for some time. Finally, in 1923 Maud chose a girl who was 18 years younger than her husband to be his second wife. When Dayer was threatened with arrest for bigamy, the family fled to Mexico.

Mexico had long been a refuge for polygamist Mormons, and Dayer had lived there years before when his father planned on taking a second wife. So, Dayer took his family to the same place, a Mormon community called Colonia Juarez. Shortly after they arrived in February 1925, Maud gave birth to a ninth child, Ervil.

Unfortunately for the LeBarons, the Mormons in Colonia Juarez had turned against polygamy. Other church members were forbidden from even visiting their home and their children were bullied in the streets. But the LeBarons did their best to ignore this, believing they were "true Mormons," and during the early 1940s Ervil and two of his brothers, Joel and Alma, briefly traveled as missionaries.

The LeBaron brothers believed they were destined for great things. Their grandfather, Benjamin Johnson, had been a staunch polygamist and friend of Joseph Smith. According to the family, before his death in 1905 Johnson had taken Dayer aside and revealed that Smith had bestowed upon him "authority over the earth." He passed this "authority" on to Dayer, who apparently was never inclined to use it.

His sons were different, though. The oldest, Benjamin, received revelations at an early age and believed he was the last Prophet – the "Once Mighty and Strong," that had been foretold in the scriptures. Alma and Ervin became his first followers and embraced polygamy as they were ordered to do. Benjamin's behavior became increasingly erratic and he was eventually diagnosed with schizophrenia. He spent the rest of his life in and out of mental institutions.

In 1944 Dayer moved the family to an even more isolated place in the desert, near Galeana, Chihuahua, which he called Colonia LeBaron. The family managed to scratch out a living growing fruit and were occasionally joined by polygamists from the United States who were hiding from the law.

Five of the LeBaron brothers (left to right) Ervil, Joel, Verlan, Alma, and Floren

Dayer died in 1951. Another of his sons, Joel, claimed that before he died his father laid hands on him and passed on the "authority" given to him by Benjamin Johnson. Four years later Joel started his own church – the Church of the Firstborn of the Fullness of Time – and issued a revelation calling for other fundamentalists to relocate to Colonia LeBaron, which he called the "Land of Zion."

The other LeBarons were skeptical of Joel's claims at first, but eventually they all came around. Ervil was given the title of "Patriarch" and became Joel's second-in-command.

Life was hard in Colonia LeBaron. The settlers lived in adobe huts with no electricity or running water, but by 1959 nearly 100 people were living there. Most of them came because of Joel, a deeply religious man who was beloved by his followers. He worked hard and was embraced by everyone for his quiet manner and peaceful demeanor.

Ervil, though, was exactly the opposite. He never worked in the orchards, continually quoted scripture, and was a hard man to like. He believed that his role as Patriarch entitled him to many wives. Officially he ended up with 13, but there may have been more. After he married two Mexican brides in the 1950s, he seduced Anna Mae Marston away from her husband, who was one of the original "Firstborners" of the church, which caused quite a scandal. His fourth wife was Lorna Chynoweth, who was 18. Lorna's mother, Thelma, had brought her husband and five of their children to the settlement. Lorna's younger sister, Rena, became Ervil's thirteenth wife. One of the girls that he married, Kristina Jensen, was only 14-years-old.

Ervil LeBaron as a young man, around the time he was maneuvering to take over leadership of the cult

Ervil also began arranging all the sect's marriages, despite Joel's objections that people should be free to marry whomever they wanted. But Ervil enjoyed the power this position brought him and later would use his own daughters as bargaining chips.

In time his religious views became more extreme. He created a doctrine he called "Civil Law," which basically meant the death penalty for anyone who broke what he considered God's laws. He became an obsessive writer, locking himself in a room and scribbling for days at a time, neglecting to shower or shave. Page after page he railed against the LDS church, as well as other fundamentalist groups. He wrote of enemies that should be beheaded and disemboweled and demanded to know if the men of his sect were prepared to kill for the Lord. He sometimes spoke of overthrowing the U.S. government and installing one of their people in the White House. When several people expressed their concern about Ervil to Joel he brushed their worries aside.

That turned out to be a really bad idea.

In 1964, after receiving a revelation from God, Joel began buying up beachfront property in Baja California. He wanted to create a cooperative where poor people could live and work. About 200 people later settled at a community he called Los Molinos. Ervil, who had never realized the secret desire that he had to be rich, belatedly realized the potential the land had as a resort property. He tried to start several businesses there, but all of them failed. He wanted to sell the land to developers for millions, but Joel refused, and tensions between the two brothers grew.

In October 1970 talk that Ervil planned to depose his brother began to spread and Joel finally paid attention to it. He announced that Ervil would be replaced as Patriarch by another brother, Verlan. Ervil publicly accepted the demotion but privately, he was furious.

In May 1971 he founded his own church, the Church of the Lamb of God, in San Diego. A number of the Firstborners followed him there, including his right-hand man of many years, Dan Jordan. The cold, calculating man had helped Ervil create the doctrine of "Civil Law."

In August 1971 a 28-page document called *Message to the Covenant People* was published by Ervil and Jordan. It stated that Joel had failed to recognize Ervil's authority and called that failure "an act of treason that carries the penalty of death in this world." Joel finally seemed to realize how deranged his brother was. When one of Verlan's wives asked Joel how far he believed that Ervil's followers would take this statement, Joel replied, "I will be killed."

And he was right. On August 20, Joel stopped by the home of Benjamin Zarate in Ensenada. Zarate and his family were now following Ervil, but Joel was still on good terms with them. Another Ervil follower, Gamaliel Rios, was also there, and a few minutes later, Dan Jordan arrived. Joel's son Ian, who was waiting outside, heard the sounds of a fight and then two gunshots. He ran into the house and found his father lying dead on the floor. He had bullet wounds in his head and throat.

Ervil believed that with Joel dead the Church of the Firstborn would simply become his, but most of the Firstborners backed Verlan, who became the next President. The Mexican police issued warrants for the arrest of Ervil, Dan Jordan, Gamaliel Rios, and others, but they had all fled to the United States. The FBI was alerted, but agents assigned to the case could make little sense of war among polygamists in the 1970s.

In December 1972, though, Ervil surprised everyone by walking into the Mexican police station with two attorneys and demanding that charges against him be dismissed. He was arrested and put on trial, but the case was hampered by the absence of Jordan and Rios. Ervil was found guilty, however the verdict was later overturned – probably by bribery – and he was released after just 14 months in jail for the murder of his brother.

In May 1974 Ervil printed another booklet, aimed at the Firstborners. This one was called *Hour of Crisis – Day of Vengeance* and had a hand holding a sword on the cover. Inside it threatened that all those who did not heed the word of God's messenger – who was, of course, Ervil – "would be destroyed from off the face of the earth through the outpouring of judgments and destructions."

On the night of December 26, 1974, a truck drove into Los Molinos. It was filled with men armed with handguns, shotguns, and Molotov cocktails. It was followed by a car driven by Rena Chynoweth, 16, along with three of Ervil's sons who had been promised some "fireworks."

The truck drove up to Verlan's three-story home, the largest in the settlement. Molotov cocktails were hurled, and it burst into flames. Other residents of the community came running and made frantic efforts to douse the flames. Verlan wasn't home and his family was able to get out in time. They had almost put out the fire when shots rang out. As the truck roared out of town windows were shattered and homes were pelted with firebombs. Two young Mexican boys were killed in the raid, 13 people were wounded, and seven buildings were burned to the ground.

More murders occurred, and that was when Noemi Zarate, one of the wives of Bud Chynoweth, decided that she was done with the sect and threatened to go to the police. She disappeared in January 1975 and was never seen again.

Ervil's next victim was a Mormon named Robert Simons. After suffering a nervous breakdown Simons came to believe he was a prophet with a mission to lead the Native Americans to the "Latter Days." One day a friend gave him a Lamb of God flyer to read and he decided to write to them. Soon after, Ervil and Dan Jordan turned up at Simons' ranch in Grantsville, Utah. During this and subsequent visits they tried to recruit him. Simons remained unmoved by Ervil's efforts and when Ervil began showing an interest in one of his wives, Simons wrote a letter challenging Ervil's authority. That turned out to be one step too far for Ervil, who announced that God had ordered the other man's death.

Lloyd Sullivan, a recent Lamb of God recruit, had become one of Ervil's most trusted henchmen. On April 21, 1975 he went to Simons' ranch. He had been there previously and got along well with the family. He told Simons that he'd had a falling out with Ervil and that he had spoken to some Native American leaders about Simons being their "white prophet." He wanted to arrange a meeting between them.

Simons was excited when Sullivan returned two nights later to take him to the meeting. They drove for three hours, finally arriving at a remote place in the desert that was marked with a pile of stones. Mark Chynoweth and Eddie Marston – the son of Ervil's third wife, Anna Mae – were waiting there. When Simons got out of the car Marston shot him in the back of the head. He was buried in a grave that had been dug for him earlier.

The bloodshed continued. Ervil's next victim was Dean Vest, a tall, bearded Vietnam veteran whose father had been a Firstborner. Drifting since the end of the war, Vest connected with the Lambs of God and helped plan the Los Molinos raid. His wife hated Ervil, though, and when Ervil heard that Vest agreed to leave the church he decided that a "blood atonement" killing was needed. He assigned Vonda White to the job. On June 12 Vest stopped by White's house in San Diego. He was washing his hands in the kitchen sink when she shot him twice in the back. She told the police that she had been upstairs when the shooting occurred and suggested that the Church of the Firstborn had done it.

With the Utah police asking questions about Robert Simons' disappearance, Ervin moved operations to Denver. The Lambs of God started a business refurbishing and selling old appliances. Victor Chynoweth also started an auto salvage business.

In March 1976, Ervil was spotted in Mexico by a Firstborner, who notified the police. He was arrested and charged for his involvement in the Los Molinos raid, but a judge eventually dismissed the charges. Once again, bribery was suspected.

After his release from jail Ervil and some of his followers moved to Dallas, where they started another salvage business. His teenage daughter, Rebecca, moved there with him. She had married one of the Chynoweth sons, Victor, but their relationship had turned acrimonious. Rebecca, who was pregnant with her second child and considered mentally unstable, began threatening to go to the police about the sect's many crimes.

In April 1977, Lloyd Sullivan discovered Rebecca's body in the trunk of Ervil's car. It was later claimed that Eddie Marston had strangled the young woman. She was later buried in the desert – and her body has never been found.

By this time the movement was falling apart. Selling secondhand washing machines was a far cry from taking over the Mormon Church or the U.S. government, and Ervil's followers were starting to notice. To make matters worse, Ervil had prophesied that a "momentous event" was going to occur in May 1977. Though the details were very vague it was suggested that their enemy, the Church of the Firstborn, would be destroyed. Ervil knew that something drastic had to happen if he was going to retain his status as leader.

On April 20, Ervil met with about 25 of his followers in Dallas. He told them that Rulon Allred, the leader of the polygamist set the United Apostolic Brethren, was to be killed. His assassination would be carried out by two women – his latest wife, Rena Chynoweth, and Dan Jordan's wife, Ramona, who was also Eddie Marston's sister.

Rulon Allred and the LeBarons went back many years. When Dayer had founded Colonia LeBaron in the 1940s Allred was one of the first American polygamists to seek shelter there. Later, when Joel declared himself a Prophet, the revelation he issued calling for other fundamentalists to join him had been addressed to Allred. The United Apostolic Brethren coolly decided to pass. Ervil had issued further demands to Allred and his group over the years, all of which had been ignored. By 1977 the Apostolic Brethren had 2,000 members and were fabulously wealthy compared to Ervin's struggling sect.

Rulon Allred, who became an enemy and Ervil LeBaron and his cult

Allred's murder was only the first part of the plan. Ervil was sure that his reclusive brother, Verlan – who had been wisely staying on the move in North and Central America since Joel's murder – would attend Allred's funeral. When he showed up a second Lamb of God team, led by "military leader" Don Sullivan, would kill him.

Ervil was sure this would succeed – he'd seen it in a vision, after all.

Allred was a naturopath – a type of medicine that uses natural remedies to help the body heal itself – with an office on the outskirts of Salt Lake City. On the afternoon of May 10, Rena and Ramona, both wearing disguises, entered the clinic. Allred, who had been attending to a patient, walked past them into a diagnostic room. Rena followed him in, pointed a gun, and fired seven times. Hearing the shots and Allred's screams, Melba, one of his eight wives who also worked as a secretary, ran into the room and found him on the floor, covered in blood. Rena and Ramona fled the scene. A friend of Allred's, Richard Bunker, had been in the reception area and chased after the two women, hoping to get a look at the license plates on the getaway car.

Instead, he was terrified to see them coming back inside.

There was a scuffle, and a gun was put to Bunker's head. He managed to get away and locked himself in a bathroom. Rena returned to where Allred was lying on the floor and fired one last shot at his head. She missed.

On May 14 the second assassination team – Dan Sullivan, Eddie Marston, and Jack Strothman – were in a pickup truck on the way to Allred's funeral with automatic weapons and a stockpile of ammunition when they ran into trouble. As they arrived at the venue, they didn't like what they saw. According to Ervil's "vision," the funeral was supposed to take place out in the open. Instead, it was in a high school and there were police and television camera crews all over the place. Sullivan canceled the attack.

The Lambs of God were obvious suspects in Allred's murder and the police discovered that one of the guns used in the killing had been purchased by Victor Chynoweth's wife, Nancy. She was arrested on May 22 and other arrests followed, including those of Lloyd and Don Sullivan. Lloyd, who had become disillusioned with Ervil, told detectives everything he knew. He gave them details about the murders of Noemi Zarate, Dean Vest, Rebecca LeBaron, and Robert Simons and even led them to Simons' grave in the desert.

Lloyd Sullivan testified at the preliminary hearing against Vonda White for the murder of Dean Vest but would not survive to testify at the Allred murder trial. He died of a heart attack before he could. That trial began on March 6, 1979. All the defendants were present in court, except for Ervil, who was at large in Mexico. Don Sullivan offered state's evidence in the case, but his testimony suffered from the fact that he had been part of the conspiracy to kill Verlan at Allred's funeral.

The prosecution had other problems, too. They could place all the accused in Salt Lake City at the time of the murder but had no real physical evidence to link them to it. Melba Allred and Richard Bunker were unable to identify Rena as the shooter. In the end the four defendants were acquitted. In a second trial Vonda White was sentenced to life in prison for killing Dean Vest.

In May 1979 Mexican police finally caught up to Ervil LeBaron. He was handed over the FBI and went on trial for the murder of Rulon Allred and conspiracy to murder Verlan LeBaron on May 12, 1980. Two weeks later a jury found him guilty on both counts and he was sentenced to life imprisonment.

Behind bars, after learning that many of his followers – even Dan Jordan – had deserted him, he wrote his last and most terrible manuscript, *The Book of the New Covenant*. It was a 500-page hit list of about 50 people who had opposed or betrayed him and deserved to die. It was smuggled out of prison and 20 copies were made by those still loyal to him.

On the morning of August 16, 1981 Ervil suffered a heart attack and died. Two days later, Verlan was killed when his car ran head-on into another vehicle. This was one death that could not be attributed to Ervil – or could it?

The Church of the Lamb of God blew apart after Ervil went to prison with the largest group reforming in Mexico around his oldest son, Arturo. Under his leadership the sect openly embraced the criminal enterprises that they had previously dabbled in, specifically auto theft. When Ervil's wife, Lorna Chynoweth, became disillusioned and decided to leave the church she was murdered on Arturo's orders – by her own son, Andrew.

Another of Ervil's followers, Leo Evoniuk, also claimed to have been given the authority to lead the church. After months of arguing, the men agreed to meet in 1983 to resolve their differences, but only one of them survived the meeting. Arturo was shot to death.

After Arturo's death the leadership of the church fell to another son, Heber. It soon became apparent that the sect had decided to act on the hit list that he created in prison. Heber revived the doctrine of "blood atonement" and over the next few years took revenge on anyone who had wronged them. The men believed responsible for Arturo's death were killed. Their sisters, who had once been married to Ervil, disappeared.

In 1987 the group split again. Heber took Ervil's wives and older children with him to the United States where they established a large auto-theft ring. The younger children stayed in Mexico with Heber's younger brother Aaron, son of Lorna Chynoweth. In August 1987 Aaron took the younger children to Dan Jordan's home, asking for shelter and sanctuary from the other family members. Although Jordan did not fully trust Aaron, he allowed them all to move in. Two months later Jordan took his wives and children and the LeBaron children with him on a camping trip. He was shot and killed at the campground. A week later Aaron was arrested after pulling a gun on Jordan's wives and children and telling them he had been given a revelation giving him authority over the family.

On June 27, 1988 the sect targeted three names from Ervil's list. At almost the exact same time – around 4:00 p.m. – followers killed four people in three separate locations in Texas. The dead included Ed Marston, Mark Chynoweth, and Duane Chynoweth. Duane's eight-year-old daughter, Jennifer, was collateral damage, killed when Chynoweth and the little girl were lured to an empty house in Houston.

It seemed the sect was destroyed for good a few weeks later when Heber and four of his siblings were arrested in Arizona for auto theft. Soon after Aaron and two of the others were arrested in Chicago and charged with having false identifications.

Richard LeBaron, another of the siblings who took part in the June 27 murders, pled guilty to his role and testified against his siblings. Several were convicted and others were indicted but could not be found.

Six of the younger children, aged 12–18, were placed in separate foster homes in Utah. Authorities hoped that by separating them the children could lead normal lives and this could end the cycle of violence that had been continuing for decades.

And then, on a single night in September 1989, all six of the children vanished from their foster homes. To this day, their location remains unknown.

Somewhere, somehow, the Church of the Lamb of God survives.

Prophet of Evil

For those of us who didn't grow up in Utah, it's difficult for us to believe that polygamy has always had its defenders. Even many Mormons who didn't practice it were content to let it continue. It wasn't hurting anything, they reasoned, and polygamists should be able to practice their religion in the way they see fit. Many good, decent, devout Mormons helped polygamists evade the law, hiding in their homes and helping them to flee to Mexico in the same way that abolitionists once helped escaped slaves on the Underground Railroad.

In 1953, Arizona Governor John Howard Pyle decided to take action against polygamy. Following allegations of underage marriages, the Arizona State Police raided a polygamist community in Short Creek. The entire town was taken into custody and children were taken away from their parents. After what came to be called the

"Prophet" Rulon Jeffs

Short Creek Raid, about 150 children were held as wards of the state for almost two years. Some of the children were never sent home.

At that time the public and the media saw this as religious persecution and were sympathetic toward the polygamists. The Short Creek community was eventually resettled, and the town was divided into two parts, across two different borders, always making it possible to escape arrest by "leaving the state" – you know, crossing the street. The Arizona side of town was renamed Colorado City, and the Utah section was called Hildale.

The publicity about the failed raid, which destroyed the governor's reputation and career, made the authorities reluctant to interfere in cases of polygamy for decades. That didn't change until very recently – and because of something else that was created by the Short Creek Raid.

The polygamists that created the two communities along the Arizona and Utah borders were the forerunners to the Fundamentalist Church of Jesus Christ of the Latter-Day Saints, which was run by the Jeffs family.

During his leadership of the FLDS, Prophet Rulon Jeffs created a divine dictatorship when he decided to do away with the Priesthood leadership council. He didn't want anyone overseeing what he could, or could not, do. After all, God had made him the leader of the church and no man was allowed to question that. He installed the "One Man Rule," giving absolute authority to himself. He died in 2002 at the age of 92, even though he had prophesized that he would live to be 350.

I guess he was off by a year or two on that one.

His son, Warren, succeeded him as "President and Prophet, Seer and Revelator." His followers called him "Uncle Warren," and to many in the incestuous community he really *was* uncle. During his four years as the leader of the FLDS, Jeffs was a depraved tyrant. He used church doctrine – which he and his father had mostly made up – to control every aspect of his people's lives and to satisfy his very long list of sexual perversions.

In 2003, Warren Jeffs moved his followers to a "hunting retreat" compound near Eldorado, Texas. The Yearning for Zion ranch, as it was called, was started to shield them from anti-polygamy laws. In April 2008, though, an anonymous call to a domestic abuse hotline spurred a police raid of the compound. There were 469 children taken into temporary custody. The initial complaint turned out to be invalid, but the raid discovered that 60-percent of the girls – ages 14-17 – were pregnant or had already given birth.

The investigation that followed soon uncovered other crimes that were happening within the community – a horror show that should never exist in modern American society.

Just as there was only one Mormon Prophet to die by lethal injection, there is only one other to make it onto the FBI's Most Wanted list. Jeffs evaded the police for years by living on the run and staying at various "safe houses" that the FLDS had across the country. He was finally captured by the Nevada Highway Patrol at a traffic stop in Las Vegas. He was caught with $55,000 in cash, $10,000 in gift cards, 15 cell phones, four portable radios, four laptops, two GPS systems, a police scanner, and a well-read Book of Mormon.

He was arrested wearing the "Gentile" clothing that he never allowed his followers to wear and carried a range of disguises, including 12 pairs of sunglasses, wigs, and fake beards. Jeffs was wanted for forcing teenager Elissa Wall to marry her cousin and as an accomplice to rape.

But the authorities would soon find out that was only the tip of the iceberg of his crimes.

Warren Steed Jeffs was born two months premature on December 3, 1955 to father, Rulon Jeffs, and mother, Merilyn. Warren was raised outside of Salt Lake City, Utah, and for more than 20 years served as the principal of Alta Academy, an FLDS private school at the mouth of Little Cottonwood Canyon. Jeffs became principal in 1976, the year he turned 21. He was known for being "a stickler for the rules and for discipline."

Rulon became the president of the FLDS in 1986, and when he died, he was survived by 20 wives and approximately 60 children, but it was Warren who took over the church. Before his father's death Warren held the position of counselor to the church leader, but he quickly adapted to his new role. Almost immediately he told high-ranking FLDS officials, "I won't say much, but I will say this—hands off my father's wives." When addressing his father's widows, he said, "You women will live as if Father is still alive and in the next room."

But within a week he had married all but two of them. One refused to marry him and was subsequently prohibited from ever marrying again, while the other, Rebecca Wall, fled the FLDS altogether. Naomi Jessop, one of the first of Rulon's former wives to marry Warren, became his favorite wife, confidante, and accessory to his crimes.

Until courts in Utah later intervened, Jeffs' new role allowed him to control nearly all the land in Colorado City, Arizona, and Hildale, Utah – which was part of a church trust called the United Effort Plan. The land has been estimated to be worth over $100 million. All the police and town officials in both communities were members of the FLDS and essentially also under Jeffs' control.

Jeffs had nearly 10,000 followers and they went along with whatever bizarre edicts that he issued. They were not allowed to watch television, read newspapers, or use the internet. All literature was forbidden, except for the Bible and the Book of Mormon. Children were not allowed to attend public school. He banned music, dancing, playing, and children's toys. He did not allow them to eat corn and even imposed an all-bean diet. He prohibited his people from owning or wearing anything red – that was a color reserved for Jesus.

He told his followers how to dress, what to eat, where to live, and who to marry. As the Prophet he was the sole individual in the FLDS church with authority to perform marriages. He assigned wives to husbands and could discipline male church members by reassigning their wives, children, and homes to other men. During his leadership he arranged over 550 polygamist marriages. Many of them were between underage girls and older men, and often in return for favors. The more young daughters that a loyal man would give up, the more young brides he would receive as a reward.

The men that Jeffs saw as disloyal or disobedient were branded as "Apostates," and they lost their Priesthood. This often meant excommunication and exile. Their wives and children were stripped away and given to another man. The stranger to whom they were reassigned had to be referred to as "husband" and "father." All photographs of the Apostate were destroyed, and he was never to be seen or spoken to again by his family. They didn't mind, though – contact with him would prevent them from getting into the Celestial Kingdom.

Warren Jeffs with one of his many "brides"

During his leadership, Jeffs excommunicated 60 men and reassigned over 300 women and children to new families. Some of the women and children were even reassigned more than once. Thanks to this game of marital musical chairs a man named Fred Jessop collected 18 wives and 100 children, even though he was sterile.

Originally, reassignment had been practiced only after the death of a husband, but Jeffs took sick pleasure in using it as a punishment. He destroyed families for many different "crimes" like talking badly about the Prophet, living like Gentiles by watching television or listening to music, violating the dress code, viewing pornography, masturbating, having sex with a wife at times other than when she was ovulating, not having control over their children, having "immorality in your heart," or anything other reason dreamed up by the Prophet. The main reason, however, was Jeffs maintaining his power by ousting men who posed a threat to his leadership.

Jeffs with some of his wives and children — although it's hard to know which ones were the wives and which were his children

It's been suggested that Jeffs was toying with other forms of punishment for these men, as well. Former member Robert Richter later claimed that he had been working on a "secret project" in which he was asked to design a thermostat that would handle temperatures of up to 2,700 degrees. Richter believed that Jeffs was building a "blood atonement" room where sinners would have their throats cut and their bodies disposed of in a crematory created to incinerate their remains.

Jeffs wasn't only threatened by men. He was also threatened by the young boys in the community who were competing for the women. With male children being born all the time there simply weren't enough females to go around — not with men having three, four, and five wives anyway. Jeffs began expelling boys as young as 13 from the church for trivial transgressions like playing music, kissing, or even talking to a girl. Known as the "Lost Boys," they were abandoned by their families to fend for themselves without money, support, and education. Not all the boys were kicked out. There are stories about some boys being taken into the desert and shot, while others died in mysterious car accidents.

Jeffs' massive Yearning for Zion Ranch in Texas

Jeffs didn't give away all the young women – he kept many for himself. He had at least 24 wives that were under the age of 17. During the later police investigation, a photo surfaced showing a child bride in Jeffs' arms, kissing him passionately. DNA evidence revealed that Jeffs had fathered a child with this girl when she was only 15.

When it came to his crimes Jeffs was his own worst enemy. He believed that nothing he was doing was wrong. He kept "Priest's Records" of everything he did. In one he wrote that God told him to find young girls who can be "worked and easily taught." As "God's mouthpiece," he also recorded almost everything he said. In one recording he was heard graphically instructing minors about how to please him sexually. During what he called "heavenly sessions," he told these girls to "set aside all your inhibitions." A girl "needs to be excited" to satisfy him, he said, and by pleasing him they were pleasing God. God would reject them if they didn't comply with his demands.

Warren Jeffs was a very sick and twisted man.

Among the evidence that was collected was the now infamous recording of Jeffs assaulting a 12-year-old girl. A group of his young wives assisted in the crime. They bound his victim's arms and legs while Jeffs raped her.

At the Yearning for Zion ranch in Texas Jeffs built an opulent Temple. It was equipped with an altar that was later labeled the "rape bed" by the press. Ritual sex sessions were performed on the altar and recorded in front of an audience. Prayers were recited both before and after the girls were tied up and molested. It was like something out of bad exploitation movie – but it was real. During lengthy trials jurors openly wept as they listened to the disturbing recordings.

The stories that later emerged from the FLDS compounds were horrifying. One day Jerusha Jeffs, age 7, was called into Uncle Warren's office and told to sit on his lap. He told her how "special" and "beautiful" she was, and he promised to help her get into heaven, as long she didn't tell anyone what he was about to do. Then he raped her.

When Brent Jeffs was five Uncle Warren took him into the bathroom at church one Sunday morning and was ominously told that what was about to happen was between "you, me, and God." Jeffs sodomized his nephew. The abuse continued for two years, and when Brent was a teenager, he became one of the Lost Boys, along with his brothers, who Jeffs had also abused. His brothers never recovered from the abuse. One died from a drug overdose and the other committed suicide.

Jeffs grilled the children about their home lives, looking for information that he could use against their parents. He also offered demonstrations to the young boys, teaching them how females were supposed to be submissive to males. He called in one of his wives for a demonstration, grabbing her hair and twisting it until she dropped to her knees.

You could say that Jeffs' reign over his followers was mercifully short at only four years, but to many of those who endured it, it stretched on for a lifetime.

In July 2004, Brent Jeffs filed a lawsuit alleging that he had been raped by his uncle in an FLDS compound in the Salt Lake Valley in the 1980s. This was the first bad publicity, but more was coming. Jeffs was charged in Mohave County, Arizona with sexual assault on a minor and with conspiracy to commit sexual misconduct with a minor in June 2005. The charges stemmed from his arranging of a 2001 marriage between a then 14-year-old Elisa Wall and her 19-year-old first cousin. She later testified that she had begged Rulon Jeffs to let her wait until she was older or to choose another man for her. The elder Jeffs was apparently "sympathetic," but his son was not, and she was forced to go through with the marriage. Wall alleged that her husband often raped her and that she repeatedly miscarried. She eventually left him and the FLDS community.

The Arizona Attorney General's office distributed wanted posters offering $10,000 for information leading to Jeffs' arrest and conviction. In April 2006 Utah joined the pursuit, issuing an arrest warrant for Jeffs on felony charges of accomplice rape of a girl between 14- and 18-years-old. Soon after the FBI placed Jeffs on its Top Ten Most Wanted Fugitives list, offering a $60,000 reward. That reward was soon raised to $100,000.

But Jeffs stayed on the run, returning safely – with local police protection – to Colorado City to perform more marriages. All of them involved underage girls and older men.

Finally, on August 28, 2006 Jeffs was pulled over on Interstate 15 in Clark County, Nevada by a highway trooper because the temporary license plates on his 2007 Cadillac Escalade were not visible. Jeffs was taken into custody and three days later waived extradition and was sent to Utah to face two first-degree felony charges of accomplice rape. Each charge carried a penalty of five years to life in prison.

But Jeffs continued to lead his sect from jail, awaiting his trial. He was still issuing commands and expecting them to be carried out. He also seemed to be spinning out of control. At one point in court the Prophet warned of a "whirlwind of judgment" from God if he wasn't released. He made many predictions of earthquakes and storms of biblical proportions. He also prophesied that the world would end before 2013 but it was hard to take that seriously since he'd been so bad at making predictions in the past. He'd already named many incorrect dates for the Rapture and had built a garden known as the "launching pad" for his ascension to Zion that was, obviously, never used.

In jail, Jeffs' luck went from bad to worse. Arizona prosecutors were next in line to indict him, and in May and July 2007 they charged him on eight counts of sexual conduct with a minor and incest.

With Jeffs in jail there was confusion over the leadership of the church, but Jeffs kept issuing new edicts. He blamed his incarceration on his followers, claiming he was locked up because they refused to repent. He ordered couples to stop having sex, and even to stop touching each other completely. If a woman wanted to have a baby, she had to have sex with one of 15 men handpicked by Jeffs, and the act had to be witnessed by two other men on the list. Jeffs' bizarre sexual appetite continued in jail. Though he had deemed it a sin worthy of reassignment, he attempted to masturbate as many as 15 times a day, always in full view of the guards.

Jeffs suffered from several mood swings in jail. He tried to hang himself in his cell in 2007 and fasted in protest until authorities placed him in a medically induced coma. In 2009 an Arizona judge ordered that he be force-fed. He wavered back and forth between resigning and claiming that he's still the rightful Prophet. In video footage he stated, "I'm not the Prophet" and said he was the "greatest of all sinners and the wickedest man."

In Utah, Jeffs was found guilty of two counts of being an accomplice to rape. He was sentenced to prison for 10 years to life and began serving his sentence at the Utah State Prison. He was also scheduled to be tried in Arizona, but the Mohave County prosecutor was forced to dismiss all charges against him because the victims no longer wanted to testify. In the meantime, charges had also been filed against him in Texas, and he was sent there to be convicted on two counts of sexual assault of a child. He was sentenced to life in prison – and he'll be eligible for parole in July 2038.

In the summer of 2019 Jeffs allegedly suffered a mental breakdown, leaving him unfit to give a deposition in a sex abuse case against him. Forcing him to testify would be "futile," his attorneys said, adding that "there seems to be a high likelihood that Warren Jeffs is not mentally competent to provide admissible testimony."

Simply a legal stunt or Jeffs' depravity finally catching up to him?

Who knows? What we do know, however, is that FLDS members continue to consider Warren Jeffs their leader. He is the Prophet, and he speaks to God. Uncle Warren is infallible and has been wrongly convicted. Like Joseph Smith, he is a martyr to the true faith.

Even as Jeffs sits in prison, many of his wives and followers remain loyal to him, following commands issued from his cell

Why do people – especially the women -- stay in Fundamentalist Mormon sects? How can they possibly believe the rhetoric that spews forth from the mouths of often deranged and disturbed "Prophets?"

The thing to remember is that most of them didn't join the cult, they were born into it. It is a lifetime of brainwashing where the abused don't even realize they are being abused. Living behind the walls of a compound they are isolated from society, living a repressed life that is duplicated for their children. Their leaders discourage and punish free thought and critical thinking. So, for many leaving the church is not an idea that ever crosses their minds.

To leave the FLDS – and other Mormon spin-off cults – is a terrifying idea because it means abandoning everything they have ever known. Trained from birth to be obedient, they depend on their leaders to tell them what to do. Women are also bound with children. If they do escape, they will be shunned by family and friends and they are also threatened with punishments that don't end on Earth. Without money or support they don't have the education or the life skills to be on their own, even if they did dare to leave the "safe" confines of the compound. They are raised with a fear of the outside world and if they venture there, they will never reach the Celestial Kingdom.

Instead of being critical of the Fundamentalist Mormons that we might encounter we should pity them instead – or at least treat them with respect. Those who have managed to escape from the compounds encourage us to try and disprove these peoples' fears of modern society. If they are treated with dignity and respect, maybe a seed can be planted in their minds that shows them that there is a chance for them to leave and perhaps live a normal life.

"Uncle Warren" is no Prophet. He is --there's just no other way to say it – a monster.

Part 2: From the Fringes of Religious Belief

One man's cult is another man's religion.

It's a simple phrase but I suppose one that is worth remembering, no matter how you might feel about what you've read – and will read – in these pages. Some of it has, and will, strike you as strange, bizarre, incomprehensible, and even insane. We ask ourselves how seemingly rational people can give up their lives, and sometimes the lives of their children, to follow a religious leader into a chaotic world of weird rules, oddball customs, and unfathomable beliefs?

It's all about finding God, right?

That's a difficult question to answer. All new spiritual movements, whether they are offshoots of established religions or are creating new beliefs, are often treated with suspicion by mainstream society. The word "cult" was originally a term used to describe a group with a single object of worship, like the cult of the Virgin Mary, for instance. It can also be used to describe the first stage of a spiritual movement – the time when a charismatic leader gathers his followers and creates a doctrine. In this sense all religions have been considered cults at one time or another.

During the nineteenth century communities like Oneida, founded by "free love" advocate John Humphrey Noyes, were treated with suspicion by the people who lived nearby. Still, American society saw his group as a bunch of harmless eccentrics. But by the middle of the twentieth century "cult" began to become a more ominous term. Worries about new religious groups eventually became a full-blown panic in the 1970s – and with good reason, based on some of the things that were happening at the time.

So, what distinguishes a cult from a religion? It is not merely a matter of belief. As strange as the teachings of some cult leaders may seem to us there are ultimately no objective proofs that anyone's religion is the "right" one.

Again, one man's cult is another man's religion.

In the pages ahead we will look at some of America's most notorious cults – the ones that made headlines when they descended into madness, murder, and suicide.

But we must remember that these represent only a small minority of the non-mainstream religious groups that have existed in this country. For that reason, we'll also take a look at some that are so strange – and so uniquely American – that I couldn't resist the urge to include them.

Strange as these cults may seem we must remember that in almost every case people freely and willingly joined them. Yes, there has been a lot of talk about the idea of "brainwashing" over the years – in which cults use insidious methods to lure and hold onto their victims – but that idea has been dismissed more times than it's been verified. It is a comfortable idea though, to people trying to understand why their loved ones have joined a group they see as crazy. It became the justification for the controversial practice of "deprogramming," where cult members were kidnapped and held against their will until they surrendered their beliefs, but little real evidence of this exists.

You see, the often broken and troubled people who join cults aren't brainwashed – they're following a natural inclination that most of us have. Any person who joins a group and finds a place where they feel they belong will begin to take on its attributes and identify with its goals, whether it's a company, sports team, political party, or yes, even a religious movement. This is essentially a tribal instinct that we all have, and one which cult leaders exploit. In most cases the people who choose to follow them are ripe for that kind of exploitation. They are usually young, perhaps already estranged from their parents, and unhappy with their lives and with "normal" society. Cult leaders often make it easier for their followers to feel part of the group by giving them new names and forbidding them to have contact with people outside the group, including their families. The fact that the cult's ideas may seem completely bizarre to outsiders actually helps the process. Once those ideas are accepted by the followers, they create a barrier between the group and the rest of the world. It's an "us vs. them" mentality that all cult leaders know how to manipulate.

Charles Manson is a perfect example of this. We're not going to delve into Manson here. We are all very familiar with his story and how his group imploded after the brutal murders in Los Angeles in August 1969. What is more important to our purpose here is to look at how he constructed his group in the first place.

After Manson was released from prison in 1967, he eventually ended up in San Francisco playing his guitar and begging. There he met Mary Bruner, a 23-year-old librarian, moved into her apartment, and convinced her to let other girls move in, too. What later became known as his "Family" began to grow. Its members would always be predominantly female. Many of the women were estranged from their real families and Manson was skilled at using their fears and weaknesses to his advantage. He loved to break down their inhibitions, plying them with drugs and introducing them to group sex so that he could mold them into a family unit.

He often said that it was his role to "unprogram" people, to erase their egos and rid them of everything they'd learned from their parents, schools, and the government. Manson taught them that life and death were illusions, that all actions were permissible, and that the most important thing was to be self-aware and live in the "now." Fear was good because a person who is afraid is the most self-aware of all.

Anyone who questioned him too closely about his philosophies was discouraged. He liked to say, "No sense makes sense."

Manson overwhelmed troubled young people with his personality. He was older than all his followers, and he became both a source of sexual attraction and a father figure to them. He convinced them that he had supernatural powers and could read their thoughts.

Manson didn't "brainwash" his followers. He didn't have to trick them into committing murders for him – they wanted to please him. He filled the hole in their life with religion, a sense of belonging, and what he called "love."

The murders carried out by the Family in 1969 were bad enough, but the terrible end of Jim Jones and the People's Temple in 1978 firmly cemented in the public mind the image of an evil cult leader who took his deluded followers to their deaths. By the time the siege in Waco started 15 years later everyone from the public to government and law enforcement officials who watched the news coverage on television saw another Jonestown happening before their eyes. When it finally happened the fire that ended the siege and claimed the lives of some 80 men, women, and children seemed inevitable.

After the smoke cleared, though, it became clear that the story of Waco was not nearly as straightforward as the media and the FBI had made it appear – as you'll see in the pages ahead.

Since Waco there has been a lot of effort made to try and understand why people join cults and to excuse the actions of many of those who do. While this neutral approach can sometimes be helpful, it tends to ignore the often terrible, controlling, and criminal behavior on the part of some cult leaders.

Far too many of them don't deserve to have excuses made for them.

I've tried to strike a balance in this book, sticking to facts and trying hard not to judge what I'm presenting. I admit that I have often failed at that, but I have tried and will continue to do so in the pages to come.

I'd rather present the stories and let you judge for yourself.

Cyrus Teed and the Hollow Earth

He called himself "Koresh," a sort-of translation of a Hebrew name for Cyrus, the name that he was given at birth. He would eventually claim that he was the man foretold by the prophet Isaiah – the Shepherd of God who would restore Jerusalem.

Cyrus Teed became the charismatic leader of one of the strangest movements of the late nineteenth century. He was raised in the Burned-Over District of upstate New York, but his religious revelations came during the Civil War when he was fighting for the Union army. While recuperating from sunstroke that resulted in his left arm and leg being paralyzed, he dreamed of creatures that lived at the earth's core. He couldn't see how such stories could be possible unless the earth's center was hollow.

And his bizarre religion of alchemy, medicine, and science was born.

Cyrus Teed – the man who would become known as "Koresh"

Cyrus Teed was born in Trout Creek, New York in 1839. The family relocated to Utica after Cyrus was born. He came of age in the region after the fires of the Burned-Over District had, for the most part, burnt to ashes. As with many other men who would claim to be American messiahs, Cyrus never received much formal schooling. At the age of 11 he was sent to work on the Erie Canal as one of the boys who drove the oxen, mules, and horses that pulled barges along the waterway.

Child labor life along the towpath didn't allow much time for leisure, but when the barges stopped to exchange their cargo at various ports the boys had the chance to explore the bustling towns that sprang up along the canal. Even though it would later be replaced by the railroads the canal was then the region's main conduit of east-west commerce and news. Working the barges in the early 1850s would have put Cyrus in the company of spirit mediums, abolitionists, socialists, feminists, labor reformers, and temperance activists – all of whom would affect his future.

Cyrus was on his way to a respectable middle-class life when the Civil War began. After a decade on the canal he had become a medical apprentice for his uncle, Samuel, who was a doctor. He married a second cousin, Delia Rowe, and had a son named Arthur who eventually became a landscape painter of minor fame and lived most of his life in Europe. When the Union army put out the call for volunteers Cyrus, an unwavering abolitionist, was compelled to join. It was during his time in the hospital, recovering from sunstroke, that he first received the revelations that would change his life.

After his discharge from the military, Cyrus began studying at the New York Eclectic Medical College. Eclectic medicine had emerged during the middle nineteenth century, alongside mesmeric healing and water cures, that offered less invasive treatments than brutal surgeries and bloodletting by leeches. Folk remedies, including some derived from Germanic occult traditions connected to alchemy and astrology, found favor with eclectic healers. They combined them with herbal recipes and chemical compounds like lead, mercury, and arsenic.

He completed his studies in 1869, specializing in electrotherapy, the use of electrical energy as a medical treatment. He built an "electro-alchemical laboratory" next to his home and conducted experiments with batteries and metals believing that he could use the occult science of alchemy to transform lead into gold and then discover the universal cure for all disease.

During this time, he also began reading anything he could find about the mysterious realm in the center of the earth. He searched for books, newspapers, and magazine articles – likely finding the work of British astronomer Edmund Halley (of comet fame), who proposed that the earth consisted of concentric spheres placed inside of one another.

But Teed's ideas were much bigger than just a hidden world at the earth's core. While working in his laboratory late one night in the fall of 1869 Cyrus experienced what he called a "divine illumination." He claimed that one of his electrochemical reactions transformed matter into electricity and back into matter again. He reasoned that a similar transmutation could affect the regenerative processes in the human body. If the brain, as he believed, was the body's chemical battery, then it contained energies that might be used as a physical battery. When a body was destroyed by disease or violence, the battery could remove the spirit from a person's body and transfer it to another body, allowing the electricity to continue in a new form.

Cyrus also reasoned that the physical process of alchemy made it possible to regenerate the body by using the mind to interchange matter and spirit. He even had scriptural backing that proved it was possible, twisting the words of Jeremiah 31:22 to fit his purpose: "How long wilt though go about, O though backsliding daughter? For the Lord hath created a new thing in the earth, a woman shall compass a man."

With this scripture to back him up, Cyrus believed that the same law of transmutation meant that a spirit could "translate" itself into different bodies – for instance, from Enoch to Elijah to Jesus to himself. Transmutation by alchemy now offered a scientific explanation for the mysteries of reincarnation, which would soon form the basis for Teed's belief that he was the new messiah.

During this revelatory night Cyrus also claimed that he was able to remove his energy from his own body and enter a "vibratory sea," where he had a vision in which God appeared to him in the form of a beautiful woman. She revealed the secrets of the universe to him, in which modern science could be applied to the occult theories of alchemy and lead to the spiritual transformation that brings about the next golden age of human civilization.

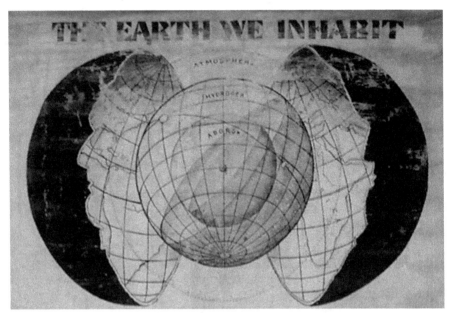

Teed's visions included the revelation that we all live inside of a "Hollow Earth," an idea that he would spend years trying to prove through science

One of the secrets revealed to him was what he called "Cellular Cosmology," the belief that the earth is practically stationary in time and space and exists as a concave sphere, with all life on its inner surface – kind of like a gigantic inverted cave. He later wrote about this controversial idea in a book called *The Cellular Cosmology or The Earth in a Concave Sphere*, which he wrote under his new name of "Koresh," the ancient Hebrew name for Cyrus.

According to Teed the known world is located on the inside of the earth's curvature, beyond which there is only the darkness of the celestial void. At the center of the sphere rotating in unison are the sun, stars, and planets. The vast, internal cavity is filled with a dense atmosphere that screens the other side of the globe. To prove this theory, Cyrus measured the curvature of the earth – a measurement that contradicted the Copernican hypothesis. He was so sure that his theory was correct that he offered $10,000 to anyone who could prove that his measurement and theories were wrong. He found plenty of people who tried, but each time scientific measurements were taken, the results were the same as Teed's – or so he claimed.

More than anything else Teed's belief in a concave earth became an article of faith, based on his religious research and study. He once wrote, "To know of the earth's concavity is to know God, while to believe in the earth's convexity is to deny Him and all His works. All that is opposed to Koreshanity is anti-Christ."

When Cyrus decided to make public his new scientific discoveries it caused the collapse of his medical practice in Utica. He didn't do much better when he moved to Binghamton in 1871, but it was there that he acquired his first loyal convert, Dr. Abiel W.K. Andrews, another doctor and Union military veteran.

Teed became a close family friend to Andrews, his wife Virginia, and son Allen. He stayed in touch with them after he left Binghamton and moved to northern Pennsylvania where he practices sporadically as a country doctor. When Delia's health took a turn for the worse, rending the itinerant prophet unable to care for her, she returned to Binghamton to live with her sister. It was Andrews who cared for Delia and diagnosed her with Pott's disease, a form of tuberculosis that eventually spread to her spine and killed her. It has been claimed that Delia was not unhappy with her husband for abandoning her, although she initially doubted his reports of a spirit who declared him the savior of the race. She later came around, stories claimed, and "fully accepted him as the messianic personality of the age, and strenuously resisted the suggestion of friends and enemies alike that Cyrus be committed to an asylum because of his extreme and radical convictions."

Did I mention those stories of Delia's acceptance came from Teed and his Koreshians? I probably should have.

Cyrus was, by this time, actively recruiting followers, preaching a stern critique of the "prostituted" Christian churches, which in his view had become the servants of oppressive capitalist institutions. He believed they would all fall into ruin, and from that carnage Teed would lead his followers in the regeneration of mankind.

Pressed to provide for his invalid wife and teenage son though, Cyrus had to make money and the medical profession was all he knew. He relocated to Sandy Creek, New York where a nearby factory and sawmill offered him a steady supply of injured workers who needed urgent treatment, no matter how strange the doctor might be.

During this time Cyrus focused on his writing – mostly about his scientific, religious theories and the hollow earth – and corresponded with Andrews and a few potential converts. He also made frequent trips back and forth to his parent's home in Moravia, New York where he formed his first communal religious society on July 24, 1877. On that date Teed and his five closest family members put their names in a document called the "Preliminary Covenant of Consociation," pledging to contribute all they possessed to furthering "God's Kingdom on Earth." Since Cyrus had no property of his own, he was flexible on the idea of communism. His father, Jesse, made sure the covenant stipulated that he had donated $50,000 to Teed's religious order and retained the right to dispose of $5,000 of its start-up capital any way that he wanted.

The commune members agreed to end bodily corruption. Cyrus believed that physical corruption was caused by carnal desires and capitalist exploitation. Since they were pooling their money together, so next, he believed, they had to commit to celibacy. He stated that regeneration would be achieved by mental will, not by procreation.

With his plans firmly in motion his next objective was to find additional converts. He established a newspaper called the *Herald of the New Covenant* that would proclaim his theories of how "true physical science is the continent of the doctrines of immortality." By November 1877, it was in print and communicating that the new prophet Elijah was preparing for the coming of the Lord. That prophet was, of course, Cyrus himself, although privately, he viewed his role as equivalent to that of Jesus Christ. His arrival was the dawn of a new age.

Despite the planning that had gone into it, the commune at Moravia never really got off the ground. Teed's parents tired of the scheme and Cyrus went back to Sandy Creek to care for accident victims from the sawmill. His flock had now fallen to just two members – Dr. Andrews and Teed's sister, Emma. They would remain staunch believers for their entire lives.

Cyrus went back to the drawing board. After discussing the situation in letters Teed and Andrews decided to propose a merger between their movement, such as it was, and the prosperous Harmony Society of Economy, Pennsylvania. The Harmony commune passed on the offer, but they did invite Cyrus and any of his associates to visit them and see the workings of the Harmony Society up close. After a study of the Harmonists, the Shakers, and the Oneida Community, Cyrus became convinced that a successful Utopian community needed a specialized industry to sustain it. Fortunately, his aging parents needed help with their mop factory and so he returned to Moravia, determined to start over again with his apostolic community. This time the commune would be organized around the fabrication of mops.

Once again, the Teed family home became the site of a communal society. This time it lasted for two years. Cyrus, Emma and her husband, their brother Oliver, and the Andrews family joined the commune. Next to enlist were members of what would become the largest demographic among Teed's followers – women attracted by what seemed to be a feasible way to leave their husbands. His goal was also to attract hard-working members and wealthy converts who, he hoped, would help sustain the others until the commune became self-sufficient.

As the commune struggled, Cyrus fine-tuned his teachings, explaining to his followers how the defects of each sex would be remedied when spiritual regenerates transformed themselves into sexually bi-gendered beings. Teed had a detailed explanation for how this would happen: energies that used to be expended in sexual intercourse could be redirected to charge the brain, which he saw as a battery. When fully charged the brain would be powerful enough to cause combustion in the pineal gland. The explosion would cause the production of male and female cells to stop completely, allowing the body to regenerate to the bisexual completion of a human.

Cyrus believed that he would be the first to "translate" from his corrupt, mortal form into an immortal body. But even a being such as himself could not do that on his own – spiritual transition was a collective endeavor. He required a group of celibates around him, directing their conserved energies to his battery rather than their own. When he achieved his immortal form, he would destroy the institutions of a capitalist society as well as the churches that supported legalized prostitution in the form of marriage. After these obstacles to regeneration were eliminated the entire human race would be brought under the rule of the New Order of celibate socialism and regenerated to bisexual immortality.

You have to admit – Cyrus Teed never thought small.

However, overthrowing capitalism with a communist mop factory proved impossible. Teed went to New York City, hoping to set up a distribution chain, but found that his mops were not in high demand.

He also discovered that the people of Moravia were not keen on tolerating the commune. The village was not inhospitable to unusual ideas – it was located in the Burned-Over District after all – but the cohabitation of married couples with runaway wives looked more than a little unseemly. So, Teed relocated again, this time to Syracuse where he set up an eclectic medical practice with his brother, Oliver. They called it the Institute for Progressive Medicine and began catering to the needs of some of the city's wealthiest patients. They specialized in "electrotherapeutic treatments for neurasthenia," a common catchall diagnosis for the psychosomatic malaise that seemed to mostly afflict the upper classes of Victorian society.

To further his reputation as a quack he also tinkered with new inventions, like the booth in which a patient sat on a stool with her feet in a water bath. After being situated in the cabinet for privacy, the patient was outfitted with a "number of electrodes adapted to the various parts of the body" and softly electrocuted with currents of various strengths. Luckily it was never developed.

Cyrus continued with his eclectic medical practice which soon got him into trouble – and made headlines in the *New York Times* on August 10, 1884. Usually, the activities of people in Syracuse wouldn't be of interest to people in Manhattan but this story was strange enough to sell to big city readers. The article claimed that not only was Cyrus defrauding the "best people in the city" of their money but he was also trying to steal their women – or so the rumors claimed. A woman named Mrs. Charles Cobb alleged that Teed had extorted money from her and her mother "under the plea that he is the Second Christ." Mrs. Cobb had been suffering from nervous prostration and Teed prescribed that Mrs. Cobb receive his electric therapy at home, in bed.

In case this has not been clear already, I should probably point out that Teed's "electric therapy" that he used for treating "nervous prostration" (i.e., hysteria) was essentially a vibrator. This kind of device was used to relieve female patients of their issues through an orgasm. Since it was too much trouble for doctors to bring a patient to orgasm with their fingers alone, people like Teed came up with an innovative device that could do it electrically. These devices were wildly popular among gentle ladies of the Victorian era.

It probably was for Mrs. Cobb, too, since she didn't complain about that. Her complaint was about Teed's strange theology and his pleas for money to fund his commune. The *Times* reported that "when he is 46, he will be translated to heaven, whence he will return in 50 days to found a kingdom where all will be love."

The Syracuse scandal destroyed Teed's medical practice, and needing another change of scenery he moved his four female followers – none of whom were his wife – to New York in the fall of 1884. They moved into an apartment in Manhattan, fell behind on the rent, and spent the winter hungry and cold. One of the women who went with Cyrus to New York wrote to Dr. Andrews and begged him to take up a collection among the followers who had stayed upstate. The women all depended financially on Cyrus, but he'd had trouble finding clients for his medical practice in the city.

Teed's mother and wife both died that year, but by spring his luck had started to change. An acquaintance introduced him to a Brooklyn society of intellectual ladies led by a spirit medium called Mrs. Peake. After sitting through a lecture during his first visit Cyrus so impressed the ladies with his questions that he soon took over the meeting. He talked until well after midnight, delighting his listeners with his convoluted scientific theories. His good looks and charm helped them to overlook his threadbare clothing and obvious lack of funds. He was so poor that he'd had to walk the 11 miles from his Manhattan apartment to Brooklyn. The night concluded with an invitation for him to return the following week to speak on the subject of mediumship.

Cyrus was elated as he made the long walk home. For the first time he'd found an audience receptive to his teachings. When he returned, he dazzled the society with his alchemical understanding of the human brain and its ability to channel and materialize spirit energies. The group had never heard such a thing applied to spirit mediumship. Mrs. Peake printed Teed's papers for the group to read, and at the following session the spirits declared that through her circle would be formed the core of Teed's church, which would be the "beginning of the divine communital system, the inauguration of goodwill to men."

I doubt that Mrs. Peake realized that Teed was just about to replace her as the leader of the Brooklyn group when she passed on those messages from the spirit world, but that's exactly what happened. By the end of April his new followers were spreading the word of his teachings. His reputation as a lecturer on religious science landed him a weekly speaking engagement on Sunday afternoons at the Faith Healing Institute, a mind-cure establishment near Central Park. The founder, Anna J. Johnson, invited Teed to contribute to the group's journal and he began writing under his new name of Koresh. Having realized that the emerging mind-cure movement was comprised mostly of female followers of Mary Baker Eddy, Cyrus shifted his teachings to appeal to women stating that his "new kingdom will be formulated through the organic potency of the woman's brain." His new proclamations of women's rights created new followers among members of the Faith Healing Institute and other mind-cure groups.

Leaving out his claims of being the next messiah, Cyrus found that his hodgepodge of celibacy, feminism, brain science, and communism appealed to many clubs – including that of Cynthia Leonard, a New York suffragist and humanitarian, who would soon become the first woman to run for mayor of New York. She had emancipated herself from her husband in Chicago and had become deeply involved in labor and social movements and women's rights. She hosted a weekly Science of Life Club in her home, and this gained Teed many new followers.

Thanks to this network of progressive intellectuals Cyrus met his next landlady, a German woman named Mrs. Egli, who became devoted to his teachings. She introduced Teed to an important new acquaintance, Elizabeth Thompson, a society matron who was a patron to many freethinking New York scientists. She was a woman of considerable influence in political circles and she began bankrolling Teed's scientific writings almost as soon as she met him.

Like Cyrus, Mrs. Thompson had a reputation for eccentricity. She didn't bother with the fineries and indulgences of women of her class. She dressed simply and spent what she saved on what she believed to be worthy causes. By doing this she claimed to follow the example of Christ. Along with her belief in a systematic reform of American society, she also believed that religion and science went hand in hand. This made her a woman after Teed's own heart.

Not only did she offer Cyrus a monthly writing allowance – as she did for a number of other writers – she was so impressed with him that she moved from Stamford to New York so she could study with him. Soon, Teed, Egli, and Thompson were living together.

Thompson also sent letters of introduction on Teed's behalf to influential friends in Washington, promised to send his books to counts and foreign ministers in Europe, and came to believe that his work would shape the next 2,000 years of human civilization. It would, she knew, form the basis of a new system of scientific government designed to enhance human evolution.

She expected Cyrus to deliver a manuscript about his work to her in nine months when it would be published. However, Teed was too busy to write. He was still leading Mrs. Peake's circle, was giving private lessons in physiology to Cynthia Leonard, preaching to various congregations, and contemplating a run for state senate. Mrs. Thompson cut off her support in July 1886 when Cyrus failed to deliver his manuscript. Even worse, Mrs. Egli had defected to the Rosicrucians. Teed was cut off again, but this situation didn't last long.

At one of Teed's lectures about brain physiology he met a middle-aged woman named Thankful Hale. She had been impressed by his lecture and offered him an all-expenses-paid trip to Chicago to speak at a mental science convention that she had organized. He accepted without hesitation.

The mental science movement was directed descended from American mesmerism. It had drifted off in multiple directions, most notably as Christian Science. Mary Baker Eddy, known for being a jealous dictator within her church, repeatedly drove off her best students. One of them, Emma Curtis Hopkins, went to Chicago and started her own version of mind-cure metaphysics. And she wasn't alone. Others entered the movement in Chicago mixing the science with Spiritualism – and some, like Andrew J. Swarts, a former Methodist minister, started their own schools. Swartz, with his wife Katie, a well-known Chicago medium, partnered with several others to start the Mental Science University, which had organized the September 1886 National Mental Science Association conference where Cyrus was scheduled to speak.

When Cyrus arrived for the convention, he discovered that it wouldn't be necessary to create his own metaphysical school, as he'd planned to do in New York – he only needed to take over the Mental Science University. This, he realized, would be simple to do by taking advantage of the divisions within the eclectic mental science community.

The conference was held at Chicago's Church of the Redeemer, which doubled as a candy factory. Cyrus wasted no time in gaining allies and was somehow elected president of the Association on the convention's second day.

His lecture, simply titled "The Brain," was scheduled for the last day of the event. He easily upstaged all the previous speakers. After several days of mind-cure testimonials and vague theories about the mind's effect on the body, attendees were stunned by Teed's array of terminology and diagrams, and by his detailed explanation of what parts of the brain controlled individual parts of the body. Other mental science practitioners were reformers, mesmerists, and quacks with little to no education in physiology, so Teed's eclectic medical knowledge was unparalleled at the convention. He even concluded his performance with the "faith healing" of a woman who could barely walk.

Katie Swartz closed out the event later that day, but like her husband she was heckled during her lecture. Teed's takeover of the Association was settled.

Cyrus moved to Chicago immediately and announced the establishment of the Society Arch-Triumphant, a spiritually oriented group that was open to students of what he now called "Koreshan" science. The Society took its name from the fringe belief in the prophecy of a unified Church Triumphant that would be established for the good of all. Among the Society's first members were Thankful Hale and Evelyn Bubbett, who had discovered Teed while attending the mental science convention with her sister. Her devotion to Koreshan science lasted until her death decades later.

Teed then conducted a purge of the Mental Science Association, first removing Andrew and Katie Swartz, and then ridiculing any Christian Scientists in the ranks until they left. He was a public antagonist of Mary Baker Eddy, blaming her movement for thousands of unnecessary deaths. Assured of the loyalty of those who remained he re-branded the Mental Science University – which was still linked to the Association – as the College of Life. He advertised that he offered advantages to students that they could not get from Christian Science, like "Metaphysics, Mental Healing, and the Mind Cure." Located at 103 State Street, the college taught the fundamentals of Koreshan Science, which was described as "a complete system of the cult, universal in its scope."

At least Teed never tried to hide the fact of what was Koreshan science was – it was a cult, based on his belief that he was the Messiah, no matter what kind of window dressing that mental science put on it.

Cyrus soon stopped practicing medicine. A failed mind-cure that ended in a patient's death landed him in court in 1888. He expounded on his mind-cure theories for the coroner's jury at the inquest. Although the Koreshan women in attendance were heard to exclaim "Wonderful, wonderful" as he outlined the cure, the jury wasn't buying it. Teed was indicted on charges of practicing medicine without a license and arrested. After being set free on a $300 bond paid by Koreshan Mary Daniels, Cyrus declared victory, calling his release "martyrdom for the cause." He still continued to list his credentials as a medical doctor on the College's promotional material, but he never practiced medicine again.

He continued to market the college extolling the virtues of Koreshan belief, including the prophecy that Teed's "translation" to his mortal body would occur in 1891. The cost of a College of Life degree was $50, which included diploma fees and tuition for a course in all five branches of study offered – metaphysics, brain pathology, gynecology, analogical biology, and analogical physiology. The latter two were the College's real specialty. There were essentially classic occult subjects, dressed up as science, which taught the laws of "universal form," or how the human body corresponded to universal cosmic design.

Among the 14 faculty members at the College, 13 of them were women. Before long Cyrus realized that one of them would be endowed with a special role in the new dispensation. Annie G. Ordway, a middle-class housewife, possessed the body into which Teed's spirit would pass after his translation. In recognition of her special status, Teed gave her the name Victoria Gratia and designated her the present of the Society Arch-Triumphant. Although the group was composed largely of women attracted to the freedoms of being sexually celibate, the elevation of one woman above all the rest caused considerable friction and the loss of some of the members, like when Teed expelled Thankful Hale at Victoria's request.

Teed's forays into metaphysics continued through his College, but he hesitated to reveal his messianic destiny to his students. He'd used the name Koresh in New York but delayed using it in Chicago until April 1887. Once the word was out, though, it was everywhere, thanks to the *Chicago Tribune* which reported that Cyrus had not only named himself as the preeminent mind-curist in the city, he also declared himself the reincarnation of Enoch, Noah, Abraham, Moses, Elijah, and Jesus. As he explained to his followers, his seven incarnations corresponded to the seven planets in the solar system, known to exist at the time. For his final embodiment – which would occur after his translation – Teed preferred the body of a woman. The *Tribune* also mentioned that Teed believed that the earth was hollow. As with other theories cooked up by Victorian-era occultists, Koreshan science made up for its lack of solid evidence of this with an attractive logic of symmetry and diagrams.

The word was out, but times had changed. What happened after the sex scandal in Syracuse didn't happen in Chicago. Koresh wasn't shunned. If anything, he became more popular. Teed used this new interest in his work to start a printing house called the Guiding Star which began to issue a newspaper of the same name. He dispatched followers like "Professor" Royal Spear to neighboring states to lecture on Koreshan science and to distribute the newspapers. This new reach drew in Teed's next important convert, Henry Silverfriend, a prosperous dry goods merchant from Wisconsin. He became a follower almost as soon as he heard of Cyrus Teed. Silverfriend sold his stake in his family store, moved to Chicago, and donated the proceeds of the sale to the cause. Just before this transaction Teed sold his printing press and equipment to Silverfriend so that creditors could never lay claim to it.

By this time Cyrus had worked out an organizational structure for Koreshanity that would remain in place long after his death. The College of Life continued to function as the scientific and educational arm of the church, while the Society Arch-Triumphant would be its vehicle of outreach. Membership in the Society was $2 per year and included all Koreshan publications. Within the Society was the elite inner circle – the Church Arch-Triumphant. It was the communal and religious order at the core of it all. Its members lived together in a six-flat apartment building on College Place. Members donated all their worldly belongings to the movement and broke all former family ties. Ella Woolsey and Thankful Hale were among the first residents, along with two of the most faithful from New York – Teed's sister Emma and Sarah Patterson.

When Dr. Andrews and his family joined Cyrus in Chicago, they also entered the communal order. It's unlikely they were happy with what they found, though. The

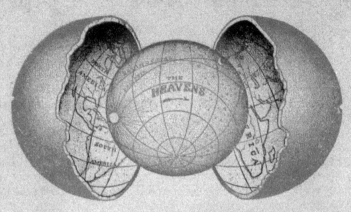

Teed thrived in Chicago for years. It was a city that was known for being home to crackpot ideas, inventors, and misfits and Teed was not only tolerated, but accepted, especially after he began touting the benefits of socialism

commune was cold and crowded. The group lacked money for heat and furniture because Cyrus had burned through their money at the Koreshan printing office.

In spite of hardships the movement grew. Silverfriend pressured Teed to create a Koreshan convention and it was held on October 8, 1888 at Chicago's Central Music

Hall. The stirring speech that Cyrus gave finally converted Andrews's wife, Virginia, who had been reluctant to join her husband in Chicago. Although Teed's speech does not survive, Virginia's remarks were so popular they were reprinted into a pamphlet called "Woman's Right to her Rightful Dominion." It compared the lives of most women in America at the time to slavery and offered a way out of bondage through Koreshan science. There were an additional 40 recruits to the Society Arch-Triumphant during the convention. By July of 1890 the movement boasted as many as 100 loyal Koreshans.

Most of them came from the distressed middle-classes of the era who found themselves falling into the widening gap that had appeared between the haves and the have-nots during America's Gilded Age. Skilled tradesmen, the backbone of the middle class, were becoming casualties of industrial mass production. Chicago was a hotbed of labor unrest at the time and working-class people were looking for diversions in metaphysics and Eastern religion. Unlike religious innovations like Theosophy, Koreshan science had something material to offer – relief from the anxieties and the terrifying social transformations that had been brought about by modern industrial capitalism. To the middle-class married women who made up the active core of the movement, it offered an alternative to the drudgery of "domestic servitude." To unmarried women Koreshan communism offered an escape from the solitary journey to old age. The movement validated the worth of women and workers as intellectuals by offering them the opportunity for education and for them to be engaged in politics in a way they had never done before.

The Koreshans welcomed anyone who agreed that women's rights and the overthrow of capitalism could not be achieved independently. The movement believed that the subjugation of women and workers went hand-in-hand. Teed added urgency to his anti-capitalist teachings, stating that the capitalist order was coming to an end and would be destroyed in an inevitable, apocalyptic confrontation between labor and capital. It was a good idea to be on the right side of history, he told his converts, if they wanted to make it into the new age.

Although mind cures and messiahs were derided in the Chicago press, socialism was taken much more seriously. The newspapers regarded Teed's experiment in communism skeptically, but with a certain amount of respect – the Koreshans unwaveringly practiced what they preached. No one doubted their commitment and the members of the movement appeared to be content and happy, despite their poor living conditions.

Cyrus soon began to spread the movement across the country. In 1891 he sent Royal Spear to San Francisco, and he began teaching Koreshan doctrine at a boardinghouse on Post Street, just off Union Square. His lectures soon attracted what a local newspaper called "three old men, a couple of young fellows, and a crowd of 30 to 40 women." His missionary efforts resulted in the establishment of a Koreshan commune on Noe Street. Teed dubbed it "Ecclesia." Another branch opened a short time later in Denver.

The San Francisco colony grew to rival the commune in Chicago. Its recruitment of several wealthy women allowed it to grow into the Koreshan Bureau of Equitable Commerce, the objective of which was to start the transition to a moneyless society in which goods could be exchanged according to credit that was given for completing assigned tasks. Cyrus knew that the country at large was not ready for such a thing but envisioned it as a system among seven Koreshan communities across the country.

The Bureau also put together a convention at San Francisco's Metropolitan Hall where Teed and other Koreshan speakers railed against corporate monopolies and capitalism, hoping to engage with California progressives in the backyard of Senator Leland Stanford, one of the era's great robber barons.

The convention received a lot of publicity – most of it bad – but managed to draw in a crowd of several hundred. The newspapers dismissed the ideas espoused by Teed and the other speakers in the days that followed, but dismissal turned to morbid fascination when word leaked out that a woman named Mary Mills had "deserted a hitherto happy family to join the converts of the pious pretender and charlatan Cyrus Teed." Mary was a society matron and wife of 33 years to Dr. James Mills, an eminent geologist. Winning her over to the Koreshan ranks was a stunning victory for the cause. Dr. Mills compared his wife's condition to that of "a fever that must run its course," suggesting that his wife was suffering from hysteria.

Eager to assemble evidence that would finally prove that Cyrus was a home-wrecking wife-stealer, the *Chicago Tribune* sent a reporter out west to cover the unfolding scandal. But Mrs. Mills refuted her husband's claims of hysteria and religious mania. "I did not take this step in the belief that I would add to my present happiness," she told the reporter. She stated that her separation from her family was "absolutely necessary if I wished to have a religious belief of my own. This state of celibacy is but a preparation for our future life when the Christ-man will dwell upon the earth." She further explained that she and her fellow Koreshans believed that Teed was the second coming of Christ, foretold in the Bible, and that "in two years he will be dematerialized and reappear in the form of a man-woman, having the attributes of both sexes. He will live on earth and spiritually produce the sons of God, who will inherit the earth."

The newspaper was thrilled to print such ridiculous claims. The *Tribune* and other papers had long been jabbing at the Koreshans for being a predominantly female religion, suggesting that Teed used his "magnetism" to prey on vulnerable women and broke up marriages to obtain followers. But that wasn't the draw – it was the fact that women who joined the Koreshans enjoyed the status and equality not offered to them at home. The Koreshan orchestra and drama troupe were coed. Women lectured on Koreshan science. And women held positions of leadership in the organization – in fact, a trio of women known as the Triangle made decisions for the group when Teed wasn't available.

While men were ridiculing the Koreshan beliefs of equality between the sexes, Teed was slowly amassing a following of women inclined toward feminism and socialism, but who refused to renounce organized religion in the way that Marxists of the era had done. In Chicago at least one Koreshan woman joined the movement to escape a physically abusive marriage. Her story is known because her husband sued Teed for alienation of affection. Most of the other stories of Koreshan women are unknown but it's likely that others saw the female-dominated movement as a safe place, no matter how strange the beliefs behind it might be.

As 1891 came to an end, Cyrus revised the prophecy of his "translation," postponing it for two years. He now claimed it would happen during the 1893 World's Columbian Exposition in Chicago, which also marked the time of the apocalyptic battle between capitalism and labor that would destroy the city. Only the Koreshans would be saved and they would enjoy immortality. Unfortunately, two of Teed's most loyal followers – Dr. Andrews and Sarah Patterson – didn't live long enough to see it. They "succumbed to mortal corruption" before the World's Fair took place.

Teed traveled back and forth between San Francisco and Chicago, but by 1892 there was trouble out west. Royal Spear had quit the Bureau of Equitable Commerce over anxieties about Teed's total lack of business skills and for his frustrating habit of justifying his frequent changes in plans by ambiguously saying, "Necessity compels me to make a change on the chessboard."

Spear and his wife remained believers in the cause and mourned the Koreshan failure in the city claiming that the three-building commune on Noe Street was nothing but a home for elderly and invalid women with nowhere else to go.

Cyrus knew that he still had many followers in San Francisco, so he gradually ordered them to pack up their communal belongings that winter and come to Chicago. Teed told reporters that his followers from Seattle, Los Angeles, and Portland – one of whom was a wealthy young heiress – were joining those from San Francisco for the trip east. This was, of course, a face-saving lie.

The College Avenue commune was not large enough for all of the Koreshans, so Teed and Victoria found a mansion in the suburban neighborhood of Washington Heights that would become the new headquarters and an apartment building in the Normal Park neighborhood that could serve as housing for the followers from out west.

The problem was, though, no one wanted the Koreshans in their neighborhood. Teed was threatened with tar and feathering soon after the jilted husband of a Koreshan woman stirred Washington Heights into action to keep the group from moving there. In Normal Park residents organized street protests and threatened to vandalize the Koreshan apartments. The police had to turn them away.

The opposition failed to intimidate the faithful and, besides, they had little choice – the group from San Francisco had arrived and were crammed into the existing commune. In May the headquarters relocated from College Avenue to the Washington Heights house which was renamed "Beth Ophrah." The property held eight structures including a barn that became the new home of the Guiding Light publishing house.

Things didn't improve after the Koreshans settled in. A suspicious device was found outside of Beth Ophrah, which a local chemist said "resembled a bomb used by anarchists a few years ago," referring to the Haymarket Square riot, a labor march that got out of hand in 1886 and killed a police officer and injured several workers. Teed also received a death threat that had him once again appealing to the authorities for protection.

The Koreshans tried to brush off these hostilities but some were too frightening to ignore, like when Teed had to be bailed out of jail after being chased down the street in Washington Heights and arrested on charges of immoral intimacy with another man's wife. Although there is no evidence to say that Cyrus broke his vow of celibacy, the people of the time could not understand the living arrangements of the

Koreshans. As far as they were concerned the communal home had to either be a brothel or a harem.

As tensions ticked upward, Teed hoped to cool things by taking a trip to visit the Shaker communes of the east. He hoped to learn from them and emulate some of the methods that had sustained the movement for so long. He and Victoria took a small group of Koreshans with him and they made a grand tour of the Shaker colony, New York, Boston, Cambridge, and Harvard.

Cyrus was restless after returning to Chicago. As the start of the World's Fair approached, he faced the same predicament that William Miller had decades before when the apocalypse that he predicted failed to occur. After the Fair came and went without Teed's translation, many of the Koreshans left. The most faithful stayed with their master, however. Of course, many of them had no choice – they had given up their property, family, and jobs to join the cause, plus the bank panic of 1893 had decimated the nation's economy.

Teed's thoughts turned toward advice that he had been given by the Shakers, suggesting that the Koreshans find a place where they could sustain themselves by farming. To do that Teed believed they would need to find a place in the south. That notion appealed to him. After all, it would not be hard to convince his followers to depart for a southern climate. The Koreshans, like all Chicagoans, had been hit hard by the economic depression and had suffered through a winter with no heat. He also saw migration as a way to escape the animosity and the onslaught of lawsuits that he was facing in Chicago. He knew that if the Koreshans were going to survive they needed to do so in an isolated spot that was far away from scrutiny and interference.

This realization, combined with the inspiring tour that the Koreshans had taken of the White City that had been built for the Fair, led Teed to decide that it was time for him to establish his own Koreshan metropolis. In October 1893 Teed went to Florida to investigate the potential purchase of Pine Island in Estero Bay. He took Victoria with him and they were accompanied by Berthaldine Boomer, one of Teed's most loyal companions. Her family was one of those who contributed hefty sums to the Koreshans. The Boomer family had joined the movement in 1888 after first studying the writings of Charles Taze Russell, who went on to found the Jehovah's Witnesses. Russell had issued prophecies about the return of the Messiah, and the Boomers came to believe that he was talking about Cyrus Teed. Berthaldine had recruited her family to the Koreshan ranks and became a close associate of Teed. He appointed her to the Planetary Court, a 17-woman advisory council that aided him in making important decisions and later became one of the tips of the Triangle.

When the three travelers arrived at Pine Island, they were disappointed to learn that the owner wasn't interested in negotiating his price for the land – $150,000 was much more than they could pay. But before leaving town they dropped off some Koreshan literature at the train station which happened to be picked up by a German immigrant named Gustave Damkohler, who was another disenchanted Jehovah's Witness. When Teed and the others returned to Chicago, they found a letter waiting from Damkohler asking them to settle on his land.

The trio again departed for Florida, accompanied by Mary Miller. When they arrived, they camped for several nights in an abandoned hotel they considered buying while working out details of the plan with Damkohler. They ended up buying 300 of his 320 acres for $200, as well as a first right of refusal on the remaining 20 acres that he'd set aside for himself and his son, Elwin. The Koreshan property was placed in Boomer's name.

They remained in Florida for the next several weeks, crammed into Damkohler's tiny cabin with the women sleeping on the only bed, Teed on the couch, and Gustave and Elwin sleeping onboard their boat. During the day they cleared the land of the thick scrub in preparation for the arrival of the Koreshan colonists. In the evening the group dined on fish, oysters, alligators, boar, and honey from Damkohler's beehives. The Koreshans were thrilled with the fruits that grew naturally in the region, including the mango trees that Gustave planted near his cabin.

Cyrus brought down an advance work crew from Chicago, with carpenters, mechanics, and farmers among them. They arrived in late January, at which point Teed left Mary and Victoria in charge while he returned to Chicago. He recruited 24 men, ranging in age from adolescent to elderly, and put them on a train to Florida. Before he'd left Florida Teed had purchased a small sailboat that could ferry the settlers from the rail station at Punta Gorda to Mound Key, an island in Estero Bay. Once they arrived the passengers waited for high tide when they could use rowboats to get around the sandbars and oyster beds in the bay. Until a stove was transported to the settlement Mary and Victoria cooked over open fires for nearly 30 men, who slept in tents and hurriedly built cabins before the rainy season started. They had no sawmill, so the cabins were built with thatched roofs which leaked throughout the winter.

The Koreshan settlement was definitely isolated. Fort Myers was located 16 miles away down a rugged, sandy road that made wagon travel impossible. The Koreshans mainly used the Estero River for travel, commerce, and communication. Until they were able to dig a well the settlers relied on the river for drinking water, but it was so sour that it had to be cut with citrus juice. They mostly ate the fish that the settlers were able to catch in the mornings.

In 1895 the Koreshans were finally able to set up a sawmill on the island. It enabled them to build many large structures, some of which remain standing today, like the Master's House where Cyrus lived with Victoria and his sister Emma. Another large construction was the dining hall and kitchen where the Koreshans ate together, held meetings, and listened to Teed's lectures. Women's dormitories occupied the second and third floors of the building.

Since land on the Florida frontier was inexpensive the Koreshans expanded their holdings by purchasing several nearby islands. The colony hit its peak population of about 200 people after Teed summoned the rest of the Chicago followers to the Sunshine State. Battling heat, mosquitoes, political adversaries, and the routine perils of the wilderness, the Estero colony succeeded and grew to include dozens of buildings including dormitories, bakery, hospital, printing house, laundry, general store, the Art Hall auditorium, and a grand residence for the Planetary Court. The Koreshans built sunken gardens and paved gravel paths through scrub pine and palmetto and created a settlement that became their utopia. Cyrus Teed had used city folks to carve a citrus

The "Master's House" where Teed lived with Victoria and his sister, Emma.

plantation out of a wild landscape and they produced a cash crop that largely sustained them.

One of the most extravagant projects that Teed undertook in Florida was a definitive vindication of his Hollow Earth Theory. He hoped to continue his surveys to show that surveys conducted by the U.S. government were nothing but "sham science." He traveled several times to Washington, D.C. to try and interest government scientists in his efforts to disprove the Copernican model of the round Earth but found little interest. However, he did make one new recruit – temporarily anyway. Ulysses Morrow was an editor from Allegheny, Pennsylvania who discovered Teed's theories and began incorporating them into his own work. He soon joined the movement and Teed promoted him to the role of "scientist" for the purposes of the survey.

Over the course of four weeks the Koreshans deployed a device called a "rectilineator" that was supposed to allow them to extend a line perpendicular to the force of gravity, beginning at the height of 10 feet. Using a variety of instruments – including protractors, levels, triangles, rulers, compasses, plumb lines, and for some reason, thermometers – Koreshans carefully ensured that the rectilineator was aligned. Fearing the device might be tampered with, they guarded it around the clock. The experiment took several months to complete.

As expected, it showed that that the world was a hollow shell that was 8,000 miles in diameter, curving eight inches per mile upward. Teed and Morrow published the results in their *Cellular Cosmogony* book which went through several reprints.

The final printing, though, only had Koresh's name on it.

Morrow's continued study of Teed's calculations later uncovered inconsistencies that demolished his faith in Koreshan beliefs. After he brought the mathematical errors to Teed's attention Morrow was kicked out of the movement.

But nothing lasts forever – not even for the "immortal," it seems.

Cyrus Teed enjoyed a few more years of spreading the Koreshan good news across the country. Aside from the short-lived commune in Denver, small cells of Koreshans had also formed in Los Angeles, Portland, and Pittsburgh. Adversaries in Chicago and Fort Myers occasionally made trouble for the movement in court and in the press, but overall things went surprisingly well.

As the Florida colony grew, Cyrus saw the advantages of incorporating the settlement as a town. This was easily accomplished in 1904. The only critic of the incorporation was Phillip Isaacs, the Koreshans' main opponent in the Fort Myers press, but no one else was really interested. Trouble really began when Isaacs was elevated to the position of Democratic Party chair in Lee County. Although the Koreshan men were registered Democrats, they'd annoyed the party by supporting Theodore Roosevelt when he appeared on the Republican ticket in 1904. Isaacs assembled a slate of candidates for the 1906 election who vowed to take away the state funds that the Koreshans were entitled to as a town. He also changed the rules of the party primary to exclude anyone who refused to sign a loyalty pledge to the Democrats. The Koreshans refused to sign without first taking out the parts of the pledge that offended them, but they didn't stop there. To intimidate their political opponents, they also offered a candidate of their own – Ross Wallace for county commissioner – and formed their own Progressive Liberty Party just for that purpose. The new party called for a standardized income across the county and the immediate public seizure of all utilities. The platform provoked Teed's enemies who raised the stakes by trying to invalidate the Koreshans' voting rights.

The Koreshans struck a chord with people who were tired of Lee County's corrupt government and soon became a force to be reckoned with. The feud between Teed and the Democrats intensified. Isaacs, who was now a judge, did everything he could to cause problems for the Koreshan settlement, while also attempting to destroy Teed's reputation with rumors and false scandals. Teed began traveling with a group of Koreshan bodyguards whenever he went into Fort Myers, but even this didn't protect him completely. After Teed tried to mediate a misunderstanding between Ross Wallace and some of his adversaries, a hotel owner named Sellers slugged Cyrus in the face.

According to Koreshan history, this event began Teed's slow decline to bodily corruption.

Teed began suffering crippling nerve pain throughout his body. Although he still managed to do some traveling, he spent most of his time at his beach house on Estero Island, being treated with ice baths and electrotherapy sessions. He knew he was dying. The "Messiah's" body finally suspended animation three days before Christmas 1908. Because he had always been so unclear about what was supposed to happen next, his followers were unsure if his translation had occurred. Some believed that his

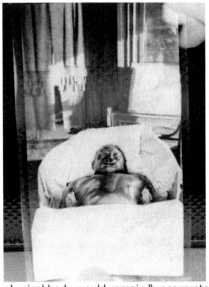

(Left) Teed's body was left in state until it finally began to decay.

(Right) Teed's tomb on Estero Island

physical body would remain "uncorrupted," after which his immortal body would pass from his spontaneously mummified corpse into the body of Victoria. Others thought Victoria would be left behind by the Master to complete the work of the new age. Another faction disagreed with both ideas, suggesting that Victoria's body was just a place for Teed's spirit to wait before returning in another form. Victoria was left out of the debate – Cyrus had tasked her with taking care of some business interests in Washington, D.C., and didn't even know that he had died until several days later.

She found out by telegram. No one wanted to shock her, but they didn't want her to hear about Teed's transformation in the newspapers. They sent a message that only said, "Suspended Animation. Can you come?" Victoria later claimed that she heard Teed's voice say, "I have passed out" just before she opened the telegram.

Most Koreshans believed that Teed's translation had not occurred at the same time as his death – suspended animation – and that his immortal body had not yet moved on to its next destination. Where his soul had gone, no one knew for sure. However, they only had to wait until Christmas to find out – sort of.

Early that morning Teed's corpse, which had been left in state, began to seriously decompose. Teed's sister Emma, was the first to remark, "That thing ought to be put in a tomb." Others, though, likened the blackened, swelling corpse to a chrysalis, inside of which their Master had started the work of regeneration. The various interpretations of the rotting body served to authenticate the Koreshans' religious beliefs.

Once the body finally decomposed the Koreshans agreed to the county coroner's demand that they entomb Teed's body. It was placed in a stone mausoleum that was designed for single occupancy. A plaque was placed on the outside that read, "Cyrus, Shepherd, Stone of Israel."

Even after his body was placed inside the corpse was guarded around the clock by his followers, who were still waiting for him to rise from the dead. Many of the Koreshans believed that he would be resurrected on Christmas Day of the following year. But the date came and went and Teed never returned.

In 1921 a hurricane struck the southwest Florida coast, washing away Teed's tomb forever.

Teed's sister, Emma, at the ruins of his mausoleum. His corpse vanished during the hurricane

The Estero community suffered without Teed. New factions formed almost immediately. Victoria was named Empress Pre-Eminent and many followers considered her divine. Other Koreshans quietly tolerated her occasional abuses of power and believed that Teed had coronated her to silence dissent from other Koreshan women who envied her power and authority. After Teed's death many abandoned the main society and started movements of their own, based on Teed's writings.

Victoria ultimately proved incapable of overcoming the divisions in the community. She eloped with a Koreshan dentist, C. Addison Graves, after which she was thrown out of the movement. She had, many said, been led astray by the "control of the nether world."

Another sinister faction formed around Edgar Peissart, who had joined the Koreshans only one month before Teed's death. During his time with the movement he claimed to be a biblical scholar but was actually a zealous seeker who had been involved with the Watch Tower Society, a Mennonite sect called the River Brethren, and the House of David – an offshoot of an English messianic society. Peissart was also a spirit medium who convinced Victoria and 28 other Koreshans to open Teed's tomb and conduct a séance with his corpse. Alerted to the plan other followers put an end to it.

Neither the in-fighting nor Teed's death could kill the community entirely. The Koreshans lasted for four more decades. They never built the grand temple or the city of 10 million that Teed envisioned for the Estero community, but it had endured much longer than most communal religious societies did after the loss of their charismatic founder.

In 1960 the state of Florida, finally embracing its eccentric son, turned what was left of Teed's utopia into a state historic site. Even though the last of his followers died in 1981, site volunteers still offer tours of the settlement and show many of Teed's personal items which are kept on display and show off charts and diagrams that illustrate his bizarre ideas and beliefs.

The final lesson to be learned from the life of Cyrus Teed and the Koreshans was not the amount of time that the movement lasted or how many followers he had. It is the ability that Teed had to recruit followers into a sect that revolved around the ideas and beliefs of one man during a time of social and economic anxiety in the country.

Cyrus Teed set the stage for other, much more insidious, cult leaders to come.

The Blackburn Cult

On October 7, 1929 the body of a 16-year-old girl named Willa Rhoads was found buried beneath her adopted parents' home in Los Angeles. She had not been murdered – Willa had died from an infection caused by an abscessed tooth – but the circumstances of her illegal burial were what caught the attention of the authorities.

Willa had died three years earlier, but her parents had come to believe that she could be brought back to life. Willa's body was mummified with ice, salt, and spices and had been buried under the floorboards of the house with the bodies of seven dogs, sacrificed to "represent the seven tones of the angel Gabriel's trumpet" and ensure her resurrection.

You see, Mr. and Mrs. Rhoads were part of what would become one of the most notorious Southern California cults of the 1920s.

In the early 1900s Los Angeles and Hollywood became a favorite topic for preacher's sermons across the country. They were the modern American version of "Sodom and Gomorrah," those two biblical cities destroyed by God because of their wickedness. This was actually a draw for people in the 1920s, that great period of excess, abandonment, and experimentation. This was the time of the "lost generation" of young adults who had been traumatized by the horrors of the Great War and who had become cynical about the values of their parents and grandparents – the people responsible for starting that terrible war in the first place.

People came to Southern California looking for a new life. Believing that the old traditions and values had failed them, they sought liberation from what they had been taught and now wanted something new. They came west to the place where the new motion picture industry was busy showing people that magic was possible – and they became easy prey for the cults, kooks, and fanatics of the fringe element who followed them to the land of sunshine.

The film stars of the 1920s immersed themselves in the occult, paving the way for the seekers that followed in their wake. According to a newspaper reporter that visited one of the studios, "Hundreds of performers are more than passingly interested in necromancy, superstition, and prognostication in general." He noted that seers – palmists, crystal gazers, and trance mediums – were everywhere. Many actors, he claimed, paid annual fees to astrologers so they could be kept informed of any planetary changes that might affect their careers.

Dr. Lewis Brown, a religious scholar who lived in Santa Monica, noted in 1929 that, "This world is full of primitive minds." He had been asked to explain why men and women of the era were so easily drawn to unorthodox, pagan, and primitive religious practices. Brown had found the region to be a fruitful field for his studies of religious movements. He estimated that there were approximately 400 cults active in Southern California in the late 1920s with memberships numbering in the hundreds of thousands. They included, he said, notable groups like Zeralda and Omar's "Love Cult" - also known as the "Sacred Schools Cult," the "Mazdazan" cult, the "Magi" cult, and the "Christian Church of Psychosophy."

According to novelist Nathaniel West, who used the dark side of L.A. for atmosphere in several of his books and stories, some of the local cults included the "Church Invisible" where fortunes were told, the "Tabernacle of the Third Coming" where a woman in male clothing preached the Crusade Against Salt, and the "Temple Moderne" where "Brain-Breathing, the Secret of the Aztecs" was taught.

There were also numerous devil-worshiping cults, long before Anton LaVey founded the Church of Satan in California in 1969. A man named Macario Timon was murdered in Oakland in 1926. In his home the police found books and manuals on the occult and prayers signed in blood. They also found a drawing of a cross at the base of a tree, surrounded by hills with an eerie sun floating above them, and cryptic symbols surrounding everything. The prayer written in blood began with "Most Powerful Lucifer..." and asked for wisdom and strength to overcome his enemies.

Purification by fire and "Garden of Eden orgies" were part of the activities of the House of Judah cult. Members prayed and chanted together in the nude and sacrificed lambs, which they burned alive, much to the horror of their neighbors.

"Bishop" Wilbur Leroy Cosper was arrested in 1926 and sentenced to six months in jail for violations of practicing medicine – mixed with religion – without a license. His cult, who gathered to wait for him outside the jail, were "lightly clad dancers, major and minor deities, a scattering of archangels, and scores of (uncostumed) followers – mostly women." They promised onlookers a "resurrection day" to celebrate their leader's eventual release.

Margaret Rowen founded the Seventh Day Adventists Mission – not to be confused with the Seventh Day Adventist church – and was adamant that the world would end on February 6, 1925. She drew an estimated 1,000 followers and a lot of publicity but was more successful as a self-promoter than as a prophet – as everyone in L.A. discovered on February 7. However, she did claim that one of her children was born as a result of "delvings in the occult, mysterious experiments in mind control, and spiritual investigations" while she and her husband were members of a cult that she never named. At the time of this interview her husband was an inmate at a state mental hospital.

In 1930, a woman under police protection told newspaper reporters that she was so terrified of the cult she had abandoned that she was afraid to say its name. It was later discovered to be "Hickory Hall." The woman who was the priestess for the group, a Mrs. Leech, "dominated the household mentally and physically... we could have no wills of our own, no thoughts except hers." When the former member had objected to cult children being spanked with sticks, she was bent over a chair and spanked by five cult members in retaliation. She later received a telegram from her former fellow cult members with a four-word message that only said, "We won't hurt you."

There were so many cults in Southern California that the Los Angeles District Attorney assigned an undercover man whose job it was to infiltrate them and keep track of what they were doing. His name was Eddie Kane, and he was momentarily famous for befriending and then exposing the fraudulent activities of a popular spiritualist named Elsie Reynolds.

A newspaper editorial in 1930 complained that "Los Angeles extends a welcome asylum to every cult of every kind that seeks to hide temporarily its ugly head until it can build sufficient strength to begin the spreading of its poisonous propaganda. The number of cults in Los Angeles are a standing joke the country over."

And it was into this fertile field that May Otis Blackburn sowed the seeds that became the Divine Order of the Royal Arms of the Great Eleven. It was a cult that was inspired by a single verse in the biblical Book of Revelation, 11:3 to be precise: "And I will grant my two witnesses power to prophesy for one thousand two hundred and sixty days."

The "two" that the cult believed were predicted in the verse were a mother and daughter who used religion, sex, and greed to separate believers from their money. This occurred while their followers were waiting on the return of their Messiah – an event that would occur at the same time their dead 16-year-old "priestess" would be resurrected. Although eventually buried, the "priestess" was initially kept on ice in a bathtub. She would occasionally be taken for rides around L.A. in the back seat of a touring car, however.

The roots of the cult began to grow in 1924 when two angels – Gabriel and Michael – allegedly appeared to May Otis Blackburn, 60, and her daughter, Ruth Wieland Rickenbaugh Rizzio, 24, whom the press would later dub a "girl of many loves." It was not a moniker meant to be kind. When Ruth was not delivering prophecies, she was convincing her many suitors to make her loans, which she never repaid.

While I'm sure this might surprise you – the account of the "angels" may not be true.

The real beginning of the cult took place many years before and the two Blackburn women had been honing their skills of deception and manipulation for more than a decade.

May Otis Blackburn – future high priestess, Queen, and Witness of God – was born in Storm Lake, Iowa on August 2, 1881, daughter to William and Matilda Otis. William was possibly killed in a railroad accident in 1885. Matilda then married a man named Edgar Holt and the family moved to Huron, South Dakota. Ten years later they moved to Minnesota and on October 3, 1897 16-year-old May married August Wieland. The couple moved to South Dakota where their marriage began to fall apart. In 1899 they split up – May later said it was because he gambled too much – and May was pregnant at the time. Her daughter, Ruth, was born soon after the separation on July 25, 1899.

Soon after Ruth's birth May received a letter from a doctor in California informing her that John Wieland had been shot and killed there after a dispute over some mines. An unidentified man arrived to tell her the same thing soon after the letter.

May was now a widow – or so it seemed.

In 1900, after placing her daughter in the care of her mother and stepfather May went to Minneapolis, where she met and married Rudolph A. Schultz on July 1, 1901 after a whirlwind romance. May had told her new husband about her dead husband, but apparently concealed the existence of Ruth. She had not abandoned her, though. A short time later May's parents and child moved to Washington state. As soon as May received word, they were settled she began asking her husband to move to the northwest so that she could be near her family, including her "younger sister," Ruth. Schultz agreed and by 1905 he and May were settled in Portland, Oregon.

The move to Portland allowed May to visit her daughter regularly, but neither May nor Matilda told Ruth who her real mother was. She had been an infant when left with Matilda and believed her grandmother was her mother. When May was finally reunited with her daughter, she introduced herself as her "older sister." Eventually she would find out, but this delay caused Ruth to only ever address her mother by her given name. When speaking to others she would refer to May as "my mother, but she never called her by any term of endearment.

In Portland Schultz began working as a waiter at the Oregon Hotel. He made $150 each month and his wife demanded $125 of it for her personal use. He agreed to her demand without question – a sign of things to come.

In 1906 Rudolph returned home from work one day and found May waiting for him with a strange look on her face. She told him that she had evidence that her supposedly dead husband, John Weiland, was actually alive. That meant she had never been widowed and her marriage to Schultz was invalid. She was leaving him, she said, because to stay with him would be a sin. Rudolph was shocked by the news and when he tried to learn where Wieland was May was evasive with him, claiming that she didn't want a confrontation between the two men. He asked May to stay but she refused. She had to return to her true husband.

But John Weiland was in no hurry to return to her. Two years later, on May 15, 1908, May's attorney published a summons for Weiland to appear and answer a complaint that he had faked his death. If he failed to appear May would seek a divorce and sole custody of Ruth. He didn't show up so on July 17 May appeared in court to explain her reasons for a divorce. She said that earlier that year her mother had received a letter from a man named "John Worthy" who claimed that he had recently buried May's husband in Alaska – almost a decade after Weiland had allegedly been killed in California.

According to the letter, John had been a hard worker and had bequeathed nearly $100,000 to May, as long as she never remarried. May told the judge that until the letter arrived, she thought her husband dead – which makes her claim to Rudolph Schultz that John had returned two years earlier a lie. Regardless, she told the court that after the letter arrived, she went to Tacoma where it was posted from, and found not the mysterious John Worthy but her husband, John Weiland, alive and well. Angry about the inexplicable deceit she returned home, intent on getting a divorce.

May was granted the divorce and in the 1909 city directory she was listed as a widow, although John Wieland was still not dead. He just returned to Alaska and went back to work.

But if Weiland had not returned from the dead to claim his wife in 1906, why did May tell Rudolph Schultz that he had? And why go through the trouble of getting a divorce when he was already out of the picture? She did it because she needed to make sure that her new boyfriend, lumber tycoon Fremont Everett, knew she was available. Everett, though, was already married – and rich. This made him the perfect target for May. She could bleed cash out of him without ever having to worry about the entanglement of marriage, and when necessary she could end the relationship with a bit of blackmail.

Everett was so entranced by May that he allowed photographs to be taken of him with his mistress. He wrote love letters to her on his company stationary, which he signed with his real name. He even replied to May's curiosity about his net worth – over $250,000, by the way – without ever considering the reason why his lover would ask.

Meanwhile, May's parents, hoping to move closer to their daughter, relocated to Grays Crossing, Oregon. It was there that Edgar died at the age of 62. Mathilda, who didn't believe in long mourning periods, took a third husband in 1913. His name was William Blackburn and he brought a son named Ward with him to the marriage.

On May 7, 1915, even while she was having an affair with Fremont Everett, May married a 27-year-old singer named George Blum. He had been working for a construction company in 1911 when he fell through a hole in the floor and was injured. He received a small settlement from the company, which May learned about in the newspapers. The marriage – and Blum's money – only lasted for a year. Soon after Blum was locked up in a prison camp and on his registration card when he arrived, he marked his marital status as "single."

By this time Ruth was living with her mother in Portland. The beautiful brown-eyed girl was a born entertainer and began acting at age 11 in 1909. In 1917, as the prettiest girl in the city, she was cast in a comedy-drama called *A Nugget in the Rough*, the first motion picture ever made in Portland. Ruth, the "nugget," was described by reporters as "a most vivacious actress." Ruth was also cast in a two-reel comedy, *The Tale of a Dress*, which was shown prior to the main feature.

It later turned out that the films were financed by the "Starlight Film Company," a Portland company that was owned by her mother. May had accumulated a great deal of money in recent years – mostly thanks to Fremont Everett – and had invested it in a new home and car, apartment buildings, and in the fledgling film company that was being used to kick start Ruth's career. Ruth never appeared in any Hollywood productions – that would be a fiction later created by her mother to make her more appealing in the eyes of the public.

Unfortunately, Ruth's career never took off in Portland. May had poured a small fortune into two films that played for a week, becoming a financial disaster and making it look as though no future films would be made. Her hopes of establishing Portland as a film making alternative to Hollywood – with Ruth as the main attraction – were

May and Ruth, the "two witnesses" who would create Divine Order of the Royal Arms of the Great Eleven — which would become notoriously known as the "Blackburn Cult"

destroyed. May then decided that if Hollywood would not come to Portland, then her daughter would go to Hollywood.

To make this scheme work though, she needed cash, something she was a little short on at the moment. She sold her apartment buildings to Fremont Everett and with $25,000 in hand the mother and daughter moved to Los Angeles in 1918.

May still wanted to work in movies and Ruth still wanted to be a star. Unable to come up with the money to start her own studio, May resorted to seeking opportunities as a director or writer but no one would hire her. She took this failure badly and spent most of her early days in Los Angeles sulking about the house she shared with Ruth. For the first time in her life she was not in charge. She was an exceptional manipulator who was used to getting what she wanted, and now she had failed. May spent hours each day doing nothing but reading the Bible.

Ruth, however, did land a few jobs as a Hollywood extra, but not enough of them to earn any real money. She decided to make some extra income working as both a "taxi dancer" and an "Oriental dancer." In the 1920s a taxi dancer was a girl who hung around clubs and danced with men for money. Dance halls didn't cater to women so they sold tickets to male customers for a dime each. A girl employed by the dance hall was obligated to dance with any man who presented a ticket to her.

There was nothing glamorous about a taxi dancer's life. The girls were often scantily dressed and earned most of their money from after-hours liaisons with male customers. Many of them were simply fronts for prostitution, but others called themselves "dancing schools" to provide a veneer of respectability. The girls played along with this and called themselves "dance instructors," as Ruth did in the 1920 census.

When not taxi dancing, Ruth worked as an Oriental dancer, or an "exotic dancer," as we'd call it today. Oriental dancers dressed in skimpy, provocative costumes that revealed a lot more skin than socially acceptable outfits would usually allow. They didn't dance with men – they danced for them – and most of the girls who did so would not have been able to find the Orient on a map.

Ruth mainly worked at the Rose Room Dance Hall on South Spring Street and worked most evenings. She preferred Oriental dancing over taxi dancing because she could be the center of attention when she was performing the "ancient dance music of Egypt" or the "dances of Cleopatra and Salome."

In 1918, Ruth met her first husband, Edgar Rickenbaugh, a 22-year-old railroad clerk from Altoona, Pennsylvania. They were married on May 27, 1919 and began sharing an apartment with May. Ruth continued working as a dancer while May stayed at home and read her Bible.

By 1921, Ruth's marriage was on the rocks. It was inevitable, really. Her husband was a jealous man, known for physical altercations, and his Ruth was paid to dance with, and for, other men. After some contentious arguments the two agreed to a divorce. They didn't have enough money for the paperwork, though, so they decided to just live apart until they could afford it. Edgar claimed the two separated on good terms and Ruth and May moved to a new, smaller apartment.

In 1922, Ruth met a young Indiana man named Arthur Carl Osborne. A likable young man, he was smitten with Ruth, and while they went on some dates, she was never serious about him. She did, however, write him many letters and he would be the first person to whom Ruth revealed that she and her mother were working on a book that would literally "make the world stand still."

The book, Ruth told him, would explain the origins of the universe, the purpose of man's existence, the nature of God, and how to find hidden treasure, for which only the "lost measurements of Solomon" were required. The book would be called *The Great Sixth Seal* and would explain the mysteries of life and health, heaven and earth, and more. Most of what the Bible contained was metaphorical, and the book that she and her mother were writing would explain everything.

She then told Osborne the real news – she and her mother were not actually writing the book; they were just taking dictation from an angel. He was coming to their home every night to dictate the book of all knowledge. This was more difficult than it sounded, she explained, because the angel often recited complicated biblical names, or the names of places May and Ruth had never heard of, which required them to consults maps and Bibles to make sure what they recorded was accurate.

Osborne was too infatuated with the beautiful dancer to doubt anything she told him.

He was, however, concerned with Ruth's health. She was often tired and felt too ill to work. He begged her to quit her dancing job, but she refused because she was saving money to obtain her divorce from Edgar Rickenbaugh. But, she said, if Arthur knew anyone who might lend her some money for a divorce, she could quit dancing and devote all her time to the book. The book would sell hundreds of millions of copies, she assured him, so whatever money Arthur borrowed would be repaid many times over once the book was published.

Arthur considered this and suggested that his employer might give him a loan if he promised to pay it back quickly. But soon after floating that idea he had second thoughts and began to avoid Ruth. He even stopped writing her. Sensing his change of heart, though, Ruth wrote to encourage him, promising him a "reward" after the divorce went through. Despite his better judgment Arthur borrowed some money and gave it to Ruth. She filed for divorce and went back to using her maiden name. The pretty young woman was now able to date again.

Arthur was happy – but not for long. Soon after she stopped dancing Ruth told Arthur that she and her mother had been commanded to start a new religious order that would be based on the book's teachings. This would require even more money. The two women had no choice but to obey this divine command, so it looked like Ruth would have to start dancing again – with other men, she stressed – unless Arthur might be able to provide a little more financial assistance.

Ruth's admirer, Arthur Carl Osborne

Arthur did. He gave Ruth every bit of cash that he could earn or borrow, adding up to $150. Unfortunately, a few months later when it was time to repay the loan, the great book was still not finished. Ruth had been telling him it would be "just a few more weeks" for two months. As more time passed Arthur was told that he had to pay back the loans, or he would be fired.

Arthur's father was aware of his son's predicament and went to Ruth and May's house to demand that Ruth pay back the money she had borrowed. May met the man at the door and a heated argument occurred. Eventually the man left, but May was still furious. She telephoned Arthur's mother and threatened to kill Arthur if he or his father kept pestering Ruth for money she didn't have. Years later Arthur downplayed the threat, saying May was "only spoofing."

But she probably wasn't.

Arthur was fired from his job and was now in debt. The relationship that Ruth had promised him was over. The broken-hearted young man went to the nearest Army

William Blackburn

(Below) May's mother, Mathilda, who usually went by the name "Jennie"

recruiting station and enlisted. Before he left for boot camp, he stopped by Ruth's house one last time.

It was empty. The two women were gone.

May and Ruth had returned to Portland. It was a place where they had family, friends, and contacts – the perfect candidates for their new religious movement's first followers. They moved into William, Mathilda, and Ward Blackburn's house, and began creating the cult that would soon have hundreds of members.

In Portland, May began creating the myth that she'd had "spirit voices" with her since she was a child and that Ruth had inherited those gifts. For many years the strange voices had asked nothing of the women – they were simply persistent, invisible companions – until they had moved to Los Angeles. The voices had finally emerged from the background and took the form of the angel Gabriel, who told them, "you are the two witnesses God has chosen to announce the end of the world." May then explained that the angel began to visit them in their home every night and sometimes during the day, giving them the words that were to be transcribed in a great book.

May and Ruth produced a tattered Bible and maps they claimed to use as reference tools when editing the dictation. They also had a prop trunk that contained bundles of parchment paper tied together with string. Scrawled on the top page of each bundle were unintelligible metaphysical scribblings. No one was allowed to touch the bundles or pick them up, May explained, the angel had forbidden it.

What the Two Witnesses had discovered was that the universe breathed in and out via a "fourth dimension, swallowing up old versions of reality and replacing them with new ones. The gear that regulated the fourth dimension was called the Tree of Life, which figured prominently in the early chapters of the Bible. When the tree was functioning properly man lived forever, because the universe replaced his aging body with a new body at regular intervals.

Unfortunately, when Adam and Eve ate from the Tree of Life, they threw everything out of whack. Not only did they shift themselves out of gear, but they threw the entire universe out of gear. When man fell, he took the universe with him. Now, the Tree of Life was causing havoc, sucking in the new and pumping out the old, instead of the way it was supposed to be. But it could be fixed! Mankind would soon have the opportunity to make things right by reversing the Tree's cycle. At that point humans would be able to live forever. The layers of death that had been accumulating since the fall of man would be stripped away, one layer at a time. The earth and the universe would be blessed by this reversal of broken time.

Ruth and May – as the Two Witnesses – announced that they had been tasked to find others to help with their divine mission. Not only would a person who understood live forever, but he or she would learn about those pesky "lost measurements of Solomon," which could be used to find hidden deposits of gold and other precious metals.

Once humanity was set right, a Divine Order of the Royal Arms of the Great Eleven would be established. It would be a spiritual family consisting of May, Ruth, and nine other women, all of whom would rule the earth as queens. Marble palaces would be erected for them on Olive Hill in Hollywood, and the queens would be given a horde of gold and diamonds that were somewhere underground near Bakersfield. The queens would not be lonely, either. The angel Gabriel would designate 11 kings of every queen – a harem that may, or may not have, included the current husbands of the designated women.

May's announcement – and I can't even begin to guess how she thought all this up – likely made many of those who heard it roll their eyes in disbelief, but a surprising number of people were receptive to her teachings. At the start the movement was able to boast between 70 and 100 followers. With a few exceptions, it's impossible to say where these early disciples came from. The first undoubtedly came from Portland between 1921 and 1924. In 1925 she made her move to Los Angeles a permanent one. Over the next five years most recruits came from Southern California or from other parts of the country.

A curious aspect of the Great Eleven was its family focus. Husband and wives brought their children and even their parents into the cult. They came from all walks of life and included former reporters, carpenters, farmers, streetcar operators, nurses, pharmacists, truck drivers, oil field workers, salesmen, hotel managers, printers, and more. Sprinkled among them was a self-proclaimed "metaphysician," as well as a few former Christian Scientists, but, for the most part, they were ordinary people who became entranced by the message that May and Ruth had started spreading.

One Portland resident particularly affected by May's story – and who would play a larger role in the future of the cult – was Martha Rhoads and, by extension, her husband William, and daughter Willa.

Martha had been born in Oregon in 1869. William was born in Iowa that same year, though he left there as a young man and traveled west to California and Oregon. He met and married Martha on September 15, 1893. The newlyweds lived in California for a time and it was there in 1897 that their first daughter, Beulah, was born.

Around 1900 the family moved to the small town of Tule Lake, Oregon where they had a second daughter, Robena. After that, they moved to Merrill, Oregon where William leased a ranch and opened a large sawmill. It was a huge success and the family prospered. The sawmill doubled its size and he sold it to the Turner Brothers before dabbling in an unsuccessful political campaign. He went back into the sawmill business after that, but he was never as successful as he once was.

By 1918 the sawmill burned to the ground, causing a major financial setback for the family. The girls had grown up and moved out on their own and now Martha's aging mother, Sarpeta, was living with them. They also lost a portion of their land as a result of a lawsuit that had been filed against them, further complicating their finances – and the rumors that were circulating about them.

William had a good reputation in the community. He was a skilled carpenter who had operated a successful sawmill, built a church, and engaged in civic activities. Martha was known as a deeply religious woman who had served as a Christian Science camp welfare worker during the Great War. On the surface they seemed to be completely respectable, but stories told about them made some of the locals uneasy.

It was said that the couple once had a son who had died when he was nine and the Rhoads had denied him a traditional church burial. They chose instead to have him buried in their front yard in what some said was an odd, ritualistic fashion. Some neighbors believed the Rhoads – specifically Martha – had started a cult in the county. Little was known about it except that it was supposed to be a faith-healing sect.

Among those concerned with the family's activities in the area was a doctor who wrote a 1909 article for a Klamath Falls newspaper in which he protested the activities of Martha and her followers. He listed three incidents during which he believed that children had died because their parents had gone to Martha for healing instead of to a physician. The doctor said that she claimed to heal not only humans but also animals, using only "thought waves."

In Portland, it was said that Martha "took up her religious ideas and more and more became engaged in practices that took up most of her time." It was also reported that "The strange religious work of the family was carried on in Portland and was found to have taken in numerous other Portland residents." At the time that May Otis was forming the Great Eleven in Los Angeles, Martha was in Portland, "engaged in other religious work there."

But Martha was doing more than healing the sick – she also raised the dead, or so she claimed.

She was said to have returned people to life at least five different times. While Christian Science, which she had once practiced, allowed for this possibility, Martha went even further. She claimed that she had raised *herself* from the dead.

Crazy or a pathological liar, it didn't matter – people feared Martha Rhoads. Even though William had always had a good reputation – and admitted that he was "lacking in enthusiasm" for Martha's schemes – he was soon being lumped in with his wife as a practitioner of the occult. He was a devoted husband who was willing to follow his wife into whatever strange predicament she might lead him.

On April 28, 1908 a baby was born to a 15-year-old girl named Iva Eaton and William Adams, 19, the son of a prominent ranch owner named Frank Adams. For many years the baby's father was kept secret. Iva lived with her grandparents and a child born out of wedlock was a great scandal at the time. However, when Iva named the baby, she chose a female variation of the father's name – Willa.

Willa's arrival was not a happy event for the Adams family. William's parents decided that he could neither marry Iva not claim the child as his own. It was clear to the Adams, however, that Iva, a teenage girl with no means of support and no immediate family, would be unable to care for a child on her own. It was decided that Iva should give the child up. The adoption could not be public. The child would have to be privately transferred to the care of new parents, who had to be people that the Adams knew and trusted. Fortunately, two such people lived just a short distance down the road – William and Martha Rhoads.

The Adams approached the Rhoads and explained the situation. A settlement of some kind was reached, and Iva was shipped off to Nevada without her child. On May 4, 1909 William and Martha took custody of the child and her adoption was legally finalized.

In 1910 the Rhoads moved to Portland. For the rest of her life Willa exchanged letters with Iva, who had married by then and lived in Nevada but was happy with her adopted parents. Willa was bright and intelligent, and a good student about whom it was said she had "a remarkable attachment to her religion."

Great Eleven priestess and queen, Willa Rhoads

In 1922, Martha first met May Otis when the high priestess was on her Portland recruitment tour. They met several times, and it was at one of those meetings that May introduced Willa to her. Willa was about 14-years-old at the time. May showed exceptional interest in the young woman and was so taken by her that she elevated her to an honorary leadership position, dubbing her a priestess and queen of the order.

She also began calling her "Tree of Life," making her a symbolic link between God and man. It was one of the highest possible titles within the Great Eleven.

For Willa, though, it would lead to tragedy.

While May was gathering followers, she was still creating a doctrine of what her new religion was going to be. Although influenced by the New Thought movement's ideas of healing and the power of the mind, May really wanted to offer a universe and a god that was all about action, not thoughts. These actions took the form of ceremonies, rites, blood sacrifices, and the assignment of magical names to her followers. May's theology was so esoteric that some of her followers would admit to not truly understanding it. They just trusted that she knew what she was doing, which says a lot about the power of May's personality – or their own desperation.

If her followers didn't understand her teaching, there was little hope for anyone outside of the cult. A *Los Angeles Times* reporter called it "the most bewildering hodge-podge of biblical and mythological references, cross-references, and statements that possibly has even been gathered together."

May presented the idea, "One body and four kinds of flesh, knitted together into one order for the body of man to include four kinds of flesh. God's body includes the four kinds of flesh, and God's body is liked together into a seamless garment of one being. And man, reflecting God in four kinds of flesh is knit into one seamless garment at one with his maker." She made allusions to the stars and talked about precious minerals in the earth, the "Holy Osucilation of God's Body" (she may have meant oscillation, but maybe not), the existence of God as a "sentient vortex," Hermetic Principles and Ancient Egypt, numerology, and "concords," which she called the relationship between the visible and invisible worlds.

Yikes – I can see what the *Times* reporter was talking about.

May believed that concords could be established by rituals but took the idea further by assigning a special name to her disciples in order to "induce a harmonious condition" between them and the solar system. She believed the name – or concord – reflected his or her role in the universe.

Magical names included "The Four Winds of the Whirlwind," "The Gravitation Upwards," "Queen of the Scaling Breath Inside of the Body," "The Trees that Take in the Seven Concords of Vegetation," "The Division Between Matter and Spirit," "The New Road to Freedom," "The Sand Bar Between Water and Land," "The Still Waters," "Eternal Circle of Taste," "The Circling of the Minor Scale in the Harmony of Music" – and there were many others. All of them seem to be a bit long to use as a day-to-day name, so I'm not clear if they were only used in ritual or how cult members were supposed to address each other.

May's concord was "The North Star," though she had also designated herself "The Heel of God," "Her Heavenly Highness, Queen May," or just "Queen May" to her friends. Most of her followers just called her "Mother."

Ruth's concord was "Grand Royal Water of the Father's Blood." This name was never explained, but in May's doctrine water was the most beautiful thing in the visible world.

The rules that May created for her followers ranged from the dramatic to the deranged. Cult members were prohibited from buying apples because they were the forbidden fruit that caused man's fall and broke the Tree of Life. The Great Eleven would not be able to restore the Tree of Life if they consumed apples because its members would be re-enacting the moment that broke the universe in the first place. Similarly, T-bone steaks were not allowed because May viewed the "T" as a concord for the cross that Christ was crucified on, which created a "negative harmonic." Walnuts were not permitted because they built an invisible wall ("wall nuts") between members of the cult, creating disharmony.

Weird? Yes, but sometimes her announcements were truly insane.

She wrote that God had changed Abram's name in the Old Testament to AbraHAM so he could have a thread to Ham. The descendants of Ham (May believed in the popular racist idea of the time that the descendants of Ham were black because of the *Curse of Ham*) became slaves in the South. To free the slaves God placed AbraHAM Lincoln in office. HAM was tied to HAM through God's invisible thread so the slaves could be freed. AbraHAM Lincoln thus balanced the South, which is why a Lincoln penny was used to pay the penny tax that balanced the books of the United States. The Lincoln penny was made of copper, a conductor of electricity, which established a concord between Lincoln and Franklin D. Roosevelt because the latter was God's "live wire," i.e., a man of lightning and great intelligence, which was why Roosevelt's presidential yacht, *USS Potomac*, was formerly a coast guard cutter called *Elektra*.

Creepy Ward Blackburn

That, May taught, was the divine thread that connected the Abram of the Old Testament to Franklin Roosevelt, as evidenced by a biblical name change, the Curse of Ham, slavery, pennies, and yachts. Not surprisingly, the car she drove was a Lincoln. Her followers believed these insights proved that she had a special relationship with God.

They just make my head hurt.

While May was in Oregon putting her religion together, she began a peculiar relationship with the man that she was soon going to marry – her stepbrother, Ward Blackburn.

Born in 1901 Ward was a year younger than Ruth, which in itself made his relationship with Ruth's mother more than a little strange. The fact that he was May's stepbrother was even stranger.

A former Portland bellboy, Ward groomed himself in a style of the time known as the "Oriental mystic" – greased back hair, eyebrows trimmed to thin lines, and a Fu Manchu mustache that dropped below his jawline. He also was known for having five-inch fingernails. Aside from that he was a smelly, sloppy man who wore the same clothing – usually a brown, ill-fitting suit – for days at a time. He was never considered particularly smart nor ambitious, and a former classmate of his once called him a "sub-normal child, with many queer traits not seen in other boys."

Ward was also a pedophile.

These were not ideal traits in a new husband, but then May had her own issues. She was 20 years older than Ward, semi-delusional and self-absorbed, and had a phobia about being touched. No one but Ruth was ever allowed to come into physical contact with her. This was likely the reason for her odd habit of requiring cash or check donations to be placed on the ground, where she could pick them up. This minimized the possibility of accidental contact. May's phobia would have made physical intimacy with anyone difficult.

But that was fine. Ward had little interest in a sexual relationship with her anyway. He liked his females to be much, much younger.

In a twisted way they were perfect for each other. Ward's low intelligence and lack of ambition worked well with May's megalomania. There would be no clashes of ego and no marital spats. May was "Mother," a Witness Chosen by God – Ward obeyed her without question.

As far as Ward's sexual issues went, some have implied that perhaps May shared them. Her fascination with Willa and the other child "queens" that ended up in the cult suggests she had issues of her own. One time May approached a mother and daughter at a store, and May asked the woman to "give" her the daughter. She promised to dress the "beautiful" little girl like an angel. The horrified woman obviously refused, but after that, lived in fear that the high priestess might try and kidnap her child.

In another report May's car was stopped in front of a Simi Valley house where a child was playing in the front yard. Her driver got out and moved toward the child but, fortunately, a neighbor with a gun appeared and chased him away.

May and Ward were married on January 11, 1924 in Santa Ana, California. When applying for a marriage license May identified herself as "Mamie Holmes" and claimed to be 30-years-old. She was actually in her 40's, and her name was not Mamie, but misrepresentations aside, she received the name from Ward that she would keep the rest of her life – and which she would make infamous.

She was now May Otis Blackburn, priestess of the "Blackburn Cult."

In the spring of 1924, May, Ruth, and the Blackburn clan left Oregon and returned to Los Angeles. They moved into a house on Acacia Street that no longer exists, and it became their small, cramped, temporary headquarters. The Great Eleven was still young, but it was starting to grow.

Ruth was now divorced and free of Arthur Osborne's affections, but being the "women of many loves," she was looking for male companionship. She found that with a young Italian-American man from Chicago named Samuel Rizzio. He was then just 17-years-old. May was 24.

Sam came from a large family. His father, Angelo, was an Italian immigrant who came to America in 1901. He was now the owner of a small grocery store. Sam's mother, Francis, spent her days caring for Sam and his seven younger siblings. They were packed into a small apartment on Pasadena Avenue.

The Rizzio family had an interesting history. While living in Chicago Angelo had been the target of the Black Hand, a loosely organized version organized crime that blackmailed and extorted wealthy Italians. They sent threatening letters to business owners and crime bosses alike, demanding money. If they didn't get it, the target of the letter might see his business burned, his house blown up, or his family and friends murdered. Apparently, Angelo didn't respond to the threats the way the Black Hand wanted – he fought back. In 1912 he found himself wanted by the police for a triple murder. He quickly packed up his family and fled to California.

Sam also had a criminal history. He was only 17 but had already served nine months at the California State Reformatory for "check irregularities." He also had – Ruth later claimed – a bad temper and a propensity for violence. That probably wasn't an exaggeration.

But Ruth loved a "bad boy" and found herself attracted to him. On May 24, 1924 they were married, Frances Rizzio tentatively approved of the marriage. She said, "We did not hold it against Ruth that she was of a different religious belief when she married Sammy." This was probably true because soon Frances and Sammy, both good Catholics, were inducted into Ruth's religious order, which they'd been assured was "Christian" in nature – even if it was a little odd. They were both assured a share of the Great Eleven's profits, which might have been the most important reason for acceptance.

Ruth with Sam Rizzio

Meanwhile, May was getting frustrated. The house on Acacia Street was too small for her needs, and she wanted to increase both the size and stature of the Divine Order. She couldn't do that with her current congregation, which was mostly made of up down-on-their-luck blue-collar workers. She needed to recruit some people with real money. To do that, she needed a proper front for her operation.

She eventually found the perfect place in the upscale Wilshire District. It was a large three-story, 10-room home that was owned by Rudolph Frederick "Fred" Vogel, a 48-year-old real estate millionaire. It was his wife, Edna, who agreed to rent the house to May. The ink was still wet on the lease agreement when May started violating it by converting the house into an apartment building to house her Great Eleven disciples. It became the cult's new headquarters.

Not much is known about what happened behind the walls of the house after the cult moved in, but neighbors frequently complained about loud "elaborate sessions" that went on until the early morning hours.

Around this same time Ward and William Blackburn opened a small office building on South Olive Street where they established a printing company. By August the *Seventh Trumpet of Gabriel* began rolling off the press. This was not the great book promised by May and Ruth – it was an eight-page pamphlet, or series of pamphlets. It was through these booklets that May shared with a baffled public her insights into the universe.

That the *Seventh Trumpet* was a series of pamphlets must have come as a surprise to May's followers, who believed that it was going to be the book that would bring about the apocalypse, eternal life, and wealth beyond measure. However, May explained that the book was still coming. They were waiting on the angels to finish it. The pamphlets were just the way for the angels to pave the way for a far greater work, *The Lamb's Book of Life*, which was later re-titled *The Great Sixth Seal*. Its publication would, in effect, break the sixth seal of the scroll described in the Book of Revelation.

Isn't it frightening how many of the cults and wacky churches within these pages are hung up on the Book of Revelation? It has to be the most misunderstood and misinterpreted book in the Bible, and yeah, that's saying a lot.

May had been promising her followers the book for two years and had often told them that it was *almost* complete. By the way, it would remain *almost* complete for another decade. To keep them happy she offered them an intermediate product in the form of the booklets.

The pamphlets were impossible to figure out, though. A newspaper reporter called it "unfathomable" and said that it appeared to be a "ritual book" that was only comprehensible to someone who was already an initiate of the Great Eleven. Anyone outside of the cult would never figure it out – there was no narrative and really, no point, to any of it.

Believe it or not, May's followers accepted her story and continued to be faithful. She had a magnetic personality and was filled with promises of future rewards. She also intimated that God would punish anyone who fell away from the Order. The punishment could take many forms, but it would almost certainly be fatal.

Everyone decided to stay – just in case.

Ruth and Sam had been married only two months before they started having serious problems. It's easy to understand why. Sam was eight years younger than his wife, who was by then a queen of the Great Eleven and treated with reverence by everyone around her, except her husband. He was a permanent guest of the order with no real importance, and worse, a Catholic. He'd been assigned to work next to William and Ward at the cult's printing press. No one knew what else to do with him.

Sam was unwilling to participate in the rituals of the Great Eleven. He was tired of the closed-door sessions where Ruth and May supposedly took dictation from an angel. He tried to convince Ruth to abandon the cult and move out of the headquarters – she refused. Ruth was a witness, a prophetess, a priestess, and a queen of the Great Eleven. To abandon this role for an ex-convict with an anger problem was unthinkable.

It also didn't help that Ruth was beautiful and was still that "woman of many loves." She still had a lot of interested suitors, and cult members claimed that an insanely jealous Sam threatened to kidnap Ruth if she didn't voluntarily leave the Great Eleven.

By July 1924 things were ugly. Sam allegedly struck Ruth on the side of the head during an argument, cutting her eyelid open. Sam left the house and when he tried to return, he was stopped by May and several other cult members. The infuriated young man stormed out of the house.

Five years later Ruth said, "He left, and I have not seen him since."

There may have been some truth to that – or maybe not. The argument with Sam, his striking her, and him being thrown out of the house may have happened just as Ruth said it did.

But what happened before – and after – his disappearance is a bit more complicated.

One of the members of the Blackburn Cult was a druggist named Eleanor Sandrosky. According to her later story, May Blackburn came into her drug store on the first Sunday of July 1924. May asked her to come to the cult's headquarters as soon as possible on an urgent matter. Eleanor, concerned, did so.

When she arrived, she was led upstairs and found herself in a room with May, Mathilda, and William Blackburn – but not Ruth. On tables and in boxes around the room were parcels tied with string that Eleanor was told contained manuscripts that would eventually be included in *The Great Sixth Seal*.

But that wasn't what the meeting was about. It was about a new and disturbing revelation that May had received from the angel Gabriel. According to May, Gabriel had told her that she was supposed to kill Samuel Rizzio and that he commanded Eleanor to give her the poison with which to do it. Sam was "draining the life out of her," May said.

But don't worry, she assured Eleanor, once he is dead, he will come back to life. May would resurrect him as soon as she published *The Great Sixth Seal*.

Eleanor left the house in a state of shock and spent the next few days hoping that another angel might appear to May and call off the murder. But it didn't work out that way.

A short time later May again approached Eleanor and asked for poison. This time, though, she said that she did not intend to kill Sam. She was simply requiring him to go through a ritual that would "rid him of another belief that prevented him from accepting his concord in the Great Eleven." During the ritual, which would take place on the beach in Santa Monica, Sam would be dressed in ceremonial robes and would perform a "whirling dervish" on sand that had been sprinkled with poison while chanting "I am a dead priest."

You have to give May credit for her imagination.

Sam would only symbolically die – it would not be the real thing. May just needed some kind of poison that would leave no trace for the ritual. The angel said that it had to be deadly, and he'd added that if Eleanor told a soul about it, her "bones would crumble, and you will drop in a heap."

Eleanor, terrified, agreed to provide the poison. When she left May said that she would have a messenger come to the drug store and pick it up. By the time Eleanor got home she was upset and angry. She believed that May was lying to her about the ceremony. Her husband, Simon, agreed. In fact, he'd already decided that May was a fraud and told his wife that they should demand the $750 back that they had donated to the cult when they had joined.

A few days later Eleanor met May at the cult's headquarters and told her what her husband had said, adding that neither he nor she believed in May's promises anymore. She said that if their money was not returned, they would go to the District Attorney and expose her.

May flew into a fit of rage, demanding that Eleanor leave her husband and threatened that if Simon went to the District Attorney he would "drop dead" before anything happened.

Eleanor fled. She had no intention of leaving her husband and knew that no real case would be made against May or the Great Eleven. May would just deny the charges, and then, maybe an angel would tell May to kill the Sandroskys next.

The next day a messenger walked into the pharmacy and told Eleanor that she was there to pick up the poison, along with a bottle of chloroform. Eleanor gave her the chloroform – which was perfectly legal at the time – but instead of poison, gave her a bottle of colored water.

The next day, Eleanor and Simon quit the cult.

In 1930, the messenger – whose name was Mary Stewart – told the authorities that she knew Eleanor had given her colored water, not poison, but she didn't care. No one intended to kill Sam, and the ceremony went on that evening as planned. It happened just the way that May had described it with the colored water – not poison, she stressed – being poured into the sand. The ceremony had lasted only minutes, and when it was over, Sam had driven them all home. May denied that she had ever been ordered by an angel to kill her son-in-law.

There would never be any way for the police to determine the validity of Mary Stewart's story. By then the bottle of liquid – whether colored water or poison – was gone forever.

And so was Sam Rizzio.

Though the large home where May had been living served wonderfully as a headquarters for the cult, May grew tired of living there. In October 1924 she moved into a new home on North Vermont, a large house that newspaper reporters would eventually describe as "pretentious."

She may have chosen this address for a very good reason – it was only a few blocks away from the majestic home and manicured lawn of the Dabney family, with whom May was about to become deeply embroiled.

Richard and Martha Dabney, from Illinois and Iowa, were married in the late 1880s, and their first child, Clifford, was born in 1890. Richard, the son of an Illinois farmer, had several siblings, the most notable of whom was his younger brother, Joseph. At age 22, Joseph was an attorney but was not content with acting as a lawyer for the rest of his life. He traveled the country and ended up in California in 1892, where he began pursuing his new interest in oil exploration.

In 1900, he and a man named E.J. Miley leased a parcel of land in the San Joaquin Valley where they drilled 10 oil wells. They were hugely successful, and the following year Joseph formed the Dabney Oil Company. He began drilling more wells and making more money – a lot of it. He became extremely wealthy but also donated millions of dollars to charity and to the California Institute of Technology.

In 1916, his brother, Richard, died. His widow and children moved to Los Angeles and took up residence on North Oxford, a short distance from the home that May Blackburn would later occupy.

Joseph Dabney continued looking – and finding – oil. Huge deposits had been found at Huntington Beach, Santa Fe Springs, and Telegraph Hill. It was a cutthroat business and many oilmen would do whatever it took to find the next big patch of oil – including bribery, extortion, and even murder.

In 1920, Joseph instructed his nephew, Clifford, to locate and procure oil lands in the vicinity of Signal Hill. He was tasked with not only finding land that might generate oil but with sending prospective sellers of rights or leases to his uncle for negotiations. If a deal was reached, Clifford would then share in the profits made from the land.

This became Clifford's primary occupation in the 1920s. It was hard work but promised tremendous wealth if he found the right places to look for oil.

This would eventually lead him to May Blackburn.

In November 1924, Clifford and his wife, Alice, were introduced to May, who – surprise – only lived a few blocks away from them. Dabney – a 33-year-old, well-dressed, and conventionally handsome man – had a surprising number of unconventional interests, especially when it came to the occult. So, he was not shocked by the stories he heard about May and her cult. He'd heard about the group's planned publication of *The Great Sixth Seal,* and he asked May exactly what the book would do.

It would explain all life's mysteries, she told him, offering her usual reply but, knowing her audience, added that it would reveal where precious jewels and minerals were hidden – including oil. It would restore the "lost measurements" and bring youth, happiness, wealth, and eternal life to all members of the Great Eleven.

Clifford wanted to know when the book would be published and if he, as a member of the cult, would be able to obtain a copy. May told him that she was merely dictating the book, not writing it, but it appeared that the solar system would be "in the right condition" for publication in February 1925.

With the date right around the corner Clifford weighed the risks and decided to gamble that May had an insight that no one else had. He and Alice joined the Great Eleven and donated $5,000 toward the publication of *The Great Sixth Seal*. A few days later the Dabneys met with May and Ruth to receive their concords, which they were told required another donation of $500.

Clifford Dabney paid in cash.

In November 1924, William, Martha, and Will Rhoads finally followed the Blackburns to Los Angeles. William was reluctant to move but his wife was anxious to take on a more active role in the Great Eleven, and he was always happy to please her. He was also pressured to leave by his foster daughter. Willa had been designated a queen in the cult and May had been pressuring her to come to Los Angeles and take her place among the other ten queens of the Great Eleven. After they arrived the family moved into one of the apartments at the cult's headquarters.

They had only just unpacked when Mathilda Blackburn came to call. She brought with her seven puppies, a gift for Willa. Mathilda suggested that the dogs be named after the seven tones of the musical scale – Do, Re, Mi, Fa, So, La, and Ti. This was a carefully planned decision. The seven tones of the musical scale played a large role in the Great Eleven's theology and were said to correspond to Willa's concord as the Tree of Life.

Willa settled into a happy life in Los Angeles. She lived in what she considered a fancy home in a nice area of the city. The weather was always beautiful, and she had much to occupy her time. But she also knew that her life would only be perfect when *The Great Sixth Seal* was published, and she took her throne in Hollywood.

But Willa's almost-perfect life was about to come crashing down.

On Christmas Day 1924, Willa became ill from an ulcerated tooth. A visit to a doctor or dentist at this point likely would have prevented what was to come, but there was no possibility that Martha, who believing in heal by thoughts and prayers, would allow it. She spent the next five days trying to correct the "wrongful belief" that was causing Willa's illness.

Her attempts failed. Willa got sicker. Her condition deteriorated with the ulceration causing her throat to constrict. She was in horrible pain as the pus from the infection continued to form in the socket of the affected tooth. As her fever rose, her face became swollen, and the infection seeped into her bloodstream.

Baffled by her failure to cure her daughter, Martha decided that Willa's death was preordained. She assured Willa that all would be well – she would be resurrected, as was promised in *The Great Sixth Seal*. Willa was confused by this at first – she was, after all, half out of her mind with pain – but eventually, she accepted the inevitability of her death and resurrection.

On December 31, though, Willa suddenly started feeling better. She got out of bed for the first time in nearly a week and got dressed. Hopes were high that the worst was over. It seemed that the faith of the cult members had saved the Great Eleven's youngest queen.

But it didn't last. On New Year's Day Willa suffered a relapse and returned to her sickbed. Some of the cult members begged her mother to allow them to bring a doctor, but Martha refused. Later that afternoon, with her parents, friends, and fellow followers around her, Willa died.

Despite her assurances to her daughter that she would be resurrected when *The Great Sixth Seal* was published, Martha actually made a few attempts to revive her right away. She had raised the dead before, she believed, and had no reason to think she couldn't do it again.

Needless to say, it didn't work.

May was at home when she received the news of Willa's passing. Unaware the girl's condition had deteriorated so quickly, she rushed to the cult's headquarters where she met Ruth. They both hurried to the dead girl's bedside, overcome with grief. It was then that Willa's parents asked May what to do with their daughter's body. Should she be buried or cremated?

But May shook her head. God had sent her a message – he needed her body for a little while.

May left but returned two hours later and announced that the angels Gabriel and Michael had told her that Willa would live again. If the cult turned her body over the authorities it would be "dissected," which would prevent a bodily resurrection. That couldn't be allowed to happen.

The bad news, May explained, was that the resurrection would not occur until after Passover, an event that would coincide with the release of *The Great Sixth Seal*. Perhaps because she did not want other cult members to know about Willa's death, May wanted the body moved to the Blackburn house. The corpse was wrapped in a blanket, quietly taken out of the headquarters, and was placed in May's car. It was propped upright between two unnamed people and driven away.

At May's house, Walter and Martha helped carry the body into a bathroom, where it was placed in a tub filled with ice. Salt was poured on the ice around the body, but care was taken so that none of the salt touched it.

May then announced that Willa's pet dogs were to be killed and placed next to her body. She explained that the puppies were the "hinges" to Willa's heart and must accompany her in life and death. The dogs were either chloroformed or poisoned – accounts vary – but all were killed and placed in the icy bathtub with Willa's body.

Willa's corpse was later moved to a bedroom that had been specially prepared for her as a "sleeping chamber" so that she would find herself in pleasant surroundings when she woke up. May had fresh flowers brought to the room each day until May 1925, after Willa had been dead for five months. That was when May announced that she was moving her home – and the cult's headquarters – to Santa Monica.

The cult's new headquarters were in Ocean Park in Santa Monica and had been donated by Mary Stewart, the wealthy cult member who had picked up the "colored water" at the drug store around the time Sam Rizzio disappeared. She also signed over a house around the corner for May's private use.

Willa's body posed a problem, however. She was still trying to keep Willa's death a secret from most of the cult – although likely more knew about it than she thought – but with nowhere else to take the corpse, May had to figure out a way to conceal it inside the new cult headquarters.

Before everyone else moved in May visited the house with Mary Stewart, William Rhoads, and possible cult member Floyd Miller, who was a carpenter. They looked around and concluded that a secret compartment could be built at the rear of the house. The hidden room could be large enough to accommodate a bathtub that could be filled with ice and Willa's body.

While Floyd framed out the secret room William Rhoads returned to May's house, where he constructed two cedar coffins – one for Willa and one for the seven dogs. Both were lined with copper, and he soldered the joints to make them airtight.

According to newspaper accounts, Willa's body was moved from one house to the other by placing it in the backseat and driving it from place to place as if she was still alive. Some historians, like Samuel Fort, who is an expert on the case, have disputed this and say this creepy and colorful tale "almost certainly" never happened. Most believe that Willa and the dogs were placed in their coffins for transport. That's probably what really happened – but would the alternative really surprise anyone at this point?

The bodies were moved without incident and hidden away in the secret chamber. It was a dismal place, though. The room at May's home had been perfumed with flowers and filled with sunshine. The new tomb had no windows, no light, and little air. But Willa wouldn't stay there for long – things were strange, but they were about to get even stranger.

A few months later, May instructed William and Martha Rhoads to buy a two-bedroom cottage on Marco Place in Venice. In February 1926, she told them that the angels had told her that Willa's body was going to be temporarily interred.

This must have been both good news and bad news to William and Martha. It suggested that an immediate resurrection of their daughter was not going to happen, but at least it also meant that Willa would be decently buried – sort of.

William and Floyd Miller began digging a burial chamber beneath the floor of one of the cottage bedrooms. They spent two days digging holes large enough for the two coffins. They were placed under the floor with the lids removed, so that Willa could escape when the time came for her return. After that, they installed a trap door to grant the Rhoads access to the burial chamber – or a way for Willa to get out.

While this work was being completed Martha went to the City Drug Company pharmacy and presented the druggist. J.J. Freeman, with a torn page from an old book that contained "an unusual formula for embalming the dead." Martha spent $26 buying a variety of herbs, spices, and ointments that would create the formula on the page.

Ingredients in hand, she returned home and began preparing Willa's body for burial. She applied the mixture but did nothing to preserve her daughter's internal organs. The corpse was then placed into the coffin but was not laid on its back, as would be expected. Instead, following Martha's unique beliefs, the corpse was placed with its knees drawn up to the chest and its hands crossed. The puppies were wrapped in white sheets and placed in the other coffin.

On February 10, 1926, the trapdoor was closed. Rites were performed, but what they were remains a mystery. Martha later stated, "We buried Willa, and the seven dogs there with the rites that I believe are called for in the seven symbols of the sounds of Gabriel's trumpet and the Sixth Seal."

For three years Martha and William lived in the cottage, sleeping each night above the slowly decaying remains of their daughter and a coffin filled with poisoned puppies.

By 1926, the Great Eleven was able to boast more than 100 local members. This began causing a housing shortage because many of these members expected May to provide them with someplace to live. She began moving them around, putting them in houses in Santa Monica, Los Angeles, and Monrovia. But spreading them out made them more difficult for her to manage, which was a large problem for someone who needed to be in control as badly as May did.

May also began to worry about public scrutiny. To "manifest the proper concords and maintain a harmonious relationship with the universe," the Great Eleven often held outdoor rituals. Conducted at night, they frequently included animal sacrifices, burials, and exhumations. Curious neighbors often complained about these activities and threatened to call the police – and after the disappearances of Sam Rizzio and the death of Willa Rhoads, May was not anxious to have an encounter with the law.

With this in mind, she decided to establish a colony in the Simi Valley, north of Los Angeles. At the time this area was sparsely populated and sufficiently remote that the cult did not have to worry about the prying eyes of outsiders. However, it was still close enough for her to easily travel there from the city.

By the autumn of 1926, she had convinced Clifford Dabney to purchase and transfer to the cult 10 hilly lots of land in an area of the valley called Mortimer Park. It was undeveloped and consisted of hills, sand, and a lot of rocks. It was, without question, the worst place in the valley to build houses, but that was exactly where May intended most of her followers to live.

But not all of them, of course. Many of the families remained in the homes where they already lived. And, naturally, May and Ruth had no intention of living in the rough, rugged valley, but they did maintain a cabin there for when they attended cult events. Their cabin was dubbed "the Watchtower." Clifford Dabney also had a cabin in what cult members began calling "The Work," which was short for the "Work of God."

Initially, Great Eleven followers camped out in tents. The winter of 1926 took a toll on them. They used fires for heat, lanterns for light, and had to carry water in buckets from some distance away. Only dirt roads traveled into the valley, connecting it to the outside world.

By 1927, work began on the shelters and cabins. May contracted with the Hammond Lumber Company to provide the necessary wood. They extended credit to the Blackburns, which turned out to be a terrible idea. They were forced to sue them for payment in 1929. They were still suing them in 1933.

The cabins slowly came together, as did the "Golden Throne Temple," a white, crescent-shaped, four-room building that towered over the other smaller structures. Through the main doors a visitor to the temple found himself in a long living room that was illuminated by stained glass windows. At the far end of the room was the "inner Shrine," which held the "Lord's Furniture Set," intended for use by the Messiah, who would appear after the cult had undone the damage to the Tree of Life. The most prominent piece of furniture was a massive throne that weighed more than 500 pounds. It had been built with gumwood and was embossed with gold leaf. It was so heavy that it took eight men to carry it onto the building. The throne's design, May claimed, had been given to her by an angel.

Other items in the Lord's furniture set included a large couch upholstered with gold satin, an overstuffed gold satin chair, and a seven-foot-tall dresser with three mirrors. A variety of cult props were also stored here, like a lion's head and a variety of knives for sacrifices.

The Temple also held a long, narrow dining room for cult meals. Next door to the Temple was May and Ruth's "Watchtower," and to the north were the stables where they kept the "sacred animals" – horses and mules – and the animals used for sacrifices.

Near the stables were the cabins for cult members, which were generously described as "simple." These structures perched rather precariously on the hillsides around the valley. The cabins had a *combined* assessed valley of less than $2,000 in 1930. They were furnished with water from a large water tank that sat on a dome-

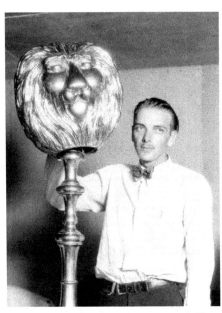

The lion's head was one of the cult's props, stored in the main temple at the settlement

shaped rock above them. There were also three springs in the area. The cabins also shared a single post office box at the post office that was 12 miles away.

I'm assuming that no one had ever promised the new members a "life of luxury."

May had high hopes for the colony. In addition to the cabins she hoped to build a much larger printing facility, knowing that she would need to provide every person on the planet with a copy of *The Great Sixth Seal* when it was finally completed. By now it was two years overdue.

She also hoped to build "The Great Argumental Parlor of Interview of the World," where "all denominations, doctors, lawyers, clergymen, scientists, and professors can gather together to discuss *The Great Six Seal*." She also planned to build a sunken garden, playground, tennis courts, and a swimming pool.

Of course, none of that ever actually happened.

It's hard for many of us to believe how the nuttiness of the Great Eleven attracted so many people to the cause, but it did. May and Ruth gathered many followers and demanded tributes of money and property from them so that they could finance and continue their great work.

Many of the cult members' experiences with the Great Eleven ended in tragedy.

Merritt Woodell was a handsome, likable young man who was brought into the cult with his parents, Charles and Deborah. Given the concord of the "King of Peace," he was easy to get along with, and many confided in him about their frustrations with the cult. The Woodell family remained living in their home in Santa Monica after the colony was completed, though Merritt spent a lot of time there. Like his father he had driven a truck for a living but had been forced to quit his job after joining the cult. He then became an occasional driver for May and was responsible for the upkeep on the colony's Temple.

One afternoon May kept looking for him at the group's Hollywood headquarters and told him that she needed him to drive her somewhere and that Merritt had been assigned a mission "by an angel." She explained that God wanted him to be shot by Ruth – but not to worry, it would only be in the foot.

Merritt nervously went along with it and drove to a drugstore, where May told him to buy some bandages. After that they drove out to the colony for the "ceremony."

When they arrived, he was taken out to a clearing by May while Ruth went into one of the buildings. She came back carrying an automatic. The gun banged loudly – but not as loud as Merritt's screams of pain. The bullet passed through his heel.

Merritt was calmed down and bandaged up but, not surprisingly, held a deep resentment toward May from that point on. Even so he never lashed out publicly against her. When later asked about the shooting by the authorities, he claimed that he'd shot himself in the foot while cleaning his gun.

He never forgave May, though. When eating alone he sometimes ate fish, which was forbidden.

But not everyone survived their encounter with May and the Great Eleven.

Frances Turner, the sister of Great Eleven member Margaret Sands, was paralyzed and unable to speak when her sister brought her to May, hoping for a miracle.

In mid-March 1928, May had Frances taken to the cabin of her mother, Mathilda Blackburn. Inside was a newly constructed brick platform that was about five feet wide. Chicken wire was suspended above the platform's surface, creating an opening of around 18 inches. Hot bricks from a nearby stove were placed on top of the chicken wire, effectively turning the platform into a broiler. Frances was then placed on the platform, which was supposed to ease her suffering.

May required the entire colony to be evacuated during the "treatment." The last thing her followers saw was Frances lying on the platform, under the hot bricks, coughing. The "treatment" lasted two days. To keep the oven hot, cooling bricks were changed out periodically with hot ones.

Frances Turner's condition made it impossible for her to speak – or scream, if necessary. Needless to say, the "cure" didn't work. She died two days later. According to William Blackburn it was "peaceful," but we'll never know if that was really true.

Her official cause of death was "leakage of the heart" and the death certificate was not signed until five days later. No coroner ever examined the body. Her estate was sold a year later. One has to wonder where the proceeds from it ended up.

No real investigation of Frances Turner's death ever occurred, but May did have the brick oven dismantled. The bricks from the oven that literally cooked a woman to death were used to make a pathway to one of the cabins.

And there were others who died.

Harlene Satoris was one of them. The Portland woman was the daughter of a prominent businessman and politician, Francis Satoris. She was a talented musician and worked in a music store, but as years passed friends said that she "began acting strangely and developed unusual beliefs and tendencies." After a failed suicide attempt Harlene was sent to an asylum. When she was eventually released her family expected her to move home. Instead she traveled to Los Angeles and joined the Great Eleven. She had a bad heart and hoped that the cult – and life in the colony – would cure her health problems.

Harlene settled in well and soon after her arrival wrote to her father and told him that May was looking for workers to help with the publication of *The Great Sixth Seal*.

Anxious to be with their daughter Francis and his wife traveled to Simi Valley. It was a primitive settlement, but Francis was intrigued by May's plan to turn the colony into something larger and more important. They decided to stay.

On May 4, 1928 Harlene was in an unusual amount of pain and her father summoned a doctor to the colony. He examined her and said that she was suffering from a serious gastric disease. He didn't believe that her condition was treatable. The doctor left and Harlene died that night.

The following morning Francis Satoris tried to contact the doctor to obtain a death certificate, but he couldn't be reached. Another doctor who came to the colony refused to sign the death certificate. Finally, the original doctor returned and listed the cause of death as "gastric hemorrhages." Later, though, Francis would tell reporters that his daughter died of heart disease.

In the end it would not be the weird claims and accusations of sex scandals, animal sacrifices, disappearances, bizarre rituals, or mysterious deaths that would bring down the Blackburn cult, it would be something as boring as civil suits for fraud.

By July 1927, Clifford Dabney was nearly broke. He had written checks to May valued at over $21,000 and, at her command, had purchased all the land for the colony and had received $500 for food and a shack in the hills. The oilman and his wife were now dependent on May for subsistence. He didn't understand how he'd gotten to this point. He was an intelligent man from a respectable and wealthy family, yet his ambitions and hope had blinded him to the absurdness of everything that May had promised him. To make matters worse, many of the oil properties that Dabney had found for his uncle weren't acquired, due to title issues or nonproductive wells. It was a huge financial setback for him. He had spent years seeking out the properties and they were supposed to generate a large revenue stream for himself and his family in the future.

Now, there was nothing – and May still demanded money from him.

Reality set in for Dabney on July 31 when he took his car into a garage for repairs and he was unable to pay the $191.07 bill. The mechanic waved it off and told him to pay it another day, but two years later Dabney would be in small-claims court after failing to pay the bill – with 15-cents to his name.

Enough was enough. He and Alice were finished with the Great Eleven. He told May that they were leaving but she refused to let him go. God, she told him, still has a place for you here. But Dabney didn't know she was serious until January 1, 1928 when he was summoned to the colony. He arrived to find that May had somehow gotten a Richfield Oil Company lease that belonged to him. He owned the rights to a field that the company paid him $400 each month for – all of which he had been donating to the Great Eleven for years.

May told him that an angel had directed him to give her the lease. If he did not, "death will surely come upon you."

Upset but terrified by the threat, Dabney agreed to sign over the oil properties. He begged her, though, to allow him to keep the payments for a while until he could get back on his feet. To his surprise May agreed and asked him when the payments were made each month. Dabney told her, which was a big mistake. Her promise was too good to be true. Each month on the date of the payment May came to his house and rode with him to the offices of the Richfield Oil Company. He received his check, endorsed it, and handed it over to May, leaving him with nothing.

Why did he go along with this as long as he did? According to Dabney, he remained in the cult only because he feared what the other members would do to him and his family if he left. Yes, he had immersed himself in the occult teachings of the order for years but grew disenchanted. He said that he became too scared to leave – and he was likely telling the truth. Eventually reports surfaced of adherents who fell out of line being beaten, attacked, pulled into cars at gunpoint, and disappearing altogether. Clifford and Alice could come and go from the colony as they pleased, but they knew their home in Los Angeles was no sanctuary from May's dedicated followers.

At this point, however, Dabney was penniless, mostly because of his donations to the Great Eleven. May refused to share any secret knowledge with him so that he could find new oil fields, and he had started to doubt that the publication of *The Sixth Great Seal* would ever take place.

He'd lost most of his fortune because of the cult and his involvement with it was causing problems in his family. He involved Alice and his sister-in-law, Bessie Mosier, in what had appeared to be an uplifting – and profitable – undertaking, but things had taken a dark turn. Recently, "an uncle" had offered Dabney $75,000 if he would prosecute May, ending all the nonsense once and for all. He finally decided he was ready to do that. He confided his plan to ruin May to Merritt Woodell – the "King of Peace" with the bad limp – telling him that as soon as May was locked up he was going to seize all the automobiles owned by the cult, as well as the homes in the colony, the rights to *The Great Sixth Seal*, and all the "Lord's Furniture."

He was not the only disaffected member. Jennie Toy, another of May's wealthy converts, was bitter that May had never delivered the riches she had promised to lure her and her husband into the cult. She also told Woodell about her plans to leave. He was, as can be imagined, still a little upset about being shot in the foot.

Evelyn Whitemore had already left the colony, along with several other members. She later said, "The things we had been taught to believe were not coming true." She had loaned May $1,200 to help with the publication of her long-promised book, and when she left the cult, she demanded the return of her money. She must have been very persistent because May gave her the deed to an old cult headquarters in exchange. It wasn't much of a loss for May, though, since it had been donated to her by another member years before.

Nellie Banks – mother of faithful cult member Gale Banks – also left the colony. In June 1929 she was contacted by a private detective who wanted to know about the inner workings of the cult. She sent the detective a lengthy letter, telling him of her contributions, and offering him notes and receipts from her transactions. She did not blame her son for the money she had lost, though. "if I have been fooled, so has my son," she said, even though Gale did not want to leave.

Later it would be reported that the detective had been hired by George Jeffrey to search for his ex-wife, Winifred Banks, and their daughter, Barbara. He had traced them as far as the cult, but they were never heard from again.

Much of the unhappiness came from the fact that the colony was falling apart. After spending some time there, one member, Aurelia Hilton, said she finally realized that May would never make good on her promises and left the cult.

The colony had been promoted as a retreat for scientists, philosophers, and great thinkers. It was the "mother colony" – implying there were others – where international members could meet to share insights and compare notes.

None of this was true. Instead, new arrivals were greeted by what Aurelia Hilton called "starving" cult members. All the money coming into the cult was pooled into a treasury from which May made disbursements – few of which were made to benefit the hot, sandy colony. Members were told they "didn't need money" because everything was provided for them, except, apparently, food. Members of the cult who were not independently wealthy – or part of May's inner circle – were utterly depending on May's generosity to survive.

Some cult members were not as lucky in their escape attempts as others. On February 27, 1928 a man was delivering an automobile to the colony, and a girl ran up to his car in a panic. She told him she was afraid for her life. Before the driver could do anything two armed men appeared and forced the girl to go with them. It was later surmised that she was a former Hollywood screenwriter who had taken a job as May's secretary. She was never seen again.

A photographer named W.C. Johnson told the police that May had once attacked him during a botched recruitment effort. She had tried to get him to join the cult by claiming to know where all the money in the world was stored and told him that the Great Eleven paid handsome dividends to its members. When he turned her down an argument began that turned into a physical altercation.

Later, one of the cult members claimed he was coerced into "strong-arm actions" against other followers. He said that he had wanted to notify the police about what was going on but he feared for his life.

After finally withdrawing from the Great Eleven, Clifford Dabney wasted little time in starting legal proceedings against May and her inner circle, filing five civil lawsuits against them. He was attempting to collect on a $4,000 promissory note from 1925 that was never repaid, as well as $17,017 that he had loaned to a business using "the fictitious name of the William Blackburn Publishing Company." He was also trying to recover the 164 acres he had given May for the colony site along with the oil lease money that May had taken and some real estate in Monterey Park.

After filing the suits, Dabney went to the police on September 15 to file fraud charges against the cult. He met with detectives Edgar Edwards and William Reed of the Bunco Squad, as well as with Captain B.W. Thomason. They listened patiently – though with increasing incredulousness – as he detailed his experiences with the Great Eleven and explained how May Otis Blackburn had taken him for all the money he had. When he was finished there was silence in the room. They weren't sure what they could do to help him. Since he hadn't been mentally incompetent when the money was paid out May technically hadn't broken any laws. Dabney was a victim of his own gullibility.

However, Captain Thomason did agree to send the detectives with him over to see the District Attorney. If there was a case to made against May, they could tell him. Dabney didn't go straight to the D.A.'s office though. He picked up his wife, Alice, Jennie Toy, and Aurelia Hilton and took them with him to bolster his story. They met with District Attorney Charles Kearney on September 17. He promised to look into things and get back in touch with them.

Over the next week the Bunco Squad detectives tried to interview other members of the cult but had little luck. They were uncooperative and most claimed to be satisfied with the Great Eleven and pleased with the progress being made on *The Great Sixth Seal*. They were, they insisted, free to worship in any manner they chose, and the police were advised not to pry into religious affairs.

It's likely that Edwards and Reed would have given up completely if not for a call from an anonymous man who suggested the police look into the fate of a former cult member named Frances Turner. She had died under mysterious circumstances, they were told. He believed that she had been murdered.

The Turner investigation didn't go very far at first. The Ventura County Sheriff's Office told the detectives that it had indirectly confirmed the paralyzed woman's death, taking a statement from May Blackburn who said Turner died after a "choking spell." Reed and Edwards made some calls but came up empty-handed. The Turner woman was dead and buried and there was little information to be turned up.

But something was bothering Captain Thomason. Up until that point he'd kept the investigation quiet, but after telling Homicide Captain Raymond Cato about Dabney's weird claims about the cult they decided that a little publicity might stir things up. On October 4 a story appeared in the *Los Angeles Times* with a headline that read, "Cult Leaders Face Charges." The article – on page 8 – revealed that May and Ruth were charged with 15 counts of grand theft, that Dabney was the complaining witness, and that several people connected to the cult had disappeared.

Captain Cato was right – there was another anonymous call, and this time, the story was a big one.

According to the unknown man on the line, there had once been a girl named Willa Rhoads in the cult. She was a priestess, and her parents, William and Martha, had also been in the cult. The girl had died several years earlier under strange circumstances and her body had been hidden.

The police demanded to know where the body was hidden.

The caller spoke quickly, "Talk to the Rhoads at 1094 Marco Place in Venice."

On October 5, Thomason, Reed, Edwards, and policewoman Lula Lane arrived at the Rhoads home. Martha answered the door and they told her that they had some questions about her daughter. They were allowed into the house and Martha called for William. They asked about the couple's connections with the Great Eleven. At first William was confrontational with the detectives, refusing to say anything other than that their membership in a religious organization hardly excused an invasion of their home by the police.

Thomason agreed but explained that they were there because they seemed to be some mystery concerning their daughter's death. He told them, "I must ask you to submit proof that she is dead or tell us where the body is buried."

Hearing this Martha let out a loud moan, sank into a chair, and started to cry.

William, still upset, threatened to throw the police out of his house. They didn't have a search warrant and he had every right to demand that the leave – but he didn't. Instead, he sat stoically next to his increasingly emotional wife as the police made their case against May Blackburn.

It was Lula Lane who finally convinced Martha to cooperate. She spoke to her quietly, and eventually Martha choked out a response. "I will give you everything," she said, "if you promise not to desecrate my daughter's grave."

But that was a promise they couldn't keep. Martha told them everything but refused to say where Willa had been buried. She assured them her daughter's death had been a natural one – why couldn't she be left in peace? Captain Thomason tried to explain, telling her that the "curiosities" of the case meant that Willa's body would have to be examined. Homicide detectives were called in and the police were not going to leave the Rhoads' home empty-handed.

With great effort Martha finally admitted, "My daughter's body is buried under the floor of that bedroom there. We buried her with her dogs, which I believe are a symbol of resurrection. They were her pets, and one of them died the day she passed away. We killed the other six and laid them in a row in a casket similar to the one in which we buried Willa."

You can imagine that L.A. homicide detectives in the 1920s saw and heard a lot of strange things – but probably not as strange as this.

Seeing their shock, Martha became defiant. She announced her intent to preserve her daughter "until Gabriel sounds the seven notes of his trumpet." Sure, that explains everything.

William took the detectives into the bedroom and lifted the trap door in the floor. The police peered into the hole with flashlights. They found a pit that was four feet square and six feet deep. They could see the lids of the coffins, which were surrounded by dirt and concrete.

While the detectives were examining the hole, William disappeared but returned with shovels and pickaxes. He handed them to the policeman and then, finally overcome with emotion, left the room. He wanted all this to be over.

Martha wailed from the other side of the room. "If you do not believe I have told the truth, go ahead. Desecrate the belief I have and dig up the body!"

And they did. Detectives dutifully stripped off their jackets, jumped into the pit, and started digging. As the men worked reinforcements arrived at the cottage, followed by reporters and the inevitable morbid curious.

They dug for nearly 30 minutes, and then chains were used to haul both coffins up and onto the bedroom floor. Police photographers captured the event and photos of the recovery began appearing in newspapers around the country in a matter of days.

Willa's coffin had not remained sealed. Water had penetrated the cracks beneath the coffin's lid and it was now half-filled with a murky liquid. Inside, detectives found

Willa's casket was removed from the Rhoads house and brought out to the front yard — in front of reporters, photographers, and curiosity seekers

Willa's body wrapped in a white blanket. She was remarkably preserved and intact, lying on her left side, with her knees pulled up to her chest.

The coffin containing the puppies was opened next and detectives saw the animals inside had been wrapped individually in white sheets and laid in a row. Martha had made no attempt to preserve their bodies, though, and Detective Reed would later remark that the corpses were "revolting."

Both boxes were pulled out of the house and onto the front lawn. Reporters, policemen, and detectives gathered around the coffins. They stood by as photographers snapped photos, but they did not open the lid of Willa's casket. If they had it likely would have sent William and Martha over the edge. Willa's body was loaded into an ambulance and taken to the Los Angeles County Coroner's office.

William and Martha were taken into custody. The circumstances of her death were unusual to say the least. She had died on New Year's Day, which seemed symbolic, and the detectives had already heard many rumors about the cult the couple was part of. It was impossible for them to take the Rhoads at their word that Willa — a cult "princess" — had died of natural causes.

Detectives, police officers, and investigators from the district attorney's office pose with the two vaults from beneath the bedroom floor before they are taken away

The October 6 headline in the *Los Angeles Times* announced: "Police on Search at Venice Cottage for Secret Grave of Young Cult Priestess – Body Preserved in Spice to Await Resurrection – Weird Confession of Mystic Rites Follows Search by Police."

May and Ruth were identified by newspapers as "high priestesses" of a "strange cult" in a remote section of Simi Valley that called itself the "Divine Order of the Royal Arm of the Great Eleven." The newspapers reported that the cult, which had recently been charged with fraud by Clifford Dabney, practiced weird rites and claimed to be guarding a second god, "a child born to one of the adherents." Everything reported was correct, except for the story about the child, which rumor claimed was the result of a "sex orgy" among the members. That titillating addition was purely the work of reporters.

May was alarmed by the news and immediately hired attorney Thomas Cochran to represent herself and Ruth. After what must have been a lengthy discussion with his clients, Cochran contacted the district attorney's office and stated that, while his clients refuted the charges of fraud against them, they were prepared to turn themselves over to the authorities. He claimed that Dabney was given more than his money's worth when it came to May's time and attention, and besides, he reluctantly

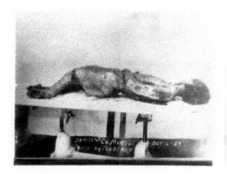 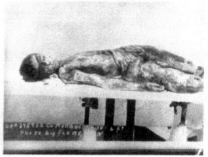

Willa's body at the L.A. County Morgue

added, surely at May's insistence, his clients would soon reveal *The Great Sixth Seal* to the public. The book would answer all the questions that had been previously considered unanswerable.

Cochran then hired a private detective named Joseph J. Wavrin to make a "complete check of the cult's activities." This was a weird and complicated case, and he didn't trust his clients to tell him the whole truth. He didn't want any surprises, he told him.

Unfortunately, surprises were coming.

May and Ruth turned themselves over to the authorities. At a hearing bail was set at $10,000 for each woman, and they were placed in the county jail pending arrangements for bond.

By October 7 news of the investigation had gone national. The lurid details about the cult – including human sacrifice, scandal, swindles, and mummification – were a gold mine for the papers. Reporters snapped photos of Ruth, interviewed Clifford Dabney, and began tracking down members of the cult who had left. All of them spoke about money that had been donated to the cult that had disappeared.

May, seeing the accusations against her that were appearing in the news, began speaking out. She countered comments from Martha Rhoads, saying that the Great Eleven never held mysterious ceremonies. She claimed the cult was scientific, not spiritual, with a primary purpose of "the study of the resurrection." She added that the charges against her, made by Dabney and others, were the result of jealousy. She and her daughter had done nothing wrong, she said before her attorney advised her to be quiet and stop talking to reporters.

Ruth found it hard to be silent when she was visited by a ghost from her past. Arthur Osborne, her first victim, was back in Los Angeles and talking to the district attorney. He even handed over some of Ruth's old letters to him, which quickly made their way into print in the local papers.

The police, hoping to convince Ruth to talk, sent Arthur to see her at the jail. At the D.A.'s prompting, he mentioned he'd heard about the case against Ruth and her mother and wondered if she wanted to talk about it. Before Ruth could reply May appeared and pulled her daughter away.

While talking to the police Arthur told them about Addie McGuffin, the widow of an oilfield worker who had gone missing after joining the Great Eleven. It's unknown how Arthur could have known about the missing woman but some have speculated that one of May's enemies saw him as an ally and asked him to pass it on to the police.

No matter how Arthur learned about the missing woman, Addie McGuffin's name was added to the list of possible victims of the Great Eleven.

It was a list that kept growing as investigators dug into the fate of Frances Turner and began interviewing cult members – present and past – about Willa Rhoads and the followers who had gone missing, like Sam Rizzio. Detectives interviewed his mother, who told them that her son had not been seen since July 24. She said that May had presented her with a letter that allegedly came from her son, saying that he was sorry for abusing her and doubting her work with the cult – but she didn't think her son had sent it. May was interviewed about Sam and she offered the same letter to the police to prove that he was alive. No one seemed convinced of its authenticity.

William Rhoads – happy that part of his life was finally over – went out of his way to be helpful to the authorities. He took them to houses the cult owned, abandoned headquarters, and to the colony in Simi Valley. Detectives obtained a search warrant for the property and explored it in the company of several reporters and photographers. They managed to see and hear a lot of very strange things in the buildings and from the cult members but left with nothing criminal.

Meanwhile, Clifford Dabney – the man that true believers from the cult blamed for starting the mess – received 12 letters containing death threats against himself and his family. He placed an urgent call to the police and demanded protection. The police obliged by assigning Detective Lieutenant J.A. Letterman to guard him and his family.

Dabney knew how dangerous it could be to cross the Great Eleven.

Throughout October and November, the public was inundated with strange news about the Great Eleven. Newspapers rabidly reported stories of concords and rituals, angels, orgies, human and animal sacrifices, mummification, temples, the apocalypse, and more. Dabney's fraud case got a lot of press. Reporters loved taking jabs at Dabney, portraying him as a rich sucker with too much money and too little common sense. There was also a lot of space given to the deaths of Willa Rhoads, Francis Turner, Harlene Satoris, and the possible deaths of Addie McGuffin, Sam Rizzio, and others. Photographs were printed of Ward Blackburn and his curious mustache, of Willa before she died, of the "Lord's Furniture Set" and the massive throne, of Ruth sometimes in her skimpy Egyptian dancing costume, and of every cult member they could track down.

On October 16, though, three of the counts against May were dropped. The authorities also decided there was insufficient evidence to hold Ruth and ordered her release. When she was taken out of her cell, she protested at first, saying that she didn't want to leave her mother alone in jail. Cult members eventually convinced her to let them take her home. Among them was J.J. Wavrin, the detective hired by Cochran, whose new job was to serve as Ruth's bodyguard.

William and Martha Rhoads were also cleared of charges after the county's chemist failed to find any poison in Willa's body. The coroner now agreed that death was probably caused by sepsis caused by the ulceration of her tooth. The Rhoads were allowed to make preparations for Willa's burial at a local cemetery, but when Martha asked that the remains of the seven dogs be returned to be buried with the girl, the coroner refused, saying that it would be illegal.

The police were still trying to round up members of the cult, most of whom were now scattered to the wind. Those that remained at the colony were in terrible shape. The normally bad conditions there had worsened with May in jail and unable to dispense money for food. They were so dependent on May that they were literally starving.

Finally, on October 30, May was released on $10,000 bail. Her attorney told reporters that she would use her freedom to revise and regroup "the first part" of *The Great Sixth Seal* so she could present the manuscript for her defense.

In mid-November Clifford Dabney – who had taken a beating in the press after telling reporters that he was afraid that May would have killed him with her occult powers if he'd refused to give her money – filed another lawsuit against May. This one was for $41,000 of property in Orange County, which included several oil lots. He said that he had signed over the property to May and Ruth under threat of death.

On December 4 May was arraigned on charges of grand theft of approximately $28,000 from Clifford Dabney and Jennie Toy. The attorney for both parties, Roy P. Dolly, requested that the court require *The Great Sixth Seal* to be produced, saying that viewing the book was the only way to know if an angel was really dictating it.

May's criminal trial began on January 14, 1930. It ran for seven weeks with the defense calling cult members still friendly to May to the stand. Thomas Cochran wanted to prove that Clifford Dabney had not been defrauded and that he was a willing participant in, and financial supporter of, a church that he later decided that he didn't like.

The prosecution sought to prove that the Great Eleven was not a church at all. It was a fraud that May presented as a church for her financial gain. Good and innocent people had died as a result of her swindle. Deputy District Attorney Ferguson called both friends and enemies of May to the stand. Those who were friendly to May were portrayed as delusional, and those who were May's enemies were encouraged to tell the jury how much money they'd lost to the cult. Ferguson stressed that Dabney gave funds to and remained in the Great Eleven because he feared for his family's safety.

Ferguson demanded that *The Great Sixth Seal* be produced, but, of course, it wasn't because it didn't exist. Aside from two *Los Angeles Times* reporters who claimed to see a couple of pages of nonsensical writing in 1924, the only person who asserted he had read any of the book was Clifford Dabney – and May had only allowed him to see one or two pages.

Cochran's excuse for the missing book was that May had shipped *The Great Sixth Seal* to Grand Central Station in the care of the missing Addie McGuffin. Since then, no one had heard from McGuffin, so the location of the book was a mystery. Why had

May sent the book away? Cochran said that the Ventura County Sheriff had recently seized the visible assets of the colony because of the lawsuits and the Great Eleven didn't want their "sacred work" to fall into the hands of the state.

When Ruth was on the stand, she claimed that angels were visiting her and telling her what to say. May didn't do herself any favors when she testified either. When confronted with endorsed checks that she had claimed she'd never accepted, she clarified that each check had been placed on the ground by the donor first. She had picked them up – but technically, had never "accepted" them.

When asked if the "Lord's Furniture Set" was hers, May said it was not. When asked whom it belonged to, she replied, "The Lord." The prosecution then produced a bill of sale showing the furniture had, in fact, belonged to May.

At one point she collapsed on the stand, causing a delay in the trial. She later told the jurors that her mission was a burden and the angels were interfering in her life. She just wanted to be like everyone else and hadn't asked to be one of the "two witnesses of God." The angels had compelled her and her daughter to take countless pages of dictation. As to anything she might have done that might be legally or ethically questionable – it wasn't her fault. "I didn't do it," she said. "It was the angels that dictated it should be done. It was God's work, and I was only the medium."

Without angels present to blame for May's crimes, the jury convicted her of eight counts of grand theft on March 2, 1930. Each charge had a potential sentence of 1-14 years in prison. May was to be sent to San Quentin but was allowed to stay at the Los Angeles county jail, pending her appeal.

Dabney's civil trials continued against May, and while they were separate from her criminal trial the verdict was beneficial to his case. On March 21, 1930 May returned the rights to all future gas and oil royalties that Dabney had assigned her. She was also forced to return $30,000 that had been taken from him.

But Dabney's victory didn't stop the death threats. The cult was still out there. They had been forced to leave the colony in the Simi Valley and were scattered across Los Angeles, looking for a new place to settle. Even though the Great Depression was now starting to settle in across the country the cult was not short of cash. They found an empty property that they could get at a low price. It had recently belonged to Japanese-American actor Sessue (Kintaro) Hayakawa, a prolific actor of more than 80 films who found his career destroyed at the end of the silent era when "talkies" became the new thing. Hayakawa had bought what was dubbed the "Glengarry Castle" in Hollywood when his career had been going strong. It became notorious in the 1920s as the site of his extravagant all-night, no-holds-barred parties, but after several subsequent owners, it was now empty. The cult soon moved in.

While the cult was finding new headquarters, May's appeal was working its way through the circus. It went all the way to the California Supreme Court in 1931. The higher court overturned the original verdict on the grounds that the evidence relating to the cult's bizarre activities had no bearing on the charges of grand theft, and that it was impossible to prove whether May had, in fact, taken the money in bad faith.

May Blackburn was a free woman.

Neither May nor anyone else ever faced criminal charges for the deaths or disappearances connected to the cult. Witnesses had vanished, evidence was lost, and the authorities were so afraid of violating the cult's "religious freedoms" that they ended their investigations.

Willa Rhoads had not been poisoned – probably – and though no one could rule out foul play for certain, neither could they find any evidence of it. There was some talk of charging the Rhoads or others with improper burial or failing to report a death but opted not to follow through with it.

Given the limited forensic tools available at the time, the state had little hope of finding anything actionable in the deaths of Harlene Satoris or Frances Turner, and those cases also went cold.

The police gave up looking for Addie McGuffin – she later appeared in 1931, with no idea anyone had been looking for her – along with all the others who had reportedly disappeared from the cult. Sam Rizzio was never found – dead or alive.

W.C. Johnson, the photographer who said he'd been attacked by May after she tried to recruit him, eventually dropped his case.

The death threats against Clifford Dabney could never be traced back to any specific cult members so there wasn't much the police could do about them.

The Divine Order of the Royal Arms of the Great Eleven had managed to prove itself immune from destruction by the authorities. To those who remained at May's side it must have seemed as if she and Ruth really were being protected by angels.

The law couldn't ruin them, but publicity was an entirely different matter.

Thanks to the newspaper stories generated by the events of 1929 and 1930, new recruits to the Great Eleven effectively came to a halt. However, were still many of the long-time members who stayed faithful to May – at least for a while.

In February 1932, Ruth filed for divorce from her allegedly missing husband, Sam Rizzio. She promptly married again, this time to Klonie "Jack" Gray, the owner of a barbershop. He was placed in charge of collecting the paychecks of all Great Eleven followers who had been put to work in a nearby tomato packing plant.

Surprisingly, with how unhappy the Rhoads must have been with May, William and Martha continued to associate with the cult until at least 1932. They may have remained for the sake of their friends, many of whom had been neighbors back home in Portland.

It should come as no surprise that even though Addie McGuffin mysteriously reappeared, *The Great Sixth Seal* did not. The imaginary "sacred work" was never anything more than a collection of notes posing as a book. However, May did go on to publish a book in 1936 called *The Origin of God*. In it May abandoned most of her former prophecies and ideas, including references to Solomon's "lost measurements," gold mines, mansions on hills, healing, resurrecting the dead, and eleven queens. Essentially, it's a book about how the whole world is tied together through harmonics to the invisible and underlying properties of the universe. It certainly isn't as exciting as her original craziness, which is probably the reason that so few cult members remained at her side by this time.

Perhaps the reason for the book's lackluster material was that it wasn't dictated by angels this time around. Instead, it was dictated by May to Winifred Banks, a still loyal follower. Winfred remained with May out of desperation – anything to forget the tragedies that haunted her life. Winifred's daughter, Grace, had been hit and killed by a car driven by a wealthy teenager. Soon after the insurance company issued a $10,000 check to the grieving mother, May turned up on her doorstep. Without offering any condolences she demanded that the insurance payment be turned over to her. Winifred immediately did so.

Around the same time Winifred's mother also died. A diabetic, she had accidentally dropped her glass syringe, shattering it. When Winifred went to May and asked for the money to replace it, May refused, declaring that the syringe had been broken because God had cured the woman of her diabetes. Winifred's mother, without her insulin injections, began a slow, agonizing death. She was completely blind before she finally passed away.

May eventually published a book — but it certainly wasn't the one she had promised for so long and created a cult around

Winifred spent years typing up *The Origins of God*. She was, of course, never paid for her time or work. To make matters worse, when the book was eventually published May ordered the impoverished woman to purchase a copy of it.

May and the cult slowly deteriorated in the years that followed. By 1948 she announced to the congregation that she had left that God was tired of Los Angeles – the "bottomless pit" of sin. She warned that the city's destruction was imminent and the only hope for the Great Eleven was to escape to Lake Tahoe, California.

May never made the trip. She died of heart failure on June 17, 1951.

Her husband and step-brother, Ward, died two decades later on June 24, 1975 from lung cancer. He had no one left. On his death certificate most of the information – like names and birthplaces of his parents, marital status, and occupation – are marked as "unknown." He'd made no preparation for his death. Perhaps he still believed what May had told him – that he'd live forever. His corpse was donated to science as a medical specimen.

Ruth divorced and married again in the 1940s and 1950s. After her mother died, she and a handful of the last remaining cult members moved to Lake Tahoe. Between 1955 and 1970, using at least four variations of her real name, she bought up numerous parcels of real estate. But it wouldn't last. In time she returned to California and the Great Eleven had come to an end.

Ruth died on December 19, 1978 in Sacramento, bringing an end to a chapter in the bizarre history of Southern California.

The story of the Great Eleven is so strange and so bizarre that it seems impossible that anything like this could happen today. Right?

While I was working on this book a story came along that, while not exactly like that of Willa Rhoads, was eerily similar. On December 14, 2019 a two-year-old girl named Olive Alayne Heiligenthal died in California. The family called 911 and paramedics tried to revive the little girl at home and at the hospital, but she was declared dead.

The next day the child's parents asked that "friends, family, and others from the church gather to pray for the miracle of resurrection (the basis for which is modeled by Jesus in the New Testament of the Bible)." The family, members of Bethel Church, stated that they believed in the stories of healing and physical resurrection found in the Bible and that "the miracles they portray are possible today."

Olive's mother, Kalley, also posted her beliefs on a GoFundMe page that was set up for the family over the following weekend. Within days, it had raised tens of thousands of dollars. She wrote:

"We believe in a Jesus who died and conclusively defeated every grave, holding the keys to resurrection power. We need it for our little Olive Alayne, who stopped breathing yesterday and has been pronounced dead by doctors. We are asking for bold, unified prayer from the global church to stand with us in belief that He will raise this little girl back to life. Her time here is not done, and it is our time to believe boldly and with confidence wield what king Jesus paid for. It's time for her to come to life."

The family began praying soon after their daughter died and then posted on Instagram to ask others around the world to join them. Needless to say, a hashtag -- #wakeupolive – followed.

I probably don't have to tell you that it didn't work. Olive wasn't resurrected. On December 20, six days after the death, the family finally gave up.

To be clear, I'm not making light of anyone's grief here. I can definitely understand why parents who have lost a child would cling to any hope, no matter how slim. I would never condemn them for seeking comfort, private or public.

But I don't feel as generous toward the people out there – at the Heiligenthal's church and online – who joined in and encouraged them to believe in something impossible. Under the circumstances that was cruel. It gave them false hope and delayed their acceptance of reality. That made it even more painful when reality inevitably arrived.

Trying to bring someone back from the dead is not widely accepted in the Christian faith – it's more widely practiced in cults like the Great Eleven. However, it should be pointed out that Bethel Church is no mainstream congregation. It's profile as a megachurch has risen in recent years. It was founded in the 1950s, but its real growth began in the 1990s when the controversial couple Bill and Beni Johnson took over its leadership. In 2005 they left the Assemblies of God denomination and became an independent church. It's become best known for Bethel Music, a music ministry that includes a record label and touring band that produces the inspirational anthems that dominate the Christian music scene. The church has also jumped into politics, supporting Donald Trump in 2016 and promoting politicians like Sean Feucht, a Republican who frequently posted about Olive's resurrection in late 2019.

At the church Bill Johnson peddles a theology filled with magic and miracles where the idea of reality is hazy at best. The church also runs a school – the Bethel School of Supernatural Ministry – that offers classes on how to conduct miracles.

Once you understand this the belief of the Heiligenthals makes sense. Just as the resurrection of Willa Rhoads seemed possible to her parents, the Heiligenthals believed that Olive could return. They'd been immersed in the culture of faith healing, prophecy, and exorcisms, and bringing their child back from the dead seemed just as real to them.

But wait – don't all Christians believe in such things? They do if they believe in the Bible, but unlike those from the Bethel Church, most Christians don't pray out loud for flagrant miracles. They tend to pray for things that might happen anyway in the course of day-to-day life. The Heiligenthals turned out to be different because they prayed out of absolute faith and followed their beliefs without reluctance or hesitation.

Of course, their prayers weren't answered and, just as Martha and William Rhoads were eventually forced to face the fact that May Blackburn would never be able to restore their daughter to them, the Heiligenthals were also forced to face the fact that the dead don't come back to life. Our universe is unfortunately governed by impersonal physical laws. It's a place where a fire is hot, water is wet, food doesn't appear out of thin air, and we can't get back those who die.

That leaves us with one hard fact: people who feed off the grief of others – like May Blackburn and the attention-seeking Instagram followers who encouraged a heartbroken family – are among the worst that mankind has to offer.

The Madness of Jim Jones

For those who grew up in the 1970s, who can forget one of the most horrific stories of the decade --- the mass suicide of the People's Temple cult in the jungles of Guyana? The name of the cult's leader, Jim Jones, became known all over America, and the inaccurate catchphrase of "drinking the Kool-Aid" became synonymous with brainwashing, suicide, and horror.

The cult's settlement in Guyana, known as Jonestown, was a place of voluntary slavery. The inhabitants had come there looking for paradise and found Hell instead. Each day with filled with backbreaking labor for all but Jones and his inner circle. The inhabitants were too busy working in the fields to realize what was happening to their lives.

Jim Jones was their leader, high priest, king, and god. He had total control of his follower's lives. Adultery committed by anyone other than Jones and his henchmen was a severely punishable offense. Even husbands and wives had to seek permission from Jones to sleep together. On occasion married couples who were caught defying their leader's ban against sex were made to engage in intercourse in front of the entire

Jonestown community. Rumor had it, though, that the congregation was peppered with Jones' personally sired offspring.

New members gave all their income and property to Jones, who had them believing that he was Jesus Christ reincarnated. In truth he was nothing more than a charismatic criminal who demanded that his people call him "Father" or "Dad" and worship him as a living deity. Whatever Jones decided was the rule of the day.

There was little, if any, racial discrimination at Jonestown – about 70-percent of the inhabitants were black. Only those who came from the worst ghettos of the inner city found Jonestown to be an improvement over their past their living conditions. Those members of the cult with no self-esteem, and who had a desperate need to belong, found life at Jonestown more than just bearable.

For everyone else, there was no escape.

Many believed in Jones' claims to be able to do anything from placing fatal curses on his enemies to bringing the dead back to life. He was an expert at manipulation and there were enough members under his spell to keep any malcontents from fleeing.

But how did a bizarre cult from America end up in the jungles of South America? And how did the community deteriorate into one of the great mass suicides in history?

James Warren Jones was born in a rural area of Crete, Indiana on May 13, 1931. His father, also named James, was a disabled World War I veteran, and his mother, Lynetta, was a smart, hard-working woman who was 16 years younger than her husband and the breadwinner of the family.

In 1934 money problems during the Depression forced them to move to the small town of Lynn, where Jones grew up in a shack with no indoor plumbing. Jones became fascinated with books and read everything he could get his hands on, especially books about people like Hitler, Stalin, and Marx, and he carefully made notes about the strengths and weaknesses of each. He also discovered the power of the spoken word. He entertained local men by swearing, and in return they gave him nickels to buy soda.

James Warren Jones – a young man with horror and depravity in his future

As a boy he became obsessed with religion. He visited all the churches in the area and his favorite was the Gospel Tabernacle, a Pentecostal church on the outskirts of town where services were wild, and people spoke in tongues. For a while he went around wearing a white sheet over his street clothes, looking like a minister in his robes. By the time he was 10 he was preaching to a makeshift altar located in the loft of his family's barn. If his audience lost interest, he simply locked the doors and refused to let them leave. He had few friends, but those he had he liked to dominate.

A friend, Don Foreman, later recalled that Jones twice pointed a gun at him and fired, narrowly missing him.

Another childhood friend, Chuck Wilmore, said, "I thought Jimmy was a really weird kid. He was obsessed with religion; he was obsessed with death. A friend of mine told me that he saw Jimmy kill a cat with a knife." Others agreed that Jones performed experiments on small animals – and later forced his friends to attend funerals for them.

Jim and Marceline soon after they moved to Indianapolis

Jones' parents separated and he and his mother moved to the industrial city of Richmond. He was working as a hospital orderly when he met a young and attractive nurse named Marceline. They got married in 1949 and moved to Bloomington where Jones began attending Indiana University. Two years later they moved to Indianapolis and Jones enrolled in night classes at Butler University.

In just two short years Marceline had started to regret the marriage. She had discovered how bad-tempered and possessive her new husband could be and had started worrying about him telling people that he had lost his faith and thought communism wasn't such a bad thing.

While in Indianapolis Jones had started attending Communist Party meetings. He became upset about the harassment that was taking place at the McCarthy Hearings in Washington and frustrated by the persecution of open and accusing communists around the country. Marceline didn't know what to make of his behavior, but she was undoubtedly pleased when her husband suddenly announced that he was going to become a Methodist minister.

In 1952, he became a student pastor at the Somerset Southside Methodist Church, but he was more keenly interested in the services being held by the flashier Pentecostals. He was occasionally invited to preach at the Lauren Street Tabernacle where he practiced "discerning" – giving people unknown information about themselves – speaking in tongues and faith healing. He specialized in removing cancerous growths, which were really pieces of animal tissue that Jones appeared to extract using a sleight of hand trick. By cheerfully faking it all Jones made a name for himself on the Indiana preaching circuit.

Lynetta Jones had instilled a concern for social justice in her son and he had become particularly passionate about racial equality. He had once had a falling out with his father – who was loosely connected to the Ku Klux Klan when Jones was young – because the elder Jones had not allowed Jim to bring one of his black friends into their home. Now Jones was dreaming of a church that white and black members could attend together. Neither the Methodists nor the Pentecostals were keen on desegregation, however, so Jones realized that he would have to create his own church.

He used an event that he organized to launch the church. He put together a large convention at the Cadle Tabernacle and arranged to share the pulpit with Rev. William M. Branham, a well-known healing evangelist and religious author. He used the convention as a platform to start a new church. It would have various names until it eventually became the People's Temple Christian Church Full Gospel.

As Jones was creating the doctrine for his church, he studied leaders of various other movements, like Adolph Hitler and Father Divine. They were both experts on how to manipulate people and Jones knew

In order to raise money to start the People's Temple, Jones went door-to-door selling monkeys imported from South America

he would need this skill. He went to visit Father Divine at his home and Divine advised him to "find an enemy" and make sure that his followers knew who, or what, that enemy was. That would unify the people in his group and would make them subservient to him, knowing they were all working toward a common cause.

As the "enemy" of his movement, Jones chose racism.

Declaring that he was "outraged" by what he perceived as racial discrimination in Indianapolis churches he established his own, pointedly making sure it was open to all ethnic groups. To raise money for its establishment Jones chose a method that I would imagine had never been tried before – he went door-to-door selling monkeys that had been imported from South America.

Strangely, Jones would later keep a chimpanzee as the mascot of the People's Temple. His name was Mr. Muggs and he was said to have the intelligence of a four-year-old child. Like his followers, Mr. Muggs followed every one of Jones' commands – and, also like his people, the chimpanzee met a tragic end on Jonestown's last day.

Jones' new church – and his unpopular racial opinions – got a lot of attention. In 1960 Indianapolis Mayor Charles Boswell appointed Jones as the director of the city's Human Rights Commission. He advised Jones to keep a low profile, but the minister couldn't stay out of the spotlight. He appeared on local radio and television and was wildly cheered at a meeting of the NAACP and the Urban League when he called for the audience to be more militant. At the end of his speech he shouted, "Let my people go!"

He made sure that his efforts were publicized when he opened food and clothing banks, started soup kitchens, took poor children to the zoo, and delivered free heating coal to shut-ins. Jones helped to integrate Indianapolis churches, restaurants, the police department, the telephone company, an amusement park, a theater, and the Indiana University Health Methodist Hospital. When swastikas were painted on the homes of two African American families, Jones visited the neighborhood and visited black families and asked white families not to move. He set up sting operations in restaurants, trying to catch them refusing to serve black customers. He wrote to the American Nazi party leaders and then passed their replies to the media. In 1961 Jones collapsed from exhaustion and was "accidentally" placed in an African American ward at the hospital. He then refused to be moved and used his old orderly skills to make beds and empty the bedpans of black patients. Political pressure resulting from this caused hospital officials to desegregate the wards.

Needless to say, not everyone liked Jones' message. He received a lot of criticism and found himself banned from some white-owned businesses. A swastika was painted on the Temple building and a stick of dynamite was once left in the coal pile. He received dozens of threatening telephone calls at home, and once a dead cat was nailed to his door. These criticism and attacks – although some believed that Jones invented some of them himself – increased his paranoia. He soon began claiming that there had been many attempts on his life.

In the meantime, Jones' church was slowly growing. His earlier attraction to communism resulted in his philosophy of "religious communalism," an idea borrowed from Father Divine and other movement leaders of the past. He expected his followers to devote their lives – and their incomes – to the People's Temple. Jones was already doing that with his own life. He turned his home into a combination of a commune and a nursing home for the church's elderly.

In addition to the son that he had with Marceline, Stephan Gandhi Jones, he and his wife created what he called a "Rainbow Family" by adopting three Korean children – Lew, Suzanne, and Stephanie – and an African-American boy they named Jim, Jr. They were the first white couple in Indiana history to adopt a black child. A few years later they also adopted a white boy named Tim, whose birth mother was a member of the People's Temple.

In 1962 Jones read an article in *Esquire* magazine that listed the city of Belo Horizonte in Brazil as one of the safest places on earth in the event of a nuclear war. He became intrigued by the idea of setting up a new Temple there and he traveled to South America with his family. On the way they passed through Guyana, which was a British colony at the time.

The family rented a modest home in Belo Horizonte, and Jones spent some time studying the local economy and trying to see if his message would appeal to the residents. Language was a huge barrier, but Jones believed he could overcome it and create an apostolic communal lifestyle in the area. He was interested in the area, but the locals were not interested in him or his message. In mid-1963 the family packed up and moved to Rio de Janeiro where they worked with the poor in the city's slums.

Jones and Marceline with their natural and adopted children — the "Rainbow Family" that Jones like to brag about

But all was not well back in Indiana. His associate pastors had sent messages that warned of the Temple's collapse without him. Plagued with guilt for leaving behind his people, he returned to the United States.

While he was away, though, something had changed in Jim Jones.

He had started to question the Bible and its inconsistencies and began to talk about these things during his sermons. The more conservative Temple members became upset, but most went along with it. Around this same time Father Divine died in Pennsylvania and Jones made an unsuccessful power grab for the Peace Mission organization during a visit to Divine's estate – even going as far as to claim that he was the reincarnation of the late cult leader. Mother Divine responded by kicking him out, but not before Jones managed to poach a small number of Peace Mission members for the People's Temple.

Now, Jones knew he needed something new to keep his followers. Looking back over that same *Esquire* article he found that one of the other "nine safest places in the world in the event of a nuclear catastrophe" was Eureka, California. That seemed a little more attainable than Brazil, so he announced to his followers that it was time for them to move to Northern California for safety. They didn't have much time to

After the People's Temple moved to Northern California, Jones became increasingly stranger with his beliefs and teachings

spare, either, he told them. He had received a vision that a nuclear attack was going to occur on July 15, 1967.

Some of the Temple members balked at the idea of a move out west, not wanting to leave their friends and families behind, but dozens more agreed. In July 1965 they began moving to California's Redwood Valley, near the town of Ukiah.

They built a church, resumed their charitable work, and aggressively recruited new members. Some of Jones' inner circle were tasked with secretly digging up information on prospective recruits by breaking into their homes and digging through their garbage. Jones would then present this information during his church services, further proving his divine powers.

Over the next few years, the Temple experienced phenomenal growth and opened branches in San Fernando, San Francisco, and Los Angeles. While still targeting poor African-Americans, it also attracted many young, enthusiastic, and college-educated whites. Jones and his followers traveled across the country by bus, preaching, collecting donations, and gaining recruits.

By this time Jones had all but abandoned orthodox Christianity. His services still seemed like old-style revival meetings with songs, call-and-response sermons, and the inevitable healing sessions, but he made no secret now of his contempt for the Bible. He would throw it on the ground and stomp on it, claiming that it was a tool to oppress women and non-whites. He derided Christianity as a "fly away religion" and denounced the "Sky God," who was no God at all. "I am God!" he often said. "What you need to believe in is what you can see... If you see me as your friend, I'll be your friend. If you see me as your father, I'll be your father, for those of you that don't have a father... If you see me as your savior, I'll be your savior. If you see me as your God, I'll be your God."

Children who were born into the Temple were baptized in the name of socialism. He taught that "those who remained drugged with the opiate of religion had to be brought to enlightenment—socialism." He often mixed his ideas together, "If you're born in capitalist America, racist America, fascist America, then you're born in sin. But if you're born in socialism, you're not born in sin."

Jones also liked to preach that he was the reincarnation of Gandhi, Jesus, Buddha, and Vladimir Lenin. And yet, somehow, his followers didn't realize that he was already going off the rails.

Maybe they should have, though, when he started talking about sex – a lot. At first, he demanded that his followers remain celibate, but later he denounced sexual jealousy and began advocating free love. He had sex with many of the women in the Temple and impregnated some of them. Church meetings became a forum for the discussion of individual members' sexuality, with women expected to praise the sexual prowess of Jones. At the same time Jones often accused his male followers of having homosexual tendencies and, to prove it, sodomized some of them. After Jones was arrested for masturbating in a movie theater, he still had no regrets about standing behind his pulpit and declaring that he was "the only true heterosexual in the church."

The People's Temple found its niche in California in the 1970s. Jones nevertheless warned his followers of the threats they faced – many of which were likely cooked up by Jones, like the time that he told a story of stopping an assassin's bullet by causing it to "dematerialize." The church in Ukiah was surrounded by a chain-link fenced, topped with barbed wire, and patrolled by armed guards. Visitors were frisked before they were allowed to enter.

Within five years of the Temple's arrival in California, Jones had started shifting his focus to the larger cities because of the limited chances for expansion in Ukiah. He moved the Temple's headquarters to San Francisco's Filmore District, a major center for many radical protest movements. Jones and the Temple soon became influential in San Francisco politics, especially when Jones helped get George Moscone elected as mayor in 1975. Moscone then appointed Jones as chairman of the San Francisco Housing Authority Commission.

It's terrifying now to look back and see how much contact and influence that Jones had with local and national politicians. He and Mayor Moscone met privately with vice-presidential candidate Walter Mondale on his campaign plane just before the 1976 election, leading to Mondale publicly praising the Temple. Since Jones supported Jimmy Carter's presidential campaign, he was able to meet with First Lady Rosalynn Carter on several occasions. They were photographed having coffee, corresponded about Cuba, and she even appeared at the grand opening of the San Francisco headquarters where Jones received more applause than she did.

In September 1976, California assemblyman Willie Brown served as the master of ceremonies for a testimonial dinner for Jones, which was attended by Governor Jerry Brown. At that dinner the assemblyman praised Jones as "what you should see every day when you look in the mirror" and that he was a combination of Martin Luther King, Jr., Angela Davis, Albert Einstein, and Chairman Mao.

The well-known politician from the San Francisco Board of Supervisors, Harvey Milk, was also an admirer of Jones. He often spoke to audiences during political rallies held at the Temple. He was one of the many local political figures that Jones hosted in his apartment for discussions.

The only conclusion that I can reach from this is that most of these politicians and local figures had never been to Jones' church or heard his bizarre teachings. Eventually they'd come to realize what Jones actually was – even before the mass suicide at Jonestown. In time, his political allies would abandon him, except for Harvey Milk, who wrote a letter to President Carter defending Jones as a "man of the highest character."

Work began on the settlement in Guyana long before the People's Temple migrated to the region

But Jim Jones didn't fool everyone.

When he first arrived in California, Jones went out of his way to create friendships and alliances with reporters, editors, and columnists on various newspaper staffs. He knew that good publicity would help him to expand the church, and strong relationships might also keep any detrimental information about the Temple out of the papers.

But the move to San Francisco caused some reporters to start taking a closer look at the church. When the *San Francisco Examiner* began to run a series of critical articles written by the paper's religion editor, Jones and his attorneys managed to get the series canceled.

He knew there would be more to come, though, and that was when he began thinking of a refuge for himself outside of the United States. He remembered his difficulties in Brazil but then considered the small, English-speaking country of Guyana. Thanks to his political connections it was easy for him to lease about 3,000 acres of jungle from the Guyanese government and to send a small group of Temple members down to start clearing the land. When they left, they had no idea of the hardships they were going to face. They were not allowed to communicate with the followers back in California about the horrible conditions in the jungle. All mail was censored, and the workers were not allowed to leave the camp. Only Jones' supervisors were permitted to travel to Georgetown, Guyana's capital.

Back at home there were growing tensions within the church. Jones was always looking for new sources of income for the People's Temple. He was always accepting donations from his members as well as their slave labor in businesses that financed the church, but many new members were hesitant about turning over their life savings and their social security and pension checks when they joined the church. Once they were wrung dry, those who'd had nothing to start with or had already given everything they owned to Temple were usually allowed to defect without much trouble. But when a member who still had a substantial source of income became disillusioned with the sect, Jones would use a considerable amount of persuasion to retain their membership. When that failed, dire circumstances followed. Some died mysteriously, while others simply vanished.

There were also the new "experiments" that Jones was attempting with his followers. One night during a meeting of the church's planning committee he announced an exception to one of his rules. Alcohol was expressly forbidden for the followers, but he explained that he had some excellent wine that had been made from grapes grown on Temple property that he wanted them to try. After everyone finished a glass, he announced that the wine had been poisoned, and they would all die within 45 minutes. Some of the committee members collapsed, as if in pain. One tried to escape but was stopped by one of Jones' men, who fired a shot at her that turned out to be a blank.

The others stood where they were – waiting to die for their "father." They didn't argue, and they didn't ask for an antidote.

Finally, Jones admitted there was no poison. He had merely been testing them, he said. Privately, he considered his "experiment" a great success.

That wasn't all. The practice that Jones called "catharsis" – when individuals were publicly criticized by church members during services – had been a Temple practice for years, but now it was becoming violent. When he decided that followers had sinned Jones decided on the punishments. Members were beaten with boards, or he staged boxing matches with those who had sinned – including children – forced to fight larger, stronger opponents. Some of the bouts resulted in serious injuries.

In early 1977, a reporter for the *San Francisco Chronicle* tried to publish an exposé of the People's Temple but met with resistance from his editors. He ended up taking the story to New West, a nationally-known magazine. Jones soon learned about the article and panicked. Convinced that he was also under scrutiny by the FBI and the Internal Revenue Service – he wasn't – he announced that the Temple was moving to his agricultural commune in Guyana.

The People's Temple Agricultural Project – which would come to be known as "Jonestown" – had been promoted as a "socialist paradise" and a "sanctuary" from media scrutiny in San Francisco.

For most of those who came to live there, it would become Hell on earth.

Jones had assured the followers who hesitated to leave San Francisco for the middle of the jungle that the commune was a paradise where the trees were laden with fruit that tasted like ice cream. Seriously, he did. It was the "Promised Land."

In truth the ground of Jonestown was infertile. It was hot, humid, the air was infested with flies and mosquitoes, cockroaches were everywhere, the undergrowth was slithering with snakes, and it rained almost every day, so the roads were always muddy, and everything was damp and mildewed.

Sounds great, doesn't it?

The initial settlers had worked hard to prepare the compound for new arrivals, but it was nowhere near ready for the hundreds of people who showed up. Cottages designed for seven or eight people were filled with more than twice that number. Followers were expected to spend nearly every waking moment at work in the fields or helping to build new structures. Anyone who failed to work to their potential was beaten by the guards or punished in some other way, like being placed in the "sensory isolation box," a wooden crate that was placed in a ditch for days at a time. Children who misbehaved were lowered into a well with an adult hiding at the bottom, pretending to be a demon.

If Jones thought he was escaping his problems by fleeing to Guyana he was mistaken. The article had appeared in New West magazine by now, featuring allegations by former Temple members who claimed they were physically, emotionally, and sexually abused during their time in the church. All Jones' political connections abruptly broke off ties to him after the article was published.

He had legal problems, too. Tim and Grace Stoen were among Jones' first followers when he came to California. Tim was an attorney and did work for the Temple, and Grace was a member of Jones' inner circle. In 1972 Grace gave birth to a boy – John Victor Stoen – and Jones claimed to be the father. Tim even signed an affidavit that confirmed that Jones was the father. He said that he had requested Jones have sex with Grace to keep her from leaving the Temple. In 1976 Grace did defect from the church, but she left John with Jones, fearing that both their lives were in danger. She began divorce proceedings against Tim the following year and Jones ordered Tim to take the boy to Guyana in February 1977 to avoid a custody dispute with Grace. After Tim finally defected himself in June 1977, the Temple kept John in Jonestown.

When Tim returned to the United States, he and Grace began trying to get John back through the U.S. courts. Jones adamantly refused to hand the boy over, despite court orders that he had to do so. The dispute over John's paternity became a symbol of the bitter conflict that had started between the Temple and its opponents. If the Stoens managed to get John back it would signal the loss of Jones' far-reaching power over his people and might start other relatives trying to bring their relatives home from Jonestown.

That fall Tim and others who had left the Temple formed a "Concerned Relatives" Group. All of them had family who were in Jonestown. Tim traveled to Washington, D.C. in January 1978 to visit with state department officials and members of Congress and presented them with a statement that detailed his grievances against Jones and the Temple. His efforts sparked the curiosity of a man who would become intrinsically linked to the final days of Jonestown – California Congressman Leo Ryan.

Ryan ended up writing a letter on Tim Stoen's behalf to the Guyanese Prime Minister Forbes Burnham, while the Concerned Relatives were starting with their legal battle with the Temple over the custody of John Stoen. Ryan would eventually become so involved in the situation that he would take a trip to Guyana.

Tragically, neither he nor John Stoen would make it out of the country alive.

As Jones' anxiety and paranoia increased, he began creating scenarios that "protected" his followers from the Temple's enemies. One day in October 1977 he had one of his men open fire on the compound, and he told his followers that they were being attacked by armed mercenaries who had come to kidnap John Stoen. A six-day siege followed, during which Jones whipped up hysteria and talked of mass suicide for the cause.

The siege was the prototype for what became known as "White Nights," which would soon begin to be rehearsed over and over again. They began with Jones bellowing, "Alert! Alert! Alert!" over the community's loudspeaker, the signal for everyone to crowd into the compound's open-air pavilion. They would then spend the next several hours listening to Jones as armed guards patrolled the grounds. During one of the "White Nights," Jones announced that they were all going to take poison and die. Followers lined up to drink what they thought was poisoned fruit punch until Jones' son, Stephan, convinced him to stop. Stephan and his mother, Marceline, were now the only ones who had any control over Jones' behavior.

Congressman Leo Ryan

His madness had started to spin out of control in Jonestown.

Even though it was overcrowded Jonestown was initially well organized. Conditions deteriorated over time, however, along with the mental and physical state of Jones. He had secretly been abusing a variety of prescription drugs since the early days of the Ukiah church, but now he did so openly. And he used a lot more. He'd also started drinking which caused an increase in his many real – and largely imagined – ailments. He suffered from violent mood swings and was often irrational. He spent much of his time locked in the cottage that he shared with two of his mistresses. It had a telephone that connected it to the compound's loudspeaker, and he would ramble on for hours at a time, slurring his words, reading the daily news, and cover his apocalyptic interpretations of it. He had become an overweight, shambling shadow of his former self, and most of the day-to-day operations of the community had been taken over by his advisors – people who continued to believe that he was God.

In spite of the security measures that Jones had in place for the compound word did leak out about the conditions in Jonestown. In April 1978, the Concerned Relatives distributed a packet of documents, letters, and affidavits about the Temple to reporters and members of Congress. Their claims were backed up by an escaped Temple member named Deborah Layton, who provided more details about crimes committed by Temple authorities and about the sub-standard living conditions in Jonestown – including that there were many members who wanted to leave but were literally being held captive.

Congressman Ryan with Jones in Guyana

By this time, Congressman Leo Ryan had heard enough about Jonestown. He decided that he needed to see the place for himself. Ryan was an unconventional politician. The Democrat had once briefly incarcerated himself at Folsom State Prison to see what the conditions were like, so going to Guyana didn't worry him. He wrote a letter to Jones requesting an invitation to visit the settlement, a visit that Jones and his followers violently opposed. His lawyers eventually persuaded him to change his mind and the date was set for Ryan's investigation of Jonestown.

When news of Congressman Ryan's impending trip to Guyana was announced a number of news reporters asked and were allowed to accompany him. It was one of these reporters, Sammy Houston of the Associated Press, who was instrumental in convincing Ryan that he needed to go to Jonestown. Houston and his wife, Nadyne, told Ryan what had happened to their son Robert, a one-time member of the People's Temple. Robert had been forced to work two jobs, with the railroad and as a probation officer, in order to keep up his $2,000 monthly contribution to the church. He was later found guilty of breaking church rules and was found dead in 1976, just hours after defecting from the Temple. When the cult moved his widow was convinced by Jones to relocate with her two children to Guyana. Nadyne Houston accompanied Ryan to Jonestown in hopes of bringing her two grandchildren back to California.

On November 15, 1978 Ryan and his delegation of aides, relatives of Temple members, an NBC camera crew, and reporters for various newspapers arrived in Georgetown. Two days later they were taken by airplane to Kaituma and then were transported to the Jonestown. On the evening of their arrival Jones hosted a reception for them at the central pavilion.

Jones put on the best front possible, but Ryan was not happy with what he found.

Many People's Temple members wanted to defect. Families were divided, with some wanting to leave and others to stay. Jones tried to persuade the defectors to stay but without success. He had told Ryan the previous evening that anyone who wanted to leave was free to do so, but Temple members were obviously upset with what was happening. The entire mood of the compound had changed overnight.

The plane that was supposed to take Ryan, the press, and the defectors away from Jonestown

Some of Ryan's party left with 16 defectors on November 18. They departed the compound by truck, heading for the Kaituma airfield, six miles away, where two airplanes were waiting for them. At the airport they were loading the defectors' luggage into the planes when two Temple vehicles drove onto the field.

It was a heavily armed hit squad that Jones had impulsively sent to kill them.

They opened fire on the delegation, killing Ryan, a defector, and three newsmen. Cameraman Bob Brown managed to keep his camera going until the moment that he was shot. The developed film would show the assassins advancing on their victims in vivid, horrific color.

But not everyone was killed. When word reached Jones that the hit squad had botched the job and that some of the victims had escaped, the cultists were all gathered at the pavilion where they found Jones seated on his familiar green throne. As his ring of armed guards, which he called "Angels," surrounded the congregation, a debate began after Jones told his followers about the killing of Congressman Ryan and members of his entourage. The subject of mass suicide was discussed – something that had been rehearsed many times since the cult's arrival in the Guyana jungles.

"How much I have loved you," Jones told them. "How much I have tried to give you a good life." There had been a catastrophe, and the community was about to be invaded. "Now, we must die with dignity. The GDF (Guyanese Defense Force) will question you. Then they will torture you. They will castrate you. They will shoot you. I can't leave any member of my family behind."

A few followers protested and tried to reason with Jones. A woman named Christine Miller cried that the children did not deserve to die. She was shouted down by others.

Jones told her and the others who were hesitant that he was simply "unable to leave them behind." If they chose not to die with dignity, he told them that they would

Cups and syringes found discarded at the scene in the wake of the massacre

die anyway. Then the guards, armed with rifles, pistols, and bows and arrows, moved in and pushed the crowd into a tighter group.

He ordered the community's nurses to prepare a powerful "potion" that was added to a large tub of strawberry-flavored Flavor-Aid – a generic version of Kool-Aid – and then instructed the cult that the babies were to be brought up first. Babies were carried to the podium and while still in their mother's arms had their mouths forced open and poison squirted inside. Some of the children were torn from the hands of hesitant mothers and dragged to the front by nurses and guards. As their sobbing parents watched the babies endured painful spasms and died in minutes.

Then the previously practiced "White Nights" suicide ritual started going awry. It was very different from when they had practiced it in the past. What was never part of the plan was when the first victims began gagging, retching, and twisting in horrible pain. A number of the cultists, realizing that this was no rehearsal but the real thing, began resisting and refusing to willingly drink the poisoned juice. Guards and other members had to hold them down while the liquid was forced down their throats. Some of the more violent resistors were injected with the poison, as were those who didn't seem to be dying fast enough from ingesting the drink.

The FBI later recovered a horrifying 45-minute audio recording of the suicide ritual in progress.

On the audiotape Jones can be heard telling members the Soviet Union, with whom the Temple had been negotiating to relocate there for months, would not take them after the murders at the airstrip. He assured his followers that intelligence organizations had been conspiring against the Temple for years and that they planned to "parachute in here on us," "shoot some of our innocent babies" and "they'll torture our children, they'll torture some of our people here, they'll torture our seniors." The U.S. government would convert the captured children to fascism --- "they're gonna just let them grow up and be dummies."

As members are heard weeping on the tape, Jones ordered them, "Stop these hysterics. This is not the way for people who are socialists or communists to die. No way for us to die. We must die with some dignity." He could be heard telling them, "Don't be afraid to die!" He told them that death was just stepping into another existence and that it was a "friend." At the end of the recording, Jones concluded, "We didn't commit suicide; we committed an act of revolutionary suicide protesting the conditions of an inhumane world."

As screams of agony and tortured moans echoed through Jonestown and the dying writhed on the ground in unspeakable pain, Jones decided that he, himself, would die quicker and in less pain. When the authorities later arrived at Jonestown, they were appalled by the number of bodies they found. Most of the dead were contorted and twisted in agony.

Only Jim Jones seemed to be at peace. He was sitting on his green throne with a bullet in his brain.

The final body count at Jonestown

The bodies of the dead. More than 900 followers of Jones and the People's Temple died that day in Jonestown

reached 912. They were found lying in piles as high as 30 deep and were so badly decomposed from the brutal heat that they were falling apart by the time that Guyanese authorities arrived at the compound. Many of the soldiers and policemen, who witnessed death on an almost daily basis, retched and vomited when they saw the carnage.

Jonestown had been turned into a horrific nightmare like nothing they had ever seen before.

There were members of the People's Temple who survived the mass suicide in Guyana.

Jones' son, Stephan, had been in Georgetown with the Temple's basketball team on the day of the slaughter. Earlier that morning, before the dramatic events took place, a group of 11 Temple members – including a mother and her three-year-old son – walked 35 miles to escape Jonestown, claiming they were going on a picnic. Two other men, Stanley Clayton and Odell Rhodes, were able to slip past the armed security guards through a combination of luck and deception. Three more Temple members, Mike Prokes and brothers Tim and Make Carter, were sent on a mission by one of Jones' aides to deliver a suitcase of cash to the Soviet Embassy. There were also another two dozen or more that fled the compound when the ritual started who wandered for days in the jungle. Some of them were never seen again, but most were rescued.

Perhaps the most remarkable story of survival belongs to Hyacinth Thrash, an elderly woman who was asleep in her cabin on the night of the mass suicide. She woke up the following morning and walked over to the senior citizens' building, where she saw bodies covered with sheets. Her sister, Zipporah Edwards, was among those who were dead. Years later she recalled, "There were all of those dead being put in bags, people I'd known and loved. God knows I never wanted to be there in the first place. I never wanted to go to Guyana to die. I didn't think Jim would do a thing like that. He let us down."

Even those Temple members who didn't die that day suffered in the aftermath of the tragedy. Many of them – including those who lost loved ones – tried to go on with their lives, only to suffer from what seemed to be a "curse" connected to the Temple.

In 1979, Mike Prokes, the Temple's media relations director, called a press conference in a California hotel room to defend what remained of the People's Temple. Soon after he went into the bathroom and shot himself in the head.

Husband and wife, Al and Jeannie Mills were prominent defectors and opponents of Jones. They founded the Human Freedom Center as a refuge for other Temple defectors and were also involved with the Concerned Relatives organization. Because of their defections and their high-profile campaigns against him, Jones often lashed out at them as traitors and threatened retribution against them. In February 1980 Al, Jeannie, and their daughter, Daphne, were shot to death in their home. The murders raised fear that Temple "hit squads" were seeking out those who had betrayed the Temple. But those rumors dissipated when the police began investigating Eddie Mills, 17, who was in the house at the time of the shootings but was left unharmed. Detectives later cleared Eddie, leaving the murders of the Mills family unsolved.

Paula Adams, a former Temple staff member, was murdered along with her child in 1983. She was killed by her ex-lover Laurence Mann, a former Guyanese ambassador to the U.S., who then killed himself.

In 1984 Tyrone Mitchell, whose parents and siblings died at Jonestown, opened fire with a rifle into a Los Angeles schoolyard. One person was killed and 10 more were wounded before he turned the gun on himself.

Chad Rhodes, whose mother Juanita Bogue, was pregnant with him in Jonestown, murdered a police officer in Oakland in 1999. He is currently serving life in prison without parole.

A "curse?" Maybe not, but it's clear that Jim Jones left a tremendous amount of damage in his wake.

He also left a mystery – and a warning.

Even after the corpses were taken away by body removal teams with gas masks from the U.S. Army, the stench of death remained in the air at Jonestown. Jones' bloodstains around his green throne and podium remained, no matter how much effort was expended to remove them. As perplexing as these bloodstains turned out to be, the authorities were even more baffled by the discovery of the gun that had killed Jim Jones. The weapon was found in a building some distance away from the spot where the cult leader was killed.

Did Jones succumb to cowardice when it came his turn to die? Did he admonish his followers to "die with dignity" and then fail to do so himself? There seems to be no way that Jones could have committed suicide, placed the gun where it was found, and then return to his throne, where the body was discovered – and yet somehow, it happened.

The events at Jonestown stay with us as a horrific example of the evil that some men do – and a reminder that we should always be waiting for the next madman to come along.

Above the throne in which Jones' body was discovered a sign hung on the wall. It was a quote from George Santayana that read:

"Those who do not remember the past are condemned to repeat it."

Remember Jonestown. It's nothing that we should ever have to witness again.

The Orange People

If there is one thing that most people remember about the strange Oregon cult leader Bhagwan Shree Rajneesh, it's that he was the holy man who owned 93 Rolls-Royces. He was the always smiling guru who encouraged dancing and sex – a lot of sex – and he advocated a combination of Eastern spiritualism and Western materialism that proved irresistible to many in the 1970s and early 1980s. He came to America to create a utopia that was based on his principles, where his followers could work together and "find themselves" while doing so.

But somehow his utopia ended up more like a prison. Amidst paranoia, death threats, voter fraud, and the largest mass poisoning in American history, the dream to which thousands had committed their lives fell apart.

"I have come to wake you up."

That was the simple sentence that became Rajneesh's theme throughout the early days of the cult that eventually grew up around him. It was a subtle yet meaningful expression that led so many people to believe that he was a man with the key to enlightenment. Many will still maintain that he gathered his people with the best of intentions and was manipulated into illegal acts by those who were closest to him, but in light of the events that surrounded his commune in Oregon, that seems difficult to believe.

Rajneesh – a childhood nickname – was born Chandra Mohan Jain, the oldest of 11 children of a cloth merchant, on December 11, 1931 in the village of Kuchwada, in Madhya Pradesh, in Central India. His parents, Babulal and Saraswati Jain, were adherents to Jainism which teaches non-violence, vegetarianism, chastity, and is traditionally tolerant of all religions. They allowed Rajneesh to live with his maternal grandparents for the first seven years of his life. He would always maintain that this was a major influence on the development of his philosophies because his grandmother allowed him to do whatever he wanted. She imposed no education or restrictions on his life. When he was seven-years-old, however, his grandfather died and he returned to live his with his parents. He was deeply troubled by his grandfather's death – as well as by the death of his cousin, Shashi, by typhoid when he was 15 – and this forced him to become preoccupied with death to the point that he vowed he would never let it affect him again.

During his school years Rajneesh was a rebellious but gifted student. He read religious scriptures, guides to yoga and hypnosis, and even books by great Russian novelists. He gained a reputation as a formidable debater. He often skipped classes and argued with his teachers. As he became more critical of traditional religion, he started looking for ways to expand his consciousness, like breath control, yoga, meditation, fasting, and the occult.

In 1951 at age 19 Rajneesh began his studies at Hitkarini College in Jabalpur, but he was kicked out soon after enrolling due to several conflicts with an instructor. He transferred to D.N. Jain College, also in Jabalpur, but after proving himself to be so argumentative that he was disruptive to other students he was not required to attend class except during examinations. He spent his free time working as an assistant editor for a local newspaper and resisting his parents' pressure for him to get married.

Rajneesh's spiritual crisis continued until one night when he was 21. He had a mystical experience while sitting under a tree in the Bhanvaratl Garden in Jabalpur. He described it as an emotional feeling of bliss and communion with the universe.

After graduation Rajneesh lectured in philosophy at the University of Sagar for a time but was asked to leave by the vice-chancellor who considered him a threat to the students' morality, character, and religion. Between other jobs he traveled around India creating his own philosophy by picking and choosing the parts of Hinduism, Buddhism, Christianity, Judaism, Tantra, and Western esoteric traditions that he liked. One of his major influences was the early twentieth-century mystic G.I. Gurdjieff, who believed that the main problem with modern life was that people were essentially asleep.

Rajneesh, echoing the words of Gurdjieff, made "I have come to wake you up" his personal mantra.

He gained a reputation as a brilliant orator who often made outrageous statements. He attacked other religions and offered lectures that were critical of socialism and even Gandhi, who he described as a masochist reactionary who worshiped poverty. He mocked the idea of chastity, flaunting his love of sex. He proclaimed that Indian religions were dead, filled with empty ritual and oppressing their followers were promises of blessings and fears of damnation.

These kinds of statements made him controversial, but they also gained him a loyal following that included many wealthy families and businessmen. They sought consultations with him about their spiritual development, which he offered in return for donations. Starting in 1964 he began to hold meditation camps and he scandalized Hindu leaders by calling for a wider acceptance of sex. He soon became known as the "sex guru" in the press.

Up until then Rajneesh had taught that people should ignore gurus and seek enlightenment within themselves, but all that changed after he began enjoying great

Bhagwan Shree Rajneesh

success. Starting in 1970 he began initiating disciples. His first follower was a woman named Laxmi Thakarsi Kuruwa. She became his private secretary and second-in-command over the many who flocked to his side. She raised the money that allowed Rajneesh to stop his travels and settle down to let his followers come to him.

Laxmi was also the first of his followers to wear exclusively orange clothing. This was a color traditionally worn by wandering holy men called "sannyasins," who had renounced all worldly possessions. Orange clothing soon began to be adopted by all Rajneesh's followers, leading them to be dubbed the "Orange People." When new followers were initiated into the movement, they were given a new name – usually incorporating the Hindi words for "love" and "bliss" – and a necklace of wooden beads with a locket that contained Rajneesh's photograph.

He moved into an apartment in Mumbai where he gave lectures and received visitors, including many who came from the West to see him. He was – especially to Americans and Europeans – the perfect guru for the times. He encouraged his followers to have as much sex as they could. He didn't care if they drank or took drugs. He didn't care what they did, as long as they expressed their love and devotion for him and took part in what he called "mad games" – sessions designed to break down their egos and get them to live in the present. Visitors were captivated by his morning and evening talks where he used dirty jokes to break the flow of his lofty discussions about enlightenment.

After joining the movement followers spent the next few months attending various group therapy sessions run by Rajneesh's inner circle. Some of them were meditation groups while others were much more confrontational. The latter was supposed to break down people's inhibitions, challenge their beliefs, and force them to face their fears. Sometimes these sessions spun out of control. Fights broke out and people were injured. Some participants were made to *literally* face their fears – a person afraid of snakes might be locked in a room with a dozen of them; a woman who had been raped might be raped again. Such practices turned out to be too much for some participants. Some left the group while others committed suicide.

Some of the many Western converts became part of Rajneesh's inner circle. Many of them stayed in India while others were sent home to spread the word. The first Rajneesh Meditation Center outside of India opened in London in 1971.

The humid climate of Mumbai proved rough on Rajneesh's health – he developed asthma, numerous allegories, and diabetes. In 1974, the money brought in from visiting Westerners allowed him to buy a six-acre estate in the city of Pune. Two adjoining houses on the property became his new ashram. This allowed him to make regular audio, and later video recordings, and to print his writings for distribution around the world. He quickly saw a sharp rise in Western visitors and the ashram soon formed an arts-and-crafts center that produced clothing, jewelry, and pottery. They also had a stage for hosting music and theatrical performances. Once the ashram was able to start offering therapy and meditation this became a major source of income.

By all accounts the Pune ashram was an exciting and intense place to be. The atmosphere was emotionally charged, and many said "carnival-like." The days began at sunrise with meditation and yoga. There were lectures hosted by Rajneesh. Most of the early therapy groups were experimental and included physical aggression and

The therapy sessions at the ashram were both extreme and controversial but western followers flocked to India to take part in them

sexual encounters between participants. Those who stayed at the ashram took part in hard, unpaid labor, and supervisors were chosen for their abrasive personalities. This was designed to provoke opportunities for self-actualization and transcendence over the physical. In spite of how awful this sounds, many disciples stayed for years.

The therapy sessions were, of course, controversial, but the other things going on at the ashram were worse. Allegations of drug use marred the ashram's image. Some Westerners were alleged to be financing their expended stays in India through prostitution and selling drugs. A few of them later alleged that while Rajneesh was not directly involved in these schemes, they had discussed their plans with him, and he had given them his blessing.

There was also plenty of speculation about Rajneesh himself. Many of his followers wanted to know more about his sex life since it was a subject that he talked about constantly. He often had "private audiences" with his female followers and frequently boasted that he'd had "more women than any man in history." He told his lovers never to talk about their experiences with him, but from what many of them later revealed it seemed that sex with him involved a lot of "looking and touching."

Rajneesh was all for sex, but he had no interest in children. He even persuaded many of his converts to abandoned theirs. He believed that the best thing for the world would be a two-year ban on having children. Her urged his female followers to be sterilized and, to demonstrate their devotion to him, hundreds of them had the operation – a decision that many later regretted.

By the late 1970s the Pune ashram was obviously becoming too small to contain the rapid growth of Rajneesh's movement. The overcrowding and the flood of Western visitors were causing resentment in the region. Many were offended by their indiscreet public behavior and the women's provocative dress – Rajneesh had encouraged them not to wear underwear because it interfered with their "natural flow of energy" – and some of them were attacked in the street. In May 1980 an attempt was made on Rajneesh's life by a young Hindu fundamentalist. It seemed time for the movement to find a new place to live and he instructed Laxmi to start searching for suitable sites in India.

Even that became a problem, however. The Indian government had also turned against Rajneesh, revoking the movement's tax-exempt status and blocking its attempts to buy land.

By 1981, the ashram was still hosting more than 30,000 visitors each year and daily lecture audiences were predominantly European and American. Some of his longtime followers started to notice a change in Rajneesh's lecture style. He had started to offer an increased number of ethnic or sexual jokes that were intended to shock and amuse his audiences. Suddenly, though, on April 10, 1981, he entered a three-and-a-half-year period of self-imposed public silence. His daily "lectures" became silent sittings with music and readings from spiritual works like Khalil Gibran's *The Prophet*.

Ma Anand Sheela – a.k.a. Sheela Silverman

This wasn't the only change that he made during that time – he also replaced his private secretary, Laxmi Thakarsi Kuruwa, with a follower who used the title of Ma Anand Sheela, also known as Sheela Silverman. She had come to Rajneesh with the radical idea of starting a new ashram in the United States. Rajneesh eventually agreed.

On June 1, 1981 he traveled to America for the first time on a tourist visa, reportedly for medical purposes. He had been diagnosed with a prolapsed disc in his back in early 1981 and in his visa, Sheela had stated that if he had a medical emergency he would be in grave danger in India and could only get the medical treatment he needed in the United States. It sounded serious, but it should be noted that Rajneesh never sought nor received medical treatment during his time in the United States. Years later he would plead guilty to immigration fraud.

After his departure from India the community at the Pune ashram began to disperse. Millions of dollars made it out of the country and Rajneesh's followers were instructed to apply for U.S. visas in groups of only two or three so that would not arouse suspicion.

The "Orange People" would soon arrive in the Pacific Northwest.

Through Sheela's husband, John Shelfer, the movement found a property on which it could settle in Oregon – the 64,000-acre Big Muddy Ranch in Wasco County. Through a foundation it paid $5.75 million for the land. It was renamed as "Rancho Rajneesh," and the guru arrived there on August 29, 1981.

When he arrived, the commune threw a large party for their new neighbors. Sheela announced that all they wanted to do was to set up a farm with about 40 workers, but locals soon realized this was a lie. Initial reactions from neighbors ranged from tolerance to hostility, depending on how far they lived from the ranch. But as hundreds of followers began arriving in their orange, red, and pink clothing – the color scheme now varied a little – tensions inevitably increased.

The commune was soon met with intense local, state, and federal opposition from the press, county residents, and the government. Within months a series of legal battles began with locals, mostly over land use. The commune leadership refused to compromise and was impatient with nearby residents. They were also intent on having their demands met and engaged in threatening and confrontational behavior. It was obvious that, at some point, the battles were going to boil over into all-out war.

Most of Rajneesh's followers seemed oblivious to the trouble that was brewing. They moved into trailers on the land and began building their new community. They worked 12 hours each day – although the word "work" was banned and replaced by "worship." They sent out urgent calls for donations to Rajneesh supporters around the world and millions of dollars poured in. Hundreds of marriages were arranged between followers to allow those who were not U.S. citizens to remain in the country.

In October 1981 the residents of Rancho Rajneesh applied to the Wasco County Court to have a portion of their land incorporated as a city. Despite the ongoing conflict with local residents and fierce opposition to the plan, the application was granted for a town called Rajneeshpuram. The group built a mall, a restaurant, an airstrip, a reservoir, and a meditation school. They had their own newspaper and their own police department – the "Peace Force." By 1985 Rajneeshpuram had more than 2,500 permanent residents, with almost that many visitors in town at any given time.

The fact that the new town had become a success escalated tensions. Over the next few years, the commune was hit with constant and coordinated pressures from various coalitions of Oregon residents, all trying to void the incorporation and force the buildings and improvements to be removed. One initiative was filed that would order the governor to "contain, control, and remove the threat of invasion by an alien cult." The Oregon legislature was pressured to act and passed several bills that tried to slow or stop the development of Rajneeshpuram, including one that stopped the distribution of revenue-sharing funds for any city that had a legal status that was being challenged. Rajneeshpuram was the only city impacted by the bill.

In May 1982, U.S. Senator Mark Hatfield contacted the Immigration and Naturalization Service (INS) in Portland. An INS memo stated that he was very concerned about how the "religious cult was endangering the way of life for a small agricultural town and was a threat to public safety."

But the "Orange People" didn't seem to care. While all the various legal battles were going on Rajneesh remained behind the scenes, having withdrawn into another period of public silence that lasted until November 1984. Videos of his earlier public

Rajneeshpuram in the early 1980s

discourses were played for commune audiences. He spent his time in seclusion, living in a trailer that was next to his covered swimming pool. He spoke to his followers only through his inner circle, including his caretaker girlfriend, Ma Yoga Vivek – Christine Woolf – and Ma Anand Sheela, who had total control of the day-to-day running of Rajneeshpuram.

In 1981, he had given Sheela his power of attorney, and she eventually announced that he would henceforth speak only through her. He later said that she kept him oblivious of everything she did. Sheela was a notoriously domineering, abrasive, short-tempered woman, and many followers expressed doubts about whether she properly represented Rajneesh, which led to a number of defections. Her bad temper became legendary. Once, during a nationally-televised debate on the news show *Nightline*, Sheela's microphone was cut off after she repeatedly shouted, "Bullshit!" Her favorite retort, though, was "Tough titties!" which she used many times in television interviews.

Rajneesh spent his days in a haze, dictating books under the influence of Valium and nitrous oxide administered by his personal "dentist." The only time his followers saw him was during his daily "drive-by ceremony" along the community's main street in one of his Rolls-Royces. He had acquired his first Rolls in India, but in America his collection grew to an unbelievable 93 vehicles. When his followers were asked why he needed so many cars they always replied that they loved Rajneesh and wanted him to be happy. He loved cars and if buying them made him happy, then why not buy them? Rajneesh had, of course, never made a secret of his love for money and what he could buy with it.

As Rajneeshpuram continued to grow the legal challenges and the animosity continued. Local ministers declared that the cult was evil, the immigration service had started to investigate the arranged marriages, and the Oregon Attorney General filed a lawsuit that alleged a violation of the Establishment Clause of the First Amendment. In other words, there was a lack of separation between church and state. During all this Rajneesh's followers didn't bother to disguise their contempt for the locals and seemed to go out of their way to antagonize them.

And then, in September 1984, a strange event occurred in The Dalles, Wasco County's largest town. More than 750 people became sick with salmonella poisoning, with 45 cases so severe that people had to be hospitalized. The outbreak was traced

Rajneesh was rarely seen by his followers, except for during his daily "drive-by" when he would wave at them from behind the wheel of one of his 93 Rolls-Royces

back to food handlers in 10 different restaurants – none of them had any connection between them.

Medical investigators were baffled by the outbreak.

Around this same time, the cult came up with a bizarre plan to rig the upcoming elections for the Wasco County Court. They imported large numbers of homeless people from cities across the United States, inviting them to start a new life in Rajneeshpuram. In reality, the real purpose of the seemingly altruistic program was to bring in enough voters to win the election and shut down the many lawsuits that had been filed against the commune.

Over the next few weeks about 3,700 homeless people, mostly men, were taken by bus to Rajneeshpuram. Among them were alcoholics, drug addicts, and the mentally ill. The result was – predictably – utter chaos. The cult members found it impossible to control the newcomers, even though they had ordered in a large quantity of the tranquilizer Haldol. Realizing their plan had failed, the cult released the homeless into surrounding towns and left many for the state of Oregon to return to their home cities at the government's expense.

The outside pressures on the community continued, but now even more destructive forces were coming from within. There was a sense of increasing paranoia within the commune. Armed security guards patrolled the streets and visitors were placed under surveillance. When Rajneesh made his daily, drive-by appearance, a helicopter circled overhead, searching for snipers.

Rajneesh began to release predictions through his inner circle, each darker and more apocalyptic than the next. He often spoke of the world being destroyed by nuclear war or other disasters in the 1990s. He frequently spoke about the need to create a "new humanity" so that global suicide could be avoided. It would be a sort of "Noah's Ark of consciousness."

Even the sexual freedom that had once been an integral part of the group was gone. Sheela announced that Rajneesh had predicted the death of two-thirds of the population from AIDS, which was just beginning to be understood as an epidemic in the mid-1980s. Cult members were now forbidden to have sex without condoms or foreplay without surgical gloves. Since no one was clear then how AIDS could be spread even kissing was eventually banned.

But the most destructive element to threaten the community was Sheela. She and her female circle, known as the "moms," lived in considerable luxury in their own house. They answered to almost no one and knew everything that was happening on the ranch. Rajneesh had long stated that Sheela spoke on his behalf and had always supported her when disputes about her behavior came up within the commune leadership. He allowed her a lot of leeway, like with expulsions of anyone who spoke "negatively" about her. Most followers believed that Rajneesh was guiding the community and knew and approved of the things that Sheela did.

This may – or may not have – been the case.

Sheela eventually overplayed her hand by turning on the rest of Rajneesh's inner circle, the only people on the ranch over whom she did not have control. Rajneesh's long-time girlfriend, Vivek, became ill after she was given a cup of tea by Sheela. She thought she had been poisoned and told others of her suspicions, but no one could bring themselves to believe it. After Rajneesh's doctor was stuck with a needle by one of the other "moms" and almost died, everyone got worried. A number of followers left the ranch.

Rajneeshpuram unraveled faster than anyone imagined it would.

Over two days in mid-September 1985 Sheela and 19 others left Oregon for Europe. On the morning of September 16, Rajneesh – who had ended his period of silence sometime before – held a press conference and announced that Sheela and her associates were a "gang of fascists." She was a criminal who had turned the community into a "concentration camp." He accused them of serious crimes including the attempted murder of his personal doctor, wiretapping and bugging within the commune and even in his home, several other poisonings of commune officials and, worst of all, an attack on the citizens of The Dalles, Oregon, using salmonella.

His followers were staggered by these revelations and demanded to know why Rajneesh had placed a woman like Sheela in charge. He claimed that the crimes had been committed without his knowledge or consent, but the extent to which Rajneesh knew about her activities remains a matter of debate. Many are convinced that Sheela was only a pawn and that everything she did was on the guru's orders. Sheela simply became a convenient scapegoat.

Regardless, Rajneesh invited the police to investigate his allegations and they were happy to do so. They searched the ranch, questioned followers, and compiled a dossier of even more crimes. The police later found a "death list" of intended victims

Mugshots of Sheela and Rajneesh

that included state and federal attorneys and hundreds of secretly recorded conversations.

The salmonella attack is considered the first time that biological terrorism occurred in the United States. Sheela's lieutenants had caused the poisonings by visiting the 10 restaurants involved and poisoning the food. This had actually been a dry run for the election. In addition to bringing in all the homeless people, she had planned to increase the community's chances to steal the election by making local residents too sick to vote.

Rajneesh continued to claim that he knew nothing of the crimes that had been committed. He had been in silence and isolation, meeting only with Sheela, and was unaware of the crimes until Sheela and her "gang" left and other followers came forward to tell him about them.

Of course, many in law enforcement didn't believe him. There were many affidavits that were never released publicly, as well as hundreds of hours of tape recordings that suggested Rajneesh was guilty of more crimes than those for which he was prosecuted. Some officials stated that Rajneesh was "not disapproving of poisoning" and that he and Sheela had been "genuinely evil." According to court testimony from Ma Ava – Ava Avalos – Sheela had played for her a recording of a meeting that she had with Rajneesh when he talked about the "need to kill people" in order to strengthen the resolve of his followers. He added that it would be necessary to kill people to stay in Oregon and that this "wasn't such a bad thing." He also said that "Hitler was a great man," although he couldn't say that publicly because people wouldn't understand – "Hitler had great vision," he said.

A federal grand jury indicted Rajneesh and several other followers with conspiracy to evade immigration laws on October 23, 1985. The indictment was returned in secret but word leaked to Rajneesh's lawyer. He tried to negotiate for a peaceful surrender of his client after rumors spread about a National Guard takeover of the commune and a violent arrest of Rajneesh. The authorities later said that they believed there was a plan to use women and children followers as human shields in the event of Rajneesh's arrest.

None of that mattered anyway because Rajneesh was already gone.

Five days later Rajneesh and a few of his followers were arrested aboard a rented Learjet at a North Carolina airstrip. They were en route to Bermuda to avoid prosecution with $58,000 in cash and jewelry and watches worth over $1 million. He was sent back to Oregon for trial.

The next day Sheela and two others were arrested in Germany and deported to the United States.

Rajneesh was charged on 35 felony counts, most of them related to the arranged marriages. He spent 12 days in jail. He initially entered a not guilty plea on all charges but, on the advice of his lawyers, entered an "Alford plea" – a type of plea in which a suspect does not admit guilt but acknowledges there is enough evidence to convict him – on two of the charges. Under the deal he was given a 10-year suspended sentence, five years' probation, a $400,000 fine, and ordered to leave the United States. He would not be allowed to return for at least five years and only then with the permission of the U.S. Attorney General.

Many of his followers wanted to stay on at Rajneeshpuram, but they soon realized that the town was not economically viable without Rajneesh as the draw. The ranch was sold and its assets were dispersed.

In July 1986 Sheela was convicted of attempted murder, immigration fraud, wiretapping, food poisoning, and various other crimes. At trial she maintained that she had only attempted to murder Rajneesh's girlfriend and doctor because she believed they were a threat to Rajneesh. She claimed to have secretly recorded a conversation in which the doctor "agreed to obtain drugs the guru wanted to ensure a peaceful death if he decided to take his own life." The jury didn't buy it and she was found guilty and sentenced to 20 years in prison. She ended up being paroled after only two years, though. When released she moved to Switzerland and set up two homes for the mentally disabled.

Her true role in what happened in Oregon remains a mystery.

After leaving the United States, Rajneesh returned to India where he was given a hero's welcome by his disciples at home. He denounced the U.S. saying the world must "put the monster America in its place" and that "either America must be hushed up or America will be the end of the world." He then went on a "world tour" which mainly consisted of him being thrown out of Crete and Uruguay and be barred from entering Nepal, Greece, Sweden, England, Canada, and Jamaica. Even though no official reasons were offered he was simply "invited to leave" each of them.

In January 1987 he returned to the ashram in Pune where he began giving daily lectures that were only interrupted by his increasingly poor health. He began claiming that his deteriorating health was caused by poison that had been given to him by the authorities when he was in the U.S. prison. His doctors and former attorneys were convinced that he had been given a mattress that had been deliberately irradiated by thallium since his symptoms were concentrated on the right side of his body. Needless to say, no actual evidence of this was ever produced.

He continued medications and lectures until the end of his life. Eventually the orange clothing of the past was replaced by white and black robes and he announced that he no longer wanted to be referred to as "Bhagwan Shree Rajneesh" – he was now "Osho" – and he wanted all his trademarks to be rebranded.

He gave his final public lecture in April 1989. After that he sat only in silence with his followers. He remained just as odd as he'd always been, though. Shortly before his death he suggested that one or more of the audience members at an evening meeting were subjecting him to some kind of "evil magic." A search was started for the perpetrators, but none could be found.

Rajneesh died on January 19, 1990 at the ashram in Pune. The official cause of death was heart failure, but in a press release from the commune it was said that he died because "living in the body had become hell," thanks to the poison he was given in the American jail.

His ashes are kept at the ashram, where his epitaph reads:

"Osho. Never Born. Never Died. Only Visited this Planet Earth Between Dec 11 1931 – Jan 19 1990"

The Ant Hill Kids

"Outside of his drinking bouts, he was a very good man."

That was probably the nicest thing that anyone could say about Roch Thériault, although most would admit that when he was sober, he could be a charming man. He liked to sing and tell jokes and could talk at length about almost any subject. After a few drinks, though, the heavily-bearded, self-styled holy man, husband of eight wives, and reincarnation of Moses became something else altogether.

Throughout these pages we have already witnessed the madness of far too many would-be messiahs and the sadistic ways that they have damaged, tortured, and killed their followers, but we have seen nothing like Roch Thériault.

The story of his horrific cult is not one for the faint of heart.

Roch Thériault was born on May 16, 1947, in a small village that is now Saguenay in Quebec, Canada. His parents, Hyacinthe and Pierette, were devout Catholics, and Roch was one of eight children. When he was six the family moved to Thetford Mines, a community built on the largest deposits of asbestos in the world.

Roch Thériault

Roch's father was a member of an ultra-conservative Catholic organization that was known as the White Berets. He often took his children with him when he went out seeking donations, each of them wearing their own small, white berets. The locals found him pushy and overbearing, and his children found it embarrassing. This was the start of the bitter hatred that Roch would later develop toward Catholicism.

There were two stories that Roch told about his childhood. The first was that his father was a terrible drunk who often beat him. The second was that he spent most of his time roaming the forests, developing nature skills, and playing with bears.

Neither of these stories was true.

His childhood was uneventful. He liked to read books and was considered very intelligent, although a little unusual. He dropped out of school after the seventh grade to teach himself the Old Testament of the Bible. Thériault became convinced that the end of the world was near and that it would occur because of a war between good and evil.

In 1967, he married Francine Grenier. He had been developing his skills as a woodworker and he built a home for his wife and two children – Roch, Jr. and Francoise – from rough-hewn pine. Three years later Thériault had an operation for ulcers and a large part of his stomach was removed. He was often in severe pain after that and was unable to digest food properly. Most who knew Thériault believed that the operation began his descent into madness. Mayhem would have been stopped – and lives saved – if doctors had known then, as they do now, that ulcers are usually caused by an infection and can be treated with antibiotics.

But that wasn't meant to be. Thériault had always been a little odd, but after the surgery his personality drastically changed. He became obsessed with his health, began studying medical textbooks, and often told people he had cancer. He started to drink heavily, claiming that it eased his stomach pains. He also became obsessed with sex, began pursuing other women, and at one point he asked Francine's parents if he could start a nudist camp on some land they owned.

You will not be surprised to learn, I'm sure, that this marriage did not survive.

But there were two sides to Roch Thériault. Despite his problems he remained a gregarious and popular man with many friends. He began a relationship with a young woman from Quebec City named Gisele Tremblay and supported himself with his woodworking skills. He became interested in the occult and joined a secret society called the Aramis Club. He became the president of its initiation committee but startled the other members when he suggested that they wear capes imprinted with the image of Satan. They were all just having a little fun – none of them were taking it seriously. Thériault left the club a short time later – and went another direction entirely.

He converted to the Seventh Day Adventist church and began practicing their holistic beliefs of a healthy lifestyle, free of any artificial foods, alcohol, and tobacco. He excelled at attracting new converts and was soon put in charge of local five-day stop-smoking clinics.

As with just about anything else he did, Thériault committed wholeheartedly, and in 1977 he had a number of young people who had fallen under his spell. The four Adventists – Jacques Fiset, Solange Boilard, Francine Lafamme, and Chantal Labrie – began visiting with him in Thetford Mines on weekends, crowding into his girlfriend Gisele's one-bedroom apartment, where he preached to them for hours as a time. Gisele, who had been subjected to her boyfriend's constant lectures about how women should be subservient to men, had little to say about the frequent visitors. She still hoped to marry Thériault, so she kept silent, even though she was very unhappy with the presence of a new convert, Gabrielle Lavalee. Gabrielle was a trained nurse who had grown disillusioned with western medicine and was interested in the holistic methods advocated by the Seventh Day Adventists. Two other girls also joined the group at this time – Marise Lambert and Josee Pelletier – along with a former drug addict named Claude Ouellette.

Thériault and his merry band started traveling around Canada, holding stop-smoking clinics and vegetarian events. As time passed his followers fell more and more under his spell. He attracted more followers, including husband and wife Jacques Giguere and Maryse Grenier. The group was now too big to fit into Gisele's apartment so Thériault rented a house in Sainte Marie, south of Quebec City. The house became the Healthy Living Clinic and sold Adventist literature and health food. Thériault obtained supplies from an Adventist wholesaler and sold them at heavily marked-up prices.

The Healthy Living Clinic became the start of what would be Theriault's personal cult. The group living together in a communal space where he offered daily motivational lectures and encouraged them all to dwell in unity and equality and free of sin. He prohibited his followers from remaining in contact with their families since this was against the movement's values of freedom.

In May 1978, Thériault convinced a woman named Geraldine Auclair to abandon her hospital treatments for leukemia and come to the clinic where he could cure her through natural means. She died at the clinic a few weeks later. The police couldn't

Thériault and his followers fled into the wilderness, where he took seven other women – in addition to his wife – as his "concubines." This turned out to only be the beginning.

find anything that they could charge Thériault with, but the Seventh Day Adventist church decided that they'd had enough of their overzealous member with the unconventional living arrangements. Thériault was expelled from the church.

He wasn't upset about being forced out of the church, although this did manage to cut off his supply of cheap Adventists goods, meaning the end for the clinic. It was just as well. Thériault had begun to talk more and more about his fear of the end of the world. God had warned him that it would come on February 17, 1979 so he needed to get his followers somewhere safe. The cult – now made up of 12 women, six men, and two children – went on the road.

They ended up in the Gaspe Peninsula, a remote area on the south shore of the St. Lawrence River. They hiked into some rough terrain of what he called "Eternal Mountain," where he told them they would all be safe from the earthquakes and hailstones that would fall from the sky and bring about the end of the world. They would wait in the wilderness for Christ's return.

Work began on an octagonal log cabin that had to be completed before winter came. They worked tirelessly but, only allowed slim rations by their leader, they were always hungry. Meanwhile, Thériault, the only one skilled in woodworking, did little of the labor and abandoned a vegetarian diet and ate all the junk food he wanted.

Some grew tired of the hardship and disappeared into the night. Those that remained were given biblical names by Thériault, appointing himself as "Moses." With his Old Testament name, he announced that he was entitled to multiple wives. He and Gisele had been married while he was still running the Healthy Living Clinic, but now he took seven other women as his "concubines." He would eventually have children with all of them.

In the midst of all this Thériault also began drinking again. And that's when the scary things started to happen.

When he was drunk, he became a different person. He often flew into violent, sadistic rages. Jacques Giguere's wife, Maryse, was often a target – perhaps because she was not one of Thériault's "concubines." Once, when she had eaten two pancakes without his permission, he punched her so hard that he broke two ribs. On another occasion, when she talked about leaving the cult, he ordered Jacques to cut off two of her toes with an ax. When Jacques hesitated, Thériault shouted, "Don't you have any balls? If you want to be a man, you have to learn to teach your woman a lesson." After that Jacques did what he was told to do.

He maintained complete control over his followers. Often, they were not allowed to speak to each other unless he was present. They also couldn't have sex without permission. None of the members questioned his judgment or openly blamed him for the physical or mental damage he did to them. When he was sober, he was kind and charismatic, which hid his increasingly abusive and erratic behavior. When drinking he was quick to punish them for both real and imagined misdeeds. He accused them of "straying," saying that God "told him what they did." If a person talked about leaving the group, he became known for hitting them with a belt or hammer, suspending them from the ceiling, plucking out their body hair, and even defecating on them.

On February 17, 1979 – the day the world was supposed to end – nothing happened. Of course, like all good "prophets," Thériault had an explanation for this. He explained that time on Earth and time in God's world were not parallel, so a miscalculation had been made. It should be noted that he never came up with an alternate date.

In November of 1978, a 23-year-old man named Guy Veer was released from a mental hospital in Quebec City where he had been undergoing treatment for depression. At some point he ended up at Thériault's commune. He was allowed to stay but because of his unusual behavior – which must have been very unusual since Thériault was borderline crazy – he was kept apart from the main group and only allowed to sleep in a shed. He was placed in charge of babysitting three children in the commune that had not been fathered by Thériault, including Jacques and Maryse's two-year-old son, Samuel.

In March 1979, a party was thrown in honor of the arrival of Thériault's two sons from his first marriage. Veer was not invited to the event. Although the details of what happened next are unclear, it seems that later that night when he was unable to get Samuel to stop crying, Veer punched the little boy several times. The blows left bruises on his body which were discovered by Gabrielle Lavalee the next morning. For whatever reason Thériault suddenly decided that Samuel needed to be circumcised that night. After squirting ethanol into the little boy's mouth as an anesthetic – it's not, by the way – he performed the operation with a razor blade.

The next day Samuel was found dead.

Thériault blamed Guy Veer for the boy's death. He later forced Veer to stand trial and assigned the roles of judge, prosecutor, and jury to various group members. Veer was found not guilty by reason of insanity, but Thériault called for a vote on whether he should be castrated. The jury voted and the decision was "yes." Veer protested at first, but Thériault talked him into it telling that the headaches that he had recently suffered from were caused by a diseased testicle. Veer eventually signed a piece of paper, giving his consent.

Veer was placed on a table and with Gabrielle assisting as a nurse and Claude and Jacques holding his legs, Thériault sliced open his scrotum and removed his testicles.

But the cult leader wasn't finished torturing the young man. Once he even tied him to a tree and whipped him until he fainted from the pain. Fearing for his life Veer finally escaped. He told people about Samuel's death and the commune was raided by the police, who arrested Thériault, Jacques, and Maryse. They also placed the seven remaining cult children, including Roch, Jr. who had taken part in the castration, under state care.

In all, seven cult members were charged in connection with Samuel's death, while Thériault and Gabrielle were also charged with causing bodily harm to Guy Veer. Thériault went to jail for two years, Gabrielle for nine months, and Claude and Jacques for six months. The police burned the settlement while its leader was in jail. The children were returned to their mothers, but on the condition that they no longer lived in the commune.

However, this was not the end of the cult. While in prison Thériault stayed in touch with his followers by telephone and made plans to leave Quebec after he was released.

When he left prison, the cult relocated to a site near the small town of Burnt River in Ontario. They purchased 200 acres in the woods. The group now consisted of Thériault, his eight wives, Claude, Jacques, and 10 children. Believe it or not, though, the cult began to grow again and by the middle 1980s boasted more than 40 members.

They began building another settlement but ran into financial problems. Thériault had arranged for the welfare payments of his followers to be paid into his own bank account in Quebec. In Ontario, though, social services classified them as an institution rather than as a family and denied them welfare. So, always a planner, Thériault sent his people out shoplifting in local stores. They were very bad at it, though, and after several were caught, they were banned from shopping in the nearby town of Lindsay.

The commune managed to raise some money by selling fruit and used those proceeds to buy equipment for a bakery. They formed a company that Thériault called the "Ant Hill Kids" because they all worked together like a colony of ants.

But those members who didn't sell enough? They were punished.

After the second community was established Thériault got bored and started drinking heavily again. He claimed that alcohol was the only thing that made his stomach pains feel better. His binges often lasted for as long as three days, and the violence that was directed at his followers during these times was severe.

Angered by their behavior or just on a whim he struck them with the blunt side of an ax or made them break their own legs with sledgehammers. He made them strip naked and stand out in the cold for hours or lie on the ground while he urinated on them. They were ordered to sit on hot stoves, shoot each other in the shoulder, or eat dead mice and human feces. A follower was sometimes asked to cut off another follower's toe with wire cutters to prove his or her loyalty. He pulled out 11 of Claude's teeth with pliers and burned Josee's back with an acetylene torch. He cut, punched, stabbed, and shot all of them at one time or another, or made them fight each other. Only one of them ever fought back and he received a brutal punishment in return. After Jacques once struck back Thériault circumcised him.

Horrifically, the abuse extended to the cult's children, who were sexually abused, held over fires, thrown against walls, and tied to trees while the other children threw rocks at them. Thériault also had a habit of masturbating in front of them.

The "Ant Hill Kids" outside of the bakery and craft store in Burnt River

Thériault was a monster. He told them that he was trying to "purify" his followers and rid them of their sins. However, once he sobered up, he expressed remorse about what he'd done, but always blamed it on God and what he had made him do. He was always gracious about tending to their wounds, and perhaps for that reason none of them blamed him for his abuse. They truly believed that their salvation depended on the suffering they endured in life. Many times, after particularly brutal treatment, they wrote him letters and thanked him for it.

The local Children's Aid Society had started taking an interest in what was going on within the commune. They had learned of his activities in Quebec and its officers visited the settlement almost weekly. The women refused to talk, though, and since the children showed no obvious signs of abuse, they were powerless to take any action.

That changed when Maryse finally defected from the cult. She had been begging Thériault to let her go, and he finally agreed. He allowed her to take her two youngest children with her but made her leave her oldest daughter, Miriam, behind. In an effort to get Miriam released, too, Maryse went to the authorities and gave them graphic accounts of the physical and sexual abuse that the children of the cult were enduring. The worst treatment was suffered by the children who had not been fathered by Thériault. They were treated like slaves, made to do menial tasks, and often starved.

The compound was raided by police and child aid workers on December 6, 1986. They removed 13 children and placed them with foster parents. Many showed signs of being extremely disturbed, and further lurid details of sexual abuse came out during interviews. Later, a judge ordered that they be made permanent wards of the state, along with four more children who were born after the raid. The exception was Miriam, who was returned to Maryse. Once this happened Maryse refused to say anything else to the police. Without her cooperation the authorities decided that they had insufficient evidence to prosecute Thériault and the other adults on child abuse charges.

The result of this was that even greater horror was still to come.

One night in September 1988, Solange Boilard began complaining of an upset stomach. She was one of the cult's original members and was devoted to Thériault. She was his second-in-command, ran the Ant Hill Kids business, and was his favorite wife.

But that wouldn't save her from his "surgeries."

Thériault diagnosed Solange with kidney problems and decided that he needed to operate in order to save her life. Solange was laid naked on a table in the bakery. There was no anesthesia. The first thing he did was, for some reason, punch her in the stomach a few times. Then he shoved a tube into her rectum and performed a crude enema on her using molasses and olive oil. He was now ready to operate.

Using a knife, he made an incision about five inches long below her rib cage and then pulled out a section of her intestines and ripped them apart with his bare hands. He then made Gabrielle stitch her up with a needle and thread while other women blew into the enema tube, which had been pushed down her throat. Solange was then ordered to get up and walk around. She never said a word during any of this. She was allowed to stagger off to bed.

Francine and Gabrielle watched over her that night. One of the last things she said was, "Well, I never thought I would suffer that much in my life."

She died in agony the next morning from the damage done to her by the operation.

But death couldn't stop Thériault, or so he believed. He had the power of resurrection. He had a hole drilled into her head and then he and other male cult members ejaculated into it, believing it could bring her back to life. It didn't, so he had her buried in a plain pine box a short distance from the commune.

He couldn't leave her there, though. He had Solange's body exhumed several times in the next few weeks. He ordered that her kidneys and uterus be removed. He also removed part of a rib, which he made into a necklace. Other bones were given to cult members as souvenirs. The rest of the group eventually convinced him to let them cremate what was left of her body.

Thériault naturally blamed his followers for Solange's death. His drunken rages became so terrifying that many of them fled into the woods to hide until his anger subsided. Perhaps feeling that she had failed him because of her training as a nurse, Gabrielle Lavalee suffered the worst of his angry attacks. In the spring of 1989, she suffered welding torch burns to her genitals, a hypodermic needle breaking off in her back, and the usual beatings. One night she complained of a toothache and Thériault seized a pair of pliers and pulled out eight of her teeth and part of her jawbone. He then went after her with a knife and he cut two of the tendons in her right hand as she tried to fend him off.

Gabrielle with Thériault in Burnt River

Gabrielle escaped from the commune and found safety in a women's shelter for a time. She was treated there by a dentist and a doctor, who put wires in her hand. But Thériault tracked her to the shelter and, amazingly, persuaded her to return to the commune.

On the evening of July 26 Thériault was drinking and began boasting of his surgical skills – causing some of his smarter followers to flee into the woods. But not Gabrielle. He asked to examine her injured hand, and when she laid it on the kitchen table, he drove a large hunting knife through it, pinning it to the table. Unable to move it, she stayed there, screaming, with her hand impaled and her arm turning purple.

It was like a scene from a horror film.

Thériault left her there for almost an hour, and then he finally removed the hunting knife. He exchanged it for a small carpet knife that he began cutting on Gabrielle with. He removed skin from her arm, between her shoulder and elbow, and when he was too drunk to continue peeling away a strip of flesh, he made Gabrielle finish the job. Once the bone was completely exposed, he severed her arm with a meat cleaver.

The next day he stitched up the stump, but he wasn't finished with her. Over the next three weeks he beat her, removed some of her remaining fingers, and cut off parts of her breast. It wasn't until he decided that her amputation wasn't healing correctly and cauterized it with a red-hot piece of metal that she mustered the courage to escape for good. She made it to a hospital but told the staff that she had been in a car accident and her boyfriend had been forced to amputate her arm.

The doctors and nurses didn't believe her – and neither did the police.

When they arrived at the commune, they found it deserted. Thériault, Jacques, Chantal, and Nicole went into hiding – along with two children whose births had been concealed from the authorities – but they were arrested six weeks later.

Thériault surprised everyone by pleading guilty to charges relating to Gabrielle's abuse and amputation, doing so because he believed that he would be able to keep Solange's death a secret.

By this time, though, Gabrielle had told the police everything.

Thériault was charged with second-degree murder and the police compiled a dossier of 84 serious crimes he committed against his followers in Ontario. When his attorneys learned of this, he agreed to plead guilty to the murder charge, on the condition that he would face no other charges. He was sentenced to life in prison.

Most of the cult members abandoned Thériault after his arrest, but three of his wives – Chantal, Nicole, and Francine – remained faithful to him, and thanks to conjugal visits he had been able to father four more children.

Reportedly, he became a model prisoner and was first eligible for parole in 1999. It was denied. Gabrielle Lavalee was there in 2002 when it was denied again. "The population, myself included, will be able to have a long night's sleep tonight," she said.

Thériault remained locked up at the Dorchester Penitentiary in New Brunswick until February 2011 when he was murdered by another inmate. Matthew McDonald was seen on video from the prison going into Thériault's cell and walking out after removing a shank from the former cult leader's neck. He then walked over to the guards and told them what he had done. According to police statements, McDonald "had expressed some animosity towards Mr. Thériault" concerning his convictions for killing one woman and maiming another. McDonald later received a life sentence for the murder.

Sometimes, it seems, revenge really is a dish best served cold. And in this case, it was served by someone unrelated to anyone who suffered at the hands of Roch Thériault. Regardless, though, I'd say that it wasn't just Gabrielle Lavalee who slept better that night.

Children of God

Children of God.

It seems an innocent name for a religious community but what this cult turned into was anything but innocent. It formed in 1968, near the time when the Manson family and an escalating crime rate brought an end to the flowers and sunshine of the 1960s.

The founder of the Children of God, David Berg, sold his followers on the idea of a spiritual revolution, peace, and happiness. He believed in an "old world" kind of Christianity in which "old world" meant sex – lots of sex. The reason why is that God loves sex because sex is love, and the Devil hated sex because sex was beautiful.

But that was where things went off the rails. Berg began advocating sex with children – reportedly over the age of 12, but many claimed some were younger –

because children should "embrace their sexuality." Sex was even used as a way to get new members into the cult. In what was called "flirty fishing," women were sent out to lure men to join them.

But the Children of God wasn't just about sex – there was an apocalyptic aspect to it, too. Members lived in a commune, banded together because they had the power to stop the Antichrist.

Even when the cult was disbanded in the late 1970s after the abuse reports piled up, it still wasn't dead, making headlines for a lurid murder-suicide and Berg's death in 1994. After that it changed again and still exists in an alternate form today.

Berg (back row, on right) was born into a family of evangelists. His mother, Virginia, would become an integral part of the founding of his own twisted ministry

Its new form claims to be built only on a love for Jesus, but the horrifying history of the Children of God can't be erased. And the layers of secrecy that surround its new incarnation speak volumes about the fact that it still has much to hide.

David Berg was born in February 1919 in Oakland, California, and into a family with strong Christian traditions. His mother, Virginia Brandt, came from a long line of noted ministers and evangelists. Her father, John Lincoln Brandt, was a Methodist minister and, later, part of the Disciples of Christ. He also served as president of Virginia College and became rich through writing and investments. Thanks to this, Virginia had grown up with wealth and luxury and traveled the world with her father. After a crisis of faith and a battle with depression she decided to dedicate her life to God. She became the Field Secretary for the National Florence Crittenton Mission, an organization dedicated to reforming prostitutes and unwed pregnant women through the creation of establishments where they were to live and learn skills. She also became engaged to Bruce Bogart, the wealthy cousin of actor Humphrey Bogart, but when she met Hjalmer Emmanuel Berg, she fell in love and they eloped.

Pressured by his new father-in-law, Hjalmer Berg enrolled in a theological seminary in Iowa and became a minister of the Disciples of Christ. But he was later expelled, along with Virginia, when the two of them began making claims that Virginia had been divinely healed – and now possessed the gift of healing herself.

The Bergs began traveling as itinerant evangelists, using Virginia's healing as a drawing card. She claimed that she had been injured in an automobile accident, that she was paralyzed and bedridden for five years, and then was suddenly healed one day and walked into church the next. She had gone from "deathbed to pulpit," as the couple liked to proclaim.

Of course, none of this was true.

The closest that Virginia had come to a "paralyzing injury" was when she fell on a curb when Hjalmer slipped on some ice and knocked her down. She had required an operation, but she'd never been paralyzed, and in fact her oldest daughter had been born during her five years of alleged invalidism. She'd led a public and active life during those years and yet no one bothered to question the story that she used throughout her life to establish herself as a "woman of God."

The couple eventually settled in Miami. There they worked with the Christian and Missionary Alliance and founded the Alliance Tabernacle, where Virginia preached regularly to huge audiences. They were eventually forced out and started their own church, the Central Alliance Church of the Open Door. Virginia mostly took her show on the road as a full-time traveling evangelist, preaching and holding revivals across the country. She was in California when David was born.

David was raised – along with his two older siblings – an in environment of evangelism, always on the move. It was much like being in the carnival business, always traveling and always flamboyant. And as it would have been in the carnival, the children were put to work. When David was a young boy, he was already being trained as a child preacher, appearing in front of large audiences.

But life would be ugly in the scattered hotels and motels across the country. By his own accounts Berg was regularly molested by adults of both sexes during his childhood, had incestuous sex with a female cousin at age 7, and became obsessed with sex and masturbation as a teenager. Every bit of this conflicted with his strict moral upbringing.

In 1941, Berg was drafted into the Army and sent to Fort Belvoir, Virginia, home of the U.S. Army Engineers. While in the service a year later he later claimed to have been diagnosed with near-fatal pneumonia. On his deathbed he promised God to serve him throughout his lifetime, and he was "immediately and miraculously healed."

In 1944 Berg met Jane Miller at the Little Church of Sherman Oaks in California. She was working there as a church secretary and youth director at the time. The two fell in love and eloped on July 22, without the blessing of her strict Baptist family. Berg finally won their approval by becoming an ordained minister and four years later became the pastor of a small Christian and Missionary Alliance church in Valley Farms, Arizona.

The Bergs went on to have four children together, and all of them played important roles in the creation of the Children of God movement. Jane – who became "Mother Eve" to the followers – was eventually discarded in favor of a young mistress named Karen Zerby.

Organized religion turned out to not be for Berg. He had a falling out with the Missionary Alliance's leadership, caused by an adulterous affair with a member of the congregation. However, Berg would later spin the story to say he was "unjustly removed" because of his strong sermons and his feelings about racial integration. He developed a deep-seated hatred toward established churches after that, and this antagonism would become one of the foundation doctrines of the Church of God.

Berg now began to embrace Communism. He returned to college on the G.I. Bill and began studying philosophy, psychology, and political science. During what he called his "communist sabbatical," he taught junior high school and drove a school bus for several years. He was still deeply involved in his faith, though. He dreamed of becoming a Christian missionary to Israel and attended a three-month "personal witnessing course" at the American Soul Clinic, an organization that trained missionaries for the foreign field. He never made it into foreign missionary work and instead spent the remainder of the 1950s with his family on the road as a traveling preacher. Since he had no affiliation with a church the Bergs had to rely on the charity of people they met to eat and have a place to sleep.

After serving in the military, Berg turned to communism for a time and then began missionary training school

In time Berg began working for Fred Jordan, who founded the American Soul Clinic in Los Angeles. For a time, he found a niche in Jordan's radical witnessing movement, approaching personal witnessing with an almost military-like zeal. This high-pressure method would become an important part of the Children of God movement because it was Jordan who taught Berg a philosophy of "salesmanship for Jesus."

Berg them went to Miami to start his own missionary training school, based on Jordan's ideas. He used the uninspired name of the Florida Soul Clinic. However, Berg and his family were ejected from Miami for using overly aggressive methods of spreading their message. They returned, at least twice. Berg blamed the problem on the Jews, explaining that after they rejected his message, they used their influence to drive him out of town.

After leaving Miami the Bergs returned to living as traveling evangelists, generally operating outside the shelter of church denominations and soliciting donations for their living expenses. They also spent some time at Fred Jordan's Soul Clinic Ranch in Texas. Most of the time, though, Berg was training his children to be involved in the ministry as they moved from town to town. The children became known as Teens for Christ, an evangelical singing quartet.

By his own accounts Berg was already in conflict with traditional ideas about sex, infidelity, and adultery. He later said that he visited prostitutes and had affairs while on the road away from his wife. He also slept with housekeepers and babysitters and even made sexual advances toward his daughters. At least six women, including members of his family, later came forward and claimed that Berg had molested them as children.

In 1965, Berg was back at the Texas ranch when he was visited by his mother, Virginia.

Virginia, who had followed in the footsteps of her evangelist father, wanted the same for her children. Her oldest son, Hjalmer, Jr., was an agnostic and wanted nothing to do with religion. Her only daughter had run away from home and eloped at 16. David, who had chosen a life of service to God, was her last hope because, as she wrote, he had "been filled with the Holy Ghost since her mother's womb."

In Texas she personally delivered a message to Berg – a "warning prophecy" that she had received about the coming last days and the arrival of the Antichrist. She also declared that he would have the "understanding of Daniel" (the biblical prophet) and would "know the number of years unto the End of Desolations."

Her messages turned out to be pivotal in Berg's life, and the basis for his belief that his own life was linked to the last days before the return of Christ. He soon developed a belief that God had a special destiny and mission for him. He began calling himself the "prophet for this generation." Berg believed that Christ would return no more than three-and-a-half years after his death in 1989.

Of course, it should be noted that Berg died in 1994, which means he wasn't a prophet – nor was he sane.

For the next few years Berg continued dragging his family around the country, pushing his children to sing and witness and to try and force people to find God. It was a bit of a hard sell at the time, and by 1968, feeling rejected and defeated, Berg, his wife, and four children found themselves in Huntington Beach, California, where Virginia was living. She died later that same year and the Bergs stayed on in California. Berg decided to try and take advantage of the talent that he had for reaching the youth and start preaching to the hippies.

In those days, Huntington Beach was to Southern California what the Haight-Asbury District was to San Francisco – it was the place in the Los Angeles area where the counterculture thrived.

Berg won many converts, using his teenage children to lure them to the Huntington Beach Light Club, which was a Pentecostal coffeehouse run by the Teen Challenge organization. In this non-church setting they were given food, shelter, and music. Berg then had a captive audience for his anti-church, anti-establishment sermons.

Berg gradually developed a small group of about 35 followers. He preached the end of the world was coming, and he encouraged his converts to move into his home and devote their lives to Christ. Their hippie lifestyle was blended into the new movement, which taught revolution against the outside world.

Applying techniques that he'd learned from Fred Jordan, Berg subjected his followers to intensive studies of the Bible, forcing them to memorize verses and references, and training them to evangelize. He used Bible verses to justify his

Berg recruited his initial followers at the Huntington Beach Light Club, a coffee house where he appealed to young people with his anti-establishment, anti-church messages

teachings that true disciples of Christ should drop out and "forsake all" – literally abandoning all their responsibilities and severing ties with jobs, schools, friends, and family so that they could follow Jesus. At the height of the hippie era – when so many were rejecting materialism and ownership – Berg's ideas sounded great. He encouraged them to return home to their parent's house, take everything they could, sell it, and then turn over the cash to him for the betterment of the movement. By this time, he had become so ingrained in their minds and belief systems that they were happy to oblige.

By early 1969 the group had grown to about 50 followers, and – just as Berg had done in Miami – he upset city officials with the movement's aggressive way of trying to recruit followers. They were eventually ejected from Huntington Beach, too. Coincidentally – or probably not – this was at the same time that Berg received a "vision" that told him that a monstrous earthquake was just about to hit Southern California, and it was best if the cult left the area.

So, fleeing the wrath of parents, politicians, and the media, Berg's "Revolutionaries for Jesus" went on the road in a convoy of vans and trailers. They first landed in Tucson, Arizona, but were sent packing after staging demonstrations and disrupting local church services. Forced to move from town to town they wandered across most of the United States and Canada, recruiting new followers as they went.

In February 1970, about 150 members of the group finally settled on 425 acres outside of the ghost town of Thurber, Texas. The land was owned by Fred Jordan, Berg's old Soul Clinic employer, who was now a televangelist. It became a temporary headquarters for Berg's movement, and he sent out teams to other places to win

Berg appealed to teenagers and young adults with his message of being "outsiders" and rebelling against the old and outdated ideas of mainstream churches

converts and set up new colonies. Eventually they regrouped in Laurentide, near Montreal, Canada.

At Laurentide, Berg settled with about 70 other members and he began creating a hierarchy for the cult, with, of course, himself on top. He then assembled his top leaders for a meeting in Virginia where he announced that he had received a prophecy from God about the "old church and the new church." He published the prophecy and it became the first official "Mo Letter," as he called all future ones. Berg had also announced that God told him to call himself "Moses" or "Mo," hence the name of the letters. To the inner circle he was called "Dad," "Father," or "King David."

In the Mo Letters, Berg justified his actions and policies to his followers and would soon proclaim himself "God's End Time Prophet" who spoke "words for today." His writings were convoluted attempts to unveil his skewed version of religion, mixed with his personal sex practices and beliefs.

In other words, pretty strange reading.

Starting in 1969 Berg had begun taking several young women in the cult as his "wives." One of them was Karen Zerby, who took the biblical name of "Maria." Berg claimed that Maria was the young "new church" that God was raising up and that Jane, his legal wife and mother of his children, was the "old church," which God was abandoning because she was disobedient and outdated. God was, as he explained, "doing a new thing."

Thanks to Berg's example and urging, sexual promiscuity – free love, partner swapping, and multiple wives – became wildly popular with the leadership of the cult. Such practices did, however, remain secret from the general rank-and-file members of the cult until the mid-1970s, when everyone joined in.

The movement continued to travel around the country, becoming a nuisance in every place they visited. They began staging what were called "sackcloth demonstrations" – when they dressed in burlap sacks with ashes on their faces – first in Washington, D.C., then in Philadelphia, and in New York, outside the headquarters of the United Nations. The press called them "prophets of doom" because of their predictions about the fall and destruction of the U.S.

They stuck with that theme for other demonstrations in Washington, D.C. Members held a public vigil where they wore large wooden yokes around their necks to symbolize mourning for the fallen nation. They also carried placards that were printed with excerpts from Virginia Berg's warning about the end of days and the arrival of the Antichrist, events that heralded by the arrival of David Berg, the "End Time Prophet."

It was during these demonstrations that the movement finally came by its name. A reporter found them camped in a junkyard behind a truck stop in Camden, New Jersey, and in an article that he wrote about them, he referred to them as "Moses David and the Children of God."

The name stuck.

Throughout 1970, the group drifted back to the camp in Texas that became known as the Thurber Colony. A school was set up for the cult's children. Rock music with religious lyrics became popular. Members of the group with a history of drug use shared testimonies and claimed that they had conquered their addictions through God. They held Bible studies and discussions and offered revival meetings for the public.

On October 31, 1970, Children of God from Thurber held a demonstration at the University of Texas Austin. They wore sackcloth and ashes, carried Bibles, and witnessed about Christ to University students. They targeted counterculture teenagers and young people, stressing to them that the end of the world was coming.

New recruits ended up at the Thurber camp. Here, members began answering only to their new biblical and tribal names. Berg divided them into 12 tribes, inspired by the Twelve Tribes of Israel, with each tribe assigned different responsibilities in the camp. They worked long hours each day maintaining the camp, preparing food, getting food from nearby towns, and caring for the livestock. Berg placed members of his immediate family in charge of each of the tribes.

The compound had a strict set of rules. No member could go anywhere without a partner. Outgoing mail was checked and censored for "security." There was also the "two-sheets rule" that noted the maximum about of toilet paper that a member could use when visiting the bathroom. Exhausted new members were subjected to relentless indoctrination on the Bible and all aspects of cult life. Their "buddy" helped them to memorize Bible passages, even when they were using the toilet. There was no "down time" when a recruit was allowed to think about anything that Berg didn't want them thinking about.

David Berg

Berg's mistress and second-in-command, Karen Zerby

Although there was always a steady income from when a new member would "forsake all" he or she owned to the cult, and from solicitations on Fred Jordan's television show, Berg always carefully guarded the finances of the group. Berg, his family, and his inner circle enjoyed special privileges, but his followers lived in grim conditions often relying on the charity of strangers and eating from dumpsters or discarded animal feed from nearby farms.

But no one complained. Converts were taught complete subservience to the cult and that the government "was of Satan." They were taught to hate and fear both established society and established religion. Few parents came looking for their recruited offspring, but those who did received written confessions of past criminal history to try and convince parents that their children were better with the group. If the parents became troublesome – or if the members were dodging the draft or in trouble with the law – the recruits would be simply moved to another colony.

It was at Thurber when things started to take another turn for the rank-and-file members. There had always been sex within the Children of God, but now all of Berg's discussions inevitably wound up delving into sexual topics, sometimes leading to orgies – with members of all ages.

Whether because of possible legal issues or something else, Berg disappeared in late 1970 with his mistress, Karen Zerby. Their whereabouts became known only to top leaders of the cult. "Shepherds" were appointed to lead individual colonies and they were supervised by members of Berg's family. Berg remained the leader of the Children of God and began issuing all his directives in the form of new Mo Letters.

In April 1971, Berg and Zerby went to London. With his financial operations now offshore, Berg was able to avoid all scrutiny from U.S. authorities who were investigating Children of God activities. He explained his move in a Mo Letter that he titled "I Gotta Split," in which he compared himself to Jesus, explaining that he had to go away in body but would be with them in spirit. In Berg's case, "in spirit" meant a series of bizarre and often nonsensical letters. They usually had no clear statements and were always contradictory, and yet cult members waited for each one impatiently. They considered the letters to be equal in authority to the Bible.

From London, Berg directed the group to spread out and establish additional colonies throughout the United States. He also emphasized personal, one-on-one witnessing. By 1972, the Children of God had stepped back from public demonstrations and had started using Christian rock music as a method of outreach. However, their doomsday message remained the same – religion was terrible, America was collapsing, and the end of the world was nigh. Music was just supposed to make the doom and gloom do down a little easier.

Members were coached on the best ways to reach people. Initiating a conversation, they told a cookie-cutter story about being lost without Jesus, being on drugs, etc. until they met the group, and their lives were changed. They criticized anyone who didn't drop out of the "system" and serve God and railed against education and jobs. This personal witnessing strategy, along with an influx of members from the Jesus People Army – another evangelical movement formed in the late 1960s – led to a rapid increase in membership. By 1972, the Children of God claimed to have grown to at least 1,400 members across the U.S. with most members in their teens or early twenties.

But all this growth came with problems.

The Children of God marketed themselves as an innocent Christian organization along the lines of groups like the God Squad or Teen Challenge. However, many outraged parents claimed their children were brainwashed or hypnotized by leaders of the group who had forcibly separated them from their families. Reports began to come in from members who left the group, claiming coercion, rape, sex orgies, forced alienation from family members, manipulation, donation fraud, and worse.

In August 1971, several worried parents of children who had joined the cult started an organization called FREECOG, or Free Our Children from the Children of God. The group, headed by William Rambur, planned to rescue their offspring by any means necessary. That included the hiring of well-known "cult deprogrammer" Ted Patrick, who was reportedly successful at "reverse-brainwashing" people who had fallen victim to cults. Patrick's controversial system involved kidnapping cult members, placing them in isolation, and "attacking the mechanisms" he believed were controlling their minds.

Despite the efforts of the group, deprogrammers, and pleas for children to come home, the membership of the cult continued to grow.

In 1972, Berg sent out a new Mo Letter titled "One Wife" that redefined the family units of his followers. In it, he told the group that God was "in the business of breaking up litter selfish private worldly families to make of their yielded broken pieces a larger unit – one family."

I'm not sure exactly what that statement means, but the point of the letter was that he thought breaking up families to extract disciples for his movement was justifiable in the eyes of God. You know, the needs of the many outweigh the needs of the few, even when it came to marriage and children.

Marriage, he added, was part of the "system" and they were meant to be broken up in situations where the relationship was deemed unmatched or unapproved, or when one of the partners was required for service in another circumstance. In other words – wait for it – a man might need to have another wife in addition to the one he had, and that wife might come from another marriage. That was okay, though; God said so.

Berg went on to say that all the children in the movement were considered to be everyone's children. This caused many of them to be placed in other homes with adults other than their parents, and even into permanent childcare. Some of them were forcibly removed from their parents and sent to other colonies, even across international borders.

But Berg was just getting started. In his "The Great Escape" Mo Letter, he directed his followers to leave the U.S. and start new colonies in other parts of the world. Since America was doomed to be destroyed in 1973 – at the same time the comet Kohutek appeared in the skies – he wanted his people to start a big fundraising push to pay for passage away from the United States. As it happened, Kohutek came and went without any fanfare – it was invisible to the naked eye – and Berg was forced to provide several alternate explanations for his failed prophecy. Some members were bothered enough by this incident to leave the group.

But those that remained had followed his orders. By the end of 1973 there were 2,400 members living in 140 colonies in 40 different countries around the world.

On the surface, spreading out the members of the cult changed the image of the group from that of a rigidly-controlled hippie movement of Jesus Revolutionaries with Moses in charge to that of a semi-democratic, eclectic spiritual movement. But beneath that veneer the group remained a tightly-controlled organization. In order to become a full member a follower had to concede that Berg was the "End Time Prophet" with the ultimate authority in all matters. Occasionally purging took place when members were made an example of or were dismissed for not obeying Berg.

Distant colonies enjoyed a small amount of independence, but they were mainly under leaders appointed by Berg from within his inner circle. All the leaders, no matter what part of the world in which the colony was found, were American, and the default culture within the Children of God was rooted in American customs.

More letters from Mo followed. In 1973, he ordered a shift away from the one-on-one witnessing methods of recent years, and members were now directed to sell copies of Mo Letters on the street. By this time the Mo Letters had become even more radical and controversial. They had to be separated into categories that included for disciples only, for friends and disciples, for leadership training, and then for the general public, which could be sold. This ensured that the more dangerous materials would not reach the public. Followers were instructed to only feed new recruits the "milk" (general public material) until they were strong enough to be able to handle the "strong meat."

Not only did selling the general public letters raise money, but it "witnessed through literature." It also deceived the people who bought them. They assumed they were donating to charity, not inflating the bank account of a cult.

In February 1975, Berg launched a "New Revolution" and he restructured his chain of command, opening new leadership positions. He also returned the emphasis of the movement to recruitment and personal witnessing. He set limits on colony sizes and implemented quotas, which forced members to leave overpopulated colonies and start new ones. By the following year the cult claimed to have 725 colonies with 4,215 members in 70 countries. Each member reported and sent money upwards in the leadership chain, receiving the Mo Letters in return.

That year also marked a change in the type of recruits that were targeted by members. Since the hippie movement had lost most of its steam at the end of the Vietnam War, Berg ordered his members to focus on bringing in members from the educated and privileged classes. He no longer wanted the dropouts of society. He also created a new level of recruit – Catacomb members. They were younger converts – many still in school – and rather than risk additional backlash from parents, Berg allowed them to become part-time members who still lived at home.

Berg also began reshaping the sexual conduct of the movement. He had already set a precedent with earlier letters about his abandonment of Jane and his taking of a mistress, about multiple wives, changing the idea of a family unit, and sex in general. He had also written a Mo Letter called "Come on, Ma! Burn Your Bra!" in which he demanded that female members stop wearing bras – or risk having them forcibly removed by colony leaders. A letter called the "Law of Love" in 1974 taught members to sacrifice anything and everything in the name of love. Berg stated that "total and complete freedom from the bondage of love" was reserved for the spiritually worthy.

Some members finally left the movement when Berg began introducing more and more radical sexual themes, but those who remained were expected to comply with his teachings wholeheartedly. Berg had managed to gradually sexualize the movement in preparation for his ultimate teachings on sex and sacrifice.

He took the next step in 1974 when he introduced a new way of getting recruits called "Flirty Fishing." Members were now encouraged to engage in sex with non-members to win converts and influential supporters. Berg began experimenting with it and then introduced the idea to the general membership in 1976 through a series of Mo Letters. Anyone who objected to the new practice was purged, and anyone who remained was expected to take part in it. By 1978, it was being widely practiced by female followers. Berg believed – or at least taught – that it was acceptable to go as far beyond the limits as necessary to show the love of God to others, even as far as meeting their sexual needs.

This new method of proselytizing attracted considerable media attention and was even profiled in *Newsweek* magazine. While problematic to start with, things got worse as Flirty Fishing became a major source of income for Berg and the movement. Eventually many of the women began working for escort agencies to meet people, and this led to sex being sold to generate a lot of money. One witness later testified

Yes, these were real — Children of God promo comics that were meant to appeal to younger audiences but still teach the tenets of the cult. There were a number of issues that served as how-to guides for "flirty fishing" and explained how much Jesus wanted followers to have sex to seeing a suitcase that contained more than $1 million dollars hidden under Berg's bed.

I can say with a lot of certainty that this was not what God had in mind when he wanted to "show his love" to people.

Flirty Fishing would come crashing down in 1987 out of fear of the AIDS epidemic. New rules were introduced that banned sexual contact with anyone who was not a member. The damage was already done, though. Several members contracted HIV and died from AIDS. There were also many children born as a result of Flirty Fishing, including Karen Zerby's son, Davidito, whose real name was Rick Rodriguez. Children that were born as a result of Flirty Fishing were called "Jesus Babies." At least 300 of them were born during the years of this practice.

Flirty Fishing also had legal ramifications. At one point, Berg had to flee Spain after he was charged with running prostitution rings. Although rank and file members were not aware of it, Berg and the Children of God had also been tried in absentia and ordered to pay $1 million in damages in a lawsuit that had been filed against them.

After legal issues and negative press, Berg advised his followers to deny that they were part of the Children of God, explaining that they were not technically lying because he was about to give the movement a new name. He suggested that they consider going underground, if necessary. "There's only one way to get them off your back, and that's just to make it impossible for them to find you," he said in one of his Mo Letters. And added, "Once this storm is over and the heat's off and the persecution dies down and/or disappears, the public quickly forgets, and maybe you can return to the streets again."

In January 1978, Berg made changes, but not the name of the movement. Instead, he began taking it apart.

He began with removing leaders of the movement who had opposed Flirty Fishing and who, according to him, had abused their authority. He supposedly dismissed over 300 of the group's leaders, declaring that he was starting a dissolution of the Children of God structure, but most ex-leaders actually remained in the movement.

Berg also made a show of announcing that the group had been disbanded. He told his followers to return home to their parents. They were advised to get jobs, look respectable, and "invade the system and the churches." During this "furlough," followers were expected to stay in touch through the mail. They would now receive Mo Letters directly at their home. The flock, he promised, would be re-gathered.

In conjunction with the reorganization – in the wake of the Jonestown Massacre and backlashes against cults – Berg then changed the name of the movement to the Family of Love.

He had consolidated his losses and gains and had kept his loyal base of followers, so Berg began making comments to the press about the charade that the movement had disbanded. In truth, it was all the same. His followers were a little more scattered, but they were still sending their money to Berg, and Flirty Fishing was still taking place.

The methods used by the movement did change somewhat, though. Methods of outreach became more covert and the group was no longer high-profiled. Staging demonstrations in sackcloth were now a thing of the past. They were no longer witnessing on the streets, but he sent his members door-to-door to busk and sing as independent missionary families.

They were also promoting a radio show that Berg started called Music with Meaning. The show began broadcasting in 1980 from Sri Lanka, hosted by someone calling himself "Simon Peter." He later moved to Greece and hosted the show there with musical guests. One of the most popular guests was former celebrity Jeremy Spencer from Fleetwood Mac who had joined the movement in 1972. Members around the world were sent scratchy cassettes of the show and were encouraged to try and get them played on local radio stations. This didn't work out well, however. The quality of the cassettes was too poor, and the show was terrible.

But it worked with some people. Jingles during the show urged listeners to join the Music with Meaning Club. Those who wrote in were sent publications that included the testimonies of the stars, all of whom had "found happiness with Jesus." Those who wrote more than once were encouraged to meet up with "representatives from the show." Those attracted to the group's message were brought into the cult in stages.

Although the Music with Meaning show made no overt message of Christ other than a few occasional mentions in a few songs, it was franchised and a Spanish equivalent – Música Con Vida – was created, along with other language versions of the show. Berg sent his daughter, Faithy, to recruit musicians on the fringes of the new Family of Love, and they became a part of the show.

Music with Meaning was the movement's first attempt at a mass-market façade. Promoting a free youth radio show about love, created by volunteers, was supposed to lend some respectability to the group. Little did anyone know, however, there was a lot going on behind the scenes of the show. The Music with Meaning team in Greece was the location spearheading the movement's free sexual practices, like orgies, wife-swapping, and pedophilia. They were under the direct supervision of Berg and were expected to carefully implement his teachings about how to raise and sexualize children.

It gave the new "Family of Love" a nasty undercurrent that would not become known for years.

Berg had been working toward his goal for a long time, dating all the way back to 1972 when he had redefined "family" and declared a Law of Love doctrine that meant that nothing was wrong in the eyes of God as long as it was done in the name of love. He had introduced sex sharing sessions as "come-union," and created Flirty Fishing. Birth control was not allowed, and sexually transmitted diseases were not supposed to faze his followers. He even taught that Jesus himself suffered from venereal diseases and it was part of the sacrifice that a disciple endured to show love. Monthly ceremonies began to be followed with partner swapping and orgies.

But the worst was still to come.

In the 1980s, suspicions arose about the movement's care of its children and its policies regarding adult-child sex. Several members had defected and had talked to the media. Berg's writings displayed an interest in and lack of concern about sexual contact with children. He claimed to be challenging modern-day taboos about adult and child sexuality, ignoring society's laws and boundaries. Berg presented laws against sex with children as the "devil's lies and propaganda and guilt complexes." He wrote, "there is nothing in the world at all wrong with sex as long as it's practiced in love, whatever it is or whoever it's with, no matter who or what age or what relative or what manner." He used a biblical quote from a letter from St. Paul to the Corinthians to justify his twisted beliefs. Paul had written, "All things are lawful unto me, but all things are not expedient." Somehow, Berg twisted this to mean that he could indulge in any kind of sex that he wanted to, but he had to watch out for the "system" because it was always trying to keep him down. The "system" was the problem – not Berg and his depravity. He wanted to convince his followers that if they hated sex, they were "one of the devil's crowd." God created sex, he told them, so enjoy it as he does.

He later also published Mo Letters about his dreams of having sex with pre-pubescent girls as well as fantasies about having sex with his own mother. Later, at least six women, including his daughters, his daughter-in-law, and two of his granddaughters, would publicly report that Berg had sexually abused them when they were children.

In the early 1980s, Berg published a series of documents about "Davidito" – Rick Rodriguez, his adopted son and child of his mistress, Karen Zerby. Allegedly written by his nanny, who called herself "Sara Davidito," they were about his home life, care, and education, but some of them contained very graphic images of children and adult-child sex. The faces of the adults were all whited-out or drawn over to protect their identities. The documents were later watered down somewhat and republished into a book called *The Story of Davidito* in 1982. The 762-page book, intended to be an example of child-rearing, included photos of the boy engaged in sexual play with his babysitters. It was reprinted and even posted online in the 1990s, but it's since disappeared. The Family removed all their publications about pedophilia and incest, explaining that the publications have been "recalled."

But the "recalling" of The Family's publications doesn't necessarily mean that they no longer follow these teachings. While the group's policies of 1995 forbid sexual contact with minors, it has not accepted any responsibility for abuses that have occurred, claiming that any abuse that occurred because of Berg's teachings were the work of individual members.

In 1984, six years after leaving the Children of God/Family of Love, Berg's daughter Deborah, and her husband Bill Davis, co-authored a tell-all book called *The Children of God: The Inside Story*. They detailed, among other things, Berg's molestation and incest with Deborah. His incestuous activity with his other daughter, Faithy, the faked story of the miracle healing of Virginia Berg, and the coercion and manipulation of follower's lives. It gave the public the first detailed look inside the secretive organization and attracted support from Christian organizations and anti-cult groups across the country.

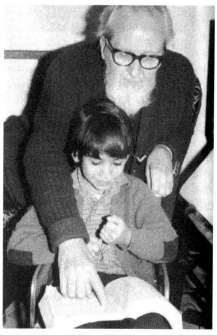

Berg with his "adopted" son, Rock Rodriguez. He was born to Karen Zerby after she became pregnant from Flirty Fishing

It wasn't enough to destroy the movement, but it did highlight the legal trouble the group was already in. By that time, it had been officially banned from several countries and its members were deported and barred from returning. They were accused of immigration fraud, sex trafficking, and other offenses. The Family called the deportations from Hong Kong, Indonesia, India, the Philippines, and other places "persecution."

Numerous allegations of pedophilia, rape, and sexual abuse were made against The Family around the world, including in Argentina, Australia, Brazil, France, Italy, Japan, Norway, Peru. Spain, Sweden, Venezuela, Great Britain, and the United States. The Family continued to maintain that it did not sanction or condone the sexual abuse of children, and yet, there it was, in the writings that had been published by their founder and leader.

There were dozens of court cases and The Family claims even now that none of the government-led investigations convicted Family Members and that there was no evidence of abuse found in the more than 750 children who were questioned by the authorities. Later, though, members who left the group admitted having lied and being instructed to lie to investigators in order to suppress evidence of abuse.

Why? They had been taught that sex with adults was not abuse.

But contrary to what they claimed the Family was not always cleared of charges in a court of law. Very few – if any – of the child abuse cases that were prosecuted against Family members resulted in an acquittal or a complete exoneration of the defendants. Most of the cases were dismissed on legal technicalities, or the defendants were tried in absentia. Some were charged with contributing to the delinquency of a minor, and several were settled out of court.

During all this David Berg kept his hold over the movement and its followers. He was still teaching his twisted philosophy, writing Mo Letters, and make wild predictions that never came to pass. In 1979 he had warned of a major stock market and financial crash. When it didn't happen, he blamed – well, really no one. He just said that it was overdue to happen.

In 1980, he began warning of the impending destruction of the United States and Europe by nuclear war. He advised his followers to move to eastern countries and to the southern hemisphere, making 1982 a time of mass exodus for Children of God flocking to South America. Of course, nothing happened.

Next, in a letter called "The Crash is Here!" he simultaneous gave advice about living as survivalists on remote farms and also about staying mobile by living in trailers. Many of the group's members moved into motor homes and onto farms. Six months later members who were living in isolation – which he told them to do – were now ordered to go to the cities where most of the world was located. We also don't want to forget that he had once predicted that California would fall into the ocean, that the Great Tribulation would start in 1989, and the Second Coming of Christ would occur in 1993.

For years Berg had been telling his followers that as the "End of Times Prophet" he was destined to die in 1989. I'm not sure what excuse he offered when he got this one wrong, but he did die in 1994 in Portugal. He was buried there but his remains were later exhumed and cremated.

By the time he died Berg had been in seclusion for so long that most followers barely remembered what he looked like. Thanks to his obsession with secrecy the photos that had appeared in movement publications had his face covered with drawings, often depicting him as a lion.

This probably made it easier for his successor to take control. Berg hadn't been in the ground for long before Karen Zerby, known in the cult as Mama, Maria, or Queen Maria, took over leadership of The Family of Love. Zerby partnered with her longtime lover, Steven Kelly, an American, also known as Christopher Smith, Peter Amsterdam, and King Peter. He became her traveling representative, allowing her to stay separated from their followers, just as Berg had done.

One of the first decisions they made was to introduce what became known as the Love Charter, a new way of life within the organization that allowed members the freedom to choose and follow their own pursuits. It tried to spell out what members could expect to receive from the group and how members were to be treated by the leadership and by other members. They were also allowed to decide if they wanted to remain as a full-time member – even though that decision could really only be made by Zerby and Kelly.

Full-time members were expected to give as much as 14 percent of their income to the movement – 10 percent to the far-reaching movement, three percent to the "Family Aid Fund" which allegedly helped needy field situations, regional services, and projects, and the final one percent, which aided local projects, activities, and literature publishing. In reality it probably went where all the other donated money went over the years – into the pockets of the leaders.

Seeing how easy it was to get money from its members, Zerby and Kelly branched out into non-profit work in the 1990s. Because of the bad publicity that The Family had faced they wanted to show that the movement was doing good work in the world. They took advantage of the newly opened Eastern Europe after the fall of communism and expanded their evangelistic campaigns. In 1996 the leadership began exploring ways in which the movement could become a tax-exempt legal entity in the United States. This would make it possible for them to solicit large donations and broaden the base of their financial support, as well as mass-market their videos and publications, which would spread their message and raise income. In addition, The Family would appear to be a legitimate and credible religious organization for those Family members who were active in charitable activities but could not attract tax-exempt donations.

The Children of God, now known as the Family of Love, wanted to be legit.

They created the Family Care Foundation as the front for their charitable organizations, of which there were several different ones registered around the world. Family members joined the foundation as "project managers," raising millions in tax-exempt funds. With their charities affiliated with what seemed to be a large, legitimate organization, the group expanded its operations, entering countries as non-governmental organizations (NGO's) and even re-entering countries that had earlier been barred from. In some instances, outreach went beyond proselytization and members credibly provided material aid to the poor.

While soliciting donations for the Family Care Foundation, Family members actively promoted their new charitable work image – working for disaster relief, humanitarian aid, music benefits for refugees, and hospital visitations.

But it was impossible to completely hide the foundation's link to the cult. It was accused – probably correctly – of being created primarily to launder funds for the movement by using its tax-exempt status. Although the foundation has always claimed to be a separate entity from The Family, it was founded by the cult's leaders to advance its goals and interests. It almost exclusively promotes Family products and assists Family followers. Members were even allowed to send their donations directly to the foundation instead of to The Family's administrative arms. Substantial tax-exempt money could – with a little creative bookkeeping – finance ventures controlled by Zerby and Kelly.

But the Family Care Foundation was not the only way that the cult made money. Aurora Production AG held the copyright to all The Family's music, video, and print publications. The owner? Steven Kelly. Family Missions Foundation received and processed the donations of its members. The board had many of the same names on it that served on the board of Aurora Production AG, including Thomas Mestyanek, one of the top leaders of The Family, and Chris Smith, a.k.a. Steven Kelly.

Activated Ministries operated as a non-profit organization based in Escondido, California. All its directors were Family members. Its president, Thomas Hack, was a high-ranking Family member and the former director of the Family Care Foundation. Activated Ministries was a licensed distributor of Aurora products worldwide, including the magazines *Activated* and the *Wine Press*, both of which promoted Family beliefs and practices. Other non-profits connected to The Family included TEAM Foundation, Brookside Farm, Cheer Up Missions, Ton-A-Month Club, Donate Car for Charity, Donate a Car 2 Charity, New York Family Mission, and The Extra Mile Ministries.

While it does appear that some amount of charity work did take place over the years, it's unknown if The Family's organizations were ever placed under scrutiny. Former members have described the use of the charities as photo opportunities, claiming that little genuine aid work was being done. Most of the donations, they have alleged, were used for group living expenses.

But the movement never stopped being controversial. Zerby was still teaching Berg's unusual and disturbing doctrines, such as encouraging the group's followers to have a spiritual sexual relationship with Jesus. All members – including the men – were told to visualize themselves as women "in the spirit" during masturbation and intercourse to accommodate the relationship. This was practiced by members starting at the age of 12 when they were taught that Jesus literally wanted to have sex with them.

In 2004, the movement was rebooted again, and its name was changed to Family International. There were more internal changes and upheavals, and secret directives were sent out to implore members to recommit to the group's mission of fervent proselytization.

The Family International – which is still the Children of God, whether they admit it or not – still exists today. The current number of members is unknown because the movement keeps that information private. According to their recent teachings they believe in what they call "new spiritual weapons." They believe that they are soldiers in a spiritual war of good versus evil for the hearts and souls of mankind. The "spiritual helpers" in their war include angels, departed humans, other religious and mythological figures, and even celebrities. On the list is Aphrodite, Merlin, the Sphinx, Elvis Presley, Marilyn Monroe, Audrey Hepburn, Richard Nixon, and Winston Churchill.

Nope, nothing weird going on there.

Karen Zerby is still leading the cult, although her whereabouts since the early 1970s have always been a closely guarded secret. Most Family members never even knew what she looked like or saw pictures of her until around 2005. She has been slightly more public since then, but not much. Her last known location was in Jalisco, Mexico, around 2010.

Tragically, this is not quite the end of the story.

The Children of God has gotten more than its share of bad publicity over the years, from Flirty Fishing to allegations of sex abuse. Actress Rose McGowan and was born and raised in the cult and later escaped to become a public figure. She has written about her experiences in her book, *Brave*.

Joaquin Phoenix also had an unconventional childhood within the cult. Living with his parents and siblings Summer, Liberty, Rain, and late fellow actor, River, they joined the Children of God in 1977 when Joaquin was only three. The idealistic Bottoms family – they'd later change their name to Phoenix – had joined the group because they believed it was a group of people who shared their values, but they later found that the cult's practices and ideas were not what they were looking for.

They were living in Caracas, Venezuela that the time. They had moved there to preach the word of God, but it was during this time that River was "initiated to enlightenment" – losing his virginity at the age of only four.

After the Children of God started forcing women into prostitution to get new followers the Bottoms decided to quit. They eventually ended up in Miami, where they started a new life and changed their name to "Phoenix" as a symbol of their rise from the ashes.

Ricky Rodriguez. He had been exploited as a child as "Davidito" and had never recovered

While not as famous – but much more tragic – another young man brought the Children of God back into the headlines in 2005. The murder-suicide of David Berg's adopted son, Ricky Rodriguez, shocked the world and stained the name of the group, especially when it came to their policies about child-rearing and accusations of child sexual abuse.

Ricky was well-known to members of the cult as Davidito, the natural son of Karen Zerby and a Spanish hotel employee that she Flirty Fished. He was later adopted by David Berg but that's not really how they knew him – it was from the book. His childhood had been recounted in the parenting manual that had been published for Berg's followers. The *New York Times*, after reviewing pages of the book that were sent to reporters by former followers, wrote that in it, "the toddler Ricky is described or else pictured as watching intercourse and orgies, fondling his nanny's breasts and having his genitals fondled."

As Ricky grew up, he developed a deep-seated resentment toward Zerby and Berg because of the sexual abuse he endured and because of the unnatural way that he had been raised. He later told his wife that he wanted his mother "prosecuted for child abuse." He also supported other women's accounts that Berg sexually abused his own daughters and granddaughters.

In 2002, Ricky, now an adult, finally left the group. He got married and tried to live a normal life working as an electrician, but he was simply too haunted by his past.

In October 2004, he moved to Tucson, Arizona, and, according to friends, he'd moved there because he heard that his mother sometimes visited the city and he wanted to see her.

He didn't find his mother, but he found someone else from his childhood. In January 2005 he arranged a meeting with Angela Smith – formerly Susan Joy Kauten – who was a close associate of his mother and one of his former abusers. She had appeared with him in the *Story of Davidito* book, engaging in fondling and sex.

He met Smith at her apartment – where he stabbed her to death.

Ricky then drove to the town of Blythe, Arizona where he committed suicide by shooting himself in the head.

In a 57-minute suicide video that he made for family, friends, and former members of the cult, he talked of his intense pain and the reason for his actions. He explained that he saw himself as a sort of "avenging angel," a vigilante for children like him and his sisters, who had been subjected to rape and beatings. He said, "There's this need I have. It's not a want, it's a need for revenge. It's a need for justice, because I can't go on like this."

The murder of Angela Smith and subsequent suicide by the tortured young man who killed her stunned the world and raised new concerns about the Children of God, which was now calling itself Family International.

But it had no impact on the leaders of the cult. A spokesperson for the group told the press that they had apologized already to former members for their pain – real or imagined – but there had never been any kind of widespread abuse in the movement.

Inferno in Waco

I still remember watching this on television. In fact, the siege outside of the compound in Waco, Texas was the reason that I first had cable installed in my office. I wanted – no, needed – to see what happened. I was at home on that Sunday morning when it came to an end, though – February 28, 1993. I watched along with most of the rest of the country as a convoy of vehicles began moving toward the sprawling wood and rock complex. As helicopters whirred overhead the back doors of two trucks opened and spilled out agents from the Bureau of Alcohol, Tobacco, and Firearms, wearing helmets and vests, and armed with shotguns and semi-automatic rifles.

The people inside watched as they arrived. They had been waiting for the attack to come for days – and even longer. The attack had, in fact, been foretold in the Bible, written thousands of years before. The conflict would end, they believed, with their leader's ascension into heaven, followed by the creation of God's Kingdom on earth.

As the agents rushed into the compound, they saw it as evidence that everything David Koresh had told them was true.

Later, we would all find out just how much of what happened that day was based on lies.

For most of us, the Branch Davidians – so many of whom died that day in Waco – will always be linked with David Koresh but it was actually a movement that predated Koresh's involvement with it. It began as an offshoot of the Seventh-Day Adventists, started by Victor Houteff, a Bulgarian immigrant and a teacher in an Adventist school in Los Angeles. At some point his interpretations of the Bible started to differ quite a lot from those of the church. He believed that in the days leading up to Christ's return – which was, of course, imminent – God would send angels down from heaven to slay all but the most righteous, leaving just 144,000 Adventists alive to serve God. In 1930 he put these ideas into a book, *The Shepherd's Rod*, and declared that God had sent him to reform the Adventist church, which had become wicked and sinful. It likely comes as no surprise that this announcement led to him being ousted from the church.

But many Adventists were interested in what Houteff had to say. He continued to preach and drew an increasing number of followers. In 1935 he established a headquarters outside of Waco, Texas that he called the Mount Carmel Center. The movement was initially named after his book and called The Shepherd's Rod, but when World War II began and Houteff wanted his followers to be eligible for conscientious objector status, he incorporated it under the name Davidian Seventh-Day Adventists, with "Davidian" referring to King David, whose throne Jesus would occupy when he returned.

After Houteff's death in 1955 his wife, Florence, took over the leadership of the movement. However, she made a serious miscalculation when she announced a prophecy that she had experienced – the Second Coming was going to take place in 1959. The sect then compounded this error by starting a huge publicity campaign to promote the news. They posted huge signs on their cars that proclaimed "Hear Ye The Rod!" and hundreds of followers quit their jobs, sold their possessions, and went to Mount Carmel to await the big event.

It was 1844, and William Miller all over again.

Nothing happened, and many people left the group and those that remained split into several factions. Florence Houteff sold Mount Carmel to Benjamin Roden, the leader of the largest splinter group. Roden, who had received a revelation that the new name of Jesus was "The Branch," called his group the Branch Davidian Seventh-Day Adventists. He also came up with a snappy slogan – "Get off the Dead Rod and Move onto a Living Branch." His most notable achievement as a leader – aside from the slogan – was establishing a small commune of Adventist missionaries in Israel.

Roden died in 1978 and his widow, Lois, took over the group. Like Florence Houteff, she announced controversial revelations of her own. In Lois' case she announced that the Holy Spirit was female. There was a lot of grumbling about her leadership within the community, much of which came from her son, George, who believed that it was his right to take his father's place. As the power struggle between them became more and more bitter, a new member named Vernon Howell arrived at Mount Carmel.

Vernon Wayne Howell – who would become much better known as David Koresh – was born on August 17, 1959 in Houston, Texas. His mother, Bonnie Sue Clark, was a single mother and only 14 when her son was born. Vernon never met his father. He

A young Vernon Howell — who would gain infamy as David Koresh

had already abandoned his mother for another teenage girl before he was born. Bonnie moved in with a violent, alcoholic boyfriend, and when Vernon was four his mother abandoned him and left him in the care of his maternal grandmother, Earline. His mother returned three years later, married to a carpenter named Roy Haldeman, and with another son, Roger.

Dyslexic, Vernon did poorly in school and was put into special education classes where he earned nicknames like "Vernie" and "Mr. Retardo." His knowledge of the Bible, though, was exceptional, and he had memorized the entire New Testament by the time he turned 12. He also had a guitar and had dreams of becoming a rock star. He dropped out of Garland High School in his junior year.

When he was 19, Vernon joined the Seventh-Day Adventist church, which his mother attended. In one version of the story Vernon was kicked out of the church because he was rebellious, but another version tells a different, slightly creepier story. It claims that he became infatuated with the pastor's daughter and, while praying for guidance, discovered that his Bible had fallen open to a passage in Isiah that stated, "none should want for her mate." Convinced this vision was a sign from God, he approached the pastor and told him that God wanted him to have his daughter for a wife. The pastor declined, and when he continued to pursue the girl Vernon was expelled from the congregation.

Regardless of what happened, in 1981 he arrived at Mount Carmel. It wasn't long before he also became embroiled in the battle over the leadership of the group, butting heads with George Roden. Vernon began claiming the gift of prophecy and began easily beating the hot-headed Roden in debates over scriptures. Vernon also strengthened his claims of leadership by sleeping with Lois Roden, who was, by then, in her late sixties. Vernon announced that God wanted him to father a child with her, who would be the Chosen One. In 1983 Los allowed Vernon to begin teaching his own message, called "The Serpent's Root," which caused controversy within the group.

It was at this point that Vernon began calling himself "David Koresh." He took his first name from the biblical Kind David and, like Cyrus Teed, began to call himself Koresh after the great Persian leader, whose name was synonymous with "farsighted."

In the middle of the uproar at Mount Carmel, Koresh announced that God had instructed him to marry Rachel Jones, which brought a short period of calm to the compound. Rachel, who was 14-years-old, was the daughter of one of the elders of the sect. She later gave him two children, a boy named Cyrus and a girl named Star.

The calm was only temporary. George Boden was furious about what was happening and made a habit of walking around the compound with an Uzi sub-machine gun on his shoulder. The community split into two factions, and his people forced Koresh and his followers off the property at gunpoint. Koresh set up camp at Palestine – about 90 miles from Waco – and lived rough for the next two years in tents and old buses. During this time Koresh took a second wife, Robyn Bunds, 17, whose parents were longtime members of the sect.

Koresh wasn't giving up on his claim for the leadership of the Branch Davidians. Even while camped on the Texas plains he actively recruited new followers, traveling to California and overseas to Great Britain and Israel. Like Victor Houteff, he wanted to be God's tool and set up a kingdom in Jerusalem. Until 1990 Koresh believed the place of his martyrdom might be in Israel, but the following year he changed his mind and predicted that he would die in the United States. It would be in Waco where the prophecies of David would be fulfilled, and Mount Carmel would be his kingdom.

Koresh with his wife, Rachel, and their son, Cyrus

Lois Roden died in 1986, but her son's hold on Mount Carmel was tenuous at best. Koresh and his people were eking out a primitive existence, but he was still pressing his claims for the leadership of the Branch Davidians – he believed that God wanted him in charge. He was also now enjoying the loyalty of the majority of the sect.

By late 1987 Roden was having trouble maintaining support among his followers. This pushed him into challenging Koresh for a macabre competition that would settle the matter of the group's leadership once and for all – each would attempt to raise a former Branch Davidian from the dead. Whichever man was successful, he would become the leader of the group.

Koresh refused to take part in the contest, but Roden went ahead with it and dug up the coffin of Anna Hughes, who had died 25 years before. The casket was placed on an altar and draped with an Israeli flag. Roden then spent the next several days muttering prayers and mumbling incantations over it.

Anna Hughes never woke up.

The Branch Davidian compound outside of Waco, Texas

In the meantime, Koresh went to the authorities and filed charges against Roden for illegally exhuming a corpse. He was told by the Waco police that no action could be taken without evidence, so Koresh decided to get a photograph of Boden's grisly work.

Early the next morning Koresh and seven followers arrived at Mount Carmel with a camera. They were dressed in camouflage gear and were heavily armed. The group was discovered by Roden and a 20-minute gunfight ensued, during which Roden was wounded in the chest and hand, but, amazingly, no one else was injured. When sheriff's deputies arrived on the scene Koresh and his men surrendered.

Koresh and the others were charged with attempted murder, but at trial Koresh denied aiming at Roden. He said that he and his men had only fired into the air to intimidate him after going there to uncover evidence of the criminal disturbance of a corpse. Anna Hughes, in her coffin, made an appearance as an exhibit for the jury. No verdict was ever reached, and the judge declared a mistrial. Two of the jurors were so impressed with Koresh that they hugged him after the proceedings had ended. The charges against him were eventually dropped. His accomplices were acquitted.

George Roden, though, ended up behind bars – in a psychiatric hospital. In 1989 Roden murdered Wayman Adair with an ax blow to the skull after Adair began making claims that he was the true messiah, not Roden. George was judged insane and confined to a mental hospital in Big Springs, Texas.

Since Roden owed thousands of dollars in unpaid taxes on the Mount Carmel compound, Koresh raised the money and reclaimed the property. Even from the hospital Roden continued to harass Koresh by filing legal papers. In one of them he suggested that unless judges ruled in his favor, God would smite them with herpes and AIDS.

With Roden out of the way the door was wide open for Koresh to finally take his place as the undisputed leader of the Branch Davidians. He led his people back to the now ramshackle compound, with an overgrown yard that was littered with garbage and abandoned cars. Their first task was cleaning it up, repairing the rickety walls and building new ones. A watchtower was built. Tunnels were dug between the buildings, and an old bus was buried on the property to serve as a makeshift bunker.

Conditions in the main building remained primitive, however. It was essentially an enormous maze of rooms, hallways, and staircases. There was no central heating or air conditioning, and only the kitchen had plumbing. Koresh liked that Mount Carmel was rambling and unfinished because he felt it was a reflection of his views on spirituality. He believed that Christianity was something that constantly changed and evolved as God spoke through those he chose as his prophets.

Their living quarters may have lacked order, but the lives of the Branch Davidians did not. Koresh expected them to live communally and donate all their income to the group. Their diet consisted of cereal, fruit, and vegetables, and they rose every morning before dawn, exercised for 90 minutes, and then spent the rest of the way working or in Bible study classes.

Of course, these conditions didn't apply to Koresh. He often slept in until later afternoon, ate what he wanted, drank beer, and occasionally smoked. When he was questioned about this – or anything else – he always had a biblical answer for everything.

When he was teaching his followers, he might talk about the Bible for 16 or 17 hours at a time. The group, already exhausted by their long day, would have to listen until well after midnight as he talked about scriptures or foretold the end of the world. At other times they were treated to performances by his rock band, Messiah.

Koresh truly believed that he was the seventh angel who was put on earth to usher in God's kingdom. Central to his thinking – like so many others we have discussed in this book – were passages from the Book of Revelation about the scroll with the seven seals, the opening of which would begin the Apocalypse. The Bible states that a lamb is the only one who can open the seals. Most Christians assume the lamb is Jesus Christ, but not David Koresh – he was convinced that he was the lamb. He also believed that his sinfulness was what made him worthy of filling this role. The first Messiah had been without sin, but the new one, having tasted all the temptations the world could offer, would make a much better judge of good and evil. Since he was now convinced that the Apocalypse would start in Texas, rather than Israel, he began preparing for the violent struggle to come by stockpiling canned goods, water, guns, and ammunition.

Around 1990, Koresh announced that he had received a new revelation – God had instructed him to produce an army of children from his own seed. To do that he had the right to take any women in the sect as his wife, regardless of whether they were married or under the age of consent. It was fine, he assured everyone, God told him to. As for the male members of the sect, they were to remain celibate and sleep in separate quarters from the women. They were consoled by the fact that Koresh

By the early 1990s, Koresh had become increasingly apocalyptic in his beliefs and told his followers that the end times were going to start in Texas

would, after his resurrection, provide each of them with their perfect partner, made from one of his own ribs.

This announcement caused a lot of disquiet among group members, especially married couples. Some of them left. Others, after a lot of prayer, decided to go along with it. Koresh eventually took on 20 wives and fathered 17 children. One of his wives was only 12. Another was Jeanine Bunds, the 55-year-old mother of his second wife, Robyn. Disgusted by this turn of events, Robyn left her husband and the cult.

It was at this same time that he legally changed his name to "David Koresh." There was a new energy around the compound as if something was going to happen. The Branch Davidians – only half-joking, began calling the place Ranch Apocalypse.

It was a joke that turned out to be eerily accurate.

When members defected from the group after Koresh's revelations, rumors began to spread about life behind the walls of Mount Carmel. Some of the defectors fed information to the press and to some government agencies, including the FBI. Because of Koresh's new policy about taking wives many were concerned about the underage girls that were living with him. The youngest of his wives was 12-year-old Michelle Jones, the younger sister of Koresh's legal wife, Rachel, and the daughter of Branch Davidians Perry and Mary Belle Jones. In 1992 Texas Child and Protective Services investigated and failed to turn up any evidence of abuse, possibly because the cult concealed the spiritual marriage of Koresh to Michelle by assigning her a surrogate husband, David Thibodeau.

There had also been reports that Koresh was beating young children and denying them food. In one widely reported incident, former members claimed that Koresh spanked his son Cyrus for several minutes after he became irritated by the boy's crying. In a second report a man involved in a custody dispute visited Mount Carmel and claimed to have seen a young boy being beaten with a stick.

However, Texas Child and Protective Services found no evidence of this either, even though the FBI later justified forcing an end to the stand-off at the compound with claims that Koresh was abusing children inside. In the hours after the deadly ending of the siege, Attorney General Janet Reno told reporters that, "We had specific information that babies were being beaten." FBI Director William Sessions publicly denied this later and told reporters that they had no information about child abuse at Mount Carmel. Which was it? We'll never know, but we do know that the child abuse charges were weak and ambiguous and, in every case, came from detractors and ex-members.

The biggest concern was about the stockpiling of weapons at the compound. Most of them were legal, but the Bureau of Alcohol, Tobacco, and Firearms (ATF) learned that Koresh and his men had been converting semi-automatic weapons into machine guns, which they were not licensed to do. Survivors would later claim they were only doing the conversions to sell the modified weapons for more money, but it was still against the law. It was the ATF that finally decided to take action against Koresh.

Koresh could have easily been arrested outside of the Mount Carmel compound. He was often in Waco, attending gun shows or drinking in bars with his inner circle, which he dubbed the "Mighty Men." Instead, the ATF decided the best way to deal with a walled compound filled with arms and ammunition and "crazed cultists" was to show up en masse with even more weapons. It would later turn out that budget hearings were scheduled, and the ATF hoped that a flashy raid would gain them a lot of favorable publicity.

Yes, that turned out to be a very bad decision.

The operation was carefully planned out. When they arrived at the compound ATF agents would split into groups. Some would move to the area where the women and children lived separately from the men, hopefully protecting them from any violence. Others would enter through a second-floor window, make their way to the armory, and secure it. They practiced the raid in mock-ups of the compound and brought in extra agents to beef up the numbers.

The plan was securely in place on February 28, 1993, but it was a disaster from the beginning.

Koresh had been tipped off about the raid. When an ATF agent approached the open front doors and called out, "Police! Search warrant! Lay down!" Koresh, who was standing in the doorway, slammed the doors closed.

It remains a matter of dispute who fired the first shot. Whoever it was, an intense gun battle broke out, and the ATF, to their dismay, quickly realized they were completely outgunned. The firefight lasted for more than 45 minutes and resulted in the deaths of four federal agents and six Branch Davidians. Many more were injured, including Koresh, who had been shot in the side and one hand. Eventually an ATF agent who was able to get through to the compound by telephone was able to arrange a ceasefire.

That night Koresh gave a phone interview with CNN. With his voice shaking with pain he said that he had tried to get the ATF to leave, telling them that there were women and children in the compound, and his people had only opened fire after the ATF shot first.

After the disastrous raid the FBI Hostage Rescue Team took command of the federal operation. The FBI now had jurisdiction because of the deaths of the federal agents. A team of negotiators began working with Koresh over the phone, trying to persuade the Branch Davidians to surrender. At first it appeared that it would happen soon. Koresh had been seriously wounded in the raid and needed medical attention. March 3 was set as a tentative date for surrender. Koresh only asked for one thing – the broadcast of a 58-minute sermon that he had recorded about the end times. The FBI agreed to the deal and the sermon was broadcast as promised. Then, at the last minute, Koresh stalled. He had received a message from God, he said, it told him to "Wait."

Meanwhile, outside the compound and beyond the perimeter set up by the FBI, journalists, TV crews, and hundreds of curiosity-seekers gathered. It quickly turned into a circus with people selling t-shirts and "Koresh burgers" and religious fanatics of all kinds wandering around shouting and holding up signs.

The negotiations were dragging on. Koresh and his inner circle kept asking for delays. His conversations with the negotiators were convoluted and filled with biblical imagery. He persisted in talking about the Seven Seals and other religious matters that only confused and baffled the FBI men, who were treating the situation as a hostage crisis – even though all the "hostages" had chosen to be there.

Koresh's wounds were causing him a great deal of pain, and as the days passed it seemed to agents that he was becoming hysterical. He sent out a couple of letters – one of which was supposed to have been from God – and warned that the Waco area would be destroyed by earthquake and flood if the FBI didn't back off. The FBI responded by increasing security around the compound, even bringing in military tanks. Loudspeakers were set up to subject the Davidians to a constant barrage of sound, including recordings of dental drills and the screams of dying rabbits. The voice of Nancy Sinatra sometimes sang "These Boots Were Made for Walking" all night long.

Soon, the older adults and 29 of the children were allowed to leave the compound. As far as FBI agents knew there were still at least 20 children still inside, most of them fathered by Koresh.

Koresh was waiting for God to tell him what to do next. According to some of the negotiators he seemed genuinely perplexed about the situation that he was in. He was sure the raid and the standoff were part of the Apocalypse, but what was actually happening did not match his interpretations about how it would all unfold.

On April 14, God finally sent Koresh a message – he was supposed to write a complete exposition of the Seven Seals that would be released to the world. When he was finished, he and his followers would surrender. Koresh immediately got to work. He had just finished writing about the first seal and was starting on the second when the FBI finally ran out of patience.

The new Attorney General, Janet Reno, who had only been on the job a few weeks, approved the recommendation of FBI officials to proceed with a final advance

The Branch Davidian compound in flames after the attack

and remove the Branch Davidians by force. They were authorized to use gas on the compound. Cult experts had advised the FBI that Koresh and his followers were unlikely to commit mass suicide, as Jim Jones and his followers had done just a little over a dozen years before. Reno told the press that her main concern was the children still inside.

On April 19 – the 51st day of the standoff – armored combat vehicles began smashing holes in the walls of the compound. Trying to flush out the group inside, the FBI pumped CS gas through the holes. CS is "tear gas," which is a chemical weapon, classified as non-lethal, that causes severe eye and respiratory pain, skin irritation, and, in some cases, bleeding and blindness.

When Davidians inside opened fire on the vehicles, the ferocity of the attack increased, and the tanks fired canisters of gas into the building. The Davidians, wearing gas masks, returned fire while others tried to go about their daily routine. Women did laundry. Others attended Bible class, while others just tried to stay away from the windows.

And then, just after noon, the fire started.

As millions of people watched the live television coverage, the fire, accelerated by 30 m.p.h. winds, whipped through the flimsy wooden compound with terrible speed. Only nine of the Davidians were able to escape from the blaze – 79 others, including David Koresh, were killed. There were 21 children still inside when the buildings burned, all of them under the age of 16.

The horrifying end to the standoff led to recriminations and controversy – and continues today.

The FBI has told multiple stories about how David Koresh died. He was shot, but whether this was by FBI sharpshooters or other Branch Davidians remains unknown.

Initially the FBI claimed that Steve Schneider, Koresh's second-in-command, "probably realized that he was dealing with a fraud" and shot and killed Koresh and then turned the gun on himself. A second account from the FBI gave a totally different story: "Koresh, then 33, died of a gunshot wound to the head during the course of the fire. No one knows who killed him or if he killed himself."

The FBI had a lot of different stories about the standoff and, over time, changed and updated many of their earlier accounts, reports, and outright lied. From the beginning the FBI was adamant that the Davidians started the fire that destroyed the compound and killed those still inside. The agency stated that three fires seemed to have ignited simultaneously, suggesting arson, and produced transcripts of incoherent recordings that may have been people saying things like "spread the fuel around," but even that has been disputed. The survivors vehemently deny that they set the fire and that they planned to commit suicide. They say that the fires started when bales of hay that were placed against the walls to stop bullets were ignited.

It's been suggested that lanterns that were being used for light – federal agents shut off electricity to the compound early in the standoff – may have fallen over and ignited the hay, but there is another possible cause, too.

Although they denied this for years, FBI officials eventually admitted that some pyrotechnic devices were used in the operation. They had been designed to release the CS gas. It is just as likely that these devices ignited the hay bales and started the fires as it is that the Davidians knocked over lanterns in three different places.

But no one knows for sure. There is a lot of speculation but no clear answers. With all the physical evidence destroyed in the blaze, the full story of what happened to David Koresh and his followers were probably never be known.

Salvation from the Stars

On the afternoon of March 26, 1997 two sheriff's deputies entered a sprawling mansion in Rancho Santa Fe, an upscale community in San Diego, California. They were responding to an anonymous report that a mass suicide had taken place in the house. As they forced their way in through the front doors and walked into the foyer, the overpowering stench in the air left little doubt that the report was true.

The deputies found 39 bodies in the house. Most of them were lying on their backs, arms at their sides, on metal bunk beds. All were dressed in identical long-sleeved black shirts, black pants, and new black and white Nike sneakers. Purple sheets that had been neatly folded into a diamond shape were draped over their bodies. Many of them had had a $5 bill, and loose change in their pockets, and each of them had a travel bag next to them that contained a change of clothing. All their heads were shaved, leading the initial report to state they were all male – 19 were male, and 20 were female. On each of their shirts was sewn a black patch with the words "Heaven's Gate Away Team" sewn into it.

As investigators began trying to piece together what had happened, they combed through the computers found in the house and discovered the dead were all members of a "UFO cult" called Heaven's Gate. It had been founded more than 20 years before by Marshall Applewhite and Bonnie Lu Nettles, who believed themselves to be extraterrestrial beings. They had come, they said, from the "Evolutionary Level Above Heaven," and promised their followers that they could also achieve this level of spirituality.

The trigger for their mass suicide had been the appearance of the Hale-Bopp Comet, which had been brightly visible in the night skies since 1996. They believed that the comet was being trailed by a UFO, and Applewhite became convinced that this was the sign that he had been waiting for – the signal for his followers to shed their inferior physical "vehicles" and travel to the next level in outer space.

I think that when the Heaven's Gate mass suicide occurred almost everyone agreed that Applewhite and his followers were seriously delusional. But it might be shocking for many to learn that UFO cults were nothing new in America. A belief in god-like beings from the stars had already been with us for decades, since the rise of popular belief in flying saucers and little gray men. Millions of Americans believed they had a message for us, and that message was a spiritual one. In the 1970s an entire movement was created around the idea that the ancient gods of our past were space aliens and they built all the great monuments of those times, like Stonehenge and the pyramids. Today most people realize that we were selling our ancestors short when it came to their ability to do incredible things, but 40-50 years ago it was not seen as unusual at all to seriously discuss the possibility of ancient aliens in polite company.

And many still believe it today, so who are we to say they're wrong?

For our purposes here, though, let's take a closer look at some of the UFO and science fiction cults that were definitely off-base when it came to alien messiahs from other planets.

Mankind United

Eerily foreshadowing the rise of the modern cult of Scientology – and just wait, we'll get to that one – was the Mankind United sect, which was created by another Los Angeles science-fiction writer, Arthur Bell. During the height of the Great Depression Bell penned a book called *Mankind United*, a turgid, repetitive text that was filled with bold type and large blocks of unnecessarily capitalized text. It told the story of a malevolent conspiracy that ran the world – the "Hidden Rulers" and "Money Changers" – who were not only responsible for war, poverty, and injustice – they were also aliens living on earth.

Opposing them was another group of aliens, the "Sponsors," who had arrived on earth in 1875. According to Bell the benevolent Sponsors were shortly going to announce their presence and would turn the world into a utopia, based on universal employment and a financial system based on credits. The workday would be four hours each day, four days a week. Needless to say, all of this sounded pretty good to tired, worn-out people who were struggling to put food on their tables.

But for the Sponsors to put their plan into place they had to receive massive support from the people. The plan would be promoted by the "Pacific Coast Division of North America, International Registration Bureau" – which was, of course, run by

Arthur Bell, the creator of the "Mankind United" UFO cult

Arthur Bell. He announced that when 200 million people accepted the Mankind United plan the Sponsors would overthrow their rival alien groups and, within 30 days, the new utopia would begin.

Of course, there were no Sponsors, no evil aliens, and no "International Bureau." The whole thing had been concocted by Bell, but it did manage to attract several thousand followers. The only true beneficiary of the group was Bell, who had several luxurious apartments and mansions, including a swanky place on the Sunset Strip that had an indoor pool, a pipe organ, and a cocktail bar. Bell was spotted in all the most swinging nightclubs and spent cash freely. He received about $50,000 a year in tax-free income, which adjusted for inflation would be the equivalent of nearly $1 million today. His followers, on the other hand, worked in various cult businesses full-time, including hotels and shops. They were paid less than $40 a month, worked up to 16 hours a day, seven days a week – which was quite a bit different than the Utopian work week they had been promised in Bell's book.

The cult gained the attention of the authorities during World War II. Bell incorporated as a church – the Church of the Golden Rule – to obtain tax exemption and began making even more bizarre claims, such as the idea that he could be beamed to several different places at once, that the Sponsors had advanced technology that allowed the dead to be resurrected on other planets, and more.

None of these turned out to be quite enough to gain popular support, and in 1951 Bell's group folded and the cult faded away completely. As some would later discover, though, he was simply a man ahead of his time. If he had started his church a few decades later, he might be able to count some of the biggest stars in Hollywood as his members.

Mrs. Keech

In the early 1950s a middle-aged woman from Lake City, Missouri named Dorothy Martin – who used the pseudonym Mrs. Marion Keech – began to receive messages from the inhabitants of the planet Clarion. The aliens communicated only with Mrs. Keech through automatic writing. She dutifully transcribed all their messages onto paper as they were beamed into her head.

The aliens had made contact with her to warn her of an impending worldwide flood that would take place on December 21, 1954. The Great Lakes would overflow and destroy the Midwest, and the entire Pacific Coast would be flooded from Seattle to South America. But the good news was that the aliens had dispatched a spacecraft from Clarion that would arrive at 11:59 p.m. on December 20. It would land on Mrs. Keech's front yard and would take her – and a select number of followers – to safety.

Mrs. Keech began calling herself the "Outer Space Subordinate" and became the leader of a small cult known as the Seekers. Only true believers would be given the passports needed for interplanetary travel and this meant that her followers had to quit their jobs, leave their spouses, and give away all their money and possessions. In addition, they had to learn the alien greeting, "I am my own porter." Followers were required to practice it by repeating it over and over in a monotone voice.

"Marion Keech," the Missouri housewife who received long distance calls from the planet Clarion

Seriously, you can't make this stuff up. If you did everyone would just laugh at you.

December 20 arrived and in the last minutes Mrs. Keech remembered that no one was allowed to wear metal on board the ship. Women removed bras with metal clasps and men cut the zippers from their trousers in a frenzy of not wanting to be left behind. They packed themselves into Mrs. Keech's house, watching for the spacecraft that would land outside.

The hands on the clock ticked toward midnight, and the appointed time came and went.

When the spaceship failed to appear, the group became deeply depressed. Many of them, including Mrs. Keech, began to weep. They were sure that the great flood was going to begin at dawn.

Then, at what eyewitnesses reported was 4:31 a.m., Mrs. Keech began to sway and tremble – a new message was coming to her from Clarion. The planet advisors announced that God had intervened on the earth's behalf and saved the planet at the last second. The spaceship that had been on its way received orders to turn around and return to Clarion.

While the cult had previously kept their plans very secret – they didn't want a rush of less deserving people to descend on the spaceship when it arrived – they now began to alert the media so they could tell the world about its narrow escape.

Mrs. Keech did numerous interviews – I'll assume with amused reporters – and said that the "lessons" the aliens had given her created so much energy in her little house that God was alerted to the earth's plight. She encouraged everyone to follow her example because channeling positive energy into the universe was undoubtedly a good thing. She changed her name to "Sister Thedra" and continued to attract followers by channeling intergalactic beings until her death in 1988.

Raëlism

The aliens made it to earth, and they took a prophet into space with them.

That's how the UFO religion of Raëlism started, but there was still a lot more to come.

The prophet who was abducted by aliens, Raël, was born Claude Vorilhon in 1946, and 27 years later the French sports car journalist and test driver was abducted by aliens from a volcanic crater near Auvergne, France. At first the small four-foot-tall green-skinned men asked him to spread messages around the world of peace, love, and unity. It seemed to be standard fare – often passed along to prophets by angels, spirit beings, and, well, aliens. Claude really ramped things up, though, and his followers began meeting in orgiastic parties of nudity and experimentation. Gender was an illusion, sexuality was whatever you wanted it to be, all beings were equal.

It should be no surprise that the cult became very popular, very quickly.

Raëlism is perhaps the largest UFO religion in the world today – only because Scientology is generally categorized as a belief in "ancient astronauts – and boasts a membership of at least 100,000 people. Raëlism began championing free love in the 1970s, highlighted boobs in the '80s and '90s, and today is a muddle of feminism, sex positivity, and women's empowerment. But I think the real achievement here is that it's still around at all.

After Raël was beamed aboard that spaceship in 1973 he began writing his first document, *The Book Which Tells the Truth*. In it he claimed that he was chosen as a messenger by the aliens, who were known as the Elohim, human-like figures from a distant planet. They were more than 25,000 years more advanced in science and technology and the Elohim created human life in their laboratories and then brought their specimens to Earth to watch them

Rael – Claude Vorilhon – outside of the UFOland museum that was created by the cult. Sorry – it closed in 1997

grow and adapt. All the great prophets in history – Jesus, Mohammed, and now Raël – were actually half-Elohim, created by having male aliens impregnate human women.

Raël created a new religion around what he was taught by his alien friends, named it after himself, and modeled its leadership and doctrines after the Catholic Church – even though he was strictly anti-Catholic in his teachings. Raël served as the pope of his new religion, and under him he appointed bishops and priests. Raëlians don't believe in just one God, though, or really, any gods at all. They have many creators – alien scientists whose version of "intelligent design" was really knowledge and superior technology. Later, when Raëlians claimed to have cloned the first humans, they would state that they had done it thanks to Elohim intervention as a way to transfer the mind to a new body and create an infinite form of reincarnation.

The movement began to gather steam thanks to a conference in Paris in 1974 where Raël hosted about 2,000 people and spoke at length of his alien encounter. His timely message of world peace and sexual permissiveness appealed to a tuned-in audience all over the world. His books would eventually be published in 25 languages.

Over time, Raël spread the message that the once-pristine human gene pool had gotten murky. It was his job to purify it again. In the beginning this meant treating sex for pleasure only, not for procreation. The Elohim planned to eliminate the need for traditional childbearing. The anatomical differences between men and women were merely designed for sexual pleasure, otherwise, gender was irrelevant. Raël taught "sex unity," or erotic plurality between all genders. His followers were encouraged to abandon their preconceived sexual preferences and monogamous boundaries. By doing so they could replenish brain cells and potentially communicate with the Elohim directly. This kind of "sexual medication" would become the center of the movement.

Even though the religion claimed indifference to gender, Raëlian women were upheld as enlightened lovers and sexual playthings, which meant that they often dressed seductively and played the vixen role that Raël had created for them. He encouraged his male followers to be more like women, cultivating feminine qualities. Raël himself was often described as soft-spoken and effeminate, dancing and singing at events with long hair and dressed in flowing clothing.

But as the religion grew and attracted New Age pansexuals, Raël apparently only ever entered into long-term heterosexual relationships. He was married three times, including in the late 1990s to a 16-year-old named Sophie de Niverville, reportedly with her mother's permission.

Around this same time Raël, then 52-years-old, established the religion's order of Angels. He claimed that he had received an alien vision that told him to gather his most attractive female followers into one group. They were to serve as hostesses to their alien creators whenever they visited the earth. After this announcement Raël received hundreds of applications. He required that their headshots be attached. In the message he received the aliens explained, "We prefer to be surrounded by individuals of great beauty corresponding to the absolutely perfect original models of the different races that we once created on earth. Physical flaws are all due to the errors of generations past, which have damaged our genetic code."

By 1999, Raël had selected 165 women to join the lower order of the White Angels, whose responsibility would be to act as missionaries and welcome agents –

Rael, Hugh Hefner, and a couple of the Angels, who posed with their leader in an issue of Playboy

and, of course, to "make Raël comfortable." There were also six elite Pink Angels that were chosen. They were to follow strict diets and to maintain genetic purity. They were not allowed to have sex with any humans, except for with their fellow Pink Angels and Raël, who was half-human, half Elohim.

In an interview one of the Pink Angels spoke about her responsibilities: "At first I was afraid that being an Angel I would be more like my mother and grandmother who are Catholics, that my job would be to wait on the men all the time, to cook dinner, arrange parties," she said. "But then I realized that when the Elohim come, it is only women allowed to go into the Embassy to speak with them, and the whole world will depend on Raël's Angels for information. We will be like ambassadors or PR people. We will learn so much!"

In September 2000 Raël was again in the headlines when he appeared with eight Angels at a press conference and volunteered them as surrogates for his new cloning venture, a company called Clonaid. Its mission was to create eternal life. Three years later the company announced that it had – thanks to the Elohim – cloned the world's first human. Stories exploded on television and in newspapers, but Clonaid failed to ever offer any proof of its success. Never missing the chance for a little publicity, though, Raël followed up on the headlines by posing with the Angels in an issue of *Playboy*.

In 2001 the cult closed UFOland, a museum that it had opened in 1997 as the largest structure in North America to be built out of bales of hay. Located on an estate owned by the group in Quebec, its purpose was to inform the public about UFO phenomenon and to attract funds for the Raëlian church. The first room featured their proposed Raëlian embassy for extraterrestrials. There were audio presentations in the other rooms about the Raëlian message, UFO sightings, and government cover-ups about UFOs. The museum was eventually closed because its revenue simply didn't justify its costs.

In May 2007 the group moved its operations to Las Vegas, Nevada, because it was a "happy and open-mind community."

The church is still in existence today and devotes much of its time to human cloning and women's issues, like repairing the damage done by clitoral mutilation, desexualizing the female body, and creating safer public environments for women. In 2014 they organized a march in New York City where women bared their breasts. "Go Topless Day" went viral and became an annual event, with women now using pasties over their nipples to avoid arrest.

None of the media outlets that have covered the event have ever mentioned that it is sponsored by a UFO cult.

Heaven's Gate

Marshall Herff Applewhite was born in Spur, Texas in 1932. He graduated from college in 1932 and married Ann Pierce. His father had been a Presbyterian minister and Marshall planned to become one, too. He spent a year at the seminary and then changed his mind, deciding on a career in music instead. He was a talented singer and musician and served as the choirmaster at a church in North Carolina for a couple of years. He also appeared in lead roles for shows like "South Pacific" and "Oklahoma."

In 1961 Applewhite, who now had two children, became a music instructor at the University of Alabama. He was handsome and well-liked, and students praised him for the way that he inspired those around him. But the early 1960s could be a difficult time for some, and he was suspended from his position after word leaked out that he was engaged in a sexual affair with a male student. He left Alabama – and his wife and children – and moved to Houston, Texas. In the larger city he was able to live openly as a homosexual. In 1966 he was appointed as an assistant professor at a private

Marshall Applewhite

Bonnie Lu Nettles

Catholic college in Houston, and in his spare time he sang in the city's opera. In 1970 he lost another college position after rumors began about an affair with another male student.

This time, Applewhite went into a tailspin. He had to be hospitalized in 1972. It was allegedly because of a heart condition but most believed that he was because he had suffered a drug-induced mental breakdown. A few rumors claimed that he had checked in to be "cured" of his homosexuality. But whatever the reason was that he was there, it was at the hospital where Applewhite first met Bonnie Lu Nettles.

Nettles had been born in Houston in 1911. She was a trained nurse, married, and had four children. She was fascinated by the occult, astrology, and tarot cards. She believed that she had psychic abilities and that her spirit guide was a Franciscan monk known as "Brother Francis," who had departed the early veil in 1818.

The two of them made an unusual couple – a tall, handsome gay man and a short, dumpy, old married lady – but they formed an immediate bond. They were convinced that they had known each other in a previous life and came to believe they had been placed on earth for a special purpose. No matter what they believed it seems obvious that they belonged together. Applewhite was deeply ashamed of his homosexuality and longed to have a deep but asexual relationship with someone. To Nettles, the charismatic Applewhite – who also now had an interest in the occult – was the perfect person with which she could reach her spiritual potential. She deserted her family for him, and they began to try and fulfill what they were sure was their common destiny.

Applewhite and Nettles began an intensive study of Christianity and alternative religions. For a short time, they ran the Christian Arts Center, located in a Unitarian Universalist Church in Houston. They hosted talks on astrology, mysticism, and other New Age beliefs. It was the early 1970s and there was a wide audience for anything of this kind.

At one point, Applewhite suffered another nervous breakdown – or "near-death experience," as he called it – and believed that God spoke directly to him during it. He and Nettles began to put more faith in dreams, visions, and the voices they heard inside their heads than in anything they read in books.

The Christian Arts Center only lasted for about a year. When it closed Applewhite and Nettles began traveling around the country in a convertible sports car. They worked odd jobs and depended on the charity of churches to survive. When their car broke down in Oregon in 1974, they had to camp there for two months.

It was here that they received the final revelation of their destiny.

Their "philosophy" – for lack of a better term – combined elements of Christianity, theosophy (especially the belief in superhuman beings called the "Ascended Masters"), and pure science fiction. They believed that Heaven was a physical place where beings lived who had reached the "Evolutionary Level Above Human." These beings – who physically resembled the bald, large-headed aliens common in UFO lore – were androgynous, communicated telepathically, and were free of all human and animal instincts, including a need for sex. Applewhite and Nettles created the belief that "Representatives" from Heaven sometimes traveled to Earth and sought out promising subjects who could move to the next level. Jesus Christ had been one of these "Representatives" and, of course, Applewhite and Nettles were his successors.

Applewhite and Nettles, or as they would later be called – The Two, and then Bo and Peep, and later, Do and Ti. Together, they would create one of America's most prominent UFO cults – and one that would end in tragedy

These two self-proclaimed messiahs began to call themselves "The Two," after the prophets mentioned in the Book of Revelation – there's that pesky book again – who are killed by a beast but rise from the dead three days later and are taken into Heaven in a cloud. The events were going to happen, and very soon. The "cloud," though, would be a spaceship.

As for the other people who lived on Earth, some of them lacked souls, while the bodies of others were occupied by evil aliens called "Luciferians," the equivalent of the demons and fallen angels found in the Bible.

The first follower of The Two was a woman named Sharon Walsh. She left her husband to join them but made the mistake of taking the family car with her when she did so. Her husband reported it stolen and Applewhite and Nettles were arrested in Texas and charged with a variety of offenses, including stolen credit cards. Applewhite spent the next six months in jail.

After his release he and Nettles went to California – a place where they would fit right in. They held numerous meetings, often on university campuses, and the posters and flyers they used to advertise their events shamelessly played up the UFO angle of their belief system.

UFOS...
WHY ARE THEY HERE?
WHO HAVE THEY COME FOR?
WHEN WILL THEY LEAVE?

People who came to the meetings were told The Two were not seeking converts, only supplying vital information. They learned that while Applewhite and Nettles looked human, they were just about to complete their physical metamorphosis, and within months there would be a "demonstration" – their deaths and resurrections – that would prove all their claims.

Unlike many charlatans and con artists who start cults, these two actually believed what they were telling people was true.

The meetings were a great success, and several dozen people joined their movement. The group had now started to call itself HIM – Human Individual Metamorphosis – and Applewhite and Nettles had taken on the weirdly childish nicknames of "Bo" and "Peep," a reference to their status as "shepherds."

Bo and Peep, with their flock in tow, continued to wander. In September 1975 they held a meeting at the Bayshore Inn in Waldpost, Oregon. It was a successful night – 23 people decided to abandon their families, give up their possessions, and join Bo and Peep. The "disappearance of these nearly two-dozen people" caused headlines across the country. Some of the initial reports actually suggested they had been abducted by aliens. This incident kept the media interested in the group over the next few years.

By now, Bo and Peep had almost 200 followers, but that number often changed. Members frequently came and went, finding it hard to live by their rules – which required cutting off all contact with family members and abstaining from sex – especially after the promised "demonstration" didn't happen. Then in 1976, Bo and Peep announced they would not be accepting any new members. They gathered all their current followers at a campground in Wyoming for a session that was designed to weed out any of those who were not worthy of moving on to the "next level." When it ended there were 70 followers remaining. The core group continued to live at the campgrounds until one of the followers inherited $300,000, which was immediately turned over to the group.

They rented two houses in Colorado and Texas, and soon after Applewhite and Nettles changed their names again. They now began calling themselves "Do" and "Ti," after the musical notes. Reports about the group's activities continued to appear in magazines and newspapers and they even inspired a television pilot called *The Mysterious Two* in 1982. It was the story of two evangelists who turned out to be aliens on a recruiting drive. The Applewhite character was played by John Forsythe, who filmed it shortly before he began starring in the hit series *Dynasty*.

Do and Ti demanded that their followers dissolve any connections to their pasts, give up all their material possessions, and donate any money they had to the betterment of the group. They were also given new names that were some variation of three letters, followed – with no explanation – with the suffix "ody." This resulted in strange names like Srrody, Qstody, Stmody, and so on.

The followers lived according to a set of rules that were designed to prepare them for both life at the next "level" and the voyage about the spaceship that would transport them there. Each day followed a rigid schedule, from which there was no deviation, planned according to the minute. Men and women had their hair cut very short and wore identical clothing, usually jumpsuits that concealed the shape of their bodies. Sometimes the clothing would get more creative, like the three months they spent wearing hoods with mirrored eye slits. They were discouraged from talking unless they had to, planning for the time when they would all converse telepathically. Applewhite handled all the finances, so when members had to leave the house for any reason, they were only allowed to carry a $5 bill and some loose change in case they needed to make a phone call. Alcohol, tobacco, and drugs were all forbidden.

The most important ban within the group was on sex. Applewhite believed that sex was the ultimate manifestation of human and animal instinct, which he was trying to transcend. In the video recording that he made to be broadcast after the group's "departure," he explained, "We are totally celibate, and there is no relationship in the nature of the male or female, there is no sexuality, there is no sensuality, that is very distasteful to us." At some point Applewhite decided to have himself castrated. Seven other male members of the cult decided to join him.

After all the publicity the group received in the late 1970s and early 1980s, they closed in on themselves and little was heard from them for the rest of the decade. In 1982 Nettles wrote to her daughter, Terrie, and told her that she had cancer and one of her eyes had been removed. Terrie later reported that her mother wrote her again in 1984 saying that she wanted to leave the cult, but there was no "graceful" way to do it. She died the following year.

Applewhite was devastated by his soulmate's death but soon reported that he stayed in touch with her telepathically. An empty chair was provided for Ti at all the group's gatherings.

In May 1993, the cult was back in the news. They ran full-page ads in *USA Today* and other newspapers with a heading that read, "UFO Cult Resurfaces with Final Offer!" Their writings had now taken on a darker, more apocalyptic tone. Civilization was about to be recycled or, to use Do's favorite term, "spaded over." The group had changed its name again and were now called Total Overcomers Anonymous.

At this point some of the original members from the 1970s who had left years before returned to the group – usually after suffering some setbacks in life – and new members joined. Some of them set up a web design company called Higher Source, which became very successful in those early days of the internet. In June 1995 some of the money they made was used to buy 40 acres of land in Manzano, New Mexico. Many group members traveled there to live in tents and start construction on an "earth ship" – made from recycled tires and dirt – that would, in theory, need no artificial heating or cooling. They made grand plans for the settlement that would grow up around it which would include a bakery and pharmacy. Work continued until April 1996, however with the "earth ship" still not completed Do changed his mind about the remote camp. The property was sold, and the group used the funds to rent a seven-bedroom mansion in San Diego.

It would become the cult's final home.

The mansion was sparsely furnished with not much more than bunk beds and dozens of computers. There were shelves filled with science fiction books and in the living room a 72-inch television on which they watched their favorite shows, including *Star Trek* and *The X-Files*. Life remained somber and rigid, although there were occasional treats. Every couple of weeks three followers went into town and returned with strawberry pancakes for the group.

After moving to San Diego, the cult changed its name again – it was now Heaven's Gate. It was a mixed bunch with ages ranging from 26 to 72. In a curious twist – especially because of the program they were rabidly devoted to – one of the members was Thomas Nichols, the brother of Nichelle Nichols, who played Lieutenant Uhura on *Star Trek*. Like most of the other members Nichols had not been in touch with anyone in his family in years.

There is little doubt that the cult's decision to finally depart from this world was influenced by Applewhite's deteriorating health. His "container," as he called it, was failing him. He told many people that he was suffering from terminal cancer, although no trace of it was found in his autopsy.

But his health was not the overriding factor in the decision – that was the arrival of the Hale-Bopp Comet. In November 1996, an amateur astronomer took a photograph of the comet that he claimed showed a UFO in its tail. Scientists dismissed the image as a star, but the story captured the imagination of UFO enthusiasts around

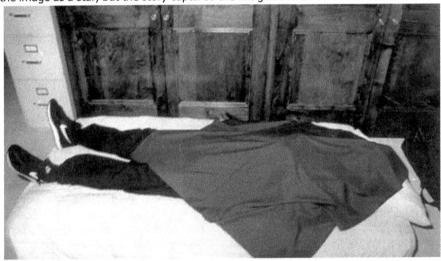

Each of the suicides in the San Diego house were laid out in the same way. The followers were identically dressed and covered with a purple cloth

the world. The Heaven's Gate cult placed a "red alert" on their website, stating that the comet was bringing "closure" to the group.

In their last days Applewhite and his followers decided to enjoy themselves a little, taking a four-day bus trip in early March 1997. On March 19, after recording their farewell messages, they went to the movies and had pizza for dinner. On March 21 they had a final lunch at a local restaurant, ordering 39 identical meals of chicken pot pie, cheesecake, and iced tea.

The suicides were planned and carefully carried out. Each member consumed a dose of Phenobarbital, mixed with applesauce or pudding. They washed it down with vodka then placed a plastic bag over their head and kept it in place with a rubber band around the neck. The deaths took place in stages over several days, with the first of the group likely dying on March 22. After their bodies were cleaned and laid out by other members, the next group consumed the lethal mixture, leaving only three female members until the end. After their own arrangements were made, they joined the others on their journey to the next level.

The bodies of the Heaven's Gate followers were found in rooms all over the house.

As the story of the mass suicide broke a few days later the media pored over the material that Applewhite and his followers left behind. They read the rambling diatribes posted on their website and watched the videos in which members, heads shaved, said goodbye to their families and explained the reasons for their actions. "We couldn't be happier about what we're about to do," one woman said with a smile. A male follower stated, "This will bring me just the happiest day of my life."

News coverage of the story portrayed Applewhite as a maniac who had tricked his followers into believing they were making a trip into space but, while seriously deluded, Applewhite wasn't tricking anyone into doing anything. Since the group's beginning, he and Nettles had argued that only the most dedicated and the most worthy would make it to the next level. They even discouraged potential followers. He wasn't asking anyone to do anything that he didn't wholeheartedly believe in doing himself. His body was found right there, among the others.

Applewhite believed in the mission and so did the people who died with him. At least one-quarter of those who died in 1997 had been with the cult since the 1970s and, for all the restrictions placed on them, seemed genuinely happy living together.

And they were, according to the videos they left behind, happy dying together, too.

It makes you wonder if any of us are really in a place to judge them.

Xenu, Thetans, and Clams
Scientology – America's Most Dangerous Cult

The Church of Scientology has been a lightning rod for controversy for decades, long before its celebrity members and recent scandals, and it attracts that controversy for a good reason. In 1950 it was founded by a science fiction author named L. Ron Hubbard who had no medical training but promised to cure illnesses of the mind and body without medication or therapy. He wrote a book based on this he called *Dianetics*. The book was reviewed by the American Psychological Association and, not surprisingly, found his claims were "not supported by empirical evidence." Even fellow science fiction author Isaac Asimov branded the book "gibberish." And yet, like so many other cults in America, the author, the book, and his methods attracted a following.

In his research for Dianetics, Hubbard found that humans are "thetans" – spirit souls that inhabit the "meat body" but are ageless beings that reincarnate. His system of Dianetics was created for the mind, so he designed the Church of Scientology for the spirit. They were meant to complement each other but have since become interchangeable as a form of therapy and a theology.

Scientology promises benefits on Earth, unlike most religions that preach of a reward in the afterlife. It is meant to teach the follower how to improve their spiritual well-being, achieve their goals, and reach their full potential in life. It does so by offering numerous books, DVDs, courses, and treatments – all of which can be yours, for a price, of course. Scientology is not spiritual in tone, but many followers believe that Hubbard's words are gospel, even if the words are confusing at times. Hubbard devised an entire language for Dianetics and Scientology that is so extensive it fills two full-sized dictionaries. He wrote obsessively, and not just about Scientology. His early career was writing for the pulp magazines of the early twentieth century, which required writers to pen extraordinary numbers of stories to make a living – stories of UFOs, aliens, and mysterious worlds. All of this would eventually find its way into the teachings of Scientology.

Hubbard "dropped his body" – what the thetans call continuing their research without the burden of the meat sack – on January 24, 1986. After a power struggle, David Miscavige became the new leader, although Scientology is more famous for its members. Thanks to their ability to promote and financially support the church, Scientology actively recruits television and film celebrities. It's become known as

"Hollywood's religion" with a cast that includes Tom Cruise, John Travolta, Kirstie Alley, Priscilla and Lisa Marie Presley, and Leah Remini – oops, more about that later – among others.

But not everyone is so easily taken in by the cult. Elvis Presley was an outspoken opponent of Scientology and was quoted as saying, "Fuck those people! There's no way I'll ever get involved with that son-of-a-bitchin' group. All they want is my money."

Elvis isn't the only one. There aren't too many religions that brand their beliefs, practices, and terminology with registered trademarks. Sometimes Scientology is a religion, and sometimes it's an applied religious philosophy, a system of ethics, or a science of the mind. There are many who believe it's nothing more than a scam and a cult – one of those would be me – but Scientologists aren't fans of questions or criticisms and are known to harass and attack their critics. Regardless of threats, many former members, journalists, politicians, and activists speak out against the church and its abuses, generating a lot of negative publicity for Scientology.

The thing is, though, Scientology really doesn't need any help when it comes to generating bad publicity – it does really well at that by itself.

Scientology continues to depict L. Ron Hubbard as a medical pioneer, scientist, humanitarian, philosopher, and war hero. In truth, he was none of those things. He was an eccentric who liked to repeat urban legends and other people's stories as his own. He was a dropout, a bigamist, and a fraud. He was deeply involved in the occult and black magic, had a criminal record for theft, and as an unindicted co-conspirator in a huge fraud case, he spent the last decade or so of his life hiding from the law.

And he was far from the superhuman of his own teachings. Dianetics and Scientology never cured Hubbard's obesity nor his chain-smoking habit. They also didn't treat or cure his many health issues, like a pulmonary embolism, pancreatitis, heart issues, or the stroke that killed him. For all his criticisms about psychiatry, Hubbard died with an anxiety drug in his system. His son later admitted in an interview that his father was a hypochondriac that was addicted to cocaine, amphetamines and even liked to use peyote.

He created an intricate world of science fiction that he claimed as fact. Dianetics and Scientology are both obvious works of fiction, but, of course, peddling science fiction isn't as lucrative as peddling self-help and spirituality, especially when you're not very good at it. As Hubbard once said, "Writing for a penny a word is ridiculous. If a man really wants to make a million dollars, the best way would be to start his own religion." And that's exactly what he did.

Born in 1911 in Tilden, Nebraska, Lafayette Ronald Hubbard spent much of his childhood in Helena, Montana. In the late 1920s, he spent time in Asia and the South Pacific after his father was posted to the U.S. Naval base in Guam. In 1930 he enrolled at George Washington University to study civil engineering but dropped out during his second year. He soon began his career as a prolific writer of pulp magazine stories. He wrote in many different genres – including adventure, aviation, travel, westerns, mysteries, and even romance – but was primarily known for science fiction and fantasy. He came to know many others in the field such as Robert A. Heinlein, Isaac Asimov, L. Sprague de Camp, and A. E. van Vogt.

L. Ron Hubbard — pulp fiction writer, occultist, cult leader, and con man

In early 1933 he started a relationship with Margaret "Polly" Grubb, who shared his interest in aviation. Polly was already pregnant when they got married on April 13 but had a miscarriage soon after the wedding. They did have two other children – a son born prematurely in 1934 who was named Lafayette Ronald Hubbard, Jr., and a daughter, Katherine May, in 1936.

Hubbard continued to write but the family was chronically short of money. He began spending an increasing amount of time in New York City working out of a hotel room, where Polly believed he was having affairs with other women.

In April 1938, Hubbard reportedly had a bad reaction to a drug during a dental procedure. He claimed that this reaction triggered a revelatory near-death experience that led to the creation of a never-published manuscript called "Excalibur." Hubbard would later claim that it was an early version of *Dianetics*.

He believed that "Excalibur" would "revolutionize everything" and that it was "more important and would have a greater impact on people than the Bible." He sent telegrams to book publishers telling them that he had written a very significant book and offered to put the rights up for auction to the publisher who bid the highest for it.

But no one cared.

Hubbard's failure to sell his "important" manuscript sent him into a deep depression. He began to believe that his other writing was slowing his progress and told his wife that he believed the book would someday be published, and he had "high hopes of smashing my name into history so violently that it will take legendary form." That was, he said, his life's goal.

Forrest J. Ackerman – who later published *Famous Monsters of Filmland* magazine and served as Hubbard's literary agent – recalled that Hubbard told him, "whoever read it either went insane or committed suicide." Hubbard also told him that he had taken "Excalibur" to New York to show it to a publisher, and the reader of the manuscript came into the publisher's office, threw the pages on the desk, and then jumped out of the skyscraper window.

The manuscript eventually became part of Scientology mythology and those who read it had to sign a sworn statement not to permit others to see it. There were also the claims that "four of the first fifteen people who read it went insane" – which is about as accurate as the claims that Hubbard later made that he had been dead in the dentist's office for eight minutes when the idea for the manuscript was conceived.

Hubbard served in the U.S. Navy as an officer during World War II. He was first sent to the Philippines but while waiting to ship out for Australia he was sent back to the United States instead. A report from his commanding officer stated, "This officer is not satisfactory for independent duty assignment. He is garrulous and tries to give impressions of his importance. He also seems to think he has an unusual ability in most lines. These characteristics indicate that he will require close supervision for satisfactory performance of any intelligence duty."

In 1942, he was dismissed from the Boston Navy Yard. His commander reported that Hubbard was "not temperamentally fitted for independent command."

And the story just gets better. Hubbard was then sent to Submarine Chaser Training and in 1943 was posted to Portland, Oregon to take command of a submarine chaser. He was on his first cruise on May 18 when only five hours into the voyage Hubbard believed he had detected an enemy submarine. He spent the next 68 hours engaged in combat until finally receiving orders to return to base. His commander noted: "An analysis of all reports convinces me that there was no submarine in the area."

The following month Hubbard unwittingly sailed into Mexican territorial waters and conducted gunnery practice by pounding the Coronado Islands, which he believed were uninhabited, and owned the United States. The Mexican government complained, and Hubbard was relieved of command.

Soon after he began reporting sick, claiming a variety of ailments including ulcers, back pain, and malaria. He was sent to the San Diego naval hospital for observation – and stayed for three months.

After his hospital stay, he was sent to Portland and was scheduled to go back out to sea. Then, on the night before his departure, he "discovered" a homemade bomb – a Coke bottle with gasoline in it and a wick – in the ship's cargo. Hubbard was given a transfer to the School of Military Government where he stayed until January 1945. He was re-assigned to Monterey, California where he ended up back in the hospital. This time his complaints included "headaches, rheumatism, conjunctivitis, pains in his side, stomach aches, pains in his shoulder, arthritis, hemorrhoids."

A few months later, the Naval Boards decided that Hubbard was only "physically qualified to perform duty ashore, preferably within the continental United States." He was discharged from the hospital in December 1945 and was transferred to inactive duty two months later. In 1950 he resigned his commission from the Navy.

After the war, Hubbard claimed that he "was abandoned by family and friends as a supposedly hopeless cripple and a probable burden upon them for the rest of my days." His daughter, Katherine, told a different story – that her mother refused to uproot their children from their home in Washington and join Hubbard in California. Their marriage was falling apart.

Hubbard moved into a Pasadena mansion that belonged to John "Jack" Parsons, a leading rocket propulsion researcher at the California Institute of Technology and founder of the Jet Propulsion Laboratory. Parsons let rooms in his home specifically to

Jack Parsons, the brilliant rocket scientist, occultist, and follower and personal friend of Aleister Crowley, the magician often known as the "World's Wickedest Man."

(Right) Sara Northrup, Parson's girlfriend who began an affair with Hubbard that would lead to black magic rituals, a business scam, and the beginnings of Scientology.

tenants who were "atheists and those of a Bohemian disposition." Parsons led a bit of a double life. In addition to working as a well-respected scientist, he was also an avid occultist and a follower of English magician Aleister Crowley. He served Crowley as a leader of one of the lodges in the magical order of Ordo Templi Orientis.

Hubbard befriended Parsons and it wasn't long before he became sexually involved with Parsons' 21-year-old girlfriend, Sara Northrup. Even so, Parsons was impressed with Hubbard and told Crowley that, although he had no formal training in Magick, Hubbard had an extraordinary amount of understanding of the field. He believed Hubbard was in touch with some "higher intelligence," possibly his guardian angel.

Parsons was obsessed with the sexual side of ritual magic and Hubbard became a willing participant. Parsons was fascinated with the idea of incarnating the Whore of Babylon described in the Book of Revelation. He believed this creature would be the bride of the Antichrist and the Mother of All Abominations. His chosen method of doing this was known as "Babylon Working," which essentially involved him impregnating a woman under occult conditions. But first they had to find just the right woman. They worked on the ritual to achieve this over several nights in February and March 1946 in order to summon an "elemental" who would participate in further sex magic. The rituals mostly amounted to Parsons masturbating in the search for spiritual advancement while Hubbard scanned the astral plane for signs and visions.

The "elemental" arrived two days later in the form of actress and artist Marjorie Cameron, who agreed to participate in the next rituals. The trio collaborated in more magical exercises, some of which included Parsons having sex with Cameron while Hubbard "magically" continued his descriptions of what was happening on the astral plane. Parsons claimed that his "Left-Hand Path" magic had been successful in creating the "moonchild," not as a physical being but as a spiritual entity. This really just meant that Cameron never got pregnant with the "Whore of Babylon." That was probably a lucky break for her.

Later that year Parsons, Hubbard, and Sara Northrup decided to set up a business partnership they called Allied Enterprises. They invested nearly their entire savings in it, although most of the money came from Parsons. They had a plan for Hubbard and Sara to buy yachts in Miami, sail them to the West Coast, and sell them for a profit. But Hubbard had a different idea. He just wanted to buy a boat with Parsons' money and sail it to Central and South America to collect "writing material." Even Aleister Crowley had warned Parsons against getting involved in business with Hubbard. He suspected Hubbard of a "confidence trick" and accused Parsons of being an "obvious victim" to a "prowling swindler."

When the so-called "World's Wickedest Man" thinks you're a crook, you are definitely bad news.

Parsons tied to recover his money by obtaining an order that forced Hubbard and Sara to stay in the country. They ignored it but had to return to port because of a storm. A week later their fledging company was dissolved. All Parsons was left with was a $2,900 promissory note from Hubbard that was never paid. Soon after Parsons sold his mansion to developers to recoup his losses.

Parsons gave up on Hubbard, but he didn't give up on the occult. In his later years he legally changed his name to "Belarion Armiluss Al Dajjal Antichrist." He was killed in an explosion in his garage laboratory in 1952 caused by his dropping a container of fulminate of mercury. His death was ruled an accident.

Hubbard and Sara remained in Florida after the company collapsed and many of his fellow writers knew what happened between Hubbard and Parsons. L. Sprague de Camp wrote Isaac Asimov and told him, "[Robert Heinlein] thinks Ron went to pieces morally as a result of the war," he said, trying to understand how the man who was once their friend could have gotten mixed up in the mess with Parsons. "I think that's fertilizer," de Camp added. "He was always that way, but when he wanted to conciliate or get something from somebody, he could put on a good charm act. What the war did was to wear him down to where he no longer bothers with the act."

On August 10, 1946 Hubbard married Sara, even though he was still married to Polly. She didn't find out that he was married again until 1947. Hubbard agreed to divorce Polly and she was given custody of the children.

Hubbard and Sara moved to Laguna Beach, California where Hubbard took a short-term job looking after a friend's yacht. He continued to write, using the money to supplement the small disability allowance he received as a veteran. Working from a trailer in a run-down part of Hollywood he sold a number of science fiction stories and pleaded with the Veteran's Administration to increase his pension because he had decided that he needed psychiatric treatment, which is ironic considering that he would spend decades calling it a "hoax."

He didn't get the treatment – unfortunately – but he did get a small increase in his pension. Nevertheless, his money problems continued and in 1948 he was arrested for petty theft. He took a guilty plea and paid a $25 fine.

Hubbard and Sara left California soon after and moved to Savannah, Georgia. It was then that he began toying with the idea of Dianetics. In March 1949 he wrote to Robert Heinlein and asked about one of the author's earlier works in which a utopian government had the ability to psychologically "cure" criminals of violent personality traits.

The following month Hubbard wrote to several professional organizations and offered his research into the human mind. No one was interested so he turned to science fiction writer and editor John W. Campbell, who was receptive to the idea of digging into fringe psychology and psychic powers. Campbell invited Hubbard and Sara to move into a house in Bay Head, New Jersey, not far from his home in Plainfield and recruited an acquaintance, Dr. Joseph Winter, to help develop Hubbard's "Dianetics." At this point the two men assumed this was for a science fiction book that Hubbard was writing.

Hubbard collaborated with the two men to create his theory and then tested it on science fiction fans that Campbell recruited. He wanted to see if the idea was a plausible one for fans of the genre. The basic principle of Dianetics was that the brain could record every experience in a person's life, even when they were unconscious. Bad or painful incidents were stored in what were called "engrams" in a "reactive mind." These engrams could be triggered later in life, causing emotional or physical problems. By carrying out a process Hubbard dubbed "auditing," a person could re-experience past experiences and then the engrams could be "cleared." The subject – now in a state of "Clear" – would have a mind that functioned perfectly, with an improved IQ and photographic memory. "Clear" could also cure a person of any physical ailments, including poor eyesight and a common cold. Hubbard asserted that both those things – and many others – were all in a person's head and weren't "real."

Hubbard claimed that a paper written by Dr. Winter was supposed to have been published in the *Journal of the American Medical Association* and the *American Journal of Psychiatry*, but instead, it ended up in the May 1950 issue of *Astounding Science Fiction*, where it really belonged. Between the stories of rockets and alien invasions was the article that would give birth to another of America's homegrown cults.

Campbell, the magazine's editor, wrote that the power of Dianetics was "almost unbelievable; it proves the mind not only can but does rule the body completely; following the sharply defined basic laws set forth, physical ills such as ulcers, asthma and arthritis can be cured, as can all other psychosomatic ills."

On May 9, Hubbard published his book *Dianetics: The Modern Science of Mental Health* and, soon after, started the "Hubbard Dianetics Research Foundation" in Elizabeth, New Jersey. Hubbard gave up all his other writing to promote Dianetics, which was poised to capture the attention of the nation. It quickly took off, only to stumble a few months later.

Hubbard after Dianetics was released to the public

The book sold as many as 4,000 copies every week, even though it was poorly received by the press and the scientific and medical communities. The *New Republic* called it "bold and immodest mixture of complete nonsense and perfectly reasonable common sense, taken from long acknowledged findings and disguised and distorted by a crazy, newly invented terminology." As we know, Isaac Asimov was not impressed, and science fiction writer Jack Williamson called it "a lunatic revision of Freudian psychology."

Even then celebrities rallied around the new movement. Author Aldous Huxley received auditing from Hubbard, and science fiction writers Theodore Sturgeon and A. E. van Vogt became trained Dianetics auditors. Van Vogt even temporarily abandoned his writing to become the head of the newly established Los Angeles branch of the Hubbard Dianetics Research Foundation. Other branches were started in New York, Chicago, Honolulu, and Washington, D.C.

It became a craze that people were willing to pay for. Van Vogt later recalled spending entire days opening envelopes that contained $500 checks from people who wanted to take the auditor's course. There was little oversight of the finances. At least once van Vogt saw Hubbard take a lump sum of $56,000 out of the proceeds of the

Los Angeles branch. One of Hubbard's New Jersey staff members, Helen O'Brien, once commented that the books showed that "a month's income of $90,000 is listed, with only $20,000 accounted for."

Hubbard played a very active role in the early Dianetics boom – aside from lifting money from the till – he spent his time writing, lecturing, and training auditors. He was charming, charismatic, and loved to be the center of attention with wild stories and tall tales that kept his audiences on the edges of their seats.

But every bit of it almost came tumbling down in August 1950.

During a performance in front of more than 6,000 people at the Shrine Auditorium in Los Angeles, Hubbard introduced a "Clear" named Sonya Bianca, who, after undergoing Dianetics therapy, had total recall. However, during the demonstration that followed she failed to remember a single formula in physics – a subject in which she was majoring – or the color of Hubbard's tie when his back was turned. Amidst laughter and catcalls most of the audience walked out.

Many of Hubbard's supporters lost faith in Dianetics. Dr. Winter became disillusioned after spending a year and failing to see anyone he was convinced was a "Clear." He also deplored the Foundation's failure to do any kind of serious scientific research.

By late 1950, the Foundation in New Jersey was in financial crisis and the Los Angeles Foundation was more than $20,000 in debt. Dr. Winter left and so did Art Ceppos, who published Hubbard's book. John W. Campbell also resigned, blaming Hubbard for the disorganization of the Foundation and criticizing him as impossible to work with. By the summer of 1951 all of the branches of the Foundation had closed.

Meanwhile, Hubbard's marriage to Sara had started to dissolve with the rise of Dianetics. As his wealth and fame started to grow Hubbard started to have affairs, and, in response, Sara had affairs of her own. As revenge Hubbard tried to report his wife as a Communist. The FBI didn't take his report seriously and, in fact, an agent made a comment on the report – "Appears mental."

Three weeks later Hubbard and two cronies kidnapped Sara and their year-old daughter Alexis, and forcibly took them to San Bernardino where he tried unsuccessfully to find a doctor to declare Sara insane. She filed for divorce on April 23, 1951 and not only accused him of bigamy but also claimed that he had subjected her to sleep deprivation, beatings, strangulation, and "exhortations to commit suicide."

In the end Hubbard granted her a divorce and full custody of their children – under the condition that she signed a document that stated he was a "fine and brilliant man."

Dianetics was on the edge of total collapse but it was saved by millionaire businessman and Dianetics believer Don Purcell, who agreed to support a new Foundation in Wichita, Kansas. Their collaboration ended less than a year later, falling apart after a judge ruled that the Foundation was liable for the debts accrued by its defunct predecessor in New Jersey. Purcell filed for bankruptcy and Hubbard immediately resigned, accusing Purcell of having been bribed by the American Medical Association to destroy Dianetics. He then established "Hubbard College" on the other side of town where he could promote Dianetics and fight Purcell in court over the Foundation's intellectual property.

Then, only six weeks after setting up Hubbard College and marrying his third wife – 18-year-old staff member Mary Sue Whipp, Hubbard closed it and took his new bride to Phoenix, Arizona. He had a new idea that would save Dianetics. He wrote to his secretary, Helen O'Brien, and told her that if they registered a church, they could charge people $500 for a 24-hour auditing session and keep the cash, all tax-free. "That is real money," Hubbard wrote. "Charge enough, and we'd be swamped."

Helen opted out, but Mary Sue was more than willing to help him start his religion. Hubbard became a millionaire. He bought his own mansion and a fleet of yachts and started one of the most controversial religions of all time – Scientology.

Hubbard created his new religion by expanding on the basics of Dianetics to construct a spiritually oriented doctrine that was rooted – conveniently – in "all great religions," boasting "a religious heritage as old and as varied as Man himself." The concept was that the true self of a person was a "thetan," the immortal entity described earlier. The thetans, according to Hubbard, created the material universe but had forgotten their god-like powers and had become trapped in "meat" bodies. Scientology was created to "rehabilitate" each person's thetan and restores its original capabilities. Hubbard insisted that humanity was kept from attaining greatness because of the forces of "aberration," which were the result of engrams carried by thetans for millions of years.

It all sounded crazy – and it would get crazier. When Helen O'Brien resigned after turning down Hubbard's scheme for his church, she told him that he had created "a temperate zone voodoo in its inelasticity, unexplainable procedures, and mindless group euphoria."

But on December 18, 1953, Hubbard incorporated the Church of Scientology, Church of American Science, and Church of Spiritual Engineering in Camden, New Jersey. Hubbard began making money even faster than he'd made it after Dianetics took off. Churches of Scientology were opened as franchises and some of the cult's auditors began dressing as clergymen, complete with clerical collars.

Scientology grew through the 1950s. Hubbard marketed it through medical claims, such as attracting polio sufferers by presenting the Church of Scientology as a scientific research foundation investigating polio cases. His income doubled, then tripled, and finally became hard to count. His family grew, too. He and Mary Sue had three children. In the spring of 1959, he used his new wealth to purchase an eighteenth-century manor house in Sussex, England, which became his permanent residence.

On the surface Scientology sounded appealing – who wouldn't want to understand one's "true spiritual nature" and be able to do all the things you could allegedly doing after being "cleared?" But Scientology's exclusive marketing hid an extremely rigid set of requirements for church members.

And hid a lot of nuttiness, too.

In order to achieve the promised enlightenment and gain the tools and mindset to overcome any challenge, the church declared that you had to read its books, use its technology, and submit to all its stringent rules. None of that was cheap – there was a reason that Hubbard was making so much money. Members had to complete the church's training, which meant studying all the texts and teaching and, of course,

being "audited." There would eventually be 12 books about Scientology, which all members had to buy, which is currently an expense of about $4,000. Whenever the church updates a book, members must buy the new editions. After buying the books members have to read them, complete the lessons, and listen to hours of Hubbard's lectures. There's a checklist, so you don't miss anything. The church estimates that if you spend about 40 hours a week learning its doctrine you'll be finished in about a year.

About one-half of being a good Scientologist is the training. The other half is from auditing. In those sessions, members are taken through what the church calls "challenging, disturbing, or traumatic memories and feelings" and are taught how to overcome them and become "Clear." They hold the electrodes of what's called an "E-meter," a device that Scientologists believe measures a person's emotional response to ideas, phrases, and even single words. Auditors use the E-meters – whose psychological use has been officially disproven in a court of law – to guide the sessions. Each auditing session, by the way, lasts a minimum of two and a half hours. The cost? $800 per hour.

If a Scientologist ever leaves the church they suffer from "disconnection," which is a lot like when the Amish leave their own communities. The church pressures friends, family, and other members to sever all ties with the defector – just as they do with anyone they see as hostile to the church. These disconnections have separated children from parents, spouses from each other, and have devastated the lives of countless people.

All of this is controversial, but it really pales in comparison to the weirdness that surrounds Scientology's other beliefs. Of course, this book has proven that no religion's beliefs are wholly grounded in science and reason. With that said, though, Scientology's strangeness – obviously ripped from the pages of a science fiction novel – seems to be in a category all its own.

Every culture or movement has a creation myth and Scientology is no exception. According to Hubbard, Xenu was once the ruler of the Galactic Confederacy, an ancient group of 76 planets. After 20 million years the planets were extremely overpopulated. Fearing that he might be removed from power Xenu gathered billions of his people, froze them to capture their souls (thetans), and transported them to Earth – which was then called Teegeeack – for elimination. He dumped them into a volcano and destroyed them in a series of explosions, killing almost all of them and sending their souls into the air.

I know you think I'm making this up, but I swear that I am not. This is a real doctrine of Scientology. I mean, someone made it up, but it was not me.

Anyway, once they were flying around in the air the souls were captured by Xenu, who filled them full of misleading information, especially all the concepts of all the world's religions. After doing this horrible thing Xenu was eventually imprisoned and Earth became a prison planet for the Galactic Confederacy.

Now you just found out something that Scientologists were once not permitted to learn until they had advanced well into the church's ranks – and spent thousands of dollars to do so. It's probably because this is a story so wild that a lot of people would immediately flee after hearing it but, after spending that much money why not stick around? Even Tom Cruise distanced himself from Scientology for a short time after learning this tenet of the church. Maybe he had no choice, who knows? Many claims have been made by former members that they were blackmailed into staying in the church. With a lot of guilty secrets that have been gathered by hours of auditing, members are told to "stay, or else."

Others make a good point – is the story of Xenu any crazier than the belief that Jesus rose from the dead and plans to come back someday, calling all his followers to meet him in the sky? I'll let the reader answer that question on their own.

The frozen thetan story plays a huge role in Scientology beliefs. Each human is actually a thetan in a "meat sack," and Scientologists try and purify these spirits through auditing sessions until they reach the state of "Clear." Of course, that only works when it's done properly, and the recipient truly wants to change. As mentioned already, auditing that results in an eventual Clear can be costly, and it's estimated to cost around $128,000. (and no, there are no extra zeros in that number)

After becoming Clear and learning how to control the powers that all thetans are capable of, the practitioner is now known as an Operating Thetan. According to Scientology these advanced beings are not limited by physical form or the physical universe. The church describes this as "a state of spiritual awareness in which an individual is able to control themselves and their environment."

From there the Operating Thetans can reach even higher levels, all of which promise increasingly awe-inspiring knowledge and power. Each level, naturally, costs even more money to attain. For example, you don't get to hear the Xenu story until you've paid to get to level three.

According to the official doctrine of Scientology, reading and reacting to other people is one of the keys to being a successful follower. The church maintains that most people are simply not good at connecting an apparent, outward emotion to its true inner emotion. In other words, they claim to know what you're thinking, even if you don't. Scientology is supposed to "take the mystery out of human behavior," and using what they call the "tone scale" teaches them how to read people and provide the appropriate emotional response. The tone scale runs from the seemingly randomly chosen numbers of -40 to 40. The higher on the scale each follower is, the better. A score of 40, which I'm sure is very expensive, is described as "Serenity of Beingness." A 1.1 is considered hidden hostility – i.e., smiling on the outside and plotting on the inside – and describes someone who cannot be trusted.

If you don't believe in Scientology you are a 1.1. However, I'd like to think of myself as a -40.

But there is not room for everyone in Scientology, no matter how much you pay. The church – like most other religions supposedly built on love and acceptance – is completely homophobic, and the tone scale even aligns by sexual orientation. If someone is gay, they automatically land in the Covert Hostility category and can only "pray the gay away" by submitting to auditing that will make them heterosexual.

Scientology has a strong focus on past lives. Because thetans are eternal beings they have past lives that have experienced trauma. As a result, people today have subconscious memories of past lives as everything from atoms, cells in the process of mitosis, early photosynthetic organisms, and clams.

Hubbard seemed to be slightly obsessed with clams in some of his writings. He argued that the hinges of the clam became the hinges of the human jaw and that by invoking your past life as a clam you can have a very real effect on your body today.

Don't believe it? Yeah, I don't either. Strangely, though, literally millions of people do, which is what makes Scientology so dangerous. Hubbard created a religion that claimed to cure blindness, make a person smarter, and even more attractive. Many claim that Hubbard's books are nothing more than self-help guides, but they aren't. Dianetics and Scientology involve some very dangerous beliefs and practices – and this has claimed many victims.

Lisa McPherson, 36, of Clearwater, Florida was a Scientologist with an undiagnosed psychiatric illness. Her condition, though, was denied by the church. After a psychotic episode that landed her in the hospital, fellow Scientologists checked her out and moved her to a hotel. Instead of allowing her to rest and relax they subjected her to intensive auditing sessions. She was given vitamins and illegal drugs to keep her awake, and after weeks of this "treatment" she suffered a pulmonary embolism. Still alive but unable to breathe, she was not taken to the hospital but to a Scientologist-friendly doctor instead. He pronounced her dead upon arrival. Her entire body was covered in bruises and she was severely underweight and dehydrated. Good news, though, when Lisa died, she was considered a Clear.

Elli Perkins, 54, was a senior auditor for the Church of Scientology in Buffalo, New York. Her son, Jeremy, began hearing voices and believed that he was Jesus Christ. After a brush with the law a court-ordered psychiatric exam discovered he was schizophrenic. According to Scientology doctrine his mother denied he had a mental illness and refused to allow him to be treated with antipsychotic medication. Instead she took him to a fellow Scientologist who diagnosed Jeremy with chemical toxin poisoning and treated him with vitamins. When Elli forced her son to take the vitamins, he believed that she was trying to poison him. Untreated and unstable he attempted suicide. When this failed, he stabbed his mother 37 times.

Roxanne Friend was not feeling well, but as a Scientologist she was taught that all illness is a person's mind and can be cured by auditing. She spent $80,000 on auditing but was still sick. She finally went to a real doctor and it was discovered that she had cancer. It was never treated, however. Fellow Scientologists kept her under house arrest, and over time her cancer became incurable. She left Scientology and sued the church for its abuses. The church settled out of court for "nuisance value," and Roxanne died soon after.

Patients are told that the church's Purification Rundown can cure liver disease, but Jerry Whitfield suffered permanent liver damage while on the program. Christopher Arbuckle died of liver failure. And the list goes on.

Scientology members love to praise themselves as "experts" in psychology and psychiatry because they have received so much "training." Their celebrity members become spokespeople for topics they know nothing about. Tom Cruise became known a few years ago for his zealous outburst against psychiatry during interviews. He publicly blasted Brooke Shields for taking medicine for postpartum depression. During one interview he claimed to "know the history of psychiatry." He denounced the medication Ritalin and denied the existence of ADHD.

Scientology claims that autism is a "fake" illness, but it was speculated that John Travolta's son, Jett, had the condition. The boy's sickness was instead blamed on environmental toxins caused by household cleaners and fertilizer. Sadly, Jett died at age 16 during a seizure – a common occurrence for autism that is left untreated. After his death Travolta finally acknowledged that he had autism.

Most Scientologists refuse treatment for mental and neurological conditions. Psychiatry may be an imperfect science, but Dianetics is not a viable alternative. Scientology demonizes psychiatry to promote its own agenda and encourages – or really, commands – followers to use its methods instead. Ironically, Dianetics is a type of therapy, but it's also pseudoscientific nonsense. It has been revealed to be ineffective at best and dangerous at its worst.

Once Hubbard created the Church of Scientology membership in the cult began to soar. But when you start a "church" that was established on the idea of thetans who were sent to Earth by an intergalactic warlord named Xenu and promise to cure every affliction in the world by auditing, which costs a lot of money to achieve success, people who don't like con artists and get-rich-quick schemes are going to start paying close attention to what you're doing.

The Church of Scientology claims that the problems that began in the 1960s were due to "vicious, covert international attacks" by the United States government. Hubbard believed that a vast conspiracy of "psychiatric front groups" were secretly controlling the government and that every attack could be traced back to this sinister cabal. Hubbard also stated that Scientology had been infiltrated by saboteurs and spies, so he began "security checking" to weed out "potential trouble sources." Followers were interrogated with the help of E-meters and were asked questions like "Have you ever practiced homosexuality?" and "Have you ever had unkind thoughts about L. Ron Hubbard?" Many were even questioned about crimes they committed in past lives.

Hubbard also tried – like so many other cult leaders – to control politics to his advantage. He advised Scientologists to vote against Richard Nixon in the 1960 presidential election and tried to establish a Department of Government Affairs that would "bring government and hostile philosophies or societies into a state of complete compliance with the goals of Scientology."

Of course, the government became aware of Hubbard about the time he started his church. The FBI had a large file on him – going back to the 1951 interview with the agent who called him a "mental case" – and police departments around the country began exchanging information about Scientology. The Food and Drug Administration went after Scientology's medical claims, seizing thousands of pills being marketed as "radiation cures." They also seized publications that promised medical miracles and forced the church to label E-meters as "ineffective in the diagnosis or treatment of disease."

Following the actions of the FDA, Scientology began receiving increasingly bad publicity across the English-speaking world. It faced particularly hostile scrutiny in Australia where the church was accused of brainwashing, blackmail, extortion, and damaging the mental health of its followers. A Board of Inquiry in 1965 condemned every aspect of Scientology and attacked Hubbard himself. He was described as "being of doubtful sanity, having a persecution complex and displaying strong indications of paranoid schizophrenia with delusions of grandeur." His writings were characterized as nonsensical, abounding in "self-glorification and grandiosity, replete with histrionics and hysterical, incontinent outbursts."

This drastically changed the image of Scientology around the world for a time. It had seemed relatively harmless to most people and had now been transformed into something evil and dangerous.

Unfortunately, though, even though the cult was banned in Australia after that, Scientology's new image didn't stick.

Hubbard found himself barred from countries around the globe after the report but he fought back by creating the church's Guardian's Office in 1966, a new agency that was headed by his wife, Mary Sue. The office dealt with Scientology's external affairs including public relations, legal actions, and the gathering of intelligence on perceived threats. When Scientology started receiving the negative media attention the office retaliated with hundreds of writs for libel and slander – once issuing more than 40 in a single day.

Hubbard introduced the "Fair Game" policy, which could be applied to anyone deemed an "enemy" of Scientology. Hubbard ordered his staff to find "lurid, blood, sex, crime, actual evidence on Scientology's attackers" who could be "tricked, sued, lied to, or destroyed."

The church continues this kind of behavior today. It does not like criticism. It claims that attacks against it are a form of discrimination. However, there is no turning the other cheek – this church retaliates. Ex-members, journalists, and others who speak about it are labeled "suppressive persons," and the church feels it's justified in overwhelming them with lawsuits, harassment, threats, and smear campaigns.

But that couldn't protect Scientology from everything. In 1967, the Internal Revenue Service decided that the Church of Scientology no longer warranted tax-exempt status as a religious organization. This had already happened to the Washington, D.C. branch in 1958 when the IRS found that Hubbard and his family were profiting unreasonably from Scientology's non-profit income. In 1971, a federal court ruled that Hubbard's E-Meter claims were scientifically unsound and that Scientology's medical aspects were nonsense. But – and here was the kicker – an E-meter could still be used in religious ceremonies, provided no claims of medical uses were made.

With that, Hubbard began using the First Amendment to his business's advantage. He sought Constitutional protection for Scientology's self-proclaimed services. Places used for auditing became "missions," fees became "donations," and Hubbard's books became "scriptures." He was now using the new rules to his advantage – until the IRS uncovered some major financial fraud.

During the IRS investigation it was discovered that Hubbard had funneled millions of dollars from the organization, laundered some of the funds in sham companies based in Panama, and tucked the money away in multiple Swiss bank accounts.

But that was just the start of what they uncovered. In 1973, Hubbard had instigated what he called "Operation Snow White," in which followers were directed to remove negative reports about Scientology from government files and track down their sources. Members posed as workers and janitors and infiltrated and burglarized numerous government organizations, including the U.S. Department of Justice and the IRS. The scheme was discovered when the FBI carried out simultaneous raids on Scientology offices in Los Angeles and Washington, D.C. on July 7, 1977. They seized wiretapping equipment, burglary tools, and over 90,000 pages of stolen documents. According to a Scientology defector followers "worked day and night," shredding documents, but they weren't fast enough. Hubbard was not prosecuted, though he was named as a "un-indicted co-conspirator" by prosecutors. His wife, Mary Sue, was indicted and convicted of conspiracy. She went to federal prison, along with 10 other Scientologists.

During the government investigation Hubbard's health declined. He put on weight, developed a large growth on his forehead, and suffered a motorcycle accident in 1973. Two years later he had a heart attack, and the next year he fell into a coma after a pulmonary embolism but recovered.

While Hubbard was traveling around the world with a fleet of boats – and living on one of them – trying to stay away from the IRS, he remained active managing a developing Scientology. But after his flotilla of boats was barred from several ports, he left the sea and moved into a hotel suite in Daytona Beach, Florida. Soon joined by Mary Sue, they moved into a condominium complex. Their presence there was supposed to be a secret but when word leaked out Hubbard moved to Washington, D.C. with a handful of aides and left Mary Sue behind. Six months later, after a security alert in July 1976, Hubbard fled to a safe house in Culver City, California. He stayed there for a short time and then moved again, this time to Olive Tree Ranch near La Quinta.

Hubbard's situation got worse in February 1978 when a French court convicted him in absentia for obtaining money under false pretenses. They sentenced him to four years in prison, but only if they could find him. Hubbard made sure they couldn't. He went into hiding in an apartment in Hemet, California and his only contact with the world came through 10 trusted messengers. He cut off contact with everyone else, including Mary Sue, who last saw him in August 1979. Two years after his conviction in France, he disappeared into deep cover with two of his closest followers, Pat and Annie Broeker.

For the final two years of his life, Hubbard lived in a luxury RV on a ranch called Whispering Winds near Creston, California. He remained in hiding while controversy raged in the outside world about whether he was still alive and, if so, where he was hiding. According to church officials he was spending his time "writing and researching," pursuing photography and music, checking on his animals, and overseeing the construction work on his ranch house. He spent millions of dollars repeatedly redesigning it and building a quarter-mile horse-racing track with an observation tower. Neither the house nor the track was ever used.

Hubbard spent the last two years of his life living in an RV on a ranch in California. He was only seen by church officials and close family members. He was in poor health, but no one could explain how he was unable to cure himself with Dianetics

He remained closely involved with the management of the Church of Scientology and secretly delivered orders and continued to receive large amounts of money. *Forbes* magazine estimated that at least $200 million was gathered in Hubbard's name in 1982 alone. The IRS soon notified the church and let officials know that it was considering indicting Hubbard for tax fraud.

But he'd never live to see the prosecution.

Hubbard was suffering from poor health during this time, including chronic pancreatitis. He suffered a stroke on January 17, 1986 and died a week later. His body was cremated, and his ashes were scattered at sea. Unable to explain why Hubbard was unable to cure himself through Dianetics, Scientology leaders announced that his body had become an impediment to his work and so he had decided to "drop his body" and continue his research on another planet.

Hubbard was survived by his wife, Mary Sue, and all his children except for his second son, Quentin, who had committed suicide years before. His will set up a trust fund to support Mary Sue, her three children, and Katherine, the daughter of his first wife, Polly.

He disinherited his other children. L. Ron Hubbard, Jr. had changed his name years earlier after he and his father had become estranged. He referred to Hubbard as "one of the biggest con-men of this century." His other disinherited child was Alexis, Hubbard's daughter with his second wife, Sara. She had tried to make contact with her father in 1971 but had been rebuffed. He claimed that her father had actually been Jack Parsons and said that her mother had been a Nazi spy during the war. Both later accepted settlements when lawsuits were threatened.

The copyrights of his works and most of his wealth were willed to the Church of Scientology. Today, Hubbard holds a place as the Guinness World Record holder for the most published author with 1,084 works, the most translated book with 70 languages, and most audiobooks. Hubbard's *Battlefield Earth* has sold over 6 million copies, with each book in the series becoming *New York Times* bestsellers on their release. However, it's been reported that Hubbard's followers had been buying large numbers of the books and re-issuing them to stores so they can boost sales figures.

The next face of Scientology — David Miscavige

I suppose that's a fitting literary legacy for a man who conned millions into believing they were aliens from other planets who could get rid of all their troubles by paying him their hard-earned cash.

After Hubbard's death, David Miscavige – a far more ruthless, cunning, and relentless kind leader – took over the church. A year later Scientology reported an income of $503 million.

Scientology is like a religious pyramid scheme. Each level costs thousands of dollars to complete. To lure you in the initial courses are cheap, then the price rapidly goes up. If you can't afford them, don't worry, you can become a member of the staff and recruit others as you work your way up. The pay is low, though, the hours are long, and you have strict targets to meet each week – or else.

And if you do meet your quotas, you still can't expect to party with those on the top of the pyramid. They're the celebrities that found their way to Scientology. Hubbard always wanted them. He even established Scientology's Celebrity Centre International as a hub for "artists, politicians, leaders of industry, sports figures, and anyone with the power and vision to create a better world." It was started in a mansion just off Hollywood Boulevard and followers received an internal newsletter that detailed its plans to attracted A-listers to the church. Hubbard once wrote, "Celebrities are special people. They have communication lines that others do not have." In other words, they had a lot of money and the fame to attract those who also had money and who would gladly give it up to the church in exchange for a spiritual awakening.

Hubbard's death occurred in the middle of the 1980s' America when the country's economy was booming and there was a national desire for fame, wealth, and celebrity. It was in this environment that David Miscavige helped the church find its poser child, Tom Cruise, and he recruited people like John Travolta, Kirstie Alley, Anne Archer, and others.

Tom Cruise has been the face of Scientology for more than three decades, and the church has made sure he's stayed with them since he first joined in 1990. Scientology became part of nearly every aspect of Cruise's life, including his personal life. It even allegedly broke up his marriage to his wife Nicole Kidman, because it suspected her of being a "Potential Trouble Source" and a bad influence on his Scientology adherence. Kidman's father was an important psychologist in her native Australia, and Scientology is notoriously opposed to any kind of psychology and psychiatry.

After Cruise and Kidman split up the church allegedly set up Cruise with a new girlfriend, only to separate them after a less-the-promising trial run. Katie Holmes, the actor's third wife, is said to have broken up with Cruise because she feared the church's influence on their daughter, Suri.

But while Scientology was doing everything to promote its star follower, it did everything it could to hide the whereabouts of another member – David Miscavige's wife, Shelly.

Shelly had been by her husband's side for decades, and at every trip, meeting or photo opportunity. The pair appeared to be the perfect couple. But according to

David Miscavige's wife, Shelly, has not been seen in public since 2007 – although church officials say she is well

defectors when they weren't in front of a camera or at an official function the relationship showed obvious signs of trouble. Marc Headley, a former member who worked closely with the couple, has stated, "I never, ever saw them kiss. I was there for 15 years, so I had plenty of opportunities to witness them together and never, ever saw them affectionate with each other."

Others said the same. Some former members noted that they obviously had a working relationship, but an odd one. Those who spent a lot of time with them agreed that they never showed any kind of affection.

And then in August 2007, Shelly disappeared.

When former Scientologist Leah Remini – who was friends with Shelly but has since produced a television show about Scientology and has emerged as the most visible and outspoken critic of the movement – inquired about Shelly's inexplicable disappearance, she was told a variety of stories including that Shelly was on a "special project" or visiting a sick relative. When she asked high-ranking Scientologists where her friend had gone, she was subjected to harsh auditing sessions, interrogations, and warnings to stop asking questions.

Actress Leah Remini has become one of Scientology's most outspoken critics

When Remini finally left Scientology in 2013, she filed a missing persons report with the Los Angeles Police Department. LAPD detectives seemed to take it seriously but quickly closed the case. They ruled that the report was "unfounded" and claimed they had met with Shelly – but didn't provide any other information.

The church assures everyone that Shelly is fine, but Remini fears the worst. Shelly has not been seen publicly since her disappearance. Ron Miscavige – David's father, who left the church in 2012 – also worries about his daughter-in-law. In an interview he stated, "Shelly, she'll never be free. These are pretty bad people, but they don't have a conscience, and that lets them do it."

The official response from the church denies any wrongdoing and then, of course, goes on the attack. Ron Miscavige, the church claims, is attempting to financially exploit his son "in a sad exercise in betrayal." As for Leah Remini, she "has been stalking Mr. and Mrs. Miscavige for years because of her psychotic obsession. It is time for her to stop."

But that's not going to happen. She isn't going to stop. I think that's become obvious.

She believes, as so many do, that Scientology is a dangerous cult with a long and sinister history of violence, strange secrets, and multiple and ongoing lies. It has left behind a trail of wreckage that includes death, financial ruin, conspiracy, and crime.
Ignore the shiny surface of Scientology – there is darkness underneath.

The End

But, of course, we know that isn't the case. New cults – masking themselves as "religions" – as well as offshoots of faiths that already exist, continue to spring up each day. They lure us with false promises, eerie threats, and promises of salvation from the End Times to come.
Always ask questions.
Never doubt your instincts.
And never follow faith blindly without knowing where it leads.

Bibliography

Arthur, Damon – "Church Seeks to Bring Girl Back to Life," *USA Today*, December 17, 2019

Bharti Franklin, Satya– *The Promise of Paradise: A Woman's Intimate Story of the Perils of Life With Rajneesh*, Barrytown, NY: Station Hill Press, 1992

Birnes, William J. and Joel Martin – *The Haunting of America*, New York, NY, Forge Books, 2009

Bruney, Gabrielle – "Joaquin Phoenix and Rose McGowan Spent Their Early Years in a Religious Cult. Then it Became Infamous," *Esquire*, October 5, 2019

Buck, Stephanie – "In this bizarre religion, the aliens who will save our planet can't decide whether they're feminist," Timeline, October 24, 2017

Chu, David – "Jonestown: 13 Things You Should Know about Cult Massacre," *Rolling Stone*

Earley, Pete – *Prophet of Death: the Mormon Blood-Atonement Killings*, New York, NY, William Morrow Books, 1991

Ebon, Martin (Editor) – *World's Weirdest Cults* – New York, NY, Signet Books, 1979

Enos, Morgan - *I Grew Up In A Congregation Of Jehovah's Witnesses. Here's What It Was Really Like.* (Huff Post Guest Article)

Fort, Samuel – *Cult of the Great Eleven*, Omaha, NE, Nisirtu Publishing, 2014

Fraser, Caroline - *Dying the Christian Science way*, The Guardian, June 6, 2019

Greer, John Michael – *Apocalypse*, London, Quercus, 2012

Horowitz, Mitch – *Occult America*, New York, NY, Bantam Books, 2009

Joshi, Vasant – *The Awakened One*, San Francisco, CA: Harper and Row, 1982

Klees, Emerson – *The Crucible of Ferment*, Rochester, NY, Friends of the Finger Lakes Publishing, 2001

Krist, Gary – *The Mirage Factory*, New York, NY, Crown, 2018

Lalani, Vimal – "The Most Horrendous Cult You've Never Heard Of," *Ishli*, December 2019

Largo, Michael – *God's Lunatics*, New York, NY, Harper, 2010

Lee, Adam – "The Strange Sad Story of Olive Heiligenthal," Patheos, January 15, 2020

Margaritoff, Marco – "The Disappeared, the Dead, and the Damned: Inside The Church Of Scientology," *All That's Interesting*, February 21, 2019

McCormack, Win – *Oregon Magazine: The Rajneesh Files 1981–86*, Portland, OR: New Oregon Publishers, Inc., 1985

Mikul, Chris – *The Cult Files*, New York, NY, Metro Books, 2009

Milner, Lyn – *The Allure of Immortality*, University Press of Florida, 2015

Morris, Adam – *American Messiahs*, New York, NY, W.W. Norton, 2019

Nickell, Joe – *Looking for A Miracle*, Prometheus Books, Amherst, NY, 1993

Quick, Donna — *A Place Called Antelope: The Rajneesh Story*, Ryderwood, WA: August Press, 1995

Roberts, David – "The Brink of War," *Smithsonian* Magazine, June 2008

Sandlin, Lee – *Wicked River*, New York, NY, Pantheon Books, 2010

Schneck, Robert Damon – *Mrs. Wakeman Vs. The Antichrist*, New York, NY, Penguin, 2014

Stollznow, Karen – *God Bless America*, Durham, NC, Pitchstone Publishing, 2013

Taylor, Troy – *American Hauntings*, Jacksonville, IL, American Hauntings Ink, 2017
----------------- - *Bloody Hollywood*, Decatur, IL, Whitechapel Press, 2008
----------------- - *Into the Shadows*, Decatur, IL, Whitechapel Press, 2013

Watts, Jill - *God, Harlem U.S.A: The Father Divine Story*, University of California Press, 1995

Personal Interviews, Correspondence, and Experience

Special Thanks to:

April Slaughter: Cover Design and Artwork
Becky Ray: Editing and Proofreading
Lisa Taylor Horton and Lux
Orrin Taylor
Rene Kruse
Rachael Horath
Elyse and Thomas Reihner
Bethany Horath
John Winterbauer
Kaylan Schardan
Maggie Walsh
Cody Beck
Becky Ray
Tom and Michelle Bonadurer
Susan Kelly and Amy Bouyear
And the entire crew of American Hauntings

About the Author

Troy Taylor is the author of books on ghosts, hauntings, true crime, the unexplained, and the supernatural in America. He is also the founder of American Hauntings Ink, which offers books, ghost tours, events, and weekend excursions. He was born and raised in the Midwest and currently divides his time between Illinois and the far-flung reaches of America.